Values and the Active Community

BY

THE INTERNATIONAL STUDIES OF VALUES IN POLITICS

A COLLABORATION IN SOCIAL RESEARCH OF

Centre for the Study of Developing Societies · New Delhi
Indian Institute of Technology · Kanpur
University of Poona
Institute of Philosophy and Sociology, Polish Academy of Sciences · Warsaw
University of Pennsylvania · Philadelphia
Institute of Social Sciences · Belgrade
Institute of Sociology and Philosophy · University of Ljubljana
Faculty of Political Science · University of Sarajevo

UNDER THE SPONSORSHIP OF

THE INTERNATIONAL SOCIAL SCIENCE COUNCIL · PARIS

Values AND THE
Active
Community

A Cross-national Study of the Influence of
Local Leadership

By
The International Studies of Values in Politics

THE FREE PRESS · NEW YORK
COLLIER-MACMILLAN LIMITED · LONDON

THE FREE PRESS
A DIVISION OF THE MACMILLAN COMPANY
866 Third Avenue, New York, New York 10022

Collier-Macmillan Canada Ltd., Toronto, Ontario

Library of Congress Catalog Card Number: 71–136613

printing number
1   2   3   4   5   6   7   8   9   10

Principal Participants

India   Centre for the Study of Developing Societies, New Delhi

   D. L. Sheth, project director
   H. R. Chaturvedi
   Rajni Kothari
   Ashish Nandy
   Ramashray Roy

Indian Institute of Technology, Kanpur

   K. K. Singh, project director
   Ali Ashraf
   S. B. Shukla
   B. K. Singh
   S. S. Tripathi

University of Poona

   V. M. Sirsikar, project director
   T. K. Attarde
   S. M. Chitnis
   A. S. Nadkarni

Poland

Institute of Philosophy and Sociology, Polish Academy of Sciences

Jerzy J. Wiatr, project director
Aleksandra Jasinska-Kania
Antonina Ostrowska
Krzysztof Ostrowski
Jacek Tarkowski

United States

University of Pennsylvania

Philip E. Jacob, international coordinator
Henry Teune, associate director of research
Thomas M. Watts

Yugoslavia

Institute of Social Sciences, Belgrade

Anton Vratusa, director
Zorana Puric, director of community studies
Slobodan Bosnic
Radivoje Marinkovic

Institute of Sociology and Philosophy, University of Ljubljana

Zdravko Mlinar, director of community studies
Janez Jerovsek

Faculty of Political Science, Sarajevo

Stojan Tomic

International Administrator

Betty M. Jacob, University of Pennsylvania

Contents

The Strategy of Comparative Inquiry: Methods of Assessment and Analysis 40
Teune

PART  Leaders' Values

3 Patterns of Commitment 67
Singh and Jacob with Puric and Jasinska-Kania

PART **THREE**   The Active Community

Foreword

International cooperation within the sciences is not new. This is particularly true of the social sciences. Scholars from different countries have long met to exchange views and discuss findings on their common objects of inquiry. Now, however, a new pattern of international cooperative research is emerging to cope with the problems of analyzing determinants of social behavior, the manifestations of which vary markedly from country to country. This venture calls for the mobilization of joint cross-national teamwork in the design and day-to-day conduct of research. By using the method of controlled comparison, scholars with specialized knowledge of particular countries are able to combine the results of parallel studies (applying identical methodology) to account for the differences and similarities that appear among nations.

In mathematics, and also in physics and chemistry, data are not nation-specific. They can be studied in any surrounding with the proper tools. In the social sciences, however, phenomena are context-bound. Hence, to test hypotheses and to formulate generalizations of even a limited range, it is necessary to study a phenomenon or relationship in a variety of situations and to compare the specific constellations of variables associated with it in these differing situations. This is the approach undertaken in the International Studies of Values in Politics.

The Executive Board of the International Social Science Council, at its 16th session in Vienna, April 1963 was presented with a number of requests to sponsor scientific research. In a policy paper setting forth its decisions, the Executive Board stated:

The sponsorship of the ISSC will not be given to projects submitted by individuals, but only to projects emanating from an institution. . . .

As any action of the Council, such sponsorship would only commit the Council as a collective body, and not individual members personally.

It does not appear possible that ISSC's sponsorship of a research project be given before the final design of this project be completed, as modifications and changes will take place constantly until the project is in actual process of being carried out.

Sponsorship should be considered a measure not to be taken too frequently, and given only to projects presenting a special interest from an international and interdisciplinary point of view.

The question of creating a Special Committee to guide the organization and administration of a sponsored research project would have to be settled separately for each case.

At the same session the Executive Board approved sponsorship of the International Studies of Values in Politics and, at a special meeting convened in Paris in 1964, set forth the guidelines for its sponsorship of this project. Finally, in January 1965, the Bureau of the Council proposed a liaison committee to assist the program in an advisory capacity, and suggested that one or more members of the ISCC should represent the Secretariat at the international roundtables. The members of this committee were: (1) Professor Sjoerd Groenman, President of ISSC, of the University of Utrecht, the Netherlands; (2) Professor S. Ehrlich of Warsaw, Poland; (3) Professor Daniel Lerner of Massachusetts Institute of Technology, Cambridge, Mass.; and (4) Professor Stein Rokkan of the Christian Michelsen Institute, Bergen, Norway.

It was my privilege to be a participant at each of these significant international gatherings, and to watch the struggle for integration of concepts and methodology in this pioneering cross-cultural program.

The Choice of the Participating
Countries

One of the most prevalent questions asked about this program has been why the project was conducted in cooperation with institutes in India, Poland, Yugoslavia and the United States. From a purely scientific point of view, could a better choice have been made?

A comparative study has to sail between two extremes. One is the extreme of similarity of social context, the other that of fundamental differences of all components in this context. If there is too much similarity, the project would miss its goal of comparing the same phenomena—in this case, values of political leaders, integration, local political decisions. If the differences in social context are present in every respect, however, the intervening variables will so complicate the analysis that a comparison of results will seem meaningless. Progress in social science can only be made step by step, even when these steps are big ones. *Qui trop embrasse. . . .* Although analytical comparison is the backbone of the social sciences, the variables must be limited to be manageable.

The choice of the above countries made sure that different political systems were included in the comparison; these systems had enough in common, however, to make this comparison scientifically realistic.

There were also a number of practical limitations. Every cross-national study must first find:

(a) interested, appropriate scholars and qualified, locally responsible institutions;

(b) support, and especially financial support, from governments;

(c) funds for the international program in general.

(a) Although there may be great interest in scientific quarters, it is extremely difficult to find sufficient well-qualified manpower to execute a time-consuming project requiring intellectual sophistication and specialized abilities—for instance, in the stage of statistical analysis.

(b) In some countries the governments may consider such a project politically undesirable or of low priority.

(c) Raising financial resources for a program of this magnitude is a crucial problem. Both governments and big private foundations have limitations on the applicability of funds for work across national borders. Consequently, financing this project involved a spectrum of different sources, even of different currencies, applicable for specific purposes.

Achieving Scholarly
Integration

Cross-national research can be executed only if there are regular meetings of the main collaborators—the directors of the participating institutes and their associates. The project's schedule, therefore, included a series of periodic roundtables supplemented by exchanges of personnel so that different nationals could take part in the research in the other countries. This feature of interchange among the principal collaborating scholars helped to establish the understanding necessary to solve some of the problems encountered in this kind of research, particularly those involving questions of cross-national comparability. The result was the development of an intimate rapport and working relationship among the participants, and constant inter-stimulation as the program unfolded. It is impossible now to discern the contributions of national groups or individuals within the design of the project. All nations and all principal individual collaborators contributed to the final product. A slow, patient, demanding process of integration led to a real product of international teamwork.

One additional factor to be considered in cross-national research is occasioned by the different scientific climates of the countries involved. Even when agreement is reached on a specific methodological instrument, such as the text of a survey questionnaire, not all the participants are necessarily in agreement on the general theoretical framework of the survey. Two people agreeing to the same items (and, implicitly, to the specific hypotheses that the questions reflect) may have quite different theoretical interests in the data to be collected. Participants in the "Values in Politics" project had to recognize and respect their different complex ways of approaching social reality; they learned not to demand complete identity of purpose as a condition of establishing common operational procedures and a common program of analysis. The lesson of close cooperation over a long period in cross-national collaboration is that it is wrong to conclude that a common theoretical background is easily attained but it is essential to have a high degree of respect for other people's ways of thinking. For this kind of collaboration some personality types are more appropriate than others.

The Value of Cross-
National Studies

This book, reporting on the development of new tools to measure (1) values across national boundaries and (2) the process of social mobilization between nations and at different levels within nations, is a good illustration of the productivity of cross-national studies of societal phenomena. These new dimensions for conducting social research have also created favorable conditions for other methodological "inventions" such as the analysis of the collected data that have established new theories on the functioning of the local power structure. Thus, the peculiar character of these cross-national materials has presented perspectives that otherwise would have remained undiscovered.

In a way, this cross-national approach systematizes the cross-fertilizing process known to sociologists who work with anthropological data. Scholars in the social sciences have to be constantly aware of the danger of parochialism, even though communication in our age runs counter to it. Cross-national research projects and the contacts among the different nations involved is a remedy to the danger of such national compartmentalization of the social sciences. By means of cross-national or cross-cultural observations, social science propositions lose their self-evidence, and are now verified in quite different contexts.

The "Values in Politics" project, because of the difficulties it encountered in trying to put the program into operation, has given the participants far better insights into the underlying basic differences in approach than other, less intensive international contacts could have effected. Meeting each other at roundtables, visiting in other countries, writing joint articles for foreign reviews—all this contributed to mutual understanding.

I would summarize the payoffs of this cross-national research as the generation of new ideas, hypotheses and instruments, changes in perspective, a control over too easily formulated generalizations, remedies of parochialism or national compartmentalization, a better understanding of different theoretical approaches in social science, and the creation of a really international social science community.

All the enumerated issues rank highly in the purposes and activities of the International Social Science Council. We were privileged to initiate the operation of this cross-national project. When the council agreed to sponsor the program, we took great risks, as the performance of a four-country study is not an easy undertaking. We took risks, however, because the results of such a project, as they are summarized, promised a new development for social science and its international integration.

Sjoerd Groenman
University of Utrecht
President, International Social Science Council

Preface

The International Studies of Values in Politics inaugurated an experiment in cross-national social research, an experiment distinctive both in the subject attacked and the strategy of conducting the inquiry. This was the first attempt to examine, on a strictly comparative basis, the impact of leaders values on social change and development at the community level. On the organizational side, it piloted a pattern of international collaboration in which design, execution and analysis were jointly determined by teams from four different countries.

From a scientific standpoint, the construction of cross-nationally equivalent measures of values and of community activeness—the first involving individual dispositions, the other collective group behavior directed toward developmental change—was a most demanding and exciting accomplishment.

In terms of theoretical and policy significance, the major cross-national differences in the determinants of developmental change were the most striking finding.

As a model for research organization, the feasibility of an international joint enterprise based on equality of participation by the respective institutions in each country demonstrated an approach that may hold doors open to further cross-national research on sensitive subjects.

Organization: A Pattern of
International Collaboration

Essential to the success of the program was its international sponsorship and the processes of multinational cooperation that were forged.

The International Social Science Council, which on this occasion, for the first time, extended sponsorship to a project other than its own programs, assured international responsibility and provided a channel for communication with the world academic community.

Specific working agreements were concluded among the cooperating institutions and provided that (1) the research design would be jointly determined by the principal participants from all four countries; (2) each national team would be mainly responsible for carrying out its own fieldwork; (3) analysis and evaluation of the pooled data would be assigned to small cross-national groups working face-to-face on specific phases of the program; and (4) conclusions would be submitted to successive international roundtables, where progress would be checked and further guidelines agreed upon.

These roundtables, held at intervals of approximately six months, in different countries, became in effect continuing seminars interspersed with periods of strenuous testing and application in the field. One of the major reasons for rotating them was to directly involve supporting staffs of junior scholars in this cross-cultural learning process. In addition to the roundtables, the principal participants were privileged to long periods of individual intervisitation with their colleagues in other countries.

This process developed in-depth relationships among the scholars, regardless of nationality or ideology. Immersed in a highly rigorous scientific experience, they became knit together as they probed for answers to problems of mutual interest. They shared each other's skills, financial resources (and financial stringencies) and cultural insights.

Cooperating with indigenous scholars obviated a need for foreign participants to acquire new language skills and prolonged cultural acclimatization; on the other hand, the perspective of outsiders offset the "culture bind" which often affects nationals as they view their own countries.

Finance: A Shared Responsibility

The project has been a cost-shared program from its inception, as it has been supported by both private and government sources. A Ford Foundation grant initiated the inquiry into the influence of social values on public policy. A Rockefeller Foundation grant facilitated an extensive field trip to locate scholars engaged in similar research, and another Rockefeller grant provided conference facilities and hospitality for the fifth international roundtable at Bellagio, Italy. The Johnson Foundation financed the European scholars participating in the second international roundtable in Philadelphia. Three grants from the Barra Foundation supported the pilot development of content analysis as a technique to identify and measure values, and also supported an examination in depth of the making of critical decisions in selected U.S. cities.

The Institute of Philosophy and Sociology of the Polish Academy of Sciences assumed full financial responsibility for staffing and administering the research in Poland, including the collection and analysis of data.

In Yugoslavia, the participating institutions also bore the full internal costs of the project, assisted by substantial grants from the Federal Fund for Scientific Work and the Republic of Slovenia Fund for Scientific Work. Yugoslav participation in the international project was developed as part of an ongoing program of joint research on Yugoslav communities under the auspices of the Federal Council for Coordination of Scientific Activities.

The Research Projects Committee of the Government of India Planning Commission supported continuing studies by two of the Indian participating institutions as pilot studies for similar research in other parts of India.

Five generous grants were made by the Department of State, Cultural Affairs Division, in soft currencies, for the exchange of scholars, international roundtables and other international aspects of the project, as well as some of the data collection and analysis in India. The National Science Foundation financed the leaders' survey and the collection of community aggregative data in the United States, the four-country comparative analysis of individual leader's values, and travel to coordinate the authorship of the international report. A three-year contract with the Agency for International Development provided financial support to develop the research instruments, field test them in India, and assess the relative influence of explanatory variables.

The East-West Center in Hawaii and the Center for International Studies at Cornell University provided facilities and grants to assist in the preparation and editing of this international report. The University of Pennsylvania served as the administrative center of the project.

Publication: A Venture in
Multinational Partnership

The fruition of the strategy of international collaborative research is a series of reports, jointly planned and prepared by the principal participants, and presenting evaluations that have grown out of intensive interchange.

The present volume is devoted to cross-national comparisons, based largely on a survey of local political leaders and aggregated community data. To follow is a presentation and analysis of the rich body of life histories of critical decisions that were conducted along parallel lines, in a set of "active" and "inactive" communities in each country. A third report will be a handbook demonstrating the special techniques of content analysis developed to identify and measure the expression of values in political communications. In addition, a number of national reports are anticipated, reports providing intensive examination of the data for particular countries, and interpreted in the light of the specific national political and social contexts.

What is distinctive about these works is the pattern of authorship. Each contributor, involved as he was in the total project, is able to report in a comparative perspective. In the present volume, for instance, authors evaluate the data on their given topic from all four countries, not just their own. While each is individually responsible for the interpretations he sets forth, the data analyses he reports have been verified by the entire group of collaborators; everyone has had a chance to challenge any part of the text and to enter reservations if the author was not persuaded. A multinational editorial committee consisting of Jacob, Teune, Vratusa, Wiatr and Sirsikar (acting for the Indian group) guided the preparation and emendation of the manuscript.

Acknowledgments

Any program of this character is inevitably dependent on many persons in government as well as academia.

The value of international sponsorship for this form of cooperative cross-national social research was initially envisioned by Professor Adam Schaff, currently President of the Board of the European Co-ordination Center of the International Social Science Council, and most felicitously and effectively implemented by the late Dr. K. Szczerba-Likiernik, Secretary-General of the Council, and Professor Clemens Heller of the Ecole Pratique des Hautes Etudes. The Council appointed a liaison committee of four distinguished scholars to provide a close continuing contact between the project and the international social science community. They were: Professor Stanislaw Ehrlich, Faculty of Law, University of Warsaw; Professor Daniel Lerner, Massachusetts Institute of Technology; Professor Stein Rokkan, Director of Research, The Christian Michelsen Institute; and Professor Sjoerd Groenman, University of Utrecht, Chairman.

Professor D. R. Gadgil, Deputy Chairman of the Planning Commission, Government of India, was instrumental in launching and guiding the research in India, and, as Vice Chancellor of the University of Poona, presided over the Indian Advisory Committee composed of: P. K. Kelkar, Director of the Indian Institute of Technology, Kanpur; I. P. Desai, Director, Centre for Regional Developmental Studies, Surat, Gujarat, representing the Centre for the Study of Developing Societies in New Delhi; Asoka Mehta, then Deputy Chairman of the Planning Commission; Prem Kirpal, Member Secretary, Ministry of Education.

The Polish commitment to this joint enterprise was secured and sustained through the efforts of the directors of the Institute of Philosophy and Sociology of the Polish Academy of Sciences, respectively Professors Adam Schaff and Jan Szczepanski.

For the participation of the cooperating Yugoslav institutions, the project is indebted to the successive directors of the Institute of Social Sciences, Belgrade, Professors Najdan Pasic and Anton Vratusa, and their associates, especially Istok Zagar; and to Professor Joze Goricar, director of the Institute of Sociology, Ljubljana.

The receptive interest but critical appraisal of Dr. John F. Hilliard of the Ford Foundation, formerly Deputy Assistant Administrator of the Agency for International Development, and Dr. F. Joachim Weyl, then Science Advisor to the Administrator, were crucial to the organization and funding of the research.

The Cultural Affairs officers in the Department of State who monitored the program, both in Washington and on the field, served with insight into the sensibilities of the scholars and understanding commitment to the principle of international partnership, in spite of the vicissitudes of changing government policies and appropriation cutbacks. Foremost among those most closely associated with the work were Guy Coriden, Director of the East European division; Wallace Littell, Michael Eisenstadt and Paul Wheeler in Eastern Europe; and Frank Bourne, Eugene Schaeffer and John Dixon in India.

An interdisciplinary American advisory committee composed of twenty-six distinguished social scientists from sixteen universities served as a continuing panel of technical experts for both the American survey and other country operations.

The administrative office at the University of Pennsylvania was fortunate to have the wise and penetrating advice of four members of the faculty who gave generously of their time to help resolve the problems of administration, funding and international communication throughout the project's four years of operations. They were: W. Norman Brown, President of the American Institute of Indian Studies; John Perry Horlacher, then Chairman of the Political Science Department; Richard D. Lambert, Professor of Sociology and Director of the

South Asia Regional Studies Program; and Donald S. Murray, Assistant to the President for Federal Relations.

The International Studies of Values in Politics is particularly indebted to its scientific advisors, whose insight, innovativeness and rigor deepened the project's substantive content and enabled it to overcome major problems of scientific procedure.

Allen S. Barton, Director of the Bureau of Applied Social Research, Columbia University, and Samuel J. Eldersveld, Chairman of the Political Science Department at the University of Michigan, assisted in the design, instrumentation and analytical procedures while participating in most of the international roundtables, as well as directly advising several of the national teams.

Adam Przeworski, Associate Professor of Political Science at Washington University, St. Louis, formerly associated with the Institute of Philosophy and Sociology of the Polish Academy of Sciences, made fundamental contributions to operationalizing the project, especially in developing the unique methodology of cross-national comparisons. He also helped structure the plan of analysis and conduct the first stage of international computer processing and data evaluation.

William A. Scott, Professor of Psychology, University of Colorado, laid the basis for the strategy of value measurement and directed the assessment of the initial pilot studies leading to the construction of the leadership survey instrument. Lester W. Milbrath, Professor of Political Science, State University of New York, Buffalo, was also instrumental in formulating key concepts and procedures for the survey.

R. D. Singh, Director of the Central Institute for Training and Research, New Delhi and Eugen Pusic, Director of the Institute of Social Research, Zagreb contributed their wealth of experience in the study of local communities within their own countries to the ISVIP design for cross-country comparative research.

The National Opinion Research Center, University of Chicago, conducted the leadership survey in the U.S. and a supplementary examination of decisional processes in the sample cities. Professors Dusan Breznik and Milica Sentic, respectively head, and deputy head of the Demographic Department, Institute of Social Science, Belgrade, helped establish the premises for the Yugoslav survey sample.

Terry N. Clark, Assistant Professor of Sociology, University of Chicago, conducted the American set of decisional case studies and outlined their implications for the structure of community influence.

The development of special techniques of content analysis applicable to the identification of values resulted from the theoretical and empirical contributions of Klaus Krippendorff, Associate Professor, Annenberg School of Communications, University of Pennsylvania;

Yasumasa Tanaka, Associate Professor of Psychology, Gakushuin University, Tokyo; Paul Novosel, Professor of Communications, University of Zagreb; and Sheldon Feldman, Associate Professor of Psychology, Swarthmore College.

The output of pilot studies, field interviews, coded data, processed analyses and ordered archives reflects the scientific skills and intellectual energy of these research assistants:

At the Center for the Study of Developing Societies, New Delhi—R. Chandidas, G. R. Lakshman, P. N. Tiku, D. K. Vajpayee; and P. D. Dabhi, N. T. Patel, Kalpana Shah, M. R. Vyas.

At the Institute of Philosophy and Sociology, Warsaw—Marek Kesy, Wanda Marchlewska, Eugeniusz Rylko, Janina Szatkowska, Jacek Szymanderski, Stanislawa Walkowska.

At the University of Pennsylvania—Marshall M. Bouton, Richard N. Brandon, James A. Caporaso, Harry C. Carr, III, J. Harriet Dietz, Leo A. Hazlewood, Steven A. Hoffman, Robert E. Hunt, Sultana Krippendorff, Gordon A. Liechty, Mark S. Levine, Gary E. Mullin, Tulsi B. Saral, Narindar Uberoi and Paul E. Wehr. Miss Dietz also served as administrative assistant with major responsibilities for implementing and coordinating the data analysis program.

At the Institute of Social Sciences, Belgrade—Aleksandra Antic, Miroslav Acimovic, Nevena Eric, Nadezda Obradovic.

At the Institute of Sociology, Ljubljana—Hristina Ferenc, Andreja Tauber.

At the University of Sarajevo—Zlato Grebo, Olga Misirlic.

The complex international administrative arrangements and responsibilities in India were effectively handled by P. R. Mehendiratta, administrative secretary for the American Institute of Indian Studies, New Delhi.

Special thanks are due to Mrs. Lucy Daghlian and Mrs. Franceline Mower for their devoted services in the preparation and reproduction of the manuscript for this book, as well as their longstanding assistance in the operation of the administrative center.

List of Tables

CHAPTER 5

CHAPTER 6

Introduction

Chapter 1 sets forth the central purposes of this study, the major variables investigated and their hypothesized relationships. It also suggests implications of the findings for theory and further research.

The second chapter focuses on the special strategies of measurement and analysis that were designed to meet the problems posed by the comparative, cross-national nature of the research.

Values and Public Vitality: The Political Dynamics of Community Activeness

This chapter was written by Jacob.

This is a study of the genesis of social action, and, in particular, of the factors of human leadership that trigger developmental action in local communities. We have tried to find out why some communities grow and others stagnate; why some demonstrate a common purposefulness and ability to satisfy social needs, while others split apart, nurse separate interests and fail to generate common civic goals; why some are more parochial and others tie in closely to broader regional or national concerns; why some are able to engage their population actively in the conduct of public affairs, while in others there is little citizen participation. We have, in a word, explored the sources of *public vitality*.

The answers sought lie mainly in the dimension of human motivation, operating within the political process. The primary focus is on the role of social values in shaping the behavior and impact of local political leaders. By "values" we mean the standards, or principles, in

All notes will be found at the end of their respective chapters.

terms of which choices are made among alternative courses of action—
that is, the normative component in the determination of action.

Two basic propositions are obviously involved in this approach
to the problem: (1) that the values that leaders hold make a difference
in what they do, and hence in their effectiveness as agents of development, and (2) that social development is at least in part a function of
political leadership.

The selection of local units of government as the level for investigation implies another assumption—that what happens at the base of the
political pyramid has much to do with the tempo of social change, and
may determine whether development occurs at all. Thus while this is a
study of the influence of leadership, it does not presume that effective
influence in social mobilization is necessarily hierarchical. Public vitality
may spring as much, if not more, from the qualities of those who lead
firsthand, as from the leadership of the few at the center and the top.

The exploration of these questions in terms that would be applicable to any general theory of social dynamics required that experience
be compared across environmental lines that might be expected to
condition the relationship between leaders values and community
action; hence the commitment to undertake as rigorously comparable
an inquiry as possible, in four countries differing greatly in political
system, economic development, social structures and cultural heritage.
In choosing India, Poland, U.S. and Yugoslavia as the bases of observation, there was also the expectation that their common preoccupation
with the role of local leadership in solving the major problems of the
society, expressed through various approaches to political decentralization, would provide a similar point of departure and frame of reference
for the investigation.

Scope of the International Studies
of Values in Politics

In brief, this was what was done in this four-year, four-nation
comparative study of the impact of leaders values on social mobilization
at the local level.

A LEADERSHIP SURVEY

In the four countries, 3930 political and governmental office
holders performing comparable functions were interviewed through a
common questionnaire, adopted after pre-tests in each of the countries.
This survey provided the data that made it possible to measure the
degree of commitment of these leaders to nine values expected to have a

strong bearing on their political conduct: (1) innovative social and economic change; (2) propensity to act as against caution and avoidance of risk; (3) economic development and improvement of standards of living; (4) economic equality or lessening inequalities; (5) widespread public participation in decision-making; (6) the avoidance of conflict in the community; (7) national interests and goals; (8) selflessness in behalf of public duty; and (9) truthfulness in public conduct.

In addition, the interviews produced information about the leaders' perceptions of their communities (problems, conflicts, cleavages, influence structure); their roles (scope of activity and influence, loyalties, reference and support groups and admired qualities of leadership); aspirations for their country; and their concept of the appropriate and actual spheres of governmental responsibility for the development of their communities.

AN INVENTORY OF COMMUNITY ACTIVITY

Information was collected from a sample of at least thirty local units in each country on what the local government was doing to promote the development of the community, and what the local population was doing through voluntary activities to support community interests or respond to general national development plans. While the specific activities necessarily varied from country to country, it was possible to measure roughly and compare the degree of activeness or vitality among communities within the same country.

This inventory of community activity provides a basis for estimating the type and amount of what is often called "social mobilization"—a combination of governmental initiatives and citizen participation. Wherever possible, variations in the pattern of community activeness were measured over time. The inventory attempted to show whether there had been an ebb or flow in vitality during the four or five years previous. To some extent it thus became an operating statement rather than a balance sheet.

IDENTIFICATION OF THE LOCAL LEVEL OF ECONOMIC DEVELOPMENT

To control for the possibility that both leaders' values and the pace of community activity might be strongly affected by the community's resource base, whether it was relatively rich or poor, it was necessary to determine measures of the level of development, measures that were applicable to the particular localities in the sample. As appropriate local data were not comprehensively available in several countries, much of the information on indices of local production and income that would permit comparisons along similar dimensions had to be collected directly in the field.

In the end, one to three measures were constructed for each country, and sufficient data were collected to enable all the sampled communities to be scored. In some countries these measures allowed the sample to be fixed in reference to the economic level of the rest of the communities in the country.

Unfortunately, trend data on these indices of economic development were not available in India, so comparable measurement of the communities' rate of growth was limited to the other three countries.

A PROBE OF LOCAL POLITICAL DECISION-MAKING PROCESSES

Life histories of critical decisions were reconstructed in a selection of communities, some of which were among the most active, and some among the least active in the sample. These identified the principal protagonists, explored the bases of their influence on the issues at hand, and, in particular, sought to pinpoint the values that motivated their actions. These case studies followed a common design and focused on similar kinds of issues. Comparisons were therefore possible between active and less active communities, and also across countries, although the number of cases did not permit stable quantitative assessment.

VALUE CONTENT ANALYSIS OF LEADERS STATEMENTS

The values expressed by local leaders in response to open-ended questions on the survey and pre-tests were identified, classified and compared, through the use of a cross-national code derived empirically from the survey data.

In addition, techniques of content-analysis were developed to measure the frequency and intensity of values expressed in speeches and general policy statements in order to get a view of leaders' value orientations independently of a directed survey situation.[1]

Values as a Determinant
of Action

Central to this investigation of the dynamics of social development is the concept of values as one of the basic imperatives of human action. The phenomenon we identify as "value" is a standard, or principle, used by human beings in justifying or opposing a course of action. The process of "evaluating"—judging or appraising action in terms of standards of what "ought" or "ought not" to be, of what is "right" or "wrong," of what "must" be done or "must not" be done, is apparently a general characteristic of human behavior. That such normative considerations are among the powerful influences actually motivating human conduct is the principal proposition being examined in this study.

Since this concept is at variance with some prevailing theories of social change, the study was deliberately designed to test its validity by pitting values against competing variables, situational as well as personal, as possible determinants of action. At the same time, the concept was accepted as the point of departure for defining and operationalizing a variable or set of variables that might help to explain political initiatives and inhibitions affecting the development process.

The most obvious expression of the human disposition to evaluate, and to apply value standards in deciding courses of action, is the immense amount of language devoted to justifying or condemning conduct on the grounds of principles. Much of this has rightly been demonstrated to be spurious. Consciously or unconsciously, people conceal the actual grounds for their actions in a cloak of widely approved "values" (the process often called rationalization) or attempt to manipulate the actions of others by persuading them that a given action will either fulfill worthy ends, or contrarily, violate cherished principles.[2] But the very tendency to seek justification, in terms of standards that others would deem acceptable, is itself a recognition of a deep-seated, widespread disposition to apply values in the process of making choices and determining conduct. The most cynical "Machiavellian" testifies to his belief in the reality and behavioral power of values when he uses value-laden appeals to persuade others to do what he wants done for his own ulterior purposes. To the extent that he is effective, he has learned what are the value determinants of his audience and how to release them.

It must be clear that what we are talking about here is something quite different from a body of desired or wanted things. People's wants, likes or preferences may be completely devoid of "value" in the sense in which we are defining it. A person may want something very much, but feel he "should not" get it because it would not be in line with a principle to which he is committed. A person may do something he thoroughly dislikes and does not want to do (for instance, protest a superior's decision and risk his job) because he feels compelled by a "value" that overrides his immediate personal desires or rewards. Both wants and values influence conduct, and influence each other. Wants are screened by values before they exert their impact on action; but values in turn are often shaped to conform to wants, as it is more comfortable for people to have what they want legitimized by their values. But they are different phenomena, and in this research an effort has been made to distinguish them.[3]

The specific content, or substance, of people's values is socially derived—though the phenomenon of value itself and the disposition to evaluate is, we have suggested, an intrinsic characteristic of human beings. Specific values are learned, acquired through the multiple life experiences that people go through. They can therefore be extremely diversified, and individuals may, as a result of their particular mix of personal experiences, come to hold particular values that, if not unique, are not shared by many others.

On the other hand, where groups of people have similar experiences, common values tend to emerge. For the purposes of understanding social behavior, two sources of common values seem particularly important. One is the dominant cultural unit with which people are associated. The other is the role or set of roles within which people function.

THE CULTURAL BASIS OF VALUES

The definition of parameters of "cultures" is usually the despair of social scientists, and often the relationship between culture and values is described tautologically, i.e., a culture is held to be coterminous with the values shared by the people belonging to it. This difficulty does not appear to have been satisfactorily met by recent analysts of "political culture," though these analysts have tried to identify such cultures through consensus on certain principles and procedures of government and common loyalties to a set of political institutions. The problem is in part a question of specifying with consistency what will be used as the empirical indicators of a culture, and also what will be taken as the threshold of consensus or common behavior necessary for a group of people to be considered members of the same culture.[4]

From the standpoint of the present study, we have simply used the country or nation as the starting point for a search for culture-based values, and approached the question empirically. Are there values that most of the respondents in a given country share, regardless of where they live or what they do or what social status they hold? If so, we assume that their cultural heritage and the experiences they have shared as fellow nationals have to this extent transcended the many ways in which their lives have differed, and have created a genuine "national culture". This culture is not necessarily distinctive. People in different countries may have quite similar values, which would be explained by common experiences that cut across national lines and therefore set different boundaries to the cultural base. Such, for instance, would be the case if respondents in several countries that were poor and economically underdeveloped demonstrated that they held many of the same values. This would be evidence of the existence of an "underdevelopment culture." On the other hand people within the same country may differ fundamentally on values which vitally affect their conduct. This would indicate the existence of subcultures, or perhaps even full-blown cultures of equal or greater potency than the national culture—for instance, a subnational group whose consensus of values was built upon color, associations, language and other experiences that set them apart from the rest of the country.[5]

The point is, therefore, that while the nation may be an appropriate preliminary point of focus for an investigation of culture-based values (especially in a study concerned with contemporary political behavior) one cannot assume that the nation as defined is sufficient. Hence, the research has been designed to secure a data base that would make possible a distinction between values transcending national lines and those characterizing particular nations; this base would also be able to distinguish those values that characterize subnational cultures.

Of the nine values for which cross-nationally comparable scales were developed, major international differences emerged on six (comparing the mean or average scores for the sample of leaders in each country). Only with respect to the values of Truthfulness, Selflessness and, possibly, sense of National Commitment might one conclude that there was sufficient similarity to suggest a *trans-cultural* basis of values.

Of the remaining six, differences on three—Economic Development, Economic Equality and Conflict Avoidance—exactly follow the respective economic levels of the countries. The strongest and most widespread commitment to the values is expressed in India; the weakest in the United States (with the stand on Economic Equality amounting to vigorous rejection of this value). These then might be interpreted as expressions of a *"development culture"*: mild concern for development (on the material side), strong opposition to equalization of wealth, and tolerance amounting to unconcern over social conflict and community dissension. The reverse would be the value profile of an *"underdevelopment culture."* Poland and Yugoslavia stand between these poles, with Poland nearer the development pole, Yugoslavia closer to the underdevelopment pole of India.

What about a distinctively *national culture* of values then? Can one identify an Indian or a Yugoslav, a Polish or an American profile? It appears that the leadership sample in each country does emerge with a particular mix or balance that to some extent is different from any other. This is most marked in regard to those values that might be expected to set the main direction of social change. Thus, the Indian group, while heavily committed to economic equality, is strongly against widespread public participation in decision-making, i.e., the "democratization" of policy formation and administration. Yugoslav leaders tend to favor both greater economic equality and greater public participation. Americans want the participation without the equality. The Polish group tends to side with the Indians against participation, but is much less enthusiastic about economic equality than anyone else except the Americans; it is the most nationally oriented of the four samples.[6]

However, the softness of these cultural generalizations based on averages must be recognized, as the averages conceal immense intra-cultural differences. Leaders differ more among themselves *within the same community* than they do nation-to-nation. This would indicate that other experiences than those that are common to a nation (or any other general cultural base) have had a stronger influence in shaping the values of these local leaders.[7] An alternative source might be the role expectations that leaders try to fulfill.

ROLE VALUES

"Role" is well-established in sociological research as a powerful behavioral determinant, and a shaper of values. What people expect of a person, in the various functions he performs, is probably the most immediate and obvious source of the norms which guide his day-to-day activities. The evidence is especially strong in the case of persons engaged in public activities. In the hierarchy of public administrative office, the expectations of superiors obviously demand respect; but in turn superiors find that they must command the respect of those that work for them by adhering closely to settled standards of appropriate conduct. In electoral office, there are the constituents of all shades of influence to consider—the party to which one belongs, and the factions within it, one's associates in the electoral body, the administrators with whom one must get along. The list goes on and on, with limits set subjectively by the person himself as he decides who he wants to listen to, but also objectively, for failure to respect the expectations of the right "reference groups" could cost him his office.[8]

In a comprehensive study of behavioral influences, the range of role values would extend to the expectations of reference groups bearing on all of an individual's activities and associations, a truly staggering inventory. What we are particularly concerned about in this study are those values that are most likely to affect the decisions of leaders in their political functions, especially those bearing on their community's social development. We have therefore sharply focused on a limited set of values perceived by people holding local public office to be the kind of considerations they would normally take into account. (See above, p. 5.)

This was controlled by a direct inquiry concerning the groups in or out of the community to whom the leader said he normally turned for support and concerning what he considered to be the primary focus of his responsibility as a leader—his party, his friends, the people in his community or the nation as a whole. The leader was also asked what obstacles he felt limited his effectiveness.

This evidence provides an empirical basis for identifying some of the role values that are relevant for the persons and the functions that are the object of this study.

THE ISSUE OF UNIVERSALITY

Values are conceived in this study as neither universal nor absolute (although some persons might consider the values they themselves hold to be so).[9] Given the great diversity of life experiences out of which values emerge, it would be expected that values would differ widely. On the other hand, to the extent that people have common needs, they may come to hold many aspirations in common, and this would exert influence in the direction of some more or less universally shared values. However, in an empirical study of this character, the existence of universal values as a political determinant is something to be demonstrated, not to be assumed. And the test of universality available to us is of course only the responses and behavior of the people we interviewed and observed; if this limited but highly diversified sample of mankind generally expressed similar values, we could declare some probability that these values were universals. Such would seem to be the case with two of the values scaled: truthfulness in public conduct, and the sense that self-interest should be subordinated to public interest by public officials. As professions of what "ought" to be, few leaders in any country could be pressed to disagree, even by "sophisticated" survey technique.

CONFLICT OF VALUES AND ITS MANAGEMENT

The diversity of sources of values gives rise to value conflicts. Such conflicts arise not only between persons and groups whose experiences have led them to hold different values; each person is himself bound also to discover internal conflict between values he has arrived at out of one aspect of his life and those that reflect another. Standards set by a culture with which he identifies may be incompatible with the norms he is expected to fill as civil servant; values he respects as a member of the local community may in concrete situations be pitted against his obligations as a party member; national goals to which he feels a commitment may run counter to considerations of family or self-interest that he also justifies as legitimate yardsticks of his conduct.

Choices of action are therefore the outcome of a balancing of values, in situations where a person can rarely find a way to satisfy all his concerns. The variety of processes devised by human beings to manage their value conflicts in the making of decisions has been extensively explored, especially in research on cognitive dissonance. For instance, the strong need for consistency felt by many may lead to rationalizing away the recognition of value conflict, while in fact definitely deciding to subordinate one value to another—assuming compatibility when there is none. On the other hand, paralysis may result when a person is unable either to sweep his value conflict under the rug, or to determine priorities.[10]

From the standpoint of political behavior, the former process is more likely than the latter (following upon the familiar maxim, "politics is the art of the possible"). But often, the leader finds himself caught, unable to affect a viable compromise between values of equal weight that refuse to be reconciled. Then no-decision becomes the decision, but as a result of inability to choose, rather than of deliberate choice.

The strategy of this study was designed to get at priorities among some of the values espoused by the leaders, as they confronted a variety of familiar situations of value conflict. This was checked against a simple expression of which of several values they considered more important *in the abstract*. Responses were sufficiently consistent (within counties) to indicate that the priorities professed by these leaders are quite stable, although they do differ among countries.[11]

VALUES AND CHANGE

The general question of the stability of values as a determinant of action needs to be considered. It is customary to think of values as among the most persistent and hence most predictable of human dispositions. Grounded as they are on a long accumulation of experience, one could hardly expect values to be volatile. To change a value, or more significantly, to change priorities among values, would require a confrontation of new experiences so radically at odds with what a person had gone through up to this point in his life that he could not integrate them into his established value pattern. And because learning is arduous and most people cherish emotional and physical security, we try to protect ourselves from exposure to the kinds of experience likely to shatter our values or challenge them too severely. Thus a built-in resistance to the new and untried reinforces the solidity of the structure of values we have come, over time, to accept. It is in this perspective that values have acquired the reputation of a conservative force in human affairs, associated with "tradition" and inhibiting developmental change.

But values, in the sense in which we are talking about them, have an equally notable association with initiative for social change; witness the ideological mystique of most revolutions, as well as the moral imperatives of reform movements and, now, the heralded commitments to "modernization" values. What is it that breaks the circle of socialization forces, undercuts the continuity of long established values, and precipitates change-inducing values? An obvious explanation is the intrusion of an outside force that cannot be pushed aside—an attack, be it military, cultural, or technological, upon settled ways. While response could well be an even deeper withdrawal into the traditional, many would feel they had to come to some kind of terms with the new experience and adapt their values accordingly.

But even without the prod of an external aggression, values might change as a result of a breakdown in the adequacy of existing institutions to deal with what people are accustomed to consider their basic conditions of life. If inefficiencies and corruption of governmental and social leadership go beyond "normal," if demands are constantly frustrated by incapacities which can be readily laid at some human door, if all of this is compounded by a rising consciousness of discrimination and sense of injustice, then people can experience great and often very sudden transformations of values, or those values that were subdued can become the basis for vigorous action.

Whether or not such changing social conditions follow set paths of development as a result of the interaction of social and economic forces is an issue that is not confronted in this study. The collaborators agreed, however, that their different perspectives on the process of social change need not interfere with an attempt to examine empirically the relationships between values and antecedent social conditions. Consequently, possible environmental sources of values and value priorities were explored (by correlational analysis) with the influence of leaders' political role and personal background. This search for explanations of differences among leaders' values actually proved less productive than expected, and threw a good deal of doubt on some prevalent theories of socialization and social causation.[12]

The central objective of this work, it should be recalled however, was to determine the influence of values on change, rather than to find out what made or changed values. Hence, the relationship of leaders' values to several multiple measures of local "dynamism," in both the mobilization of resources and of social participation, has been examined by both bivariate and multivariate procedures.

The striking differences among countries in these relationships suggests that the role of values in the determination of social change is *not* uniform, and that no single line of causation of social development is demonstrable. The import of this finding for the theory and practice of social planning is clearly of first importance.

Only in India is there a clear association of leaders' values with social mobilization in communities, an association apparently unaffected by economic resources, social structure, political differences or other factors. If a leader tends to be more strongly committed to nation and less concerned than others with avoiding conflict in the community, his community will be more likely to undertake innovative activity; leaders whose values tend in the opposite direction will be likely to head communities whose activity moves in the conventional paths of agricultural society.

But in the other three countries, other determinants of development predominate, as will be seen. Thus the influence of values must be analyzed *in conjunction with* basic environmental conditions—the initial proposition of this study is modified accordingly.

In concluding this section, the empirical commitment of the study should be reemphasized, particularly in view of the paucity of cross-nationality comparable material on values and their social effects.[13] The entire effort was devoted to systematic operationalizing of the concept of values, and of all the other variables analyzed, in terms of explicit empirical observations. The result is findings that, however limited in scope and depth, are derived from real life and have a known relevance to expressed valuations by a broad spectrum of local leaders in four countries. "Values" as they are identified and analyzed in this study, amount in fact to the responses of 3930 live people stating how and why they would act on a variety of issues in their positions as elected or appointed officials governing their communities.[14]

The Active
Community

"Being active" is the general phenomenon we seek to explain, in terms of values and other influences on human conduct. But it is *corporate* action with *social purpose* that particularly concerns us. People working together, pooling their resources and energies, to accomplish certain common ends—this is the kind of behavior whose motivation we seek to understand. For it is this quality of social dynamism that lies at the core of the processes of human development. Indeed, it is the effective application of human energy to the manipulation of resources, in coordinated effort, that *is* development.

The immense differences across the world, and the changes from time to time, in the amount and direction of social dynamism is one of the persistent enigmas that has challenged social science. Curiously, the phenomenon itself has not been generally and systematically defined. We therefore decided to anchor this investigation in a representative set of activities at a level at which people had opportunity for close interaction if they were so inclined—the lowest unit of government at which decisions having significance for the lives of the people are made.

POLITICAL UNITS AS COMMUNITIES

A political basis was selected for the arena of social action because government has become a major pivot of collective efforts: government is (or tries to be) on the one hand an instigator, mobilizer and directive power; it is on the other hand, a target of people who want to extend the effects of their own personal initiatives and involve others, voluntarily or involuntarily, in their enterprises. It is a convenient turnstile at which to check the vigor of social dynamism.

Admittedly, such a political unit may not correspond to what is widely conceived of as a "community," where people are knit together by feelings of mutual attachment and a sense of common affiliation. Prolonged debate occurred among the collaborators in the project as to whether a more appropriate choice for observing social action would not be groups that had developed into "real" communities to which people felt they "belonged." It was decided, however, that part of the problem to be investigated was the extent to which social *action* was necessarily related to social *community*. Could we take for granted that communal integration was the womb of vigorous group effort to meet the needs and advance the well-being of the community? Or might it be that social conflict would more likely generate outputs of resources and activity? Significant evidence could only be secured if we compared social units that differed both in activism and in sense of community, with the assumption that it was possible to secure reliable measures of each.[15]

DIMENSIONS OF ACTIVENESS

The properties of community activeness as we have conceived it are, on the one hand a joint effort, and on the other, the pursuit of interests presumably of benefit to the general community.

For the purpose of this study we have excluded the personal activities of individuals in seeking a living, caring for their own families or otherwise looking out for their private welfare. We have also tried to draw a line between activities that are *voluntary*, or at least locally initiated, and those that are made *obligatory* by government fiat from outside the community; we have also differentiated between those that involve the mobilization of resources from within the community and those that merely parcel out resources pumped in from the outside. While the data did not always yield to these neat distinctions, they do basically demonstrate what the locality was willing to put out, on its own, for a public purpose. It should be emphasized that this was not a measure of altruism, but of the degree of mutual interest at work in the community. (Nor, it should be added, was social or political compulsion completely barred, provided that it was imposed from within the community, as in the case of local taxes.)

Community activeness was then further broken down into what the local government did, and what the general population did. Money raised and spent, efforts to get grants from the state or national governments, (or in some instances efforts to go it alone in a mood of self-reliance) the establishment and improvement of public institutions —this was the dimension of "resource mobilization" by public authority. The second dimension—"public involvement"—was indicated by the amount of popular participation in social, cultural and political activity—membership, contributions, volunteer labor, etc.

It should be immediately pointed out—anticipating the detailed report of findings later—that in fact community performance was by no means consistent along all these lines. Instead of a single unidimensional coherent measure of activeness, it turns out that there may be several. A community may be high in output on some activities, low on others; factor analysis demonstrates that there are several distinct *clusters* of activities, with certain communities scoring high on one, while, on another, an entirely different set of communities will be top performers. Thus there are different *types* of activeness. It further turns out that communities exhibiting one type of dynamism usually also have other characteristics that distinguish them from communities that are active in other directions.[16]

This means that the pattern of social development and the *character* of community vitality (quite apart from the question of its *degree* of vitality) differs substantially from community to community within the same country. So the task of explanation suddenly becomes more complex. We have not only to account for why some communities are more active than others; we must find out why some are active in one way, and others in another, and what the implications of these different modes of dynamism are for these communities as they attempt to cope with their own problems and relate to those of the rest of the country.

The complementary aspect of community life with which we must be concerned is its cohesion, or integration, since the relationship of social unity to social dynamism is not, we have urged, of necessity a direct one.

To think of social cohesion as something that people *feel*, in contrast to what they *do* together, leads to a search for common loyalties, common values or both, which result in mutual attachment among those sharing these loyalties and values, and a sense that they all belong to the same "community." The mark of such a concept of integration, is in short, *collective identity*—people being able to point to this social unit, this group of people, as "my community," "my nation," "my country."

Without speculating about the full range of factors that may induce this identity and determine how narrow or broad the human base of the community with which people identify may be, this study has centered on the *congruence of leaders' values* as one plausible measure of both the degree and the scope of this kind of social integration. The assumption made is that widespread consensus among leaders on values they consider relevant to decisions affecting their communities indicates that their communities are well-integrated; if leaders are widely divided on their values, it is assumed their communities are poorly integrated.[17]

Such congruence of values is not tantamount to a sense of identity with a community. If, however, persons happen to share as one of their values, a strong concern for nation, or, alternatively, a strong concern for the welfare of their local community, congruence on *this* value would come close to designating the area of collective identity and also the intensity of attachment (especially if concern for one community were pitted against that for another: nation vs. locality, for instance, or country vs. region). This was precisely the intention in setting up several of the value scales.[18]

In the meantime, it *is* possible to compare and to relate integration at the *community* level, *in the sense of collective action*, with integration at the *leadership* level, *in the sense of shared values*, i.e., community activeness or dynamism with the homogeneity or heterogeneity of leaders' values. In these terms, the findings are impressively negative. There is *no* connection between these two forms of integration, given the different levels of observation.[19] While the important limitations of the data must be recognized, these two forms strongly suggest that "integration" is not a single, discrete phenomenon. Communities may be integrated in one way and not in another. It is misleading therefore to talk in general terms of whether a community, a country, a society is "integrated" or not. We must specify the kind of integration we are talking about before we presume to measure it.[20]

Returning in conclusion to the question of community activeness, we are now prepared to urge that this is an empirically identifiable phenomenon, probably with several dimensions that may vary across countries, but with sufficient coherence and commonality to offer a basis for comparison among communities within the same country, and, in the case of at least one composite index, to compare communities in different countries with some assurance that we are dealing with the same phenomenon (see Chapter 8). Activeness, while it may be taken as a form of community integration or an expression thereof, must however be sharply distinguished from other concepts of integration, such as shared or compatible values, or a sense of communal identity. Our evidence indicates that leaders of active communities are as likely to be widely split on their values, as leaders of inactive ones.

Power and Responsibility: The Political Context of Development

The choice of countries and the choice of level for a study of values and public vitality was governed in part by the expectation that the character of the political system would have a lot to do with the shaping of political conduct. The different social objectives of government, influencing in turn the extent to which government assumed responsibility for directing the course of social and economic development, would obviously create markedly different roles for political leadership. What leaders did, and what was expected of them would not be the same in socialist systems and in ones that preserved a large sector of private enterprise.

Another important systemic difference, and one considered of immediate relevance to the dynamics of development, is the extent to which the powers of political action are centralized or widely distributed. One thesis holds that effectiveness in the initiation and execution of major social change requires highly concentrated direction. Unity of vision, comprehensiveness of planning, coordination of effort throughout the society, and, especially, discipline in the making of difficult choices of which needs to satisfy and which to sacrifice—these are often held to be feasible only if the powers of government are exercised primarily by a limited vanguard of the gifted and the committed. But an almost opposite premise is advanced by those who see the crucial issue of development as the generation of widespread initiative and effort throughout the society. Social responsibility, it is urged, emerges only as people have the power to make decisions affecting their lives. They will not respond to someone else's decisions as vigorously as they will to decisions for which they feel personally responsible. Hence a political system that decentralizes political power, and places it as much as possible in the hands of local units, is likely to be more successful in mobilizing the society for development and getting it to the point of accepting changes required for "progress."

Each of the four countries involved in this study has, in different ways, been putting this issue of the power base of responsibility to the test of political experimentation. As described in Chapter 6, Poland, among the four, clearly retains the maximum centralization of political authority over the processes of development. Yugoslavia ideologically, and in practice, has gone furthest in commitment to decentralization. In India, the attempt to develop local responsibility through the inauguration of the three-tiered *panchayat* system has moved at different tempos in various states, and, with some differences, in the tier at which more important decisions are made. In actuality, the really critical decisions over allocation of resources and the strategy of social and economic development, are still made either at the Center or by the governments of the various states, with the panchayats having sometimes more, sometimes less say about implementation. The situation in the United States is difficult to assess; nominally, the division of powers between national and state governments leaves a very large discretion to the states, which, in turn, some of them have passed on to the municipalities or to other local authorities. At the same time, the federal government has assumed an ever widening range of functions, and these have become crucial in the manipulation of the development process.

These differences in system are reflected in the *perceptions* that local leaders have of the amount of power at their disposal, and whether this degree of autonomy is sufficient for the effective development of their communities. The leadership survey tapped the significance of perceived autonomy within countries and across countries. Coupled with this was a query concerning what the leaders considered to be the appropriate sphere of governmental activity in regard to their community's problems, and specifically whether central or local institutions should be primarily responsible for dealing with them. A third, less direct line of evidence was secured by inquiring what obstacles the leaders felt interfered with their effectiveness.

The results of the study of *formal* autonomy do not neatly confirm either the centralist or decentralist positions. Under the most centralized system (Poland) there is absolutely no nexus between local leaders' values and the pace and direction of community activeness, whereas in India, such a connection clearly exists. In Yugoslavia and the United States the economic level of the community emerges as a preponderant determinant of the pattern of activeness, but there seems to be no reason to assume that this is associated with differences in local decision-making powers. Affluence and poverty act *independently* of political system to control the dynamics of development.

The picture of *perceived* autonomy is one of no significance. In only scattered instances does the opinion of local leaders that they lack enough power to cope with their community's problems seem to be associated either with the direction of their own values or the various expressions of community activeness.

The broad conclusion for all four countries seriously *undercuts* the view that political responsibility flows from a base of political power, or from a *belief* that one is functioning at a point in the political system where significant action is possible. At least this is the conclusion for the relationship between *institutional* power (the autonomy of the local organs of government) and *collective* responsibility (the acts of the local government and of the local community). Whether this also applies to *personal* power, the individual's sense of his own influence, is examined in another part of the study.

Resources: Impetus
or Constraint?

The dominant place of economic factors in the analysis and explanation of socio-economic development, and especially of that phase currently labeled "modernization," virtually demands that any research bearing on the dynamics of social change plug into the design an adequate measure of the resource base from which the individual or the group operates. This is all the more necessary if one expects to demonstrate the importance of noneconomic factors in the development process, in line with the kind of challenge that has been made by exponents of one kind or another of political development theory,[21] or

by some economists as they have grappled practically with the phenomena of underdevelopment and economic stagnation.[22]

In weighing the developmental impact of economic factors against
the social values of leaders, for instance, some of the alternative possibilities are:

(1) The values of leaders might themselves primarily reflect the affluence or
poverty of their communities, their personal economic status, or both.
Were this the case, an observation that some of these values related to
community activeness could not be taken as evidence that the values
were themselves a prime, independent influence. The finding would need
to be interpreted as merely indicating that values were a path by which
the basic factor of wealth was bringing its influence to bear.

(2) If the values of leaders could be shown to be independent of resources—
i.e., rich or poor alike held to the same values—they still might have
different effects upon communities, depending upon the resources that the
leaders had to work with. The area of *possible* activeness might be severely
constrained by the community's poverty; no matter how dynamic and
change-oriented its leaders were, and how hard they tried to mobilize
social effort, accomplishments would be meager and could drop the
community into the ranks of the apparently stagnant.

(3) On the other hand, a community endowed by good fortune, by its heritage
of past efforts or by outside largesse from government or foundations,
with the rudiments of high level productivity or the good life, could
put on an impressive demonstration of activeness, which had nothing to
do with the characteristic of its leadership (values or otherwise). The
impetus of resources might be sufficiently generating of social outputs to
overcome otherwise inhibiting factors in the makeup and dispositions of
leadership and citizenry.

(4) But if it were demonstrated that the pattern of leaders' values made a
difference in activeness, *after* holding constant for the economic level
of the community, then the conclusion would be warranted that the
influence of values was strong enough to overcome whatever constraints
were imposed by lack of resources, and able to add to the impetus
provided by such resources available.

What comes out of this study is a striking *dissimilarity among
countries* in the influence on local development of the economic factor,
i.e., the present resource base of the community.

Briefly, in India the economic factor has *no* association with development; nor does it in Poland (though apparently for quite different
reasons). In the United States and Yugoslavia, the economic status of the
community is one of the most compelling influences on activeness. In
particular, it completely displaces leaders' values as an independent
influence. If communities are held constant for economic level, an
apparent connection between certain values of leaders and the com-

munities' activeness disappears. This corresponds to alternative 1 in the list of patterns of influence presented above; whereas India represents alternative 4 and Poland probably represents alternative 3.

The evidence strongly implies that the assumption that economic conditions predetermine social change is not applicable everywhere. Such a theory would certainly not explain the dynamics of local activeness in some of the underdeveloped areas of Asia, such as the segment of rural India examined in this study (thus confirming the contention of Myrdal that one cannot presume that European experience will automatically apply to areas that differ culturally, institutionally and in economic circumstances from the West).[23] In such places, completely alternative explanations need to be sought, or else the architects of development strategy will probably find their plans frustrated and their inputs of resources ineffective in triggering the mythical "takeoff."

On the other hand, it is equally significant that in countries as disparate in political system and economic condition as the United States and Yugoslavia, wealth (relatively speaking) should exercise so controlling an influence on social behavior. In each, it is the "haves" among communities who sparkle with activeness and push even further ahead—a testimony to the proverbial prediction that "to those that hath shall be given," regardless of whether the system is socialist or capitalist in the versions of those systems that are represented respectively by these two countries. This experience seems to support a circular interpretation of community dynamics in which economic differences precipitate an ever widening gulf in the incentives and capabilities for development between communities that are affluent and those that are poor, but this is *only* supported in specific locales, probably within the stream of Western industrial or preindustrial societies.[24]

But even this pushes generalization too far—witness the case of Poland, where it seems apparent that firm political decision at the top could manage the input of both human and material resources so as to overcome whatever economic deficiencies stood in the way of active community development in a favored area.[25] Political authority thus can reverse or at least offset the constraints imposed by lack of resources in a particular circumstance, though whether the result will be self-sustained indigenous effort remains to be seen.

The basic implication of these findings is that the precise effect upon the process and pattern of development of resources or the lack thereof is dependent upon other conditions which must be examined empirically. General models of development that presume a fixed and uniform interaction of material inputs and outputs must be held suspect insofar as the local level is concerned.

*The Social Matrix of Local Development: Cleavage, Conflict and
the Structure of Influence*

Looking into the heart of the community itself, can one find, in the pattern of its human relations, an additional set of factors that explains the way it functions, how it copes with its needs and whether it has acquired the quality of public vitality? Two lines of sociological inquiry stressing the importance of social structure in the shaping of social conduct are of particular significance. The first envisages the structure of community power and influence as decisive. The second focuses on the sources of cleavage in the community and the pathology of its conflicts.[26]

For the most part, the analyses of community power structure have been descriptive and have taken for granted that knowing *who* was influential would explain *why* decisions were made. Underlying this approach is a largely unexpressed tie to class and interest-group theories that assume that social action is determined by collective aspirations, usually following well-defined lines of property, occupation, religion, ethnic association, or status. Although in the more refined models, it is recognized that lines of interest can overlap, so that individuals serve more than one interest-group master, the prevailing notion still seems to be that, in the arena of politics at least, group interests are tightly knit, self-serving and therefore mutually exclusive.

Because of this assumed one-to-one relationship between groups and interests, the search for the determinants of action then indeed need go no further than to identify "who gets what, when and how," to use Lasswell's apt phrase. If a single interest group is able to secure control of the political authority, its interest and its alone will govern. If power must be shared, decisions will be bargained out, interests adjusted and compromised to a point approximating the effective influence of the different groups in coalition. Astute leadership might even go so far as to take into account interests of the "outs" as a means of forestalling a serious challenge to power, thus at the same time testifying to the going influence of the opposition and the skill of the "in" leadership in containing it.[27]

What is not clear from the community power studies and even from their interest-group corollaries is how far the power-interest-decision linkage is empirically validated, and particularly how applicable it is cross-culturally to explain the dynamics of political action and social development at the local level.

A second problem is to distinguish between the effects on action of who is in power as against the structure of power *per se*. For instance, does it make a difference in what a community does if influence is dispersed or if concentrated in a few hands; if the influence of the influential is general or if specific to certain areas (one group having influence in financial matters, another in education and social services, etc.)? Again, community studies have tended to provide descriptions of structural characteristics, but are sparse in evaluating their effects and particularly in balancing such effects against the impact of interests. These sets of determinants—structures and interests—are clearly entirely different kinds of phenomena, yet they are often discussed under the common heading "social structure," to the confusion of analysis.[28]

In the ISVIP, an attempt was made to measure four aspects of the community's social structure and relate them independently of other variables and of each other to the pattern of community activeness. The first was the range of activity and influence of the local political leaders, leading to an overall estimate of the concentration of political influence. This was based mainly on self-inventory by the survey respondents in default of resources for a thorough sociometric study in all countries. However, the decisional case studies furnished an opportunity to check the reliability of the leaders as informants, in selected communities.[29] In the United States a complementary study of public decision-making in the entire sample produced data that permit the construction of a specific index of decentralization.[30] Further studies in India related to ISVIP broaden the base of evidence on the structure of influence in some of the communities in the sample, but not on all.

The second structural variable is the reference groups to whom the leaders turn for support. This has previously been mentioned as a source of inference for the "role values" likely to influence leaders in their decisions. But the way the inventory of support groups was constructed also makes possible a strict structural analysis of the significance of such factors as: (1) how far local leaders are locally oriented or linked to influences outside the community; (2) how close to the seats of local power are particular interest groups in the community (the wealthy, the poor, the workers, the peasants, the intelligentsia); (3) how dominant a political party is in the hierarchy of influence; and (4) how independent the bureaucracy of any of the facets of local political power is.

Third, the sources of divisions in the community were examined through the eyes of the leadership, and again the case studies provide a modest check on the reliability of the leaders as informants. A profile of cleavages was derived from this information and it was then possible to determine whether activeness was inhibited or promoted by the amount of division felt over such issues as income differences, political views, religious beliefs, race or ethnic origin.

Finally, the incidence of conflict was assessed, again as perceived by the local political leaders, and specifically related to the question of its effect upon community development. The leaders were asked to what extent conflicts interfered with the development of their communities.

The result of these multiple inquiries was evidence bearing on both the structural pattern of influence in the narrow sense, and the underlying bases of contending interests within the community. By approaching the latter area the way we have, no prejudgment was made about what the interests might be of the principal reference groups of the leaders, or how the major lines of social cleavage would affect the exercise of political power. Furthermore, care was taken to avoid prejudging whether community conflict would necessarily follow the cleavage lines. A distinction was drawn between cleavage and conflict with an allowance for the possibility that people might be divided, but not to the point of outright intergroup conflict over the issues that divided them.

Thus, what we have here is source data that carefully distinguishes four possible components of influence: (1) the base activity of leaders; (2) the reference-support groups of those in political authority; (3) the social cleavages that underlie local interest groups; and (4) the lines of social struggle that reach the point of outright conflict. The interrelationship of these components is not assumed *a priori*; it is to be ascertained empirically.

Reporting first on whether there is a common identifiable "power elite" that governs active communities in all countries, the answer is unequivocally "No." Neither the areas of leaders' influence, nor the nature of the interest-groups to whom they turn for support coincide to mark a cross-nationally similar class or interest basis of "developmental" leadership attached to communities that are the most responsive to social change. Indeed, there is only the most fragmentary evidence for any kind of an elite profile for leaders of change-oriented communities in *any* of the countries. What there is tends to be negative evidence—areas in which such leaders claim to have *no* influence (political organization in the United States, agriculture, public utilities and social services in Yugoslavia), and interest groups which they tend to *shun* (local officials and other supposedly influential people in the community in India; and in Yugoslavia, surprisingly, the local committees of the League of Communists and the Socialist Alliance, organizations expected to be the spearheads of developmental change). In Poland and the United States, the leaders of active communities do tend to identify a positive support base, but in neither situation is the base groups with a special, self-serving interest. In Poland, it is local officialdom (both appointed and elected) to whom the leaders of the active turn; in the United States, they look to civic and reform groups, groups having interest in the general uplift of the community rather than in acquiring special advantages for themselves.[31]

This would seem to suggest that when it comes to the engineering of social change, local political leadership loses whatever characteristics it may normally possess as the spokesman for special interests, and ceases to perform as the agent of a particular class, caste, racial, ethnic or other socio-economic pressure group. One might almost conclude that the mark of developmental leadership is class neutrality. Such leaders are capable of severing bonds that would stand in the way of the performance of responsibilities in the "public interest," an interest that to them implies one form or another of economic and social betterment for the entire community. They must then find or build a support structure that cuts across the prevailing lines of social cleavage in their home constituencies, or turn to the outside for their source of influence. Neither of these alternatives is easy to do, a fact that may explain the negative nature of the evidence. The leaders of the active communities have cut their normal ties, but have not yet located a firm and well-defined alternative support structure. They know whom they do *not* want to be dependent on or beholden to; they do not clearly identify new lines of political or social responsibility that they can follow with confidence. To some extent therefore, developmental leadership, having become classless, is also leaderless.[32]

In contrast to the local structure of power, the cleavage pattern, and, particularly, the incidence of conflict has significant impact on community activeness, but only in two countries. Also, the effect of conflict is opposite in the two countries. In Poland, lack of perceived conflict and lack of political cleavage account for activeness more than any other variable. Social harmony and political uniformity is the seedbed for social and political vitality. In the United States, however, conflicts among social groups operate to instigate community activeness. Further, with respect to cleavage, the active communities tend, as might be expected, to be ones where there is little division between employers and employees. In neither India nor Yugoslavia did either cleavage or conflict emerge in any consistent way to explain the pattern of activeness.

The implications of this extraordinary heterogeneity of social behavior at such a fundamental level as the consequences of cleavage and conflict are most difficult to assess. It would be convenient if one could dismiss the findings on the grounds that methodological deficiencies, or differences in the implementation of the survey, had systematically biased the results in one or more of the countries. However, reexamination of the entire process of constructing, testing and administering the questionnaire, and of coding and analyzing its results, has turned up no evidence that would fault the reliability of the findings for one country against another, or of these particular items against others. In fact, the conflict questions have the advantage, from the reliability standpoint, of having been posed in a variety of formats and perspectives, and permitted cross-checking for consistency of response. The cleavage questions have the further quality of considerable specificity of reference.

We are faced with the necessity of explaining why leaders' perceptions of cleavage and conflict have such a different bearing on social change and development in these four countries. The following alternatives come to mind:

(1) Conflict and social cleavage are at odds with what is expected in Poland to be the condition of a satisfactorily developing community; so that where social change is taking place in response to, and in line with the officially prescribed plan, it would be inappropriate for local leaders to admit to conditions that would amount to a confession of failure on their part.

Alternatively, the situation might be interpreted as demonstrating that in fact, this kind of developmental push results in social unity; that many of the normal sources of cleavage do not arise, with a corresponding evaporation of causes of conflict. A true "classless" society is in process of formation, and the leaders are accurately reporting this fact.

(2) In the United States, leaders are problem-oriented and pragmatic. They act when they see a problem that must be solved, and only then. Their communities are the same way. Spend money, put forth effort for the common welfare only when you have to. But "enlightened" leadership may anticipate problems more quickly than others; hence action flows from their perception of conflict in the community, even if actual conflict may be much more intense elsewhere than in the active community.

Furthermore, because initiative for development as in Poland, stems much more from within the community than from the central government, the leaders' perception of conflict acts as a trigger for social mobilization in the U.S., whereas in Poland it would be a sign that the "plan" had not yet reached down and moved the community very far in the intended developmental process (or that the community perhaps had even been declared a development outcast because of the intensity of its conflicts).

(3) In India and Yugoslavia alike, conflicts and cleavages are so generally accepted as constants in community life that leaders are not likely to differ very much in their estimates, whatever community they lead. Development, if it is to occur, will be triggered not by awareness of conflict, but by a readiness to live with it and not be worried by it—by a *value* in other words (for development as against conflict avoidance) rather than by a perception. Significantly, this approach characterizes the two

countries at the lowest level of development in our sample; and those where multiple lines of cleavage and conflict have pervaded the societies for a long time.

In conclusion, it must be apparent from the evidence that, once again, human beings have defied sociological generalization. Conflict theorists cannot presume that uniform lines of social response follow upon the stimulus of given types or degrees of conflict. Social change in one direction or another may or may not occur as a result of one form or another of division in a community, or conflicts emerging therefrom— at least to the extent that they are perceived or admitted by the local political establishments. The change impetus of conflict at the community level must be calculated within a much broader context, inclusive of the resource base, the system of political authority and some of the values of leadership. Conflict does not operate on its own as the precipitant or inhibitor of development action.

The Demography of Developmental Leadership

The search for the roots of political behavior customarily includes a close look at certain personal and social attributes of "political man"— voters, politicians, revolutionaries and other participants in the processes of manipulating power and determining public policy. These "vital statistics" purport to explain political action in terms of biology (sex and geriatrics), one's status of privilege or deprivation (economic or social), social exposure and mobility, acquisition of knowledge (and the capacity for its rational use that supposedly goes with formal education), and the nature of the life-sustaining occupations in which people are engaged. For the political leaders who are the object of this study, characteristics of the public life that has so engrossed them figure in such a demographic analysis; for instance, does it make any difference to the way they act if they are newcomers to politics or oldtimers, professional administrators ("bureaucrats") or politicians, members of one political party, or another, or none?

There were certain constraints that limited the kind of personal background data that the ISVIP could collect. For instance, comparable and reliable information about personal income, which is often used as an indicator of economic status, was not available in all four countries participating in the study. Nor could particular types of occupation be held to identify similar levels of social status in each of these countries. Consequently, an alternative approach was adopted to identify status—

if a person's customary occupation was nonmanual, it was assumed that his status would generally be recognized in his community as higher than that of one who was a manual worker. We found social mobility was indicated if the leader's primary occupation was nonmanual and his father's manual, or vice versa. In India, it was possible to secure caste as an additional dimension of "status."

Designation of political role or function, with an eye to establishing the familiar distinction between "bureaucrat" and "politician," proved difficult in the socialist countries, where positions as appointed or elected officials are easily interchangeable and the civil service is not set apart in the political systems as a career independent of politics. This explains in part the large differences in the proportion of leaders identified as administrative, elected or party officials in the four countries, despite the explicit parallelism of procedures in the selection of the respondents.

In the end, the data collected permitted reasonably comparable measurement of the following personal characteristics of leaders:

age—sex—stage of education completed—occupational mobility (between generations)—geographical mobility (indicated by length of residence in the leader's present community and whether he was born in or near this community)—present political position—duration of political or public career—political affiliation (party or no-party).

Thus, the investment in demography was substantial in this inquiry—substantial enough to leave the researchers in a state bordering on dismay when it was discovered that none of these variables contributed consistently to an explanation of community activeness across the four countries involved in the studies; few of them could be counted on to explain, for all four countries, the difference in values held by the leaders. Even on a strictly national basis, these indices, whether of a biological, cultural or political nature, were found to be sparse and uncertain.

There is one major exception—*education*. Here is a factor that has a demonstrated common influence on the value-orientation of leaders in all the countries in the ISVIP studies; while in two of the countries—India and Yugoslavia—the amount of leaders' education carries over and becomes a significant community characteristic associated with the amount of innovative community activeness. There is, however, a vital distinction in the thrust of the educational variable as a personal and as a social (community) imperative. On a personal basis, the amount of education evidently has much to do with shaping the *kind of change* leaders want to see happen, and most particularly, the kind of change they would prefer not to have happen. The more highly educated leaders tend to be more favorable to political democracy (i.e., open to broad public participation in decision-making), but they are consistently more *opposed* than the less educated *to economic equality*. For whatever reasons, the greater the amount of their education, the less concerned leaders are about lessening inequalities between the rich and the poor.[33]

Despite the nonegalitarian disposition of the more highly educated leaders, they are apparently influential in the less developed countries in forwarding the social mobilization of their communities. At least, the evidence from India and especially Yugoslavia demonstrates that communities whose leaders have had more advanced education are more "active" in the ways that would appear in line with the usual notions of modernization. This is definitely not the case, however, in Poland and the United States, at a higher level of national economic development.

These findings—both the negative and the positive—and their implications for development policy and theories of social change are more fully appraised in later chapters. At this point, we must simply caution that it is not easy to come up with the earmarks of developmental leadership—those prized "change agents" who supposedly spark the processes of social growth and betterment—by feeding demographic statistics into the computer.

Country, Community, or Man:
The Level of Social Impulse

The major elements in the paradigm envisaged in this study have now been set forth. To bring this together in a manageable map of the project, the following tabulation of variables, and some of their hypothesized interrelations may be useful.

   I *Community Activeness*, the major dependent variable, combines the dimensions of:
      (1) resource mobilization by local government
      (2) popular involvement in public life.
   II *Values of local leaders*, hypothesized as major explanatory variables for community activeness. Values considered especially relevant to developmental action include:
      (1) Change Values: commitment to innovation in social policy, and action propensity in personal life
      (2) Economic Norms: commitments to economic development and raising the standard of living, and concern for economic equality
      (3) Process Interaction Values: concerns for public participation in decision-making and for the avoidance of conflict

(4) Identification Values: commitments to nation and to selflessness

(5) Moral Values: selflessness and honesty (truthfulness) as norms of public conduct.

Congruence of leaders' values—the extent of consensus or diversity is viewed as a further factor of potential significance.

III *Other personal characteristics of leaders* are considered both as control variables for the explanation of activeness, and independent variables in explaining leaders' values. They include:

(1) Biological characteristics: age, sex

(2) Socio-economic status

(3) Ethnicity, religion, other cultural attributes

(4) Education

(5) Political or governmental career

(6) Perceptions of role; loyalties.

IV *Community characteristics* are considered both as control variables for the explanation of activeness, and environmental variables in explaining leaders' values:

(1) Ecological characteristics: size, population, density, urbanization

(2) Resource base: level of economic development, rate of economic growth

(3) Social structure: lines of cleavage, patterns of conflict

(4) Structure of political influence: leadership activity, sources of support, reference groups.

V *Cross-national systemic differences* are the residual source of explanation for variations in patterns of community activeness or in leaders' values, which cannot be consistently explained by the above variables in all four countries:

(1) Differences in the structure of local politics:

(a) institutionalization of developmental functions for local government

(b) scope of local autonomy: formal and perceived

(c) processes of political decision-making.

(2) Other cross-national differences:

(a) features of the national political system and ideology

(b) level and character of national economic development

(c) cultural and historical traditions.

The cross-national dimension is of course the crux of the design. One must imagine a three-dimensional frame of reference, with all of the posited two-dimensional relations among variables seen in the further perspective of "country-ness." If the evidence shows uniformity of interrelationships within countries among variables in the first four categories, certain broad, trans-national and potentially universal generalizations would be warranted about the imperatives of development action and the motivations of leaders to press for social change. But if these patterns differ country-to-country, then we must conclude that some distinctive national characteristics are at work in the development process. If behavior patterns are similar in two or three countries, but not in all, then we must look for related features that are common to those countries, but do not apply in the others.

For the most part, characteristics of nation have not been abstracted or measured, so that when conclusions point to the national level as the place where patterns of explanation diverge, we come to a kind of general repository of unidentified residual influences; though as we have pointed out, we can be rather specific about cross-national distinctions in crucial features of the structure of local politics.

One reason for abdicating the task of specifying particular national characteristics more exactly was the limited number of countries it was possible to cover in the study, which made quantitative distinctions unreliable. The sample was sufficiently diversified however, so that any cross-national uniformities would immediately establish a strong presumption that there was no chance or circumstantial occurrence, although patterns that were distinctive of particular countries would lead to a search for the peculiar features of those countries that might open up a second level of explanation and form the object of a revised and extended plan of research. The range of national characterization is so great that some such process of narrowing down to the most probable developmental influences is necessary before systematic and parsimonious empirical work can be undertaken to pinpoint particular features of national cultures that nudge or inhibit developmental processes.

However, the analytical models we have followed[34] permit rather definite estimates of the overall amount of influence exerted on the local development process and on leaders' values at different levels— that is, how much the shaping of values and the instigation of community activeness can be attributed to uniform factors that cut across nations, rather than to those that operate only in a particular country; to factors that are distinctive of certain areas or communities within a country rather than to characteristics of the country as a whole; and finally to factors that are characteristics of certain kinds of individuals, regardless of the community, region or country to which they belong.

If there is one key finding that should be stressed over others, it is *differentiation*. Differences are very great *between nations* in the values of leaders, in the patterns of community activeness, and in the mix of factors that account for the public vitality of the people. But differences are even greater *within nations*. The nation is by no means that overwhelming architect of homogeneity that nationalists have proclaimed and humanists feared. In the supposedly most "integrated" countries, people are profoundly at odds with each other in their own immediate communities. And the lines of division do *not* cut neatly and sharply between traditionalist and "modern" man. The direction of social change is not to be determined by the outcome of a struggle between two well-defined camps. Differentiation of values, of conflict lines, of response to being rich or poor, is more complex; at the moment, predictions to guide the course of development should be founded on readings taken very close to the grassroots, country by country, region by region and even community by community. Effective developmental leadership is discoverable, but it is not cut from a common pattern. It is human, sensitive, responsive to the surroundings, but not slave to them, pragmatic and, hence, individualized, personal and adaptive.

This means that to the extent that leadership and development are related, different kinds of persons are effective as developmental leaders in different kinds of circumstances. There is no ideal "development man."

But even this qualified conclusion about the nature of leadership for development should not be taken as confirming a consistently significant place for leaders of some kind in the determination of development. Our evidence shows that, to the contrary, the human factor may be quite overwhelmed by other influences—the impetus or constraint of resources, or entrenched political authority and direction. In some countries, it may well be that many human beings have lost the capacity to master their own destinies. They will simply ride or drown in whatever wave is thrown up at them by the social, political and economic forces surrounding them. "Development" will come, or not come, by secular tides, and not by human initiatives.

Which is it? The determinism of man, or the determinism of the inchoate pressures of social system that will shape the course of social change? Perhaps it is testimony to the realism of the ISVIP that its evidence doesn't permit a clear verdict.

Notes

1. See Appendix C, pp. 391–392.

2. A classic exposition of the hiatus between expressed values and the genuine determinants of conduct is that of Karl Mannheim, *Ideology and Utopia*, New York: Harcourt, Brace, 1952. Trans. by Louis Wirth and Edward Shils.

3. The issue posed here is clearly and succinctly outlined in Allen H. Barton, *Measuring the Values of Individuals*, Columbia University, Bureau of Applied Social Research Reprint No. 354, pp. 63–68. For a fuller exposition of the point of view taken in this study, see Philip E. Jacob and James J. Flink, *Values and Their Function in Decision-Making*, The American Behavioral Scientist Supplement, Vol. V. No. 9, May, 1962; also, Philip E. Jacob and James V. Toscano (eds.), *The Integration of Political Communities*, Philadelphia: J. B. Lippincott, 1964, Chapter 8, "The Influence of Values in Political Integration."

In general, the concept of values being advanced here follows, we believe, the direction set forth by Clyde Kluckhohn in Talcott Parsons and Edward Shils (eds.), *Toward a General Theory of Action*, Cambridge, Mass.: Harvard University Press, 1951; and is consonant with the concept of "value-orientations" developed by Florence Kluckhohn and Fred L. Strodtbeck (see their *Variations in Value Orientations*, Evanston Ill. and Elmsford, N.Y.: Row, Peterson, 1961).

4. One of the most definitive attempts to define the relationship between culture and values is F. Kluckhohn and F. Strodtbeck, *op. cit.*

The concept of political culture has been extensively exploited since its elaboration in the cross-national study by Gabriel Almond and Sidney Verba, *The Civic Culture*, Princeton: Princeton University Press, 1963. See, for instance, the presentations in Lucian Pye and Sidney Verba (eds.), *Political Culture and Political Development*, Princeton, N.J.: Princeton University Press, 1965.

5. Subnational cultural distinctions relevant to this study include those following status lines. See in regard to India the contention of Myron Weiner that there are evident deep and pervasive cultural differences between what he identifies as the "elite" and the "mass." "India's Two Political Cultures" in Pye and Verba, *op. cit.*

The broad distinction often drawn between "modern" and "traditional" cultures with corresponding differences in values, is of course highly relevant to an analysis of the value determinants of development. Among the voluminous literature positing such a distinction, impressive empirical evidence is set forth in Joseph A. Kahl, *The Measurement of Modernism*, Austin, Texas: University of Texas Press, 1968, and in Alex Inkeles *et al.*, *The Modernization of Man*, Cambridge: Harvard University Press, forthcoming. See also Inkeles, "Participant Citizenship in Six Developing Countries," *American Political Science Review*, December, 1969. But the validity of the distinction has been strongly challenged. See for instance several of the papers presented, notably that of D. R. Gadgil, before the Seminar on Planning for Social Development, India International Center, New Delhi, March, 1968.

6. Cross-national comparisons of values are reported in Chapter 3, including a detailed elaboration of the nationally distinctive profiles.

7. Intranational differences appear most sharply in the analysis of variation in Chapter 5.

8. A succinct statement of role theory as it relates to the formation and implementation of values is Thomas C. Cochran, "The Challenge to the Historian of Social Role," New York: Social Science Research Council, 1962. For fuller treatment, see Robert K. Merton, *Social Theory and Social Structure*, Glencoe, Ill.: Free Press, 1957, especially pp. 368–380; Ann Marie Rocheblave-Spenlé, *La Notion de Rôle en Psychologie Sociale: Étude Historico-Critique*, Paris: Presses Universitaires de France, 1962; and Theodore Sarbin, "Role Theory," in Gardner Lindzey ed., *Handbook of Social Psychology*, Cambridge, Mass.: Addison-Wesley, 1954, Vol. I.

9. In an early discussion of the design, William Scott contended that the concept of value necessarily implied that the holder of a value should consider it imperative upon everyone everywhere, to the extent that anyone who acted against the value would be regarded as sinful. See his memorandum, "Assessment of Values," ISVIP Doc. USA/6; also his *Values and Organizations*, Chicago: Rand McNally, 1965.

Several of those associated with the project, however, insisted that such a view was not representative of their countries, and would unduly narrow the range of normative influences to be investigated in a cross-national study. Thus, we would identify as values, any standards the respondents cited as relevant to *their* conduct, even if they took the point of view that it might be entirely legitimate for others to act differently.

10. Some evidence suggests that cultural differences may affect the extent to which people are motivated by a need for consistency, as well as their ways of handling value conflicts. See H. C. Triandis, "Some Cross-Cultural Studies of

Cognitive Consistency" in R. P. Abelson *et al.* (eds.), *Theories of Cognitive Consistence: A Source Book*, Chicago: Rand McNally, 1968.

11. See Appendix C, pp. 392–394 for description of the techniques used for measuring priorities, and for some of the cross-national comparisons.

12. The positive findings as well as implications of the negative findings are presented in Chapter 4. This study was necessarily confined to latitudinal analysis, as we had inadequate previous data with which to compare our measures. However, some replication of the ISVIP survey in Poland 1969–1970, and partial replication elsewhere will make some longitudinal comparisons possible in the near future.

13. See the critique of the state of research on development, especially in the area of attitudes and values, by Gunnar Myrdal, *Asian Drama*, New York: Pantheon, 1968. Vol. I, Chapters 2 and 3.

14. The question of how these professed values relate to implicit values that are not verbalized has not been satisfactorily resolved, because we have not been able to arrive at reliable indicators of the latter. Values as we conceive them presumably must have some form of overt expression—they are after all an element in the decision-making process. But any specific action is an inappropriate and quite possibly inaccurate indicator of a particular value, because it is likely to be the result of multiple influences, including factors other than values, as well as of a combination or mix of several values. This is why the familiar adage, "to know a man's 'real' values look to what he does," points to a mirage.

This is why we prefer to fall back on a test of consistency to determine the genuineness of a person's professed values. Does he tend to set forth the same value priorities as he evaluated actions and justifies his own conduct in a variety of situations? Is he consistent in his professions regardless of audience—to constituents as well as to interviewer, in public as well as in private?

For the most part however, the validity of the values must be judged by the internal consistency of the survey responses. The questionnaire was prepared and administered in such a way as to avoid obvious connections between questions. It also included a number of open-ended and semiprojective items, which invited the respondent to give free vent to attitudes and feelings on matters to which some of the specific questions were also addressed. For assessment of the degree of consistency, as well as other indications of validity and reliability, see Chapter 2 and Appendix C (Validification).

15. One problem with using political units as the base for inventorying social activity, was that often they were set up solely for administrative purposes and the lines of popular participation in indigenous social functions simply bore no relationship to the area encompassed in the unit. In one state of India, even political activity (voting, party organization, etc.) was geared to constituencies that were completely different from the "development blocks," which were the basic units for administrating and conducting the governmental development activities at the local level. This severely limited the procuring of relevant data on activeness and community integration; but in the end no better solution covering the considerations mentioned and the need for a fairly explicit yardstick of cross-national comparability in choosing the sample base was found.

Terminological note: we have tended to use the word "community" in this study to refer to the locality in which the survey of leadership was conducted and the data on social and political activity gathered. Specifically this means development blocks in India, powiats in Poland, municipalities in the U.S. and communes in Yugoslavia. See Appendix B for an exact description of the samples chosen. It thus does *not* imply a group of people with a "sense of community"; and it does *not* refer to community in the Indian meaning of a well-recognized kinship group, to which one belongs by virtue of family, ancestry and status.

16. See Appendix D.

17. Congruence of leaders' values is analyzed in Chapter 5, along with an appraisal of implications regarding the amount of integration at three levels—local, national and inter-national.

18. A more serious deficiency in our data is the lack of information about the values and loyalties of the general population. We can offer no empirical evidence that the leaders reflect the outlook of their respective communities, and that they share the same values to the same degree as their fellow-citizens. One of the essential tasks of further research is to establish the correspondence, or lack thereof, between the values of leadership and of the general community, and, further, whether the leadership tends to be more or less united on the decisive values than those that they lead.

A complementary study in six Polish towns indicated considerable difference between the values of leaders and the public. This was further examined in a replication of the ISVIP inquiry, undertaken in Poland 1969–1970.

19. See the section on "Effects of Diversity" in Chapter 5.

20. For a summary of alternative concepts of integration current in social science inquiry, see Philip E. Jacob and Henry Teune, "The Integrative Process: Guidelines for Analysis of the Bases of Political Community," in Jacob and Toscano (eds.), *op. cit.*

Actually nine different concepts of integration were elaborated in the course of developing the research design, but resources permitted intensive concentration only on the variables of community activeness and congruence of local leaders' values.

Attempts were also made to develop reliable measures of the extent to which the local communities were integrated within the broader context of the nation as a whole. How strong, in other words, were the ties to country? Satisfactorily interrelated community *action* indicators of responsiveness to nation could not be secured. On the other hand, several of the survey questions provide insight concerning the degree of loyalty that leaders express to nation, and in other ways exhibit a "national orientation."

21. See, for instance, Gabriel Almond and James Coleman (eds.), *The Politics of the Developing Areas*, Princeton, N.J.: Princeton University Press, 1960; Lucian Pye, *Politics, Personality and Nation Building*, New Haven, Conn.: Yale University Press, 1962; Lucian Pye and Sidney Verba (eds.), *op. cit.*

22. See Albert O. Hirschman, *Journeys Toward Progress*, New York: 20th Century Fund, 1963, and notably, Gunnar Myrdal, *Asian Drama*, New York: Pantheon, 1968, especially Volume III, Appendix 2 "The Mechanism of Underdevelopment and Development: Parts II and III.

23. Myrdal, *op. cit.*, Prologue, Sec. 5, 6; Appendix 2, Sec. 14, 20, 21.

24. The fact that the economic growth of Yugoslav communes is highly correlated with their level of development ($r = 0.98$) strongly reinforces this conclusion for that country; in the U.S., the association is less powerful ($r = 0.28$). Implications for theories of economic determinism derived from ISVIP data are necessarily tentative: their refinement and further generalization depends on the extension of similar research to other countries and levels, making possible greater control of relevant variables.

25. See Chapter 10.

26. A third approach defined *leadership role* as a critical social determinant, looking to the area in which a leader feels he has or should have competence to act. To the extent that this concerns local political leaders and government officials, perceptions of role are discussed as an aspect of local political autonomy (see above, pp. 18–20, and Chapter 6, pp. 180–181). The significance of political role for community activeness in the light of ISVIP findings is assessed in Chapter 9.

27. The relationship of community power studies to the analysis of decision-making is effectively reviewed, on a cross-national comparative basis, in Terry N. Clark (ed.), *Community Structure and Decision-Making*, San Francisco: Chandler, 1968.

Winicjusz Narojek provides a searching critique of research on community power in Poland, in *Studies in Polish Political System*, Warsaw-Wroclaw: Ossolineum, 1967. Narojek also contributed an important critique of the ISVIP design and leadership sample from the perspective of community power analysis. See ISVIP Doc. PO/19.

An inventory and appraisal of relevant community power studies in the U.S. was prepared by Thomas M. Watts for ISVIP. See Doc. USA/14, May, 1965.

28. Probably the most precise data on the influence of the structure of social power stems from work in group dynamics. See, for instance, Dorwin Cartwright (ed.), *Studies in Social Power*, Ann Arbor Mich.: University of Michigan, 1959.

29. See Chapter 6, pp. 211–212, footnote 2.

30. The analysis of this study is not yet completed, and its results have not been correlated with the original ISVIP survey data. Preliminary findings for 20 of the 30 communities in the sample are reported by Terry N. Clark, in "Community Structure, Decision-Making, Budget Expenditures and Urban Renewal in 51 American Communities," *American Sociological Review*, August, 1968.

31. See Chapter 10.

32. It is possible, of course, that our survey simply failed to locate the relevant reference groups of the developmental leaders. They might be located outside the sixteen possibilities about which we specifically inquired, though this list covers a broad range of likely candidates, both inside and outside the community, and inside and outside the formal "power structures."

33. See Chapter 4.

In addition to education, the factors of age and length of residence in the community are related specifically to the value of economic equality in all four countries: older leaders are more disposed to *favor* equality than younger ones, as are the people who are more deeply rooted in a community.

Thus, there *is* a kind of "demography" of leadership with respect to the egalitarian dimension of social change. The young, educated, newly arrived leader has relatively little concern for this issue; whereas his older, less educated, homegrown colleague is much more committed to lessening the economic and social inequalities around him.

34. See Chapter 4 for the model of analysis at the individual level to account for differences in the values of leaders; Chapter 9 sets forth the model used at the community level to explain activeness. The ISVIP did not undertake, however, a formal and systematic process of testing explicitly formulated hypotheses. The models were constructed so as to permit explanation of a wide range of possible relationships between variables whose identity was first defined *conceptually* and

then operationalized in terms of empirical indicators shown to have an acceptable degree of homogeneity. Data were evaluated *after* collection to determine the exact dimensions of the variables and the degree of their association. See Chapter 2 for exposition of the methodological procedures and assumptions underlying them.

The Strategy of Comparative Inquiry: Methods of Assessment and Analysis

This chapter was written by Teune.

This project confronted major methodological problems stemming from the comparative, cross-national nature of its design. It was necessary above all to establish the equivalence of different variables in the four countries and the means of measuring their interrelationships. The problem was complicated by the distinctive character of the data: observations both of individuals and of various forms of collective behavior in local political units under widely differing social and political systems.[1]

This chapter describes and evaluates the models for measurement and analysis that were adopted to meet these problems. Essentially, the approach to measurement was based on the behavior of indicators within each country; this behavior provided a base line for establishing validity and reliability, and, therefore, equivalence of measurement across countries. The approach to analysis was based on testing the universality of the generalization in which "countryness" is treated as a summary label, either for unspecified variables and/or for a pattern of interaction among variables.[2]

The nature of the data gathered to test the relationships in this research allowed for a different approach to comparative research problems than that followed either in comparisons of total systems or of individuals from more than one system. First, observations were made *within* countries, and, secondly, these observations were transformed into variables and interrelated *within* each country. Thus it was possible to "compare" these within-country relationships across countries, for example a relationship between economic level and activeness *within* the United States with the relationship found in Poland. By focusing on within-country relationships, it was possible not only to validate measurement instruments within each country separately, but also to use *relationships* within each country rather than a *single* characteristic of each country, as the basic datum in the cross-national analysis.

Measurement: Direct
and Inferred

The problems of measurement posed by cross-national data depend on the nature of the measurement instrument. Two measurement models were used—direct and inferred. In the use of direct measurement instruments, where observations are arrayed or ordered in a common language, the issue is whether or not observations from different countries can be expressed in a common language—whether the ordering is standard for all countries. In particular, is there a common origin point and a standard way of ordering all observations? In inferred measurement, where inferences are made from observations to some underlying dimension, the comparative issue revolves on whether the same kind of inference rule can be used in each country to connect the observations to the underlying dimension. An example of direct measurement is the question on conflicts in the community. Does a response of "very much" as against "some" equally differentiate among Indians and among Poles and among the leadership in different communities within these countries? An example in inferred measurement is the question asking whether the respondent agrees or disagrees with the statement, "The economic development of the nation should take precedence over immediate consumer gratification." Does agreement indicate the same concern for economic development in the United States and Yugoslavia?

The diagram below presents the types of measurement statements for the major categories of variables used in this research at the individual and collective levels. The major variables of this study—values and activeness—are based on inferred measurement.

	Individual Leaders	Local Political Units

Direct	Perceptions
	Socio-economic
	   characteristics
	Behaviour
		Ecological
		   characteristics

Inferred	Values	Activeness Economic Level

Direct measurement statements are based on the application of a standard or common measurement language to all members of a set of objects and, as a result, the objects are arrayed on a property in terms of categories (nominal scales), in terms of each other (ordinal scales) or in terms of some arithmetic standard (interval, ratio, or absolute scales).[3] Perceived influences of leaders is expressed in a common measurement language. Leaders were asked whether they had "a great deal of influence," "some influence," or "no influence" in ten areas of local policy. "Great influence" was scored 2; "some influence," 1; and "no influence," 0. Although the numbers 0, 1, 2, are arbitrary designations, in the correlational analysis, an assumption is made that the distance, or differences in magnitude of "influence," is approximately equal (nearly equal) between these points.[4] Almost all of the variables derived from the questionnaire in this study, except values, are expressed in a direct measurement language.

The conventional problem with direct measurement statements in the social sciences is demonstrating that the properties observed meet the requirements of the common language, that is, "a great deal of influence" is one more unit of "influence" than "some influence." This problem is compounded in cross-national research by the fact that the expression of the observations in the measurement language must meet the requirements of that language for all countries. Not only must a scale differentiate "influence" in the same way for Indians, but also for Poles *and* Indians. The comparative measurement issue derives from an assumption that the same language of measurement can be equally applied in all societies or countries. Some research assumes that it can; others hold with the orientation of some area specialists that "great influence" is not equally different from "some influence" in two different cultures.[5]

Whether or not this is a "comparative" problem depends on what is derived from the measurement statements. For descriptive comparisons, where percentages in categories, country rankings, or how much more or less each country has of a particular property, is derived, it is indeed necessary to demonstrate or to assume that a common measurement language is appropriate. In particular, in comparing how much more influential Indian local leaders are compared to Polish local leaders, it is necessary to assume a common point of departure, and equal intervals in the designation of "great influence" as "2" and "no influence" as "0." If, however, what is to be compared cross-nationally is the *relationship* between the leader's influence and his national commitment, expressed as a correlation, then it is not necessary to know that the interval sizes are the same for all countries. The comparison of correlations between two variables in India and in the United States does not require that the origin point and the interval size be standard for both countries. When a correlation is computed in each country, the scores are adjusted to the mean of that country (standard scores) and the strength of the relationship is expressed. Even though Indian leaders may indeed have a higher influence score than American leaders, because of their different perceptions of what "great deal of influence" means, this does not necessarily affect the nature of the associations expressed in the correlations between influence and value-scale scores within each country.

In dealing with relationships within each country separately, we assume that the scales differentiate the population in the same way in each country, not that the scale scores are identical. All that need be assumed is that the response "great deal of influence" differentiates those who respond "no influence" in all countries in the same way. In restricting much of the analysis between countries to a comparison of the relationships found within countries, the strong requirements concerning the general applicability, and thus comparability of a common language of measurement need not be met. Indeed, limiting comparisons across countries to within-country relationships, the argument of "area specialists" concerning national or cultural influences on measurement scales is partially accepted without necessarily reducing the possibility of testing cross-national generality.

Although direct measurement statements are technically interpreted in a literal fashion, ("This is what the Indian leader says in response to this question") in practice these statements are often used to infer some underlying traits. Thus, a leader who says he has "a great deal of influence" on ten policy areas is actually presumed to be more "influential" than a leader who says he has no influence in any of the areas. This is how the direct measurement scales are often interpreted. In this research no tests were made to check the validity of this kind of interpretation, either with other indicators (construct validity) or with some form of predictive or concurrent validity, such as comparing the scores of leaders holding positions "known" to have more influence (mayors in the United States or presidents of powiat councils in Poland) with those known to have less influence (administrative heads). The variables based on these scales, therefore, must be evaluated in terms of their "content" or "face" validity.[6]

The reliability of direct measurement statements is not formally established. Efforts were made, however, to assure the standardization of the recording of observations in all countries, by the use of a common international code with supplementary instructions constructed from pre-test experience. Insofar as "accuracy" assures "stability," variables based on the direct measurement model can be assumed to be reliable both within and across countries.[7]

The problem of the "comparability" of the variables based on direct measurement models, which include almost all of the variables derived from the questionnaire except the items used to construct the value scales, can be judged by whether, in all countries, (1) the accuracy of error in the measurement statements are roughly equal; (2) the interval size is approximately the same; and (3) the scales differentiated leaders in approximately the same way. The accuracy, as has been mentioned, was achieved by an international code, coding instructions and a variety of internal checks conducted at one or more centers or jointly. As the analysis is based on relationships within countries, equality of interval size is assumed for each country, but not for all countries. On the basis of pre-tests it was possible to assure that most of the direct measurement statements derived from the questionnaire differentiated individual leaders in approximately the same way in all countries. Further, most of the questions were scored dichotomously; the individual "agreed" or "disagreed," he said he was "active" or "not active." These scores were used to construct proportions or percentages of leaders for community scores.[8]

The primary variables of the research design, values, activeness and the central intervening variable, economic level, received a great deal of attention in the measurement procedures. Not only were these variables of primary importance in the design, but also there was evidence for believing that "cultural" or "national" influences on their measurement would be substantial. As these variables defined the research problem, inferred measurement models were used. These were in part grounded on "auxiliary" theories.[9]

In inferred measurement, direct measurement statements— responses of a leader to a question, or some characteristic of a local government unit—are treated as *indicators* of some underlying phenomenon. In addition to indicating the phenomenon being measured, an indicator will also reflect some other phenomena. This is conceived as "error." The validity of measurement statements is assessed by determining how much error is contained in the indicators. The task is to select those indicators that contain the least error and thereby maximize the validity of the measurement statements.

The measurement model used to assess both the values of leaders and the activeness of local political units was an additive probabilistic model, where scores on particular indicators are added or combined to produce the most probable magnitude of some underlying property. Procedurally, this model requires the following steps: (1) collecting several indicators of the property, each of which is treated initially as a hypothesis that the higher the score of an object on this indicator (a direct measurement statement), the greater the probability of its possessing the designated attribute; (2) testing the hypotheses[10] by intercorrelating each indicator with all other indicators; (3) discarding indicators either on the basis of their low correlation with a score based on the total set of indicators, or their low inter-item correlation with other indicators in the set; and (4) scoring the individuals or units on the basis of the selected indicators. Different procedures were followed for weighting the indicators in the overall measures for activeness and values.

In measuring values, responses to several questions were used for each value. (These were selected from at least two pre-tests in each country.) These items were intercorrelated, and those items that were best intercorrelated with the total set of items were retained; others were excluded. Each item was scored in terms of four response categories ("strongly agree," "agree," "disagree," "strongly disagree"). Although these response categories allowed for magnitudes of differences to be expressed for each item, the items selected for the value scales—those used in scoring—were each given a weight of one. The procedures that were used for activeness (and economic level in Poland and Yugoslavia) were to factor analyze the indicators and score the political units on identifiable factors.[11] For values no attempt was made to assure "discriminant validity," that is, that a particular indicator did not also correlate highly with items from other value scales. A factor analysis of the value items, however, to some degree demonstrated the independence of the value scales.[12]

The problem of comparability of measurement is one of establishing the equivalence of measurement statements. Whether two measurement instruments can produce equivalent measurement statements depends on the interchangeability of their results, that is, whether an individual's score on one academic performance test, for example, can be expressed in terms of a score of another test. To determine whether any two instruments are indeed interchangeable would require knowing the validity and reliability of both instruments, and a transformation rule whereby the score on one test can be expressed in terms of the scale of the other.[13] In practice, of course, it is possible to test the interchangeability of two or more instruments if the same population is measured by both instruments. The problem in comparative research is that there are two or more independent populations.

In inferred measurement, the issue of comparability is whether a single inference rule can be used regardless of the "systemic" context of the indicators.[14] Can a general rule of inference be used so that agreement on the "importance of avoiding violence" indicates the importance of conflict avoidance in all countries? Do expenditures of local governments indicate activeness in the same way, despite differences, for example, in local governmental powers to tax and spend?

The practical problems confronted in this research that called for special strategies of measurement include the following: (1) an indicator in one country may not indicate the same disposition or behavior in others; (2) certain indicators provide little or no variance in some systems and thus are of little use in differentiating objects, the purpose of measurement; and (3) indicators in some countries simply do not exist in others. In measuring values, it was possible, of course, to use constant stimuli, that is, similar questions, in all countries. In the measurement of activeness, however, where not only is the behavior of local governments highly prescribed by the political system, but the behavior recorded also differs, it was not possible to start with a single indicator that was common for all four countries. Thus, it was necessary to rely entirely on indicators that were specific to each country, such as membership in agricultural cooperatives in India, and membership in the Socialist Alliance in Yugoslavia.[15]

The issue for this research, however, is how to test the ability of the instruments used in all four countries, whether based on the same items or indicators or not, to produce equivalent, and thus interchangeable and comparable, measurement statements. The problem is not whether common indicators can be used for all countries, but whether measurement statements are interchangeable across countries. This is a critical issue when the measures deal with values that are supposedly heavily enmeshed in a culture, and with the behavior of local governments that have specific and often unique political system constraints on what they can do.

The goal, as Sears has pointed out, is to develop empirical criteria by which equivalence can be assessed, other than prevailing intuitive criteria.[16] The test of equivalence used in this research is the coherent behavior of indicators *within each system*. Thus, validity, based on the behavior of indicators within each country, was used to infer the equivalence of the measurement statements and their comparability across countries. It should be recalled that insofar as the comparative analysis is confined to relationships within systems, it is not necessary to have equal magnitudes of difference expressed by the measures, but only an approximately similar amount of *variance* expressed within each county.

ESTABLISHING THE EQUIVALENCE OF THE VALUE SCALES

Although various procedures were followed in the pre-tests to obtain items for measuring values in all four countries, what is important for the question of comparability is how the equivalence of the value scales was established for the scales actually used in the analysis.[17] The strategy followed was to combine cross-national and nation-specific value items. The cross-national hypothesis took the form: *"in all four countries* 'agreement' with this item indicates the value of economic development." The form of the nation-specific hypothesis was that *"in India* 'agreement' with this item indicates the value of economic development." The pre-tests demonstrated the advantages of constructing the value scales from a combination of cross-national and nation-specific items. First, it was difficult to find a sufficient number of items that intercorrelated with each other, for both all respondents treated as a single population, and for the population of each country separately. If only cross-nationally identical items had been used—the same items correlated both for all respondents and for those from each country—it would have been necessary to limit severely the number of items in the scales, to obtain a satisfactory level of intercorrelation.[18] Secondly, it became apparent that certain items intercorrelated very well in one country, but in no others; this reflects the importance of the national context in which these values were being assessed.

The final nine value scales were constructed for each country, following the procedures stated above. First, those items that intercorrelated *both* for the international (pooled population) and for every national population were selected; second, any other items that were intercorrelated with the cross-national set were added to the scale for a particular country. For example, if four items intercorrelated for the entire population of leaders and for every national population, these became the cross-national or "international" set. If a particular item intercorrelated with these four items in India, it was added to the four items to form the Indian value scale. If another item, different from the Indian item, was intercorrelated with the cross-national items in Yugoslavia, it qualified for the Yugoslav value scale as an item specific to Yugoslavia.[19]

Specifically, the steps in this procedure were: (1) to intercorrelate all common items for all respondents (pooled analysis); (2) to discard those items that did not correlate well with the other items; (3) to intercorrelate both the cross-national items and the nation-specific items for each country separately; (4) to discard those cross-national items that did not correlate well in specific countries; and (5) to select nation-specific items for each country that did correlate well with the cross-national items. The cross-national items, thus, were used to assure the reliability of the scales across countries, and the additional nation-specific items were used to increase the validity and reliability of the scales for each country. By using a combination of cross-national and nation-specific items, it was possible to have a sufficient set of items for reliability by increasing the number of items for each scale, and to improve the validity of each scale by allowing items relevant to particular national contexts to be retained. In fact, each individual was scored on two scales, on the cross-national set of items only and on the combination of cross-national and nation-specific items. Of course, since these two scales were based on largely the same observations, they are highly intercorrelated.

Reliability and validity of the value scales is assessed by the inter-correlations.[20] To the extent that the items are intercorrelated, they can be inferred to be valid. To the extent that the items are numerous and intercorrelated, they are considered reliable.[21] To the extent that the scales are valid and reliable measures of the values intended in each country, they can be considered to provide equivalent measures of values in the four countries, and the measurement statements—the particular scale scores—may be considered comparable.

The results of the attempt to obtain valid, reliable, and, thus, equivalent measures of values in each country must be evaluated against the difficulty of obtaining valid and reliable scales of any human psychological dimensions. In this context these value scales, especially considering the fact that they were obtained in highly heterogeneous cultures, not only across nations but also within nations, are satisfactory, with perhaps the exception of the scale of conflict avoidance in Yugoslavia.[22]

An additional structured question for the assessment of values was asked. The scores derived from it are direct measurement statements. The question asked for a partial ranking of eight of the nine values measured by the value scales. Because the leader was asked to select only the three values that he considered most important, and then the one of those three he felt most important, the scores based on this question and the value scale scores are not consistently highly correlated with the value scales.

There were two open-ended questions designed to measure values: "wishes and hopes for the future of our country" and "the qualities of good leaders." As in the case of the other open-ended questions, a limited number of questions was first coded in each country, an international code was constructed, and the responses were finally re-coded according to the international code.[23]

ESTABLISHING THE EQUIVALENCE OF ACTIVENESS
AND ECONOMIC LEVEL

In the value scales, identical items were used as a base for establishing their common content validity and their potential comparability. In the case of activeness and economic level, however, none of the indicators could be interpreted as common. The problem was to construct comparable measures of activeness from indicators that were entirely nation-specific.[24]

For activeness, it was necessary to establish the content validity of the indicators in each country separately. The hypotheses contained in the auxiliary activeness theory were "in India an indicator of activeness is . . .", "in Poland an indicator of activeness is . . . ", etc. Once a set of indicators had been gathered, they required evaluation: (1) to what extent are these measures reliable and valid, and (2) how can one know they are comparable? It must be pointed out that the goal is a valid and reliable *differentiation* of local governments on activeness *within* each country, *not* a differentiation of local governments in all four countries on the basis of a cross-national measurement language.

The construction of instruments to measure activeness made use of factor analysis. What was done was to first gather and select a large number of indicators about social and governmental behavior of local political units, hypothesized to reflect popular involvement or resource mobilization, which, taken together, defined activeness. These items were then intercorrelated, and those that did not cluster with other items hypothesized to reflect either popular involvement or resource mobilization were discarded. The remaining items were factor analyzed and the factors (orthogonal rotation, varimax criterion) were examined to see which factors best fitted with the predicted clusters. Insofar as the items loaded on the factors that were predicted, the factors could be considered as valid measures of activeness and its dimensions. Further, to the extent that the measures were valid for each country, they could be considered comparable across countries, and the scores on activeness in each country equivalent in their differentiation of local political units.[25]

This procedure for establishing the equivalence of measures, based on different indicators as well as on different cases, is a weak variant of the measures of congruence among factor structures. A stronger version that could have been followed would have been, as was done for the value scale items, to specify which indicators were "substitutable" across all four systems and then to have used one or more of the expressions of factor congruence across countries.[26] The procedure that was followed, however, did indeed yield a structure of indicators of activeness that was highly similar for all four countries, despite the vast differences in the local political system and the even greater apparent differences in nature of the indicators.

Analysis

The major question of analysis deriving from the "cross-national" nature of these data is the interpretation of "countries." In particular, the goal of analysis is how best to extract the uniform relationships among nations and how to interpret those relationships that are nation-specific. What are the general determinants of local governmental activeness and the values of local leaders, and what are nation-specific determinants? Further, if the variables related to activeness or to particular value profiles are specific to each country, how can these differences be interpreted?

GENERAL STRATEGIES

Two possible approaches to the question of interpreting systems, ("systems" being defined in this research as countries) characterize social science inquiry. One position is that countries are so unique that any relationships found within them must be interpreted only in terms of the characteristics of the country and, consequently, generalization must be limited to the domain circumscribed by specific countries—a theory of Indian politics or of Polish social structure. Another interpretation is that a country and the relationships found among the components of a country is but an instance or case of some more general processes, and can be expressed in a general theory. In this view, the uniqueness described as "Yugoslavia" is interpreted as a name for a set of variables not yet identified.

This research takes the latter position and seeks to explore how far the activeness of local governments or the values of local political leaders can be explained in general, cross-national terms. Analysis, though focused on relationships found within each country, is used to ascertain the generality of these relationships.

UNIVERSALITY OF GENERALIZATION. Two alternative approaches to testing cross-national generality of relationships are available: to treat the entire set of leaders and local governments as a single experimental population, or, to treat the population of each country as an independent case, testing the generality of the relationships. The latter is the approach used throughout this research.

The decision for testing the relationships with data drawn from each country separately is based on the following considerations: (1) evidence, on the basis of pre-tests and preliminary investigations, that the measurement instruments must be adapted to the contexts in which they are applied, particularly in the case of measures of characteristics of local political units, and (2) the recognition that country-specific factors would indeed be important, and their influence would have to be determined before an assumption of a single population could be justified.

By using data from very different kinds of political systems, with different levels of economic development, and cultural backgrounds, the generality of the relationships is put to a "hard test." Because a substantial range of variation is used to test generality, if the same relationship is found in these four sharply contrasting countries, there is strong evidence for their universality. Alternatively, if the relationship had been found to hold across very similar countries, such as industrialized or Western European countries, there would be serious doubt that the relationship could be generalized to less developed or Latin American countries.[27] The disadvantage of treating the data as four separate sets of data, however, is that some pan-national or general factors may be obscured. The country-specific factors might be highlighted particularly because different observational operations are coterminous with the data from each country, not randomized across countries, as would be the case in a pooled analysis.[28] As far as possible the comparability of these independent "tests" was assured in the international design and organization of the research.

COUNTRY LEVEL VARIABLES. In stating that the value of conflict avoidance is positively related to activeness in the United States and negatively related in Poland, we have, in effect, made a statement that there is something about Poland and the United States that makes their local governments' behavior different. The question is: what differences at the country level account for the difference in relationships within these countries—the economic development of the country, political structures that encourage or discourage conflict, or cultural patterns of expressing conflict?

If specific country differences can be expressed as variables, it is possible to begin to explain differences in relationships found within these countries. If the relationships are the same, there are, of course, no differences that can be explained by country differences. With the small number of countries in this research, it is possible only to suggest the dimensions of country differences that may account for differences found in relationships within them. This is attempted in the sections explaining differences in patterns of relationships for the values of leaders and the activeness of local governments. With further research, it should be possible not only to specify that there are differences in relationships within countries, but also to account for some of these differences systematically with country level variables.

GENERALIZATION: DESCRIPTIVE AND EXPLANATORY. Although most of the findings reported concern explanatory relationships between variables within countries, there are also some descriptive comparisons in which the characteristics of the four national leader populations are compared, particularly in terms of their values. The mean scores on value scales, for example, are based on the Indian or Polish leader population and compared. Again, if there are differences between the populations, it is possible to ask why.

In comparing relationships, the important question is, how much of the "total" variance in local governmental behavior or leader characteristics of each country was included in the study? In terms of descriptive comparisons, comparing characteristics of the four local leader samples, it is necessary to know the segment of local governments and leaders from which samples were taken. The following chart displays the strata from which the observations were taken in each country.[29]

Table 1—General Characteristics of Local Political Units Sampled

	Type of Local Government	Size	Geographical	Character
India	Taluks	—	Gujarat Maharashtra Uttar Pradesh	Rural
Poland	Powiats	—	National	Mixed Urban/Rural
U.S.	Cities	25,000–250,000	National	Urban
Yugoslavia	Communes	—	Bosnia Serbia Slovenia	Mixed Urban/Rural

ANALYSIS OF RELATIONSHIPS WITHIN SYSTEMS

Two levels of analysis are reported: the local governmental units (community) and individual leaders. The analysis is drawn from two data files: a file of individual leaders' responses to the questionnaire grouped by country; and a community file, containing the aggregated responses of leaders in a particular local government, activeness scores, economic level scores, and a few other items of information. The individual file is composed of about 900 leaders per country; the community file of 30 local governments per country.

The primary form of analysis relied on for the community file, reported in the chapters on activeness, is the correlation coefficient. For individuals, the primary type of analysis is the comparison of group differences based on value profiles. In addition, correlations were used to relate a leader's values with some of his other characteristics. The details of the analyses used are given in the sections reporting substantive results.

Although the sampling requirements for using a level of statistical significance are not equally met in all countries, a .05 level of significance was chosen as a minimum common standard for "accepting" a relationship between variables or a difference between group means. Properly speaking, the sample is drawn from a universe of local governments rather than of local political leaders. Further, in only two countries was there a nationally based sample. The conventional .05 level of significance is an arbitrary choice. There was no basis for establishing different, but equivalent, levels of significance for the four countries. The .05 level of significance is probably not a "conservative" level, if the inequalities of error across countries, and the possible sources of error within countries are considered.

BIVARIATE CORRELATIONS. At the community level, approximately 170 variables were intercorrelated with each other. Correlations were used as a basis for establishing whether a relationship existed in a particular country and to assess the strength of the relationship. The correlation coefficient used (Pearson's) is based on certain assumptions about the linearity and distribution of the scores. The justification for using the correlation coefficient lies in the nature of the scores.

Many individual responses to the questionnaire were scored dichotomously; a score of "0" was assigned for responding in one category, such as "not active," and a score of "1" for another response, such as an affirmation of conflict in the community.[30] Dichotomous scoring was followed for all the open-ended questions, "mentioning or not mentioning" some item of content. When dichotomous scores are summated into a community score, the community score is a percentage of leaders responding in the same way. This score, based on a count of individual responses, is thereby transformed into an "interval" scale community score. Those individual scores that are assumed to be "interval," reflecting quantitative differences, such as how much influence, how much cleavage, or how strongly committed to a value, are the *mean* response for the leaders in each community.[31] In addition, there are, of course, community variables based on interval type indicators of activeness and economic level, such as governmental expenditures and per capita income. These scores were normalized for each country.

Insofar as the community level variables are concerned, percentages of leaders responding, the mean scores of leaders, and the measures of activeness and economic level approximate the requirements of an "interval" scale necessary for correlations, and, in the case of activeness and economic level, also a normal distribution. Further, the correlations between the community variables and activeness were also plotgraphed, and the nature of the relationship was inspected for linearity. Although it is difficult to detect curvilinear relationships by inspection of 30 cases, some were found to be clearly not linear, most notably in the case of urban population and activeness in Yugoslavia.

At the individual level, most of the scores were "0," "1," a mean score based on the value scale items, or a mean score based on a combination of responses. The use of correlations with dichotomous data is controversial. The major part of the analysis of values at the individual level, however, is based on comparisons between mean scores of groups rather than on correlations between variables.[32]

PARTIAL ORDER CORRELATION. The influence of a third variable on the pattern of correlations between one of the independent variables and activeness was examined at the community level. Three such are reported: economic level, because of its general importance in the research design; "perceived conflict," because of its apparent importance for the way in which variables were found to be related to activeness; and the influence of leaders as a control for the actual influence of the local leadership on community affairs. The question that partial order correlations can answer is to what extent a relationship between two variables can be accounted for by their homogeneity or shared variance with a third variable.[33] With a partial order correlation, the extent to which two variables are correlated because of their mutual interdependence with another variable can be evaluated. For example, in the United States the *value* of economic level correlates with activeness because of their mutual dependence on the *actual* level of economic wealth. The influence of a third, or fourth, or fifth variable can be said to be held "constant."

The partial order correlations presented in this report are first-order partials on only economic level, community conflict, and leadership influence. An additional variable was partialed—sum total of divisions between groups of people in the community—but it is not reported because the impact of this variable on the other correlations was negligible in all countries, indicating that total divisions in the community operate independently. Several second-order partials were run—economic level and conflict, economic level and divisions, and conflict and divisions. The results of these analyses were similar to those found when economic level and conflict were partialled and are thus not reported.

MULTIPLE REGRESSION. The most general question concerns the "goodness" of fit of the over-all design. To answer this question, two multiple regressions at the community level were run.[34] These multiple regressions were not used to test hypotheses, but rather to evaluate the overall fit of the design.

The first regression analysis was a free run general search for the structure of the explanation of activeness in a step-wise multiple regression, which first picks the best correlated variable with activeness, presents how much of the total variance it explains, produces partial order correlations holding this variable constant, examines the partial order correlations, picks the variable with the highest partial correlation, holds constant for this variable as well as for the preceding one, and continues this process until the variables are exhausted. The second type of multiple regression was to force or predetermine the steps, according to the sequence suggested in the design, in order to provide a basis for evaluating the "goodness of fit" of the research design in each of the countries, and to what extent each departed from it.[35]

The step-wise regressions, whether forced or not, are highly unstable. The results are dependent, first, on the first variable that enters the analysis (an entirely different result can be obtained if the first variable to enter the analysis is changed) and second, on the precision of the data, particularly when the steps are not theoretically predetermined. A very minor difference in the correlation coefficient will produce a substantial difference in the structure of the analysis. Little social science research has the precision of data necessary to determine a stable structure of multiple regressions. Because of these general cautions about regression analysis, and because the number of cases is small (30 local units in each country), the results of these regressions are interpreted conservatively and then only in general descriptive terms.[36]

DIFFERENCES BETWEEN GROUPS. Three kinds of between-group differences were examined in order to establish relationships within countries: (1) differences between means of groups of leaders, based on typologies of values; (2) differences between the "extremes" of leaders on a single value scale; and (3) differences between the variances of the leaders in an entire country compared with variances found within the local communities. The tests of differences between leaders was based on means and variances. The differences between leaders with different typologies of values and those holding extreme positions on the value scale of conflict avoidance was designed to determine whether leaders holding different values or value configurations are associated with differences in other individual characteristics, such as education, and on differences in the kind of communities in which they hold their positions. The analysis of variability, however, is primarily directed to cross-national analysis—to see whether differences in variances among leaders grouped by community and grouped by nation provide the most homogeneity of values.

VALUE PROFILES AND EXTREME TYPES. Types of leaders were constructed on the basis of five of the value scales and the extremes on the value scales of Conflict Avoidance. Differences among these groups were compared on 29 variables, including some characteristics of the communities in which the leader operated. A "difference of means" test was run on a pair-wise basis, where each typology is compared with another typology separately and the two extremes on the value scale are contrasted. The test of difference between group means included an examination of the variances in the two groups to check the assumption of equality of variances.[37] If the variances were not equal, an adjustment was made.

There are two issues in these comparisons of group differences within countries. The first is the interpretation of 30 community scores to score approximately 900 local leaders in each country. Individual characteristics were aggregated to obtain community scores. The scores for economic level and activeness, based entirely on community level observations, were used as the community scores for individuals. The problem lies in the freedom of the individuals to vary (degrees of freedom). As the sample is based on local governments, and as the degrees of freedom are affected by the number of communities, these relationships need to be cautiously interpreted. Secondly, there is a question of the "advisability" of selecting individuals on the extremes of the value scales and comparing them, rather than taking the entire population. The "cut-off" points are critical. However, in addition to the comparisons of extremes, correlations with selected variables across the entire body of leaders are used to aid interpretation.

NATIONAL AND LOCAL VARIABILITY. In the analysis of the congruence of values, an index of value homogeneity is constructed by averaging the variances on all nine value scales, both for each country and for each community within the country. The question is whether a national population of leaders is more homogeneous in their values than the international population, and whether leaders within communities are more homogeneous in their values than a national population.

To answer these questions, analysis of variability is undertaken (F ratio) to see whether differences in variances are statistically significant. When appropriate, adjustments are made for the fact that some of these groups characteristics are based on the same population.

ANALYSIS OF RELATIONSHIPS ACROSS COUNTRIES

The central question for comparative analysis is: to what extent are relationships between variables similar or different across countries, and, if different, what explains the difference? The focus is first on similarities and differences in the relationships between specific variables, secondly on the relative importance of general categories of variables, and thirdly, on the multivariate patterns that best explain either activeness or leadership values in each country.

TWO AND THREE VARIABLE RELATIONSHIPS. In cross-national comparisons of differences between groups of leaders, the question of whether any variable is significantly associated is reported for each group of leaders for all countries. In this way, it is possible to see which variables are or are not significantly related to a particular value profile or to a position on a value scale. Although the analysis is confined to differences on single variables, an evaluation of the relationships found is often given in terms of categories of variables—socio-economic background, perceptions of the community and so on.

In the cross-national comparisons of the explanation of activeness, comparisons are largely restricted to variables that are significantly correlated in at least one country. If a variable is significantly correlated in one country, its behavior in the other countries is discussed. But most of the comparative interpretations of the cross-national and nation-specific explanations of activeness are based on categories of variables—macro socio-economic characteristics, the socio-political structure, and leaders' values. Both the number and the strength of the correlations of variables in one of these general categories are used to evaluate the relative importance of that category for each country. Further, the importance of a group of variables is appraised by examining what happens to the correlations when a variable from another category is controlled.

MULTIVARIATE PATTERNS. Although much of the discussion is a presentation of specific relationships found across countries, the goal is to build a pattern of relationships to explain activeness at the community level and values at the individual level in each country. These multivariate patterns are presented and comparisons across countries are made in general rather than statistical terms.

One attempt is made to present a hypothetical, causal, one-way set of relationships for activeness in each country. These linkages of relationships are considered central to the explanation of activeness in each country. In addition there is comparison of the multiple regressions on activeness to confirm some of the major components of the patterns.

In the explanation of leader values, an attempt is made to extract a general pattern from the group differences. Group differences are examined in several ways to provide a basis for interpreting the dominant patterns in each country.

NATIONAL VALUE DIFFERENCES. There are comparisons of country differences in mean value scale scores. These differences are subjected to a difference-in-means test and statements about whether the Indians are more committed to the value of economic equality than Americans or Yugoslavs are made.[38] Whether or not these kinds of comparisons are justifiable depends on the nature of the scales. When differences in means are subjected to statistical tests, then assumptions of equality of intervals and a common origin point, as discussed earlier in this chapter, are made.

In the cross-national comparison of value profiles, where national means are used to partition leaders into value typologies, comparisons of national differences in *frequency* of value types are made. Again, the validity of this kind of cross-national comparison hinges on the cross-national nature of the scales, the criteria used in the typology for partitioning and the variances within each country. The results should be understood in terms of the scaling assumptions made.

LIMITATIONS ON INFERENCES IN ANALYSIS

The primary function of a research design is to structure data so that hypotheses can be tested and relationships evaluated. No research design is decisive for the substantive purposes of the research. The nature of the design limits the inferences that can be made from the data. Three characteristics of this design should be considered in evaluating the results of the analysis: (1) most of the observations are at one point in time, rather than cross-time; (2) most of the variables are treated in an exploratory manner rather than as tests of hypotheses; and (3) most of the collective or group characteristics—nation and community—are based on aggregation rather than on structural characteristics of the groups.

CROSS-SECTIONAL OBSERVATIONS AND CROSS-TIME INFERENCES. The substantive question of the design is, how do leaders' values affect the activeness of the community in which they hold positions? The optimal data for this question are changes in leaders and changes in activeness for several points in time. The actual data, however, relates activeness of local governments at the time of the survey of leaders and some period prior to the survey (five years) with the characteristics of leaders in the last three months of 1966. The data can be used to infer what kinds of leaders are associated with community activeness. If it can be assumed that the type of leaders a community has is stable, then it is possible to make some kind of causal inference about the associations. In explaining leaders' values, however, cross-sectional survey data must be interpreted as associational rather than causal. In the case of socio-economic background data, the inferences made between, for example, high formal education and a high score on a particular value, are usually causal by implication, because education is prior in time. Aside from these background characteristics, inferences must be restricted to concomitant relationships.

EXPLORATION OF RELATIONSHIPS. The design was oriented to a set of general questions about values, leadership and activeness. What conflicts, for example, influence activeness in what kinds of ways, were not specified. As a result, the focus is on the relationships that were found, rather than relationships not found, on general types of variables, rather than specific ones, on configurations of relationships, rather than on particular ones. The data are able to partially confirm something about categories, types of variables.

AGGREGATION OF COMMUNITY LEVEL VARIABLES. In the individual analysis, the groups are analytical aggregates, that is, share some set of common characteristics. In the community analysis, however, an assumption is made about the characteristics of the local leadership in a political unit. As is discussed in Appendix B the leadership is defined in terms of roles. It should be recognized that the characteristics of the leadership or leaders in a community are not based on some demonstrated interaction between the individuals, leading to collective behavior. Thus, inferences about the leadership should be treated with the caution required by the fact that individual characteristics are aggregated on the basis of membership in a particular community, rather than on the basis of evidence that the individuals acted as a collective leadership group.

Conclusion

The design of this research, both in the measurement instruments and the procedures of analysis, took into account the characteristics of the four political systems used to establish relationships between variables. The measurement instruments were made sensitive to the contexts in which they are applied. The analysis of data allowed full play for country differences. The fact that this research dealt with those characteristics of individuals and collectivities that are an integral part of these vastly different countries necessitated deviations from conventional research procedures. The results of the research, of course, are the critical factors in evaluating methodological strategies. But in addition to the substantive findings themselves, there is experience with these approaches to the methodological problems that must be faced in comparative research.

Notes

1. These comparative problems are treated more generally as comparisons among any kind of social system, whether the broad conglomerates of cultures, societies, or nation-states or specific organizations, political parties, economic firms or families, in Adam Przeworski and Henry Teune, *The Logic of Comparative Social Inquiry*, New York: Wiley, 1970. A definition of the "comparative problem" largely in measurement terms can be found in A. L. Kalleberg, "The Logic of Comparison," *World Politics*, 19 (October 1966), 69–82.

2. Specific operational procedures are described in Appendices A and B. A standard research design with standard variables for all countries and a common form of analysis was adopted with minor national variations.

3. These scales are based on the measurement concepts propounded by S. S. Stevens, in "Mathematics, Measurement, and Psychophysics," in S. S. Stevens (ed.), *Handbook of Experimental Psychology*, New York: Wiley, 1951, pp. 1–49. It is recognized that these concepts are controversial.

4. This assumption is widely practiced. See W. A. Scott and Michael Wertheimer, *Introduction to Psychological Research*, New York: Wiley, 1962.

5. For an example of research based on direct measurement assumed to be equally appropriate in five countries, see G. A. Almond and Sidney Verba, *The Civic Culture*, Princeton, N.J.: Princeton University Press, 1963. In contrast Smith and Inkeles base their scales on the median response in each country, thus adjusting their measurement within each country. See D. H. Smith and Alex

Inkeles, "The OM Scale: A Comparative Socio-Psychological Measure of Individual Modernity," *Sociometry*, 29 (December 1966), 353–377. There is evidence that "intervals" are perceived differently across cultures. For cultural influences on cognition, see H. C. Triandis, "Cultural Influences Upon Cognitive Processes," in Leonard Berkowitz (ed.), *Advances in Experimental Social Psychology*, New York: Academic Press, 1964.

6. See D. T. Campbell, "Recommendations for APA Test Standards Regarding Construct, Trait, or Discriminant Validity," *American Psychologist* 15 (1960), 546–553.

7. Coding was done according to an international code constructed by the participants on the basis of pre-tests. This code was supplemented by "instructions and notes."

8. See below for a description of the aggregation procedures followed.

9. Blalock states, ". . . anyone wishing to test a general theory must construct an auxiliary theory appropriate for the particular population, measuring instruments, and research design with which he is dealing." H. M. Blalock, *Theory Construction*, Englewood Cliffs, N.J.: Prentice-Hall, 1969, p. 154. For the auxiliary theory for activeness, see Chapter 8, "Activeness: Concept and Assessment." For values, see Chapters 1 and 3. The measurement instruments for economic level, however, were based on existing interpretations of economic development, but measuring this at the local level required different kinds of theoretical assumptions.

10. Technically, what is being determined is the additivity of the indicators. In order that the assumption of additivity be met, the indicators should be monotonically related. These are familiar psychometric procedures. See E. E. Ghiselli, *Theory of Psychological Measurement*, New York: McGraw-Hill, 1964; or J. C. Nunnally, *Psychometric Theory*, New York, McGraw-Hill, 1967. These psychometric models were applied to local political units in assessing their activeness and economic level.

11. See Chapters 7 and 8 for a discussion of specific procedures.

12. The value items were factor analyzed and the "discriminant validity" of several of the scales were affirmed. See Appendix C. The scale scores, however, were constructed without consideration of their independence.

13. Standard scores are usually used where the distribution of a theoretical population defines the origin point, and specific scale scores are expressions of distance from the common origin point. The problem of the "comparability" of the population on which the means and standard deviations are based remains.

14. See Przeworski and Teune, *op. cit.*, Chapter 5.

15. It is possible to increase the level of abstraction to "participation in agricultural programs" or "social mobilization." But again, the question is, do these indicators indicate that general dimension. Activeness is defined as a combination of two "more specific" dimensions.

16. Robert Sears, "Transcultural Variables and Conceptual Equivalence," in Bert Kaplan (ed.), *Studying Personality Cross-Culturally*, Evanston, Ill.: Row, Peterson, 1961.

17. See Chapter 3 for a discussion of the specific scales; Appendix C for reliability coefficients; and Appendix A for a description of the pre-tests.

18. Alex Inkeles, for example, because of his criterion of cross-national scalability, occasionally had to rely on few items for a scale. The price for this kind of "comparability" is a loss in validity and reliability. See Alex Inkeles *et al.*,

The Modernization of Man, Cambridge, Mass.: Harvard University Press (forthcoming).

19. For a detailed description of this procedure, see Adam Przeworski and Henry Teune, "Establishing Equivalence in Cross-National Research," *Public Opinion Quarterly*, 30 (Winter 1966–1967).

20. This is a version of "construct validity" where the behavior of indicators is evaluated against each other. The homogeneity of the items or indicators is one expression of validity and reliability. See for example, Scott and Wertheimer, *op. cit.* and W. A. Scott, "Attitude Measurement," in Gardner Lindzey and Eliot Aronson (eds.), *Handbook of Social Psychology*, Vol. 2, Reading, Mass.: Addison-Wesley, 1969.

21. The Kuder-Richardson formula was used for computing scale reliability. This formula takes into account scale length. In general the greater the number of items, the higher the reliability. G. F. Kuder and M. W. Richardson, "The Theory of Estimation of Test Reliability," *Psychometrica*, 2 (1937), 151–166.

Coefficients of reliability for the nine values scaled are presented in Appendix C, Table 1.

22. The norms for intercorrelations among items are not clear. One estimate is given in E. J. Webb *et al.*, *Unobtrusive Measures*, Chicago: Rand McNally, 1966.

23. See Appendix A for the code, and Appendix C for the reliability procedures followed.

24. It could be argued that the logic of using common indicators or different indicators for the construction of comparable measures is the same. This is the position taken in Przeworski and Teune, *op. cit.*, 1970, Chapter 6.

25. See Chapter 8.

26. For a discussion of these alternatives, see R. J. Rummel, *Applied Factor Analysis*, Evanston, Ill.: Northwestern University Press, 1970, Chapter 20. The use of these procedures for establishing equivalence is discussed in Przeworski and Teune, *ibid*.

27. These differences in comparative research design are discussed at length as "the most similar and most different systems designs," in Przeworski and Teune, *ibid*.

28. We are indebted to Harry C. Triandis for pointing out the various ways in which country specific analyses obscure pan-national patterns.

29. See Appendix B for a detailed statement of the sampling procedures and nature of the sample.

30. It is possible to conceive of dichotomous scores as reflections of some underlying quantity of an attribute, such as "active" or "not active" in a particular area of local policy, where "0" and "1" are interpreted as degrees of activity, rather than a "true" dichotomy.

31. Although interval scale characteristics are often assumed in the analysis of psychological dimensions, at best, what can be achieved is a ranking of "more" or "less" rather than how much more or less. "About the best that can be done in psychological measurement is to represent an attribute by an ordinal scale." Scott and Wertheimer, *op. cit.*, p. 104.

32. Using means, of course, assumes something about the nature of the scores, but these requirements do not include linearity. Further, "There is plenty of pragmatic justification in psychological experience with personality assessment, for instance, for treating one's measures as if they constituted interval scales,

even though the data collection procedures themselves do not warrant it." Scott and Wertheimer, *op. cit.*, p. 102.

33. The use of partial order correlations is controversial, as they require that the data meet strong assumptions about error, independence of relationships, and linearity of relationships. Despite these requirements, which also apply to multiple regressions discussed in the following sections, there is consistency of the results obtained in the partials on three variables—economic level, conflict, and leader influence—and the fact that generalization was usually confined to categories of variables rather than to specific variables justifies in part using partial order correlations to support generalizations that are made in the activeness chapters.

34. Actually several multiple regressions with different sets of variables were run and evaluated. A different regression is reported in Jacob, Teune, and Watts, "Values, Leadership and Development," *Social Science Information*, 7 (April, 1968), 49–92.

35. See Chapter 9 for the sequence of variables.

36. For some additional problems, see, Robert Gordon, "Issues in Multiple Regression," *The American Journal of Sociology*, 73 (March 1968), 592–616.

37. This is Bartlett's test for equality of variances. Use of cutoff points is problematical, especially if certain cases in the middle are excluded from analysis. We have no way of estimating these regressive effects.

38. See Chapter 3.

PART ONE

Leaders' Values

Values of local political leaders, whose influence on social mobilization and change is the main object of inquiry, are examined in Chapter 3. Results of the leadership survey in four countries yield significant cross-national comparisons, and demonstrate striking differences in leaders' motivations for change.

Sources of these differences are analyzed in Chapter 4. There is little cross-national similarity in the factors associated with the varying profiles of values, but education does have a strong and consistent influence on the disposition toward economic equality.

Chapter 5 considers the diversity of leaders' values, within and across countries, finding that the greatest heterogeneity occurs within the local community, and that countries differ very little in the degree of national homogeneity reflected in the values of local leaders. The influence of value consensus, or the lack of it, on community activeness is assessed, and the sources of consensus and diversity are explored.

●

CHAPTER 3

Patterns of Commitment

This chapter was prepared by Singh and Jacob in collaboration with Puric and Jasinska-Kania.

 he search for leaders' values that might explain community activeness led in three directions. First, we looked for general standards used to judge the merits of public action or the personal qualifications of leaders. Secondly, leaders' aspirations for the future of their country were solicited. Thirdly, specific values involved in the kind of decisions made by local governments were identified and scaled for measurement.

The result was a set of value profiles reflecting fundamentally different orientations toward social and political change. Leadership was found to differ significantly from country to country, community to community, and especially within communities, in the nature of these value commitments.

This chapter describes the values that were explored, compares the overall, or average commitment to these values of the leaders interviewed in the four countries, demonstrates the basic linkages among values that underlie the profiles, and then analyzes in detail the typology of dispositions toward change. The actual impact of values on community activeness is assessed later, in Chapters 9 and 10, while the procedures of measuring values are set forth and appraised in Appendix C.[1]

The Horizons of Leaders' Values

Open-ended questions made it possible to map out two dimensions of the universe of values within which the leaders saw themselves and others like them to be functioning. The first was the dimension of commendable political conduct. The second was the pattern of concerns for the nation and its future.

THE "GOOD" LEADER

In pre-tests, respondents were asked to identify leaders of whom they approved or disapproved, and to state why they felt the way they did. Similarly, they were asked to describe specific actions or decisions of which they approved or disapproved, and to explain why.[2] Many respondents proved reluctant to criticize, and their answers (to the negatively worded questions) added little but the obverse of what they said positively.[3] Also, values mentioned to justify evaluations of political actions largely correspond to those expressed to justify judgments about leaders. So, in the final survey, this line of inquiry was telescoped into the following single question:

What kinds of people would you like to see as political leaders: That is, what do you think are the most important qualities for a good leader to have? Obligatory probe (after respondent's answer): Anything else?

A detailed classification of the responses was made according to an international code agreed upon by the four-country teams after each had coded samples of responses from other countries, as well as their own. The qualities most frequently mentioned are presented in Table 1.

The value of "honesty" is high on the list of admired qualities for all countries. It could rank as the stock mark in trade of political leaders, the seal of approval recognized everywhere. The label seems to cover various shades of meaning, judging from the context of replies; but as applied to public conduct, most respondents imply that leaders should be basically truthful and should not exploit their positions for personal gain at the expense of others.[4]

Another common standard of leadership, is the person's "people orientation"—his ability to get along with others, and his interest in

Table 1—Qualities of Leadership

	India n = 955*	Poland n = 888*	U.S. n = 905*	Yugoslavia n = 1179*
	% Respondents			
Honesty	52	52	56	66
Selflessness, dedication and public service	53	40	34	16
Intelligence, education, professional knowledge	19	66	55	50
Impartiality	15	9	13	8
Good relationship with people	36	29	25	33
General leadership abilities (energy, organizational ability, decisiveness)	17	16	29	16

Note 1: The table reports the percentage of respondents whose comments were classified in a given category. A respondent was classified only once in a category, regardless of the length of his response or the number of different subjects mentioned relative to that category.
The complete code, and classification of responses by frequency of mention (rather than on the basis above) is presented in Appendix A.

*Note 2: The number of respondents indicated on this table and other tables reporting the responses to the open-ended questions varies slightly from the number reported for responses to some other questions, including the items used in constructing the value scales. These discrepancies arose as a result of multiple data processing in different centers, and other reasons. The number reported is in each case the actual input used for the given computation.

their welfare. It is evident that these two rather different qualities are linked in the valuations of most leaders. Popularity and sociability are expected to reflect a genuinely outgoing concern, not just a congenial personality or charisma. A "people's man" is one who cares, as well as one who offers a glad hand.

When it comes to the ideal of selfless dedication to public service, however, the standards of leadership expressed in different countries vary greatly. In India, this ranks with honesty as the most desired quality; in Poland too, a large number of leaders cite selflessness as an important prerequisite of meritorious conduct. But in Yugoslavia, an unusually small percentage seem to consider this quality a vital component.

Instead, Yugoslav leaders put a high premium on intelligence and professional qualifications, a value also honored by Americans, and especially by Poles. Note that 66% of the latter indicated their respect for one form or another of "know-how". For most Indians, however, such technical attributes were far outranked by the moral qualities; this indicates a fundamental difference in concept of leadership and the expectations associated with it. Furthermore, respondents differed in the kind of know-how expected: in the United States and, to some extent, in Poland, the emphasis was explicitly placed on learned skills directly related to the leader's specific tasks; in India, it was general "education" or "intelligence" that was given merit, if such qualifications were mentioned at all.

Organizational abilities, and the qualities of energy and decisiveness often associated with "strong" leadership, are most commonly admired in the United States, if one can take the ISVIP responses as representative. In none of the countries, on the other hand, is there much regard for such traits as impartiality and tolerance—what might be called the integrative and mediative dispositions and abilities.

A striking omission from the list of admired qualities is ideological commitments. Concerns for a particular kind of political system or social order, or even for such broad goals as economic development or the lessening of economic inequalities are rarely cited as a basis for commending or disapproving of leaders, regardless of the kind of national objectives being sought, or the amount of controversy in each country over the direction of the society. Evidently, leaders as leaders do not consider political orthodoxy of any type a relevant consideration when evaluating leaders as leaders. What a leader believes is good for his society does not distinguish him as a good or a bad leader in the eyes of his fellow leaders. "Character" and personal abilities alone constitute the crucial admission requirements into the club of admired political leadership in all four of the countries studied. The profession of "public servant" or "politician" seems to have its own self-determined performance standards, which do not include commitment to a particular ideology or vision of the public good.

ASPIRATIONS FOR NATION

The national, or ideological dimension of the leader's universe of values is nevertheless significant. Given the prevailing belief that the national state must be the overriding institutional framework for political action and the source of authoritative decision, the political leader's aspirations for his country should indicate how far and in what direction he feels he should and can move in his chosen role of politician or official.

Drawing upon the basic research techniques developed by Hadley Cantril and Lloyd Free, we replicated a portion of their inquiry relating to the national future. On pre-test, a similar set of questions also was posed relating to the future of the leader's immediate local community.[5] Responses were sufficiently similar between the national and local levels to warrant limiting the final survey to national aspirations; redundancy between the expression of hopes and fears enabled us to concentrate on the former. To permit direct comparison with the Cantril–Free surveys, which were conducted in all four of the countries involved in this project, wording was kept identical:

What are your wishes and hopes for the future of our country? If you picture the future of (name of country) in the best possible light, how would things look, let us say, ten years from now?
Obligatory probe (after respondent's initial answer): Anything else?[6]

The responses, summarized in Table 2, demonstrate that social and economic development objectives dominate the aspirations for the

Table 2—Wishes and Hopes for Country

	% Respondents			
	India *n = 955*	*Poland* *n = 888*	*U.S.* *n = 905*	*Yugoslavia* *n = 1179*
Improved welfare and standard of living	50	72	48	54
Industrial development; employment	32	49	11	18
More and better social services (education, health, family and welfare services, culture and recreation)	36	36	28	14
Aspirations concerning form and operation of government (democracy, socialism, freedom, etc.; more effective, honest government)	16	8	33	21
National unity, strength, self-sufficiency, independence prestige	38	17	20	10
World peace; better, cooperative international relations	3	15	60	14

Note: See notes for Table 1, p. 69.

national future, with marked and plausible adaptations to the particular conditions of each country; for instance, in the extent to which industrial development, social services, or a higher standard of living is stressed. The most striking international differences are political, concerning the quality or character of government, the emphasis on national unity or self-sufficiency, and the concern for peace.

The Identity of Developmental Values

Within the broad horizons of leaders' values, nine specific values were selected as immediately relevant, in all four countries, to local government decisions concerned with local development. These were values that we presumed might influence leaders to favor or to resist social and political change.

The identification of such values was largely empirical and extended over a two-year period before the critical values were precisely defined and operationalized. Some values, initially thought to be important, were dropped; others were reconceptualized in the light of pre-tests that demonstrated ambiguity; a few new scales, not originally contemplated, were added to measure values that were frequently cited by leaders as they discussed their activities in open-ended interviews during the preliminary phase of the research. The following descriptions of these values reflect what the investigators intended to measure; this is modified by evidence drawn from inter-item correlational analysis of whether the respondents in fact demonstrated consistency in their answers, in the manner expected.[7]

Table 3 presents a classification of the nine values in terms of their presumed relevance to the motivation and processes of social change.[8]

Table 3—Values Related to Developmental Change

    I Acceptability of Change
       1 Commitment to innovation
       2 Action propensity
   II Economic Values: Objectives of Change
       3 Concern for economic development
       4 Concern for economic equality
  III Process Values: Leader-Group Interactions
       5 Citizen participation in decision-making
       6 Conflict-avoidance
   IV Identification Values: Object of Commitment and Loyalty
       7 National commitment
       8 Selflessness (commitment to the social welfare)
    V Moral Values Applicable to Public Conduct
       8 Selflessness
       9 Honesty (truthfulness)

COMMITMENT TO INNOVATION

The general disposition toward change was measured by a set of questions that pitted acceptability of new ideas and the need to seek new solutions to problems against the desirability of following past practices, or of being satisfied with things as they are. The scale was intended to be a measure of commitment to innovation and change as a value *per se*.[9]

ACTION PROPENSITY

This scale sought to assess the individual's *personal* disposition to act despite risks or uncertainties. It also appears to gauge feelings of self-containment and satisfaction with what one has, as opposed to a need for acquisition and achievement. Certain of the questions have been demonstrated, in other studies, to be indicators of rigidity or fatalism.[10] Some of the nation-specific questions used in this scale emphasize caution as opposed to risk-taking.

Originally, it was contemplated that this scale would discriminate between leaders committed to change and those committed to traditional ways. There were certain reservations, however, about its conceptual relevance, as the items tended to tap a personality dimension rather than a value; further, many items did not correlate well with questions relating specifically to the desirability of *social* changes, as against personal action. Consequently, the Innovation scale was devised to overcome these shortcomings, and to provide a more direct measure of orientation to social development and change in the community; the Action Propensity scale remained as a measure of personal life dispositions.[11]

CONCERN FOR ECONOMIC DEVELOPMENT

This scale was expected to measure commitment to material progress and well-being, and, secondarily, the desirability of subjugating immediate gratification of needs to long-term economic gains.

At one point, it was thought that these two elements were conceptually distinct and should be split into separate scales; but pre-testing demonstrated that this was not justified. Items that intercorrelated best were a mixture of those concerned with the general goals of economic development, efficiency and technical competence, and the priority of future growth over fulfilling immediate needs.[12]

CONCERN FOR ECONOMIC EQUALITY

This scale was originally conceived in a broader context, and was designed to measure egalitarianism in general. Questions included on pre-tests referred to such themes as impartiality, differential rewards for special capabilities and equality between the sexes. However, it became apparent that political leaders did not view equality as a single discrete value, applicable across the board to all types of human relationship. They might be strongly egalitarian in some areas and might completely reject equality in others.

It was agreed to concentrate on economic aspects of equality—the attitude toward disparities in wealth and material well-being. Around this theme, a fairly homogeneous set of items was developed.[13]

Nevertheless, it is possible to interpret the scale in two ways. One is that it does in fact measure varying degrees of commitment to equality as a principle of social organization in regard to material benefits and rewards; these degrees range from advocacy of leveling the differences between rich and poor, to a position specifically justifying unequal economic status. The second interpretation is that the value measured here is not equality *per se*; instead, it is the desirability of *reducing* differences. According to this view, no commitment to outright leveling can be inferred from responses to the questions in this scale. Even the strongest proponent should not be considered "egalitarian;" only one who favors less economic disparity in the society than others is considered as such.

There is evidence that ideological orientations may have affected the manner in which some respondents understood these questions. For instance, in Yugoslavia, the second of the above interpretations seems to correspond to what most respondents believed they were being asked to evaluate. Some related the questions to the socialist principle of rewarding people according to their work or achievement, and actually explained that they understood this principle to be consonant with *reducing* economic inequalities in the society.[14]

There has been considerable disagreement over the developmental implications of this value. From one standpoint, commitment to a lessening of economic inequalities should help to implement programs designed to benefit the poorer sections of the society, and be a spur to development in these areas. But it has been contended that such a commitment would dampen individual initiative for producing and increasing wealth. Even where national objectives favor social ownership and control of the means of production, prominent leaders are concerned lest the value of economic *equality* (in contradistinction to "*reducing* disparities") provides a rationalization for inefficient and uneconomic enterprise. Concern for the masses and improving the lot of the underprivileged might, it is alleged, deter all-out efforts aimed to spur the process of nationwide economic development.

PARTICIPATION IN DECISION-MAKING

This scale was intended to measure concern for popular involvement or citizen participation in the political process. Many of the questions deliberately pose alternatives of restricted, as opposed to full public participation in decision-making; these questions ask whether decision-making should not be restricted to experts, professionals, or otherwise trustworthy and knowledgeable individuals, and cite such grounds for limiting the role of the general citizen as its being time consuming, inappropriate in a complex society and a precipitant of social conflicts.[15]

Initially this scale was identified with the concepts of self-management and citizen initiative, as well as participation. But this conceptual heterogeneity called for greater clarity. An attempt was then made to treat the concern for expertise independently from citizen participation. Later analysis showed, however, that while the former cohered into a scale, the citizen participation items alone did not provide a satisfactory independent set. Accordingly, a selective combined analysis was undertaken, and yielded a highly scalable set of questions.

Items analysis of Yugoslav responses raised the possibility, however, that in that country the scale might be two-dimensional, incorporating two different values—the concern on the one hand for citizen participation and, on the other, a quite independent evaluation of the role of experts as decision-makers, especially when technical matters are involved. Apparently, many respondents did not consider expert participation in conflict with democratic decision-making. Some favored joint participation by citizens and experts; they envisaged problems that involved both political and specialized dimensions. Others, thinking in terms of general policy issues, would relegate experts to a supplemental role. The pivot of the contention is that there are really *two* scales embedded in the set of questions purporting to measure commitment to "participation."[16]

In interpreting the relationship between the value of participation and community outputs, two parameters should be considered: the level of economic development of the country and the cultural norms for or against participation. In developing countries, with few resources and without strong norms for participation, a heavier dependence on experts and knowledgeable individuals may well be required to promote community activeness. To the extent that the value of participation, as measured, implies rejection of expertise and dependence on the common man, it may be counterdevelopmental. However, complete rejection of public participation would mean that the leaders, having little faith in the common man, would have to rely on a very narrow human base for the initiation and even the carrying out of development programs; sustained effort would have to depend on the continuous availability of both qualified and stimulating leadership. Therefore, a middle position on this value may turn out to be most conducive to community development.

CONFLICT AVOIDANCE

This scale aimed at measuring the extent to which leaders were willing to proceed with programs in spite of possible opposition and frictions within the community. The questions often pit the desirability of community consensus and agreements against desirable collective actions that may undermine harmony and induce social conflicts. As originally conceived, the scale was to measure concern for "consensual harmony." Later it was sharpened to accent the avoidance of conflict in the context of social and economic development.[17]

A high commitment to conflict avoidance would, on the face of it, seem to stand in the way of community development. It would militate against decisions or programs that were controversial. Leaders would be more likely to direct their efforts to the promotion of the social integration of the community than to its "modernization;" they would tend continually to evaluate programs of change in terms of their implications for social harmony, rather than their potential contribution to social and economic advancement in the community.

NATIONAL COMMITMENT

This scale was intended to measure concern for national interests, as opposed to local interests and problems. Most of the six international questions deliberately pit local interests against those of the nation, and ask the leader to which interest he gives priority. Two questions specific to Poland relate only to local identification, without providing national contrast, while two of the U.S. questions provide only a national reference. Two of the nation-specific questions used in Yugoslavia pose a contrast between local and national interests.

As originally conceived, the national-local dichotomy was assumed to form a psychologically continuous dimension. The first pre-test, however, indicated that in some countries a leader could be equally devoted to both local and national concerns, particularly if the latter carried any overtones of patriotism (duty to nation). The items were subsequently split into a purely locally oriented set, and a set that maintained the counterposition between local and national interests, in order to avoid forcing the respondents into an unrealistic and misleading position. The items finally selected represent the best intercorrelated set.

Despite our endeavor to create a scale that effectively measures a single, discrete value whose opposite poles are on the one hand a strong commitment to nation, and on the other a primary concern for the interests and problems of the community, there is considerable evidence that the leaders in fact do not see these as being conflicting positions, and insist that there can be genuine harmony between local and national interests.[18]

Under these circumstances, it is probably safer to interpret the scale as a measure of "more" or "less" national commitment, rather than to assume the scale measures national *vs.* local commitment.

Despite uncertainty as to the exact implications of the scale in this respect, its relatively high statistical reliability and its strong explanatory power in relation to other variables in several countries make it among the most important of the value measures that were constructed.

SELFLESSNESS

This scale identifies one's willingness to sacrifice for others and to subordinate one's own interests in the interest of a higher cause. The scale remained virtually intact through the various pre-tests. While some items stress selflessness as a virtue in its own right, others pit specific forms of self-interest against the good of the community.[19]

The values of National Commitment and Selflessness may be thought of as defining a single self-community-nation dimension. Leaders who are selfless are as likely to be identified with the community as with the nation. Local, or community identification, therefore, should not be considered a selfish orientation. Self-interest is as likely to detract from local as from national commitment, and, in either case, will, it is assumed, militate against strong developmental initiative directed toward public welfare.

HONESTY

This value, as identified by the scale items, is a commitment to truthfulness in public conduct. Questions pit the importance of public disclosure of facts against such alternatives as loyalty to superiors, preservation of one's own interests and the successful implementation of community programs.[20]

Honesty was added to the list of values subsequent to the analysis of the open-ended questions that demonstrated how important a characteristic of good leaders it was considered in all four countries. The present set of questions is quite homogeneous from both a conceptual and a statistical standpoint.

As in the case of Selflessness, the value of Honesty (truthfulness) represents a moral imperative that when carried over into public conduct should affect the kinds of actions that a leader feels he can legitimately undertake. But the effect on development of strict adherence to these two values may differ. While commitment to self-interest rather than to community or nation will usually undercut vigorous social action, it is not at all clear that candor in public life always fosters progress. An overriding commitment to honesty can reduce efficiency and imperil the achievement of community goals, however laudible it may be from the point of view of inspiring confidence in leadership and promoting cooperation of the people with their leaders. While outright dishonesty may be self-defeating, unbending honesty may not be an unmixed blessing in attempts to carry out a strategy of development change.

Directions of Commitment—The Common and the Different Among Nations

Table 4 reports the average score on the nine developmental value scales of the local leaders who were interviewed in the four countries. The extent to which leaders in each country were alike in their value commitments is also indicated, by the standard deviation.[21]

When viewed in the perspective of averages, there are certain outstanding similarities among countries in the values espoused by these leaders.

1. They tend to be committed to Innovative Change, Economic Development and the moral values of Selflessness and Honesty. (The scores are above 2.50, which is theoretically midpoint between the maximum possible acceptance of the value and the maximum possible rejection.)

2. Leaders in all countries except the United States tend *not* to be action prone, the Indians least of all.

3. In none of the countries is there a decisive position on the value of National Commitment, though the Poles are the most nationally oriented and the Americans least so.[22]

On Conflict Avoidance, Participation and Economic Equality, the national means show far greater variation. Commitment to Conflict Avoidance and Economic Equality is strongest among Indian leaders, weakest among Americans. Poles and Yugoslavs hold a position in-between. The ranking of countries on these two values is parallel, ranging from high to low acceptance as follows: India, Yugoslavia, Poland, United States.

While the value of Participation is accepted in the United States and Yugoslavia, it tends to be rejected in Poland and especially in India.[23]

Putting these findings together, a prototype of local leadership in each country can be drawn to portray the "average" leader (which of course does not reflect the great differences among individuals).

Table 4—Value Commitments of Local Leaders[1]

	India n = 946	Poland n = 889	United States n = 905	Yugoslavia n = 1178
Innovative Change				
Mean	3.47	3.33	2.83	3.27
SD	0.420	0.386	0.388	0.375
Action Propensity				
Mean	1.60	2.15	2.48	2.06
SD	0.469	0.393	0.407	0.357
Economic Development				
Mean	3.64	3.11	2.83	3.45
SD	0.367	0.437	0.417	0.354
Economic Equality				
Mean	3.50	2.74	1.72	3.03
SD	0.429	0.463	0.428	0.496
Participation				
Mean	2.13	2.26	2.74	2.74
SD	0.457	0.390	0.417	0.435
Conflict Avoidance				
Mean	3.13	2.42	2.13	2.85
SD	0.566	0.468	0.351	0.392
National Commitment				
Mean	2.57	2.70	2.29	2.34
SD	0.604	0.382	0.346	0.383
Selflessness				
Mean	3.41	3.23	3.15	3.21
SD	0.307	0.422	0.374	0.386
Honesty (truthfulness)				
Mean	3.38	3.13	3.28	3.48
SD	0.466	0.351	0.374	0.322

[1] Mean scores are adjusted so that maximum commitment to a value equals 4.00 and the minimum commitment (i.e. maximum rejection) equals 1.00.

THE INDIAN LEADER

Indian leaders are united in a high commitment to moral and economic development values. They are, however, almost equally divided between local and national identification.

Regarding the matter of the interaction and change values however, there is a most interesting contrast of positions. Though concerned for their community, and highly committed to social harmony and the avoidance of conflicts, they reject people's participation in decision-making. Thus, concern for the community does not go along with faith in the judgment of the people.

This may be interpreted in two ways. First, Indian leaders are psychologically oriented towards the preservation of the *status quo*, insofar as programs of development requiring change would divide the community or create hardships for the people. Secondly, Indian leaders tend to place faith in persons who enjoy a position of trust, and accept the advice of these people, rather than turning to the common man. This latter characteristic makes it possible to resolve the apparent contradiction between the leaders' strong commitment to the values of Economic Development and Innovative Change on the one hand, and their profound concern for the avoidance of conflict in the community on the other. On the advice of trusted and well-informed individuals, leaders may be willing to go along with new programs of development, even at the risk of community conflicts. The fear of conflict is balanced against a respect for the persons in whom trust is placed. Thus, in India, the personal characteristics of the leader, his sociometric status and his acceptability by the people are important, not only because the leader is a guide and a coordinator, but also because he is perceived as a legitimizer of social action.

It may be mentioned, however, that authority is viewed as benevolent by the Indian people. Individuals in positions of authority are expected to take into account the different interests and viewpoints in the community. Confidence in such individuals stems from the belief that they are in a better position to provide guidance and leadership than the general public. Should they by their actions belie such expectations, they would not enjoy the confidence of the people. Thus, while people's participation in decision-making is rejected in favor of the involvement of knowledgeable and trustworthy individuals, it is the people who in the final analysis decide who to trust and who to disregard.[24]

It is noteworthy that the Indian leaders place a premium on thoughtful, carefully calculated action, and want to avoid the risks of quick decisions. This is consistent with their high concern for the consequences of action for the community. It also shows that the leaders do not sense any contradiction between a strong commitment to social change on the one hand and a desire to consider carefully the consequences of personal action before making a decision, on the other. The reasons for this are commented upon at length in a later section.[25]

THE POLISH LEADER

The most accepted values of the Polish leader are Innovative Change, Economic Development, Honesty, Selflessness and Economic Equality. Like the Yugoslav leader in his acceptance of these values, the Polish leader falls between the Indian leader (who is most inclined to accept change and development) and the American leader (who is relatively least committed to them).

The Polish leader is not inclined to accept economic development without reservations. He will strongly agree that "the economic development of the nation should take precedence over immediate consumer gratification," but he will reject the statement that "less should be spent on social welfare programs so that more resources are available for economic development." Strongly committed to the value of change, he will not fully accept the proposition that "changes are desirable even if they do not seem to contribute as much as one expects."

He is less inclined to accept honesty (truthfulness) if it may lead to misunderstandings, if it will interfere with getting his work done, or if it will harm someone.

He also accepts Economic Equality, provided it is not connected with governmental control of the living style of citizens. He strongly *disagrees* with the statement that "the government has the responsibility to see that nobody lives well when others are poor." He is committed to the value of decreasing economic inequality, provided this does not infringe the principle of socialist society "to everybody according to his *work*" (he rejects the statement "difference in salaries should depend upon the size of the family").

The most specific characteristic of the Polish leader is his orientation toward national goals. He gives them priority over the local goals, but he sometimes also tends to accept some local values ("A proper political leader puts the interests of his community foremost," and "Although national affairs are important, people here should first worry about their own community problems"). Thus, in his national identification, he does not clearly juxtapose national and local values.

His commitment to the nation is correlated with the values of Change and Action Propensity. His values favor receptivity to national initiatives for change and economic development, and implementation of national directives. He is not very prone to action involving risk, but is less afraid of risk than the Yugoslav and Indian leader. Also, he is not afraid of conflicts. He thinks that conflict avoidance should not restrain him from the achievement of community programs. He is more inclined to accept decision-making by experts and knowledgeable individuals than broad citizen participation in the decision-making process.

THE U.S. LEADER

The U.S. leader is in some ways quite different from leaders in the other countries. More local than national in his identification, he rejects the values of Conflict Avoidance, and Economic Equality, and stands the lowest among the leaders in all four countries in his commitment to Selflessness and Economic Development. However, while less committed to innovative change than the others, he is more action-oriented. All of this seems to suggest that the frame of reference for action for the

American leader is the self, rather than an abiding commitment to the community or the nation. This does not mean that the American leader is not interested in the nation or the community. What is implied is that although he may be interested in one or both, this interest is not a consequence of normative compliance; rather, it is a matter of personal choice. Thus the rejection of social restraints and the assertion of his own freedom of action seem to constitute the core of the American leader's value orientation. This indeed is not a startling influence if one takes into account the importance given to independence training in early life and the desirability of exercising independent judgment, a trait that is stressed in the process of socialization.

The value patterns of the American leaders seem to be quite consistent with the above interpretation. For instance, reliance on expertise or authority figures is rejected, perhaps because it reduces the leader's freedom of action. The leader's identification with local, as opposed to national, interests seems to free him from restraints that may operate on him from an external and distant source (the nation). The relatively low commitment to economic development and to economic equality may be similarly interpreted. While the first involves long-term personal sacrifices, the latter implies a commitment to removal of economic disparities. Both are social commitments that limit the individual's freedom of action. The relatively lower stress on Selflessness seems also to conform to this interpretation, as it implies less willingness to subordinate personal self-interests to that of the community or the society.

The cognitive style of the American leader thus appears to be quite distinctive. While his normative commitment to change is relatively low, he is definitely change-oriented in the sense that many of the normal social restraints that seem to weigh heavily on the leaders of the other countries are less operative upon him. His relatively high Action Propensity shows that he is psychologically mobile and prone to accept changes that may conform to his personal orientation toward the social environment.

The high commitment to the value of participation, however, does confirm the faith that the American leader has in the judgment of the people, and to this extent demonstrates the importance he gives to collective responsibility for self-management. He is probably much more concerned about public affairs than the others and his actions are likely to reflect a genuine concern for the people and their welfare.

THE YUGOSLAV LEADER

The value profile of the Yugoslav leader resembles that of the Indian and Polish leaders. His most distinctive characteristic, however, is strong commitment to people's participation in decision-making; he resembles the U.S. leader in this respect. This, together with high concern for Honesty (value of public disclosure) and Economic Equality, indicates a basic orientation toward the public. His concern to avoid conflict, second only to the Indian leader, bears out this interpretation. His commitment to the public and the community makes him accept social restraints, and, to that extent, limits his personal freedom for action (he is low on action propensity); this commitment also brings about a relatively higher commitment to self-sacrifice.

While the Polish leader would tend to accept new ideas and to implement programs in accordance with national directives and expert advice, the Yugoslav leader would be more concerned about their consequences for the public. Like the American leader, he seems to have faith in the people, but his commitment is more to the community than to the individual or the self. Unlike the Indian leader, however, he seems to be less trustful of authority, although he is strongly committed to the values of innovation and economic development.

Additional comments secured from Yugoslav respondents permits further insights concerning their values which need to be considered in drawing a sensitive profile.[26] Although the Yugoslav leader expressly declares support of Innovative Change, his attitude is not categorical. The social justification of change must be quite obvious for him to assume a determined stand favoring it.

Dedicated to the idea that economic differences between people should be reduced, the critical question for Yugoslav leaders, however, is *how* to reduce them, considering the prevailing commitment to the principle that everyone should receive remuneration on the basis of the results of his work.

While concerned about consensus among members of the community, the leaders are not adherents of consensus at any price. Most of them reject the idea that a leader should abandon actions, or desist from making proposals of importance for the community, if they generate disagreement.

In supporting the participation of citizens in decision-making, the Yugoslav leader does not pit this social factor against the participation of experts, but rather feels that it is necessary for both public and experts to take part in decision-making, each one having his own place and role. Experts should have the last word on the technical aspects of problems, because they are specialists on the problems under consideration. At the same time, leaders reject the attitude that "participation by citizens in decision-making is not necessary if that decision-making is entrusted to reliable and capable leaders."

Also, in the case of national versus local interests, the Yugoslav leader generally opposes pitting one interest against the other. He feels identity of interests is indispensable, in the sense that the local community cannot develop unless society in its entirety develops, and *vice versa*, that the local community is a part of society and if it lags behind, so will society.

Interpreting the Yugoslav responses on the Action Propensity scale, it seems clear that the attitude is not so much one of unwillingness to take action for social change, but a reluctance to commit the resources of society without sufficient forethought. Given his high sense of responsibility for the community, he does not want to gamble with the social capital, no matter what his personal dispositions may be.

Linkages Among Values: An
Intercorrelational Analysis

So far, the discussion has stressed the distinctiveness of the value patterns of the leaders in the different countries. Here, an attempt will be made to highlight the cross-cultural similarities in the pattern of intercorrelations and to offer reasons that may account for them.

Table 5 presents a summary of the intercorrelations between the values in all four countries. It is noteworthy that out of a total of 36 cross-national sets of interscale correlations, 14 are completely consistent cross-culturally (for all four countries, the values are correlated significantly and in the same direction); 13 are comparable for three countries (with the fourth country showing no significant correlation or a correlation opposite to the others). This clearly shows that, irrespective of the wide differences in the value positions in the four nations, the leaders exhibit a remarkable identity in the pattern of associations among the different values they profess. Perhaps this implies that in many respects values have a similar meaningful bearing on the behavior of local political leaders, regardless of the systemic, developmental, or cultural characteristics of their countries. It is noteworthy in the seven cases in which the correlations between values are reversed, three are found in the United States and three in Yugoslavia.

Six of the values correlate significantly with Action Propensity in all countries. The direction of these correlations is negative for all the values except Participation. In brief, the *less* action-oriented individuals in all countries tend to be selfless, to be committed to economic development and economic equality, to reject popular participation in decision-making but to favor conflict avoidance, and to be change-oriented. How can these correlations be explained?

The answer may be found in the relationship between Action Propensity and the interaction values, namely Participation and

Table 5—Cross-National Comparability of Value Patterns

Inter-Correlation of 9 Value Scale Scores for Total Leadership Samples in Four Countries

Value	Country	APRO	ECDEV	EQUA	PART	CONF	NATL	SELF	HON
Innovative	India	S −	S +	S +	S −	S −	# −	S +	—
Change	Poland	S −	S +	S +	S −	—	S +	S +	S +
	U.S.	S −	S +	S +	# −	—	# +	S +	S +
	Yugoslavia	S −	S +	S +	S +	S +	S +	S +	S +
Action	India		S −	S −	S +	S −	S +	S −	—
Propensity	Poland		S −	S −	S +	S −	S +	S −	S −
	U.S.		S −	S −	S +	S −	S +	S −	—
	Yugoslavia		S −	S −	# +	S −	—	S −	S −
Economic	India			S +	S −	S +	S +	S +	S +
Develop-	Poland			S +	S −	S +	—	S +	S +
ment	U.S.			S +	S −	S +'	S +	—	—
	Yugoslavia			S +	S +	S +	S +	S +	S +
Economic	India				—	S +	—	S +	S +
Equality	Poland				S −	S +	—	S +	—
	U.S.				S −	S +	S +	S −	S −
	Yugoslavia				—	S +	—	S +	S +
Participation	India					S −	S +	—	S +
	Poland					S −	S +	S −	S +
	U.S.					S −	—	—	S +
	Yugoslavia					—	—	—	S +
Conflict	India						S −	S +	S −
Avoidance	Poland						S −	S +	—
	U.S.						—	—	S −
	Yugoslavia						—	S +	S +
National	India							# −	S +
Commit-	Poland							S +	S +
ment	U.S.							—	S −
	Yugoslavia							S +	S +
Selflessness	India								S +
	Poland								S +
	U.S.								S +
	Yugoslavia								S +

Honesty

Code: S = significant at .01 level ($r > .081$); # = significant at .05 level ($r > .062$). A pattern of association is circled if it is identical in all four countries.
Signs have been adjusted to denote the nature of the relationship between *positive* commitments to each value. Thus + means that a positive commitment to change is associated positively with a positive commitment to economic development. A *negative* sign means that there is an inverse correlation, e.g., a positive commitment to change is associated with a tendency to *reject* action.

Conflict Avoidance. Action-oriented leaders tend to be less committed to the avoidance of community conflicts and the involvement of experts or knowledgeable persons in decision-making. The theme common to both seems to be the individual's desire to be free from social constraints. By his indifference to the maintenance of harmony and the need for expertise, the action prone leader is apparently asserting his freedom for action. The questions that comprise the action propensity scale do in fact pose problems that require a choice between restraint, caution and purposeful deliberation, on the one hand, and the spontaneity of expression on the other. Apparently, a feeling of commitment to the community or to particular individuals is psychologically opposed to the freedom of expression and spontaneous action. It is probably for this reason that the action prone leaders reject commitment to moral constraints (values of Selflessness and to some extent Honesty or truthfulness) and also to the economic values. The value of Economic Development requires sacrifices for long-term gains and the value of Economic Equality has implications for the limitation on incomes and the leveling of differences.

Why, it may be asked, is the action prone leader opposed to change? If the arguments given above are valid, one might expect the two to be positively rather than negatively correlated. The explanation may lie in the fact that a commitment to social change does not necessarily mean that the individual is *personally* quick acting, impatient or inclined to disregard risks. On the contrary, a commitment to change, should it arise out of the leader's concern for the welfare of the community and its development, may be accompanied by careful consideration of the consequences of action. A responsible leader should hardly be expected to be an advocate of new ideas or ways that are of doubtful value and do not fulfill desired social objectives. Moreover, a number of items in the change scale juxtapose the past with the future, and stress the desirability of finding new solutions, rather than continuing with the past regardless of its merits. A commitment to action propensity, on the other hand, without a concomitant concern for change, probably characterizes leaders who are primarily interested in the present, the here and the now.[27]

The change-oriented leader in all four countries tends to be selfless and committed to economic development and economic equality. He also values honesty in public life (correlations in India not significant) and is concerned with conflict avoidance in India and Yugoslavia (correlations in Poland and the United States not significant). Change-oriented leaders tend also to reject people's participation in decision-making in all countries except Yugoslavia. There, the change-oriented leader tends to favor people's participation.

The conclusion suggested by these correlations is that commitment to change reflects a basic commitment to the community and the society. The fact that the moral values generally correlate with change shows that leaders concerned about principles share a similar concern for social progress, while the association with the economic values definitely points to the leadership being favorable to economic changes. Change orientation is also associated with national identification in all countries except India.

Concern for Conflict Avoidance is positively associated with the values of Economic Development and Economic Equality in all countries. Thus leaders concerned about economic development and the minimization of the gap between rich and poor are also interested in preserving community harmony. This interpretation is sustained with reference to the value of Selflessness. The selfless leaders tend to be more concerned about the avoidance of conflicts than the others (except in the United States). On the other hand, except for Yugoslavia, Conflict Avoidance is negatively associated with the value of Participation. Concern for people, as reflected in the desire to minimize conflicts among them, does not necessarily assume faith in the people's ability to manage their own affairs.

The value of Participation is positively related to Honesty. This should be expected, as those committed to public participation should be expected to believe in the desirability of sharing facts and information with the public (the principal connotation of "honesty" in this study).

Belief in Economic Equality, or in reducing disparities of wealth, is positively related to Honesty and Selflessness in Yugoslavia and India; but the reverse applies in the United States, where the relationship is significant but negative. Equality is also positively related to Economic Development and Conflict Avoidance; but it is negatively related to Action Propensity and Participation (correlation not significant in Yugoslavia). Its relationship to National Commitment is significant and positive only in the United States. In other words, only in the United States is belief in economic equality related to a national orientation. In other countries the correlations are not significant. The value of Economic Development is, however, related to a national orientation everywhere except in Poland and is related positively to the moral values in all countries except the United States.

Honesty and Selflessness are positively associated and show a comparable pattern of intercorrelations with the other values, except the value of Participation. While high commitment to Honesty is positively related to Participation in all countries, as already reported, Selflessness is *unrelated* to Participation in all countries except Poland, where the selfless leaders tend to favor the involvement of experts and knowledgeable individuals in decision-making.

Profiles of
Change

The management of change tests the fiber of leadership in any society. It becomes critical in countries where expectations outstrip capacities for improvement in either the material conditions of life or psychic satisfactions, or where events have unhinged the settled patterns and jolted a comfortable sense of security. The political and social future of the four countries, each confronting its own particular crisis of development, will inescapably be influenced by the kind of approach that its leaders are prepared to take toward change.

The purpose of this section is to explore those combinations of values, or "profiles," that characterize leaders who are disposed to seek change. The assumption here is that human beings do not segregate each of their values into airtight compartments; rather, they are constantly sifting and mixing them as they confront life experiences. Certain values tend to get pulled together into persistent, interrelated patterns, a kind of value "syndrome" that reflects a basic set of mind toward many of the issues the person faces, and that conditions the leader's role performance in public life.

To uncover some of these syndromes, leaders were grouped according to their scores on the five scales that were most comparable cross-nationally: Commitment to Innovative Change, Economic Equality, Popular Participation, Nation and Honesty. Those that stood above and below the average (mean) for all leaders in their country on all five values were identified. The possible combinations of high and low on these five values made 32 groups. A classification of 16 types omitting the value of Honesty (on which there was relatively little variance) was also made. In addition, a corresponding tabulation was made with the score of 2.50 as the dividing point, as this is the midpoint between maximum possible agreement with items in a scale, and maximum disagreement with these items.[28]

From this analysis, a set of value profiles has emerged, which distinguishes three major motivations for change, each of which has historically been a prime factor in major social or political upheavals.

The first is pivoted on the value of Economic Equality. From Aristotle to Marx, disparities of wealth have been propounded as the principal seedbed of political change, the rich and the poor as the classic protagonists. In the ISVIP, a profile that combines a high commitment to change with a high commitment to removing or reducing economic disparities would denote a leader whose desire for change is undergirded by a sense of purpose to reorder the social and economic system. It would be a great exaggeration to consider such persons as genuine radicals in a revolutionary sense, as most of them are office-holders in a going political establishment. But they qualify as "equalizing innovators" concerned primarily with redressing what they see as inequities in the distribution of wealth.

The second motivation for change stems from a commitment to government by the people—reflected in the value we have identified as Participation. Here is the ideological heart of the great political revolutions in the name of democracy. "The littlest he has as much right as the greatest he"—to be heard, to be listened to, and to *decide* what should happen in his society; so appeals the political radical from Athens to the American Declaration of Independence to the present time.

The third historic motivation of change has been nationalism with its insistence on the supreme value of a nation and its corresponding right to independence. Both the demand for internal solidarity under the aegis of overriding national interest, and a mood of collective self-reliance asserting a necessity for complete freedom from external control have been integral elements of the nationalist impact on the political order. The profile that identifies this kind of motivation is one that couples a commitment to the value of Innovative Change with a high concern for national interests and goals.

What is by no means clear is whether these propellents of change reinforce each other. Does commitment to nation further the forces of economic egalitarianism and political democracy, or does it tend to go conservative once the national union is in being, and foster authoritarian politics and a socio-economic structure of privilege? Nor is it a foregone conclusion that economic and political radicalism go hand in hand. However, on the assumption that leaders who are dedicated simultaneously to the lessening of economic differences, to the broadening of political participation and to the advancement of the national interest may be more prone to instigate change than those who are only committed to a single one of these values, a profile of a "general innovator" was constructed; leaders whose value syndrome combined any two out of the three change-linked values were also identified.

Tables 6A and 6B present the resulting distributions of six types of leaders in the four countries. In Table 6A the distribution is determined by whether the leader basically accepted or rejected the various motivating values (whether he scored above or below the conceptual dividing point of 2.50); Table 6B gives the distribution relative to the mean score of leaders interviewed in each country.

One can see from the relative distribution (Table 6B) that the proportion of change-oriented leaders of different types is unusually similar in the four countries, except for a larger group of "equalizers" in India. Just about one out of four leaders in each country links a commitment to change with a relatively strong concern for economic equality, political participation or national interest. Of even greater interest is the fact that there is no appreciable cross-national difference in the proportion of leaders who combine various types of motivation for change. The number who combine the economic and political participation values, or the economic equality and nationalist commitments, shrinks to about half of those who subscribed to each of these imperatives

Table 6A—Types of Innovators—Classification I[1]

	India n = 954	Poland n = 888	United States n = 905	Yugoslavia n = 1178
Total number (all respondents scoring high—above 2.50—on Change scale)	925 (97%)	874 (98%)	754 (83%)	1150 (98%)
Orientation to Change				
Equalizing (high on Change and Economic Equality scales)	772 (81%)	706 (79%)	16 (2%)	776 (66%)
Participant (high on Change and Participation scales)	150 (16%)	329 (39%)	457 (50%)	572 (45%)
Participant-equalizing (high on Change, Economic Equality, Participation)	147 (15%)	253 (28%)	11 (1%)	481 (41%)
National (high on Change and National Commitment)	411 (43%)	571 (64%)	150 (15%)	355 (30%)
National-equalizing (high on Change, National Commitment and Economic Equality)	406 (42%)	457 (51%)	4 (—)	291 (24%)
General innovator (high on Change, National Commitment, Economic Equality and Participation)	98 (13%)	173 (19%)	2 (—)	220 (19%)

[1] This table presents the number and percentage of leaders in each country who have scored above 2.50 on the value of innovative change (that is, they have indicated that they tend to agree with the desirability or necessity of change) and have also scored above 2.50 on one or more other values that are often held to be associated with the desire for political and social change (an indication of a commitment to economic equality, citizen participation in decision-making, national interests, or a combination thereof). The categories necessarily overlap.

Table 6B—Types of Innovators—Classification II[1]

	India n = 954	Poland n = 888	United States n = 905	Yugoslavia n = 1178
Total number (all respondents scoring above their national mean on Change scale)	575 (60%)	491 (55%)	363 (40%)	535 (46%)
Orientation to Change Equalizing (above mean on Change and Economic Equality scales)	397 (43%)	240 (27%)	196 (22%) (note 2)	275 (23%)
Participant (above mean on Change and Participation scales)	244 (26%) (note 3)	206 (23%)	192 (21%)	312 (26%)
Participant-equalizing (above mean on Change, Economic Equality and Participation scales)	169 (18%) (note 3)	92 (10%)	93 (10%) (note 2)	157 (13%)
National (above mean on Change and National Commitment scales)	275 (29%)	258 (29%)	214 (24%)	257 (22%)
National-equalizing (above mean on Change, National Commitment and Economic Equality scales)	154 (20%)	122 (14%)	115 (13%) (note 2)	176 (15%)
General innovator (above mean on Change, National Commitment Economic Equality and Participation scales)	91 (10%) (note 3)	57 (6%)	52 (6%) (note 2)	114 (10%)

Note 1: This table presents the number and percentage of leaders in each country who have scored higher than the mean of the leaders sampled in their country on the value scale of Innovative Change, and higher than their national mean on one or more other value scales, measuring values that are often held to be associated with the desire for political and social change. The categories necessarily overlap. It should be stressed that these categories are based on the leaders' value commitments *relative* to other leaders in their own country. They do not reflect whether the leaders in actuality reject or accept the indicated values.

Note 2: In the case of the United States, none of the leaders actually accept economic egalitarianism; hence, this category cannot be compared cross-nationally in a substantive sense.

Note 3: In the case of India, virtually all leaders reject the value of public participation; hence, cross-national comparison must be discounted accordingly.

separately. (In this consideration, we must again allow for the extra dose of economic egalitarianism in India.) This means that the potential for change is scattered and reduced. Were all leaders who stood for one kind of change also eager to press for another, the radical segment would be both larger, and, if our assumption of reinforcement is tenable, more radical. The shrinkage goes on through another stage of reduction. When all three of the strands of radicalism are combined, less than 10 % of the leaders whose profiles indicate commitment to change on all these fronts are left.[29] Thus, in the anatomy of contemporary local leadership, the imperatives of radicalism are dispersed and their potential for reinforcement is thereby dissipated. While one group pushes in one direction, another is headed elsewhere. This scattering of innovators seems to occur as much among the leadership of countries where political authorities assert firm and strong ideological commitments to change, as among those where there is no such official line; it is as likely in countries where the material conditions of life are desperate as in the richest country in the world. Thus local leadership is not an auspicious recruiting ground for the shock troops of change. The question is whether there is sufficient coherence among the fractions of change-oriented leaders to enable them to mediate development efforts initiated from the outside.

The problem appears in a somewhat different light when the "true-to-life" profiles are examined. Here national peculiarities are striking, and the prognosis must be modified for each country accordingly.

When the actual, rather than the relative, positions of the leaders are considered, the extraordinary social conservatism of Americans comes to the fore. Less than 2% are even modestly committed to change in the direction of economic equality. To be sure, half of the American leadership simultaneously favors change and broad political participation; but virtually no one sees a connection between the achievement of political democracy and the achievement of economic equality. One man-one vote: Yes; One man-one dollar: No. For 50% of these leaders, every man has an equal right to take a hand in government, however incompetent he may be; but he has no right to expect the government to help him out of poverty, to set limits to the riches that the few are able to extract, or generally "to give to each according to his need." Of course this finding is scarcely newsworthy, considering the deep-rooted American tradition of economic individualism, although it is a testimony to the immobility of the *laissez-faire* predilections of grass-roots leadership in the United States. One might have expected emergence of at least an identifiable nucleus of social radicals as cities grappled with acute problems of the economically depressed. But the conditions of political success do not seem to favor or require a commitment to fundamental economic change.[30]

This is not the place to speculate about the implications for international development of the vacuum of change-orientation at the base of U.S. leadership. What is immediately evident, however, is the immense gulf that separates (one might even say isolates) the Americans from leaders in the other countries on the issue of social change. With

81% of the Indians, 66% of the Yugoslavs and 79% of the Poles committed to developmental change and economic equality as determinants of public policy, someone is clearly out of step. The perspectives on the direction of change are so different that even understanding, let alone acceptance, of the other's point of view, will be hard to achieve. The problem is accentuated by the fact, just discussed, that nothing in the lifetime experience of these leaders, including the propulsion of their country into every nook of world responsibility, seems to have altered this facet of their value profile.

The door to changing the character of the American political leader's evaluation of change seems to be closed also by virtue of the near unanimity on this issue in the American political community. If there were wide enough and large enough division to generate continuing debate, there might be a prospect of adaptation and evolution toward a different evaluation. As it is, the social conservatism of the American leader seems to have all the solidity of bedrock and will need to be recognized by all concerned as one of the fixed points in plotting the direction of developmental effort throughout the world, as well as in the United States itself.

This rigidity of the American leader on the issue of economic equality, and his unyielding opposition to social change related thereto, would appear to stand in marked contrast to the psychologically mobile and pragmatic disposition that characterizes his general value profile.[31] However, it will be recalled that the dominant thrust in his value orientation was toward individual freedom of action; from this point of view, any moves toward economic equality, especially as they would in all likelihood entail the increase of governmental restraints, would be seen as inhibitions of personal initiative. Thus, the American leader's unresponsiveness to demands for social and economic change may reflect a deep fear of losing elbow room to exercise personal independence. His flexibility stops at the point where social organization and policy might threaten his opportunities to be flexible, i.e., to be his own boss or to choose his bosses.

The prospects for dynamic interaction in the political process appear strongest in Yugoslavia. Here local leadership is bipolarized on the issue of change, and one can therefore anticipate vigorous, intensive debate emerging out of the confrontation between the corps of general innovators and a powerful group of "conservors", when one takes into account the considerable amount of effective decision-making exercised at the local level. Table 6A demonstrates the broad base of change-orientation in Yugoslavia: high commitment to reducing economic disparities (though somewhat less than in India), a commitment to political participation as great as in the United States and a substantial core of nationally-oriented leaders. When evaluated, and after the inevitable shrinkage due to lack of overlap, there remains one in five Yugoslav leaders whose desire for change goes hand in hand simultaneously with all three of the hypothesized change propellants.

However, turning to the tabulation of conservors (Table 7) and comparing leaders within each national group (i.e., identifying those who are *relatively* more or less in favor of the status quo than their fellow nationals) one finds a surprising 13% "diehards" in Yugoslavia, a percentage relatively larger even than in the United States. These are

Table 7—Types of Conservors

	India n = 954	Poland n = 888	United States n = 905	Yugoslavia n = 1178
Total number (scoring below national mean on Change scale)	479 (40%) [29]	397 (45%) [14]	542 (60%) [251]	643 (54%) [28]
Orientation to Status Quo				
Non-equalizing (below mean on Change and Economic Equality)	186 (19%)	231 (26%)	252 (28%) [117] (13%)	390 (33%)
Non-participant (below mean on Change and Participation)	162 (17%)	179 (20%)	217 (24%) [16] (2%)	368 (31%)
Non-equalizing/non-participant (below mean on Change and Economic Equality and Participation)	87 (9%)	84 (9%)	80 (9%) [16] (2%)	214 (18%)
Local conservor: all (below mean on Change and National Commit- ment)	178 (19%)	221 (25%)	241 (27%) [103] (11%)	379 (32%)
Local conservor: non-equalizing (below mean on Change, National Commitment and Economic Equality)	95 (10%)	121 (14%)	148 (16%) [103] (11%)	239 (20%)
General conservor (below mean on Change, National Commitment, Econ. Equality and Participation)	51 (5%)	47 (5%)	48 (5%) [14] (2%)	158 (13%)

This table presents the number and percentage of leaders in each country who have scored lower than the mean of the sample of leaders in their country on the value scale of Innovative Change, and lower than their national mean on one or more other scales measuring values that are often held to be associated with opposition to political and social change and with a desire to maintain the status quo. The categories necessarily overlap.

In brackets are noted the number who scored lower than the conceptual midpoint on the scales (2.50); that is, they tended to reject the value. Breakdown into categories using 2.50 as cut-off is omitted for countries other than U.S. because the numbers are insignificant.

people who, compared to others in their country, tend to disagree with the need and desirability of change, and also to minimize the values of political participation, national interests, and the reduction of economic differences.

Thus the stage is set for an effective, although uncomfortable and perhaps bitter dialogue over the fundamental direction of Yugoslav polity. Two groups articulate different views of what should be the essential nature of this society, each one a minority bidding for the support of the others.

This diversity of values may well be the condition for creative experimentation in political and social development.

The validity of the original assumptions on which this typology of "radical" or change-oriented leadership was based should now be reviewed in the light of the actual responses secured in the four countries. To what extent is it true, for instance, that a concern for economic equality generates or is associated with a desire for political or social change? Some support for this classical assumption comes from the correlations between the Change and Equality scales, which are significant in all four countries: India $= 0.235$; Poland $= 0.090$; U.S. $= 0.110$ and Yugoslavia $= 0.133$ (p is greater than .01 when $r = .081$ with $n = 1000$). On the other hand, when the frequency of leaders holding different profiles is analyzed, only in India is there a substantially larger percentage of change-oriented leaders who are economic egalitarians (43%) compared with conservatives (21%). In the United States there are actually more conservatives than progressives who are egalitarian (32% *vs.* 22%). In Yugoslavia, conservors are as likely to favor reducing economic differences as innovators are (23% *vs.* 23%); in Poland, to be sure, more innovators than conservors support greater economic equality (27% *vs.* 19%).

But the "pure" economic radical emerges predominantly in the country at the lowest level of development, where economic disparities are very great. For the others there can be no presumption that a sense of injustice about economic inequalities will provoke a general desire for change, or, conversely, that a desire for change in general will be likely to generate reforms directed to economic leveling. The fact that this seems to be as true in countries where governments are committed to a socialist ideology as in countries where the sanctity of the rewards of private enterprise is upheld suggests that the sources of social radicalism in leadership are more effected by socio-economic conditions than by political or social systems and ideologies.[32]

Derivations of Diversity: Cross-National Perspectives

The immediate conclusion sought from a cross-national study is, obviously, the differences that exist between nations. The whole point of the design of this study, with its efforts to assure comparability of respondents' political roles, community base and concepts of value in four countries having very different systems of government and socio-economic conditions, was to find out if political leaders tend to bear the stamp of the country they lead or are more or less alike everywhere. Within the limitations of the sample, this is a test of the universality of values, or more precisely, of the extent to which people performing similar political functions hold similar values.

If there are important differences in leaders' values among the nations, a second question arises: Why? What is it about the national context that could account for these differences? Is it due to peculiarities of the country's political system or ideology? Or is it a reflection of its wealth or poverty, the stage or nature of its economic development? Or are the differences of political values associated with certain character-istics of social structure or cultural heritage?

In relation to the first question, the evidence of *dis*similarity, right across the board, is, at least from a statistical standpoint, signifi-cant. On almost every value, the leadership sample of each country differs from that of every other. Small though some of these differences appear, they are sufficient, considering the large number of our re-spondents, to exceed what might reasonably be expected by chance.[33]

However, the differences are of an entirely different order of magni-tude. On some values, notably those classed as "moral," the differences among countries are so small that it is difficult to see conceptual significance, even if they are statistically significant. On others, such as those related to economic equality, political participation and broadly the "change values," some of the cross-national contrasts are so striking that they form unmistakable national profiles. One simply could not transpose typical American and Indian leaders, or even Yugoslav and Polish leaders. Given the cues, an observer would be likely to detect the national origin of the "typical" or average respondent—the American by his conservatism and localism; the Indian by his economic egali-tarianism and antipathy toward popular involvement in decision-making; the Yugoslav by a combination of enthusiasm for "partici-pacija" and probable commitment to lessening economic inequalities; the Pole by his strong national orientation and rather dim views of equality as a goal and participation as a process of change.

Despite the extent of these national differences, the divisions among leaders *within* countries are sharper and more critical. On the central issues affecting the direction of social and political change, the leaders split along much the same lines in every country. Each country has its radicals and conservatives of various types; its men of principle and its opportunists; its conflict-avoiders and its "push-men." The proportion in each camp varies between countries, sometimes very greatly; the language of politics expressing the disposition of each of these contending groups also may have a peculiar national coloration. (For instance, the amount and kind of change advocated or opposed in the United States bears no resemblance to what is at issue elsewhere.) But basically the game is the same, the bones of contention similar, and the value profiles that distinguish the contenders much the same in all four countries.

In terms of political behavior and the dynamics of social change some of these *intra*national differences can have a determining effect. The word "can" is used deliberately, because as we will show later, the relationship of values to outputs of individual and social action is *not* the same in all countries. The point stressed here is that the gross international differences, let alone the minor ones, should not be allowed to overshadow the significance of the deep value confrontations within each country, confrontations that tend to be common to the countries in this study. While the mythical "average" leader shows his nationality, there is quite enough heterogeneity in each country to sustain vigorous political struggle and to divide leaders on essentially the same issues in every country.

The problem now is to explain the differences, international and intranational. This will be the subject of the detailed analyses in the next two chapters, dealing respectively with the differences in profiles and the differences in the amount of congruence or homogeneity among leaders' values. At this point we can suggest the general strategy of explanation that seems feasible and the main direction of the conclusions emerging from the data presented in this chapter.

First, where inter-national differences have been found to be statistically significant and are *greater* than the *intra*national differences, we must assume that something about the country has a bearing on the values held, and that this must figure in the explanation. This could either be something peculiar to one country, or a characteristic common to several countries (but not all four). Within the confines of this study, we can draw tentative conclusions about the influence of the political system and the development level of the country, as their differences in these respects are fairly specific.

Where *intra*national differences are greater than inter-national ones, we must turn, for explanations of leaders' values, to the characteristics of the communities or regions where they live, to the type of position they hold, or the expectations that they or people they respect have of their role, and, in the end, to personal characteristics such as age, education or social background.

If we discover that certain of these characteristics are associated with a value profile in one country and not in another, the search for explanation must go back to the national level and must try to see which feature of that country tends, let us say, to make younger leaders more conservative, whereas elsewhere the older ones are more resistant to change.

First, in the matter of the gross international differences, there is no clear association between political system or ideology and the social values we have measured. If one classifies the four countries according to their commitment to socialism, or the extent to which they are pluralistic in political organization, or whether they have unitary or federal systems, or how far they have gone in practice with decentralizing political authority and responsibility, there is no corresponding ranking of the leaders' commitments to any of the nine values. With regard to the value of participation, the positions taken by U.S. and Yugoslav leaders might be interpreted to reflect particular national political traditions and belief systems. But the ideological source of the belief in popular democracy is so different in the two countries that this finding actually serves to refute, rather than to sustain, the view that the system determines political values. We can find nothing in our data to support the view that values are a function of the political system in which local political leaders operate.

What has been said about the limited influence of their nations' political culture on leaders' values applies equally to social institutions characteristic of the four countries studied. It is difficult to find correspondence between a national value profile and a distinctive feature of a country's social structure, perhaps because the internal differences in values so generally outweigh the inter-national ones. This suggests that the socialization of political leadership is largely a process that takes place *below* the national level, and that the forces of socialization are sufficiently diversified within nations so that leader's values are not easily identified as "Made in the USA," or in Poland, Yugoslavia or India. The sources are more likely to be a complex of local and role influences than purported national culture or "character." This will be explored in more detail in the Chapter 5 to follow.

Certain possible exceptions to this generalization have emerged from our data and were previously reported (see section on Directions of Commitment, pp. 78–84). In India, for instance, the negative attitudes toward participation and action may have their roots in customary patterns of authority and leadership deeply embedded in village and even family practice. Antipathy of American leaders toward economic equality may reflect the powerful national heritage of economic individualism, a heritage not of ideas alone but also of social relations and economic practices that dominated the country even despite the Great Depression and the supposed introduction of a welfare state.

It is difficult to derive from these special instances of national culture-based values any general finding of the dynamics of acculturation; this indicates the consequences that might be expected to flow from a given type or feature of social structure. These instances are nation-specific. They do not lend themselves to cross-national classification; hence, one could not say this nation has more or less of a certain social characteristic than another.

In a very rough way, however, it is probably possible to compare the *rigidity* of social structure in these four countries and to test the assumption often advanced that such rigidity will reinforce or be reinforced by "traditional" values opposed to social changes. Our evidence suggests just the reverse. If one judges that India has the most rigid set of social institutions (particularly at the local level) and that American society is the most fluid (measured in terms of ability of individuals to move out of or into one social group to another), then the maximum *resistance* to change of leaders occurs in the latter. Indian leadership is, as we have seen, along with Yugoslavia, the most change-motivated. But this is far from a solid conclusion. We advance it merely to offset some of the confidence in structural explanations of political behavior and social development, and to suggest that "traditionalism" is an inadequate explanation of economic and political paralysis, if one means traditionalism to signify this acceptance of longstanding ways of social organization and group life.

A word here is necessary about transnational cultural differences; is there, for instance, an East and a West in the values professed by political leaders? In the light of our evidence, the answer is, in one word, "No." To talk of East-West differences is meaningless, unless there is a contrast between the Indian profile on the one hand, and a common profile characteristic of the three Western countries on the other.

When we consider the economic differences among countries, a much sharper pattern of explanation emerges. There is evidence of a definite *developmental ordering* of leaders' developmental values. In India and the United States—at the extremes of living standards—leaders are poles apart in their commitments to economic equality and economic development; Yugoslavs and Poles, in the middle on their welfare commitments, are also in-between in regard to national economic level. (Actually the rather modest difference in economic level between these two countries also matches the rank order of their leaders' developmental commitments, Yugoslavs being more committed to economic equality and change than Poles, while at a lower level of affluence.) Indian and U.S. leaders also differ the most in regard to the value they attach to avoiding conflict, though why this should tie in with the economic disparity between their countries is not readily apparent. It should be stressed that only some values are linked to the development index. How rich or poor the nation is seems to matter little for the moral predilections of the leaders, nor, strange as it may seem, for their propensity to take action. A context of poverty or affluence may shape the *direction* in which leaders move, but it does not shape their sense of urgency in moving—the object, but not the pace of change they espouse.[34] If a country is well off, its leaders may pay homage to the need for change or "progress," but few of them perceive the need for change in terms of basic economic or social adjustments.[35]

Coming now to the moral values, where international differences are minor (though usually statistically significant), we have found neither a systemic, a cultural nor a developmental classification of nations that ties in with the existing differences. Knowing a man's country will not help at all in knowing whether he is likely to be selfless or self-seeking in public office, candid or expedientially discreet in his public accountability. These are issues that commonly confront politician and official whatever the apparatus of their government or the needs of their society. We must look to the nature of the person, or the expectations of office he seeks to satisfy, or both, to find explanations of why leaders differ in these respects. This is far from saying that the moral values are universal. All political leaders do *not* agree on what is morally right and what is wrong, though there is great agreement in what they profess on these than on other values. What is plain, however, is that political leaders in one country would have no difficulty at all in establishing empathy with leaders in other countries on these issues. They would recognize a professional kinship in the need to consider such issues in making decisions, however different the subject matter of what it was they had to decide, or the political and social conditions in which they operated.

Our search for explanation of international differences in leaders values dead-ended at the point of national characteristics—political or social. Also, it failed to find a transnational cultural base to account for the values professed by political leaders. But there can be little doubt that the material conditions of life cut across and within nations to exert a powerful impact upon these commitments that shape the direction of social and political change sought by leaders. The leadership of the rich looks one way, that of the poor another. They lead different worlds and their values show it.

Notes

1. See also Chapter 2, "Establishing the Equivalence of the Values Scales," pp. 47–49. The universe of leaders' values was also explored in two pilot studies, one using content analysis of public statements, the other employing semiprojective techniques developed by David C. McClelland and his associates to measure need-achievement. For the former, references are cited in Appendix C, pp. 391–392. While it was not possible to incorporate the achievement motivation inquiry as part of the full survey, the pilot study indicated a definite association between "n-ACH" and certain of the values scaled on the basis of the ISVIP survey. See David G. Winter, "Identification of Motives in Political Behavior: The Relevance of the McClelland Studies," ISVIP Doc. USA/21.

2. The approach taken here is similar to that used by the Educational Testing Service in exploring the value "space" of school children, doctors, lawyers and other groups. See Paul Diederich, *The "Critical Incidents" Technique Applied to Medical Education*, research memorandum for the Educational Testing Service, Princeton, N.J., May, 1954; also "Methods of Studying Ethical Development," *Religious Education*, May–June, 1955, 162–166.

3. The fact that the responses to the negatively and positively worded questions were correlated was taken as evidence of the validity of this kind of question in measuring values (response consistency). In the final questionnaire one question could be used with assurance that it tapped both aspects of these values.

4. In a pre-test in India, Kailash K. Singh found that actual commitment to honesty as a standard of public conduct was best revealed by a "discrepancy score," based on the difference between a leader's professed regard for honesty as a qualification of leadership, and his estimate of how honest other leaders of his acquaintance were. The greater the discrepancy, the less confidence one could place in the sincerity of the man's avowal.

5. In India, a special survey of village leaders in Uttar Pradesh secured detailed descriptions of what they imagined would be the "ideal" village, block or district, and how this would differ from things as they were at present. See ISVIP Doc. IND/8A.

6. The authors are grateful for permission to use these questions and for continuing guidance and encouragement from the late Professor Cantril throughout the ISVIP.

Responses were coded in categories that correspond generally to the code developed by Cantril and Free. But the code was modified to take account of references emerging in the ISVIP survey that did not clearly fit in the Cantril code. Reliability was tested by cross-national coding of national samples. The two codes are reproduced respectively in Hadley Cantril. *The Pattern of Human Concerns*, New Brunswick, N.J.: Rutgers University Press, 1965, Appendix A; and in Appendix A of this volume.

7. The basis of identification and measurement was leaders' responses to sets of concrete, forced-choice statements in several formats, each set intended to elicit the varying degrees of commitment to a particular value. The procedures of scale construction, and the tests employed to determine reliability and validity within countries, and comparability among countries, are described in Appendix C. Also presented in Appendix C is a critique of the value scales, based on meticulous item-by-item analysis of Yugoslav responses to the scale questions, and supplemented by a sample study of respondent explanations of the answers given. The validity and unidimensionality of certain of the scales for Yugoslavia is challenged on the grounds that some of the questions did not convey the same meaning to all respondents.

In addition to the nine values selected for this analysis, the value of *political responsibility* was conceptualized and scaled, but at a stage that precluded satisfactory pre-testing in all four countries. As applied in three countries, the scale items test the willingness of the leader to maintain adequate role performance as against demands to compromise with social pressures. A special report on these data is in preparation.

The construction of political responsibility scales for three countries was undertaken by J. Harriet Dietz, who found substantial homogeneity in the responses to many of the relevant questions. Factor analysis generally confirmed the coherence and cross-national equivalence of these scales; and also showed that they identified a broad value dimension indicative of what leaders felt to be the nuclear body of principles that should govern public conduct. See her paper, "The Measurement of Political Responsibility", Seminar on Values and Motivation in Political Behavior, Department of Political Science, University of Pennsylvania, 1968. Unpublished.

8. This classification scheme was developed by Kailash K. Singh who, as a social psychologist, was concerned with the role of values in motivating persons and groups to seek or to resist change in their societies. Focus is on individuals and their interactions; values are seen as essentially a psychological force working upon and through individuals to affect the character of the society.

An alternative scheme of classification, elaborated by Z. Puric, is based on a view of community change and development as "a process of democratization of social relations under conditions of improvement of economic conditions of life through long-term economic planning and integration of communes." This classification stresses the *logic* of sociological interrelatedness of values as explanatory variables of this type of developmental change. See ISVIP Doc. YU/76.

9. The scale consists of four international items (identical for all countries) and several items that were used only in particular countries. See Survey Questionnaire, Appendix A. The rationale for including both identical and nation-specific questions in the scales is presented in Chapter 2, pp. 47–48. Procedures used in scale purification are outlined in Appendix C.

10. See instruments developed by Joseph Kahl (*The Measurement of Modernism*, Austin, Texas: University of Texas Press, 1968) and Milton Rokeach's "dogmatism scale" (*The Open and Closed Mind*, New York: Basic Books, 1960).

11. Five internationally identical items are included in the scale with one or two additional nation-specific items. See Appendix A.

An analysis of Yugoslav responses by Puric ("Patterns of Commitment" ISVIP Doc. YU/198) notes that respondents differed in their understanding of certain of these questions: while some *did* interpret them as referring to a *personal* propensity, others thought the questions referred to a general social value. Furthermore, many answers did not conform to the anticipated direction, resulting in rather low reliability for the scale. This was attributed not to personal inconsistency on the part of respondents, but to the ambiguity of the questions. This may qualify the assumption that the scale specifically measures a personal disposition toward action. Some respondents evidently were indicating their attitude toward hasty, as against deliberate action to solve social problems.

12. The scale consists of four international items and one to three nation-specific items.

13. Five international questions, and one to three nation-specific ones compose the scale.

14. See Yugoslav critique of the value scales, Appendix C. Also, Puric, "The Propensity to Reduce Disparities in Wealth," ISVIP Doc. YU/196.

15. The scale consists of seven international items and one to three additional nation-specific questions.

16. See Yugoslav critique of the value scales, Appendix C. It should be noted however that the reliability coefficient of the single scale taken as unidimensional is high (see Table 1, Appendix C); on factor analysis, most of the participation items included in the scale loaded on a single factor in all countries.

17. The scale consists of four international items and one to three nation-specific questions.

18. In the case of Poland and the United States, factor analyses resulted in splitting the national commitment scale into two, or even three factors, though these factors do not neatly discriminate separate value dimensions that can be identified as respectively national or local. An intensive analysis of the U.S. data, using an elaboration model, as well as item and factor analyses, supports the conclusion that this scale is multidimensional. See Sheila Babbie, "National and Local Value Orientations," Department of Political Science, University of Hawaii, 1969. Unpublished.

The situation in Yugoslavia is explained in the aforementioned critique of the value scales (Appendix C), and Puric, "Patterns of Commitment," *op. cit.*

19. The scale includes five international questions and one to four nation-specific questions.

20. Seven to ten questions are included in the scale, of which seven are identical for all countries.

21. The homogeneity of leaders values is analyzed in Chapter 5. It must be kept in mind that the survey data on which this analysis is based are not strictly representative of the total local political leadership in each country. The nature of the samples is explained in Appendix B.

22. It should be noted that modest though the international differences are on these values, they are generally sufficient to be statistically significant, because of the large size of the samples.

23. Inter-nation differences on the three values just discussed are statistically significant, except as between United States and Yugoslavia on the value of Participation.

These international comparisons assume equal reliability of the response, in all four countries. There is a possibility that some leaders, especially in India were more susceptible than others to an acquiescence "response set," that is, an inclination to agree with a statement for the sake of agreeing, rather than because it represented what the leader really believed. The various authors of this volume are not agreed whether the evidence is sufficiently precise to conclude that the value scores are systematically biased in this respect. Nor are they agreed that a procedure of discounting the scores could be demonstrated to have any greater reliability than the responses actually given.

The scales most likely to have been affected are Participation, Conflict Avoidance and Action Propensity. The consistent and conceptually coherent interrelations between the positions taken on these values and other issues by the Indian leaders suggests that the reservation in any case is not of such proportion as to muddy the broad comparisons presented.

Another apparent tendency among the Indian leaders was to take the most categorical positions in responding to the value questions; they tended either to accept strongly or reject strongly a statement. The extent to which this produced a national bias in the scores has not yet been determined.

24. Refer to Kailash K. Singh, *Values, Leadership and Development*. Report to the Research Programmes Committee, Planning Commission, Government of India, Kanpur, India: Indian Institute of Technology, 1968, pp. 43–44.

25. See p. 86 for a discussion of the relationship between the value of Change and Action Propensity.

26. The interpretation which follows was prepared by Z. Puric, on the basis of her analysis of the supplementary comments of Yugoslav respondents, "Patterns of Commitment," *op. cit.*

27. A penetrating analysis of factors affecting the relationship between commitments to Innovative Change and Action Propensity by U.S. and Indian leaders in the ISVIP sample was conducted by Leo A. Hazlewood. See "Community Cleavage and Action for Change: Local Elites in India and the United States," Report to the Seminar on Values and Motivation in Political Behavior, Department of Political Science, University of Pennsylvania, 1967. Unpublished. Hazlewood constructs and tests an axiomatic theory, relating the action orientation of the leader to his drive to avoid conflict and division in the society. He concludes that "the perception of cleavage and the conflict avoidance trait . . . account for the greatest amount of variance in the action trait. Theoretically,

together they form the cornerstone for any attempt to explain action propensity-change orientation. Indeed, one might suggest that it is the interaction between these two variables which either 'triggers' or acts as the initial 'multiplier' in the reciprocal causal system."

28. The first classification distributes leaders on a relative basis, as compared with others sampled in their own country. The second uses a conceptual criterion, and divides leaders into those whose answers indicate they are essentially committed *to*, or *against* a given value. The choice of a dichotomous basis for classification was dictated by the need to secure sufficient numbers for comparing groups, after three or four successive steps of division. This had the result of arbitrarily dividing the large body of respondents who scored in the middle range on the value scales, and placing them in either the "high" or "low" group, even when their scores indicated they were not intensely committed in a particular direction. It should be stressed, therefore, that in the analysis which follows, it is *group tendencies* which are being distinguished. There is no assumption that a set of "black-and-white" criteria have been applied, which justify describing particular individuals as unmistakably one type or another.

To the extent that distributions on the values scales were normal, this method of classification which ignores a middle position, calls for caution in assessing significance. Not only must the degree of statistical differentiation and correlation be high, but conclusions should meet a test of conceptual coherence as well. There is some disagreement among the authors as to how much confidence to place in this typology of value profiles and the analysis of explanatory variables which is reported in Chapter 4. See the aforementioned Yugoslav critique, Appendix C.

29. How strong the commitment of even this "change-minded" core group is a question, because their qualification for inclusion in the profile, it will be remembered, is merely that they have scored higher than the average of their fellow leaders on each of the values.

30. This profile is consistent with the responses given by the American sample to the query: "What do you think are the most important problems facing this community now?" Most of the leaders talked about tax problems, attracting industry, urban renewal and improvement of a wide variety of utilities and services. Some complained about immediate problems of government administration, inefficiencies or "politics." Practically no one mentioned poverty, jobs or other basic welfare issues; only one in ten was concerned with racial conflict, and very few with any other form of social conflict. To the local politician, social or economic conditions simply posed no issue that would call for reform or change of any fundamental character.

31. See page 82.

32. It is obvious that such observations caution against placing undue reliance on the typology of change-orientation presented herewith, and particularly on the predictive interpretations that have been derived. It should be noted however that the tabulations are based on cross-frequencies, and hence represent actual associations between different values made by the respondents themselves. A person is listed as an "equalizing innovator" only if he himself scored high on both the change and economic equality scales—high in relation to others in his national group, or high absolutely, that is, with responses placing him as definitely more strongly in agreement with the various value statements in the scale than in disagreement. Hence, these profiles reflect, as faithfully as is possible, the genuine combinations of values held by the respondents; the tables do give

the actual distribution of a country's respondents among these various profiles. But see fn. 28 above, *re* limitations of the classification procedures used.

33. This conclusion is stressed because it seems at odds with the results of certain other intensive cross-national studies. For instance, a dominant finding of the Harvard University Project on Socio-Cultural Aspects of Development, conducted by Alex Inkeles and associates, is the similarity across nations of attitudes and values related to occupation, social relations and public life among people involved in a changeover from rural to factory life. "It strongly suggests," they conclude, "that men everywhere have the same structural mechanisms underlying their socio-psychic functioning, despite the enormous variability of the culture content which they embody." David H. Smith and Alex Inkeles, "The OM-Scale: A Comparative Socio-Psychological Measure of Individual Modernity," *Sociometry*, Vol. 29 December, 1966, p. 377.

It should be noted however that the Harvard and ISVIP projects differ in the kinds of values, as well as the character of the respondents studied, so that the dissimilarity among nations found in ISVIP may reflect its deliberately chosen *political dimension*. It may be that political values are more susceptible to national differentiation than the social dispositions that Inkeles was tapping.

34. Apparently the inter-national developmental ordering of values just reviewed, is matched by a corresponding association of certain values with the economic level of communities within most of the countries. See Chapter 9.

35. We have noted that in a strict sense, there are few "true" conservatives in any country. Even in the United States, most leaders are at least verbally committed to the desirability of some kind of changes. One might almost say that talk of change is part of a common cross-national vocabulary of political leadership.

The crucial differences arise in what leaders want to change and how fast they want to bring it about. It is here that the "developmental ordering" appears, between nations and within them.

CHAPTER 4

The Shaping of Values

WHY LEADERS HOLD THE VALUES THEY DO

This chapter was written by Watts, in association with Jacob. The analyses for the chapter were conducted by Watts in collaboration with Jasinska-Kania; and reexamined by Puric on the basis of a special review of Yugoslav data.

This chapter explores the sources of leaders' values, and the reasons why leaders differ in the values they hold.

The data available permit an appraisal of four sets of explanatory variables. First is the nature of the *community environment* in which the leader operates—its wealth, size, activeness, homogeneity, and the general structure of leadership influence. The implication is that leaders' values will reflect their ecology. A second set of possible influences stems from the *personal background* of the leaders—their age, education, social status, mobility and other characteristics registering their "socialization." The *way a leader perceives his environment* is a third factor that may account for his values. In this connection, our data indicate, on the one hand, how the leader perceives the social dynamics of his community (its conflicts and divisions, for instance) and on the other, how he perceives the powers and appropriate functions of government. Finally, we expect that a *leader's political role* would have an impact on his values—both his formal position in the local political system and his informal roles, as indicated by the policy areas where he is active and influential, the groups to whom he turns for support, and the interests for which he feels responsible.

In keeping with our basic approach to cross-national research, explanation is first sought for differences in values among leaders *within* each country; the patterns of explanation are then compared across the four countries.

Analysis is directed at explaining the composite *profiles* of values of different leaders, rather than any specific value. It will be recalled (see Chapter 3) that in constructing a general configuration of a person's value orientation, his posture on the four scales of Innovative Change, Participation, Economic Equality and National Commitment was ascertained, relative to the other leaders sampled in each country. This resulted in a typology of leadership based on sixteen value profiles. Distributions are noted in Table 8.

Twenty-nine variables were selected to represent the four general explanatory factors previously mentioned (see Table 1). The means of these variables were computed for each of the 16 groups of leaders in each country.[1] The significance of differences on these variables between various types of leaders was then determined.[2]

First, in order to determine whether there were major cross-national uniformities in the shaping of leaders' values, five pairs of profile groups were chosen for analysis on the following bases: (1) that they included a number of leaders adequate for statistical comparison in all countries; (2) that they provided a substantial range of difference on several of the values composing the profiles; or, alternatively (3) that the difference between the two types of leaders was on only one component of the profile, e.g., the leaders in both groups differing only on Economic Equality, but holding a similar position on the other three values.[3]

Second, because of the particular interest of this study in change and motivation for change, a separate analysis was undertaken of the eight groups who shared a relatively high commitment to Change to determine what variables if any were associated with the *particular* kind of change they desired, as reflected in their position on other values. This is reported in the section, "Change-Oriented Leaders" below.

Finally, a special analysis was undertaken to identify those leaders who were distinguished by extreme positions on the value of Conflict Avoidance, this being one of the values shown to be most relevant to community activeness and developmental change in all countries.

Table 1—*Variables Analyzed in the Explanation of Leaders' Values*

I *Characteristics of the Community*
1 Economic level (measure I)
2 Size
3 Activeness (measure I)
4 Community conflict (mean amount perceived by leaders sampled)
5 Variation in range of leaders' influence
6 Congruence of leaders' values (on nine scales)

II *Demographic Characteristics of the Leaders*
7 Age
8 Years of education
9 Intergenerational occupational mobility
10 Political career (duration)
11 Length of residence in the community

III *Leaders' Perceptions*
(a) of Community Conflicts and Divisions
12 Conflicts—total (sum of conflicts perceived by each individual)
13 Conflicts—political
14 Divisions—total (sum perceived by each individual)
15 Divisions—over income
16 Divisions—over political issues
17 Divisions—over change
(b) of Local Government Responsibility and Powers
18 Sphere of local government responsibility
19 Spheres in which local government lacks autonomy
IV *Political Role of the Leader*
(a) formal
20 Appointed official
21 Elected official
(b) informal
22 Activity (total areas for the individual leader)
23 Influence (total areas claimed by the leader)
24 Support extended—primarily to party
25 Support extended—primarily to nation
26 Support sought—total reference groups mentioned by individual
27 Support sought—from local party unit
28 Support sought—from local elected officials
29 Support sought—from local administrative officials

The nature and significance of this "intense commitment"—as well as of the position on conflict—is the subject of the last section of this chapter.

The first two sets of analysis were subject to limitations inherent in the bimodal basis of classification used to construct the value profiles. As previously noted (Chapter 3, fn. 28) this arbitrarily placed respondents who held a middle position in either the "high" or "low" group, and allowed small differences in scores to determine whether a particular individual was classified as one type or another. An inescapable element of artificiality was thus introduced except where the actual distribution was itself bimodal. However, a breakdown into three or four positions would have resulted in too many categories, with too few respondents in some of them for statistically significant comparisons, given the various possible combinations of four values in the profiles. The object of this analytical stategy, considering the limitations of the classification scheme, was therefore to compare characteristics of groups of leaders having maximum differences in specific values, and determine whether the distinctions were sharp enough statistically (as well as sufficiently reasonable conceptually) to warrant concluding that we had uncovered genuine "explanatory" variables.

General Patterns
of Contrast

The composition of the value profiles and the distribution of the groups of leaders being contrasted in the first round of analysis is set forth in Table 2.

The first pair, leaders who are relatively in favor of broad political participation, are locally oriented, want to preserve the status quo, and suspect the goal of economic equality (type A) are compared with their exact opposite, leaders who, while less participationist, are more nationally oriented and innovative, and favor reducing economic disparities (type B). Type A leaders are particularly numerous in the United States; type B in India.

The second pair of contrasts differs from the first only on one value—participation. Type C is similar to type A except that he is "low" rather than "high" in his concern for political democracy. Type D is like type B except that he is more eager for wide participation by the citizenry in decision-making. The former is an important type in Yugoslavia, as well as in India and Poland.

Types E and F differ from C and D respectively on the value of economic equality. Type E is less favorable than C to equalizing disparities in wealth; Type F, in contrast to D, has a higher commitment to economic equality as a societal goal. Both types E and F are more frequent in the Yugoslav sample than in the other three countries.

The type G leader is a "conservor", but he favors citizen participation in decision-making. He is more nationally than locally oriented and is committed to economic equality. This type is particularly significant in the United States. Type H leaders are most prevalent in India. They tend to think locally rather than nationally, have faith in experts, are committed to innovative change and are more equalitarian on economic matters.

The last two types compared differ on two values—commitment to participation and commitment to economic equality. They hold the

Table 2—Ten Contrasting Value Profiles: Composition and Leader Distribution

| | Value Profile | | | | Frequency | | | |
	Partici-pation	Nation	Change	Economic Equality	India	Poland	U.S.	Yugoslavia
Type A	High	Low	Low	Low	43	74	100	81
Type B	Low	High	High	High	103	65	63	62
Type C	Low	Low	Low	Low	51	47	48	158
Type D	High	High	High	High	90	57	52	114
Type E	High	High	High	Low	50	65	53	96
Type F	Low	Low	Low	High	39	59	50	96
Type G	High	High	Low	High	69	40	110	59
Type H	Low	Low	High	High	123	83	40	56
Type I	Low	High	Low	High	36	36	87	58
Type J	High	High	Low	Low	52	73	72	95

Note: Because the profiles are constructed on the basis of the position of a leader relative to the mean of respondents *in his own country*, the designations "High" and "Low" do *not* represent equivalent cutoff points on the value scale scores in all four countries. Thus a U.S. leader classified as "High" on Economic Equality is probably lower than most leaders in the other countries, on this value, i.e., less egalitarian. The distribution of leaders holding other profiles is noted in Table 8.

same orientations on national commitment and change/oriented to nation but skeptical of innovation. Type I, however, is committed to expert decision-making and is above the mean on the value of Economic Equality. Type J, while a participationist, has a *low* commitment to economic equality. The latter type appears to be particularly significant in Yugoslavia.

THE POVERTY OF CROSS-NATIONAL EXPLANATION

The ultimate question with which this analysis is concerned is whether differences in value commitments, such as those just described, are attributable to essentially the same factors in all or several of the countries, or whether the pattern of explanation varies country to country; this possibility could support a conclusion that the genesis of political values is a process basically governed by the peculiarities of a nation's culture or political system.

The evidence indicates that there is actually very little cross-national uniformity in the factors that are associated with the different value profiles of leaders. Although there are some 115 instances in which there is a statistically significant difference on one of the 29 variables, linked to one of the five contrasted pairs of profile groups in one country (see Table 3), there are very few cases in which the same variable helps to predict value differences consistently in most or all of the

Table 3—Variables Associated with Contrasts in Value Profiles

Type of Value Profile Contrasted

	A vs. B	C vs. D	E vs. F	G vs. J	I vs. J	Total
India	6	8	6	4	3	27
Poland	3	6	4	2	4	19
U.S.	6	1	6	3	10	26
Yugoslavia	3	16	16	5	3	43
Total	18	31	32	14	20	115

countries. Furthermore, it will be seen that *what* is explained by a given variable differs from country to country. While the economic level of the community is a factor that is associated with the value differences between groups A and B in Yugoslavia, it is linked to the contrast between groups G and H in India. Length of residence in the community helps to explain the difference between groups C and D in India and Poland, between groups E and F in the United States and Yugoslavia, and between groups I and J in India and the U.S. The general conclusion must be that *there is no overall pattern of explanation of the different value orientations of local leaders applicable to all countries*, at least in terms of the 29 variables included in this analysis. The implication is either that we have not discovered the variables that have universal potency in shaping values, or that the power of national differences (so far unidentified) is greater than the power of community environment, personal characteristics and political role in molding the value commitments of political leaders.

This general finding may be modified by three important exceptions, where a given variable is associated with a particular kind of value difference in most or all of the countries:

(1) *Education* uniformly differentiates type I and J. The significance of this, as will be explained more fully later, is that education is apparently a powerful influence everywhere in disposing leaders to reject economic egalitarianism while embracing political participation. These are precisely the components in which profile I differs from J.

(2) The *range of activity and influence* of the leader uniformly distinguishes profile group C from group D; this is generally true also between groups E and F. Leaders with profiles D or E tend to have a wider area of activity and influence. These leaders are more highly committed to public participation, to nation and to change. Commitment to the value of economic equality is evidently not affected by this particular variable.

(3) *Appointed* officials are more likely to hold profile B than A in Poland, the United States and Yugoslavia. In India the reverse seems

to be true, the number of such officials holding profile B being significantly lower. This, it will be recalled, is the group that is more committed to the whole society, innovation, and lessening economic differences, but is less enthusiastic about citizen participation in decision-making.

This exhausts the positive findings that are similar in all or most of the countries studied. There is however an impressive array of factors that are uniformly *not* influential in distinguishing leaders holding different value profiles. The following variables do not tie in with a given contrast of values in more than one country; several have no explanatory power in any country:

Total amount of conflict in the community as perceived by its leaders:
Congruence of values among community leaders
Variance in the range of leaders' influence
Occupational mobility
Leader's personal perception of community conflict
Leader's personal perception of political conflict in the community
Total amount of cleavages perceived by a leader
Political cleavages perceived by a leader
Cleavages over change perceived
Attitude toward local government responsibility
Perceived lack of autonomy for local government
Leader holding an elected office
Support groups—local elected bodies
Support groups—local administrative officials

The implications of this finding may be more trenchant than the positive observations, although it appears more damaging to theory about political socialization of leaders rather than suggestive of alternative explanations. What this means is that any propositions purporting to explain political values in terms of factors such as these must face the fact that such propositions do not apply to a large sample of local leaders in four very diverse countries. It suggests that assumptions of cross-national uniformity in general theories explaining political ideology and values as the result of ecological context, conflict patterns, or political function and role are strongly challenged.

The remainder of this section is devoted to a more detailed appraisal of those variables that were found to have some power to explain value differences, either cross-nationally or in particular countries.

THE INFLUENCE OF LEADER'S BACKGROUND

The background characteristics of education, age and length of residence in the community are most frequently associated with differences in the value profiles. But of these, education alone, as noted above, is consistently related in all the countries to a value contrast, and indeed only to one particular contrast (type I *vs.* type J), where the difference is triggered by the issue of economic equality (see Table 4). The general

Table 4—Influence of Leaders' Background on Value Profiles

Variable	A vs. B	C vs. D	E vs. F	G vs. H	I vs. J
Age					
India					
Poland	L H			H L	
U.S.	L H		L H	L H	H L
Yugoslavia			L H		
Education					
India					L H
Poland					
U.S.	H L		H L	H L	
Yugoslavia		H L	H L		L H
Occupational Mobility					
India					
Poland					# #
U.S.					H L
Yugoslavia			H L		
Duration of Political Career					
India	H L				
Poland					
U.S.	L H				H I
Yugoslavia		L H			
Length of Residence in Community					
India		L H			H L
Poland		L H			
U.S.	L H		L H		H L
Yugoslavia			L H		

This table reports differences of means (at .05 level or above) between the designated value-profile groups. H indicates the higher mean and L the lower for a given variable. # indicates a difference of means somewhat lower than .05 but in the same direction as other countries.

finding is that in all countries the highly educated leaders tend to have a value profile in which there is a greater commitment to participation in decision-making than that of the less educated, but a lower commitment to economic equality. However, it is the difference over the equality value that is the controlling one; there is a consistently powerful and direct association in all four countries between education and the value of economic equality.[4]

Age and length of residence in the community have a bearing on the distinction between types E and F. Type F leaders tend to be older in all countries and to have lived longer in the community. (They are also less educated.) Although these associations are statistically significant only in the United States and Yugoslavia, the direction of the association in the other two countries is consistent.

Background characteristics as a set have a peculiarly important influence in the United States in distinguishing type I from type J. Leaders who are relatively nationalist, conservative, committed to expertise in government and who value economic equality tend: (1) to be older; (2) are occupationally more mobile; (3) have had longer political careers; and (4) have lived longer in their local community than those who are more democratic politically but less interested in reducing economic differences among people.[5]

LEADER'S ROLE

Three aspects of the informal role of the leader have some general bearing on this value profile (see Table 5). If we know something about the range of his activities, his perception of his influence over what happens in his areas of activity, and the extent to which he places the welfare of nation above loyalty to party, friends or local constituents, then we ought to be able to predict certain profiles of his values.

The explanatory power is strongest, it has already been noted, in differentiating type C from D, and E from F. A leader who is a *generalist* —active and influential in a comparatively wider number of areas— and one who considers the *nation as his primary reference group* is more likely to be committed to change, to widespread participation and to the value of nation (the common components of profiles D and E). Thus, while demographic elements in the personal background of the leader seem to lead to a choice of profiles in which the critical issue is economic equality, it is the nature of his political role that is decisive for the desirability of change and the sense of commitment to nation.

In terms of formal role, mention has already been made of the fact that significantly more appointed officials in all countries except India have a profile in which there is high commitment to nation, change and lessening economic disparities, but not to political participation (type B), whereas the reverse occurs in India, where more appointed officials are profile A, the complete opposite of B. However, this finding must be viewed with caution as the distinction between appointed and elected leaders is not equivalent in all countries and is indeed quite blurred in Poland and Yugoslavia.[6]

In Yugoslavia, the other role variables appear to have considerable significance. A distinctive touch in Yugoslavia is the importance of a leaders' attachment to the party in impelling him toward a value profile oriented to innovation, participation and nation.

Table 5—Influence of Political Role on Value Profiles

Variable	A vs. B		C vs. D		E vs. F		G vs. H		I vs. J	
Appointed office										
India	H	L	H	L						
Poland	L	H								
U.S.	L	H								
Yugoslavia	L	H			L	H				
Elected Office										
India										
Poland										
U.S.									L	H
Yugoslavia										
Range of Activities										
India			L	H	H	L				
Poland			L	H	H	L				
U.S.			#	#	#	#				
Yugoslavia			L	H	H	L				
Range of Influence										
India			L	H	H	L				
Poland			L	H	H	L				
U.S.			#	#					H	L
Yugoslavia			L	H	H	L			L	H
Support Extended: primarily to Party										
India					L	H	L	H		
Poland			L	H						
U.S.										
Yugoslavia			L	H						
Support Extended: primarily to Nation										
India			L	H	H	L	H	L		
Poland			#	#	#	#				
U.S.			#	#	H	L			L	H
Yugoslavia			L	H	H	L	H	L		
Support Sought: Total No. of Reference Groups										
India			L	H					H	L
Poland										
U.S.							H	L	L	H
Yugoslavia			L	H	H	L				
Support Sought: from Local Party Unit										
India										
Poland					H	L				
U.S.										
Yugoslavia			L	H	H	L				
Support Sought: From Local Elected Officials										
India										
Poland									H	L
U.S.										
Yugoslavia			L	H						
Support Sought: from Local Administrative Officials										
India	L	H								
Poland									H	L
U.S.										
Yugoslavia			H	L						

This table reports differences of means (at .05 level or above) between the designated value-profile groups. H indicates the higher mean and L the lower for a given variable. # indicates a difference of means somewhat lower than .05 but in the same direction as other countries.

COMMUNITY ENVIRONMENT AND PERCEPTIONS OF CONFLICT

It is apparent that, except in Yugoslavia, neither the ecological context of the leaders, nor their perception of the social dynamics of their communities bear much relationship to their profile of values (insofar as the selected variables adequately represent these two sets of phenomena). (See Tables 6 and 7.) One can tell little about the values that an Indian, Polish or American leader is likely to hold by knowing the wealth, size, activeness or other characteristics of his community, or, alternatively, by knowing what he himself thinks is the state of conflict or cleavage in his block, powiat or city.

In Yugoslavia, environment and perceptions are more enlightening. Leaders with profiles B, D and E tend to emerge in communes that are

Table 6—Influence of Community Characteristics on Value Profiles

Variables	Contrasted Value Profile Groups									
	A vs. B		*C vs. D*		*E vs. F*		*G vs. H*		*I vs. J*	
Economic Level										
India							H	L		
Poland	H	L								
U.S.										
Yugoslavia	L	H	L	H	H	L				
Size										
India	L	H	L	H						
Poland										
U.S.										
Yugoslavia	H	L	L	H	H	L				
Activeness										
India	L	H	L	H	H	L				
Poland										
U.S.										
Yugoslavia										
Conflict										
India										
Poland			L	H						
U.S.										
Yugoslavia										
Variance in Influence of Leaders										
India										
Poland										
U.S.										
Yugoslavia										
Congruence of Leaders' Values										
India										
Poland									H	L
U.S.					H	L				
Yugoslavia			L	H	H	L				

This table reports differences of means (at .05 level or above) between the designated value-profile groups. H. indicates the higher mean and L the lower for a given variable.

Table 7—Influence of Leaders' Perceptions on Value Profiles

Variable	A vs. B	C vs. D	E vs. F	G vs. H	I vs. J
Conflict (perceived by individual leader)					
India					
Poland					H L
U.S.					
Yugoslavia			H L		
Political Conflict (perceived by individual leader)					
India					
Poland			H L		
U.S.					
Yugoslavia					
Divisions (total areas perceived by leader)					
India					
Poland				L H	
U.S.					L H
Yugoslavia				L H	
Divisions over Income					
India			L H	H L	
Poland					
U.S.			H L		
Yugoslavia			L H		H L
Divisions over Political Views					
India					
Poland					
U.S.					
Yugoslavia		H L		L H	
Divisions over Change					
India					
Poland					
U.S.					
Yugoslavia				L H	
Sphere of Responsibility for Local Government					
India					
Poland					
U.S.	H L	H L			
Yugoslavia		L H	H L		
Perceived Lack of Autonomy of Local Government					
India					
Poland					
U.S.					
Yugoslavia		H L		L H	

This table reports differences of means (at .05 level or above) between the designated value-profile groups. H indicates the higher mean and L the lower for a given variable.

more affluent; D and E are more likely to come from the larger communes. The type E leader perceives more conflict than F, but less cleavage around differences in income; G is sharply distinguished from H by perceiving less cleavage overall, and less cleavage specifically along political lines and divisions over change (type G being those who, though committed to the status quo, favor citizen participation, are more nationally than locally oriented, and are more committed to reducing disparities in wealth).[7]

The Change-Oriented
Leaders

The influence of leadership in inducing social activeness and developmental change is the central concern of this study. Hence, it is important to understand why some leaders become more committed to the value of change than others, and, in particular, to discover the sources of different motivations for change.

The preceding chapter reported that most of the local leaders interviewed in the International Studies of Values in Politics professed a desire for change and said they were disposed to seek new solutions for their community's problems. But they differed fundamentally in their motivations for change. Some of the change-oriented leaders were committed to reducing economic inequality, but not to broadening political participation; others were just the opposite. For some, the need for change was tied to a concern for the interests of their nation, a concern that might or might not be associated with values of economic egalitarianism or participant citizenship. Only a minority of the leaders sampled in each country actually combined a concern for all three of the values historically associated in the west with major social and political change. Most directed their desire for change to specific and limited aspects of the system in which they functioned.

This section attempts to explain these differences in commitment to change. Leaders whose profiles of change orientation differ were compared in terms of the same 29 characteristics used in the previous analyses.[8]

Six sets of comparisons on change profiles were made (see Table 8) for specification of the relevant value profiles:
  (1) nation-oriented innovator (types 1 to 4) *vs.* local-oriented conservor (types 9 to 12)
  (2) national technocrat (type 4) *vs.* general innovator (type 1)
  (3) national technocrat (type 4) *vs.* equalizing innovator (local) (type 7)

Table 8—Profiles of Change Orientation

Degree of Leaders' Commitment to

Type of Orientation	Value Change	Value Nation	Value Participation	Value Economic Equality	India n = 945	Poland n = 898	U.S. n = 905	Yugoslavia n = 1182
Innovative: National (Centralist)	Innovative (leaders score High)	Nation-centered (leaders score High)						
1 General innovator			High	High	90	67	52	114
2 Participationist			High	Low	50	65	53	96
3 Equalizer			Low	High	103	65	63	62
4 Technocrat			Low	Low	31	71	46	40
Innovative: Local		Local-centered (leaders score Low)						
5 Populist			High	High	78	35	41	43
6 Participationist			High	Low	25	49	46	59
7 Equalizer			Low	High	123	83	40	56
8 Technocrat			Low	Low	75	56	22	65
Conservor: Local	Conservor (leaders score Low)	Local-centered (leaders score Low)						
9 Equalizing participationist			High	High	44	41	43	44
10 Participationist			High	Low	43	74	100	81
11 Equalizer			Low	High	39	59	50	96
12 General conservor			Low	Low	51	47	48	158
Conservor: National (centralist)		Nation-centered (leaders score High)						
13 All types			High and Low	High and Low	193	186	301	268

(4) national technocrat (type 4) *vs.* participant innovator (local) (type 6)

(5) national technocrat (type 4) *vs.* local populist (type 5)

(6) participationists (national and local-oriented) (types 2 and 6) *vs.* equalizers (national and local-oriented) (types 3 and 7)

These various combinations were selected in order to establish (by controlling successively for various components of the change profiles)[9] whether there is a basis for distinguishing: (1) those whose desire for change is primarily linked to a commitment to the nation (comparisons 1 through 5); (2) those whose interest in change is mainly concerned with achieving or maintaining democratic decision-making processes (comparisons 4 and 6); (3) those who look for change primarily out of concern to reduce economic inequalities (comparisons 3 and 6); and (4) those whose eagerness for change is goaded by a combination of motivations (comparison 2). In other words, are the nationalist, the political democrat, the social egalitarian and the totally or generally progressive leaders basically different kinds of people, coming from different kinds of backgrounds and communities? Is it possible to predict why some persons have one compelling reason for social change and others have another; why some are preoccupied with a single target of reform, while others want society altered, root and branch?

NATIONAL INNOVATORS AND LOCAL CONSERVORS

In the first set of comparisons, leaders who simultaneously profess the greatest eagerness for change and the strongest commitment to national goals and interest, "national innovators," are contrasted with those who are less disposed to support new approaches to problems and are more strongly devoted to local interests, "local conservors." This comparison holds constant commitments to participation and economic equality. Table 8 notes the frequencies of these different profile types.

Possible explanations of why leaders differ in these respects are derived from Table 9, which reports differences of means (if statistically significant) on 29 variables for the four contrasted sets of profiles. To establish that the differences in values between national innovator and local conservor are attributable to a particular factor, a significant difference on that factor should occur in each of the four sets compared. If the explanation were applicable across countries, then significant differences on the same variable would also appear for all four comparisons in each country.

It is readily apparent that no cross-country explanations are tenable. Only in Yugoslavia can a case be made that there are *any* factors that consistently discriminate between nationally oriented innovators and locally oriented conservors. This is the country that has the greatest bipolarization of its local leadership on the issue of change.[10] As size and economic development are positively related to community activeness, this is a finding of significance for Yugoslav development. In addition to the two community characteristics, intergenerational occupational mobility may have something to do with disposing leaders toward change and nation. It appears that the more upwardly mobile the leader, the more likely he will be a national progressive.

In India, larger and more active communities (in the technique-innovative sense of activeness) are environments favorable to the genesis of national innovators, but only when leaders also favor public

Table 9—Differences Between National Innovators and Local Conservors

Profile Type	Differentiating Variables in:							
	India		Poland		U.S.		Yugoslavia	
Type 1 (general innovator) vs.	2	H	4	H	15	H	1	H
Type 9 (equalizing participant conservor)	3	H	13	H	16	L	2	H
	20	L	23	H	18	L	4	H
	29	H	25	H			8	H
							9	H
							11	L
							21	L
							25	H
Type 2 (participant innovator) vs.	2	H	3	H	8	H	1	H
Type 10 (participant conservor)	3	H	18	H	19	H	2	H
	6	H	23	H	21	L	3	H
	10	L			24	L	6	H
	29	H			25	H	8	H
					29	H	9	H
							18	H
							23	H
Type 3 (equalizing innovator) vs.	3	H	15	L	2	H	1	H
Type 11 (equalizing conservor)	16	H	26	H	6	H	2	H
	23	H	27	H			9	H
	25	H					23	H
							25	H
							27	H
Type 4 (national technocrat) vs.	5	L	24	H	3	H	1	H
Type 12 (general conservor)	11	H			12	L	2	H
	12	L			23	H	3	H
	25	H			29	H	11	L
	27	H					24	H
							27	H

This table reports differences of means between value-profile groups of leaders on 29 variables where significance at the .05 level has been demonstrated by two-tailed t-tests.
Variables are identified by the numbers used in the table of variables presented above (Table 1, p. 109).
H indicates that the mean of the variable for the national progressive is higher than for the local conservative; L indicates that it is lower.

participation in decision-making. The type of community does not help explain a national-innovative orientation among leaders who tend to reject participation.[11]

GENERAL INNOVATOR AND NATIONAL TECHNOCRAT (TYPES 1 AND 4)

Among change-oriented leaders, the general innovator is highly committed to all three values that we have held may be generative of social and political change: nation, popular participation in decision-making and economic equality. The national "technocrat" is less concerned with the latter two values, and tends to prefer the expert to the common man as decision-maker, and to avoid economic egalitarianism. But he has a high regard for national interests and is committed to innovative change to advance them.

Table 10—Differences Between General Innovators and National Technocrats (profile types 1 and 4)

India			Poland			U.S.		Yugoslavia		
var.	8	H	var.	1	L			var.	3	L
	12	H		12	H				8	L
	29	H		19	H				11	H
				20	H					
				23	H					

H indicates that the mean for "total" progressives on the given variable is significantly higher (at .05 level) than the mean for national technocrats; L indicates that it is lower.

From Table 10 it is immediately apparent that again there are no dominant cross-national explanatory patterns. However, in India and Yugoslavia there is a common association between less education and being a general innovator; a similar but less significant association prevails among Polish and American leaders.

Beyond this one association, explanation follows national lines. The Indian general innovator perceives more conflict within his community and is more likely to rely on local administrative groups for support than the national technocrat is. The Polish general innovator is more likely to be found in poorer powiats, will have lived longer in his powiat, will believe there is less local autonomy, is more likely to be an appointed official, and will see himself as having more general decision-making influence than the national technocrat will. Since there are few genuine general innovators in the United States, (that is, leaders who stand unequivocally committed to economic equality as well as to the other change-related values), few quantitatively significant explanatory associations could be expected and none were found. The Yugoslav general innovator is likely to be found in *less* active communes. Like his Polish counterpart, he has longer local residency than the national technocrat, but otherwise has none of the corresponding traits.

EQUALIZING INNOVATOR AND NATIONAL TECHNOCRAT (TYPES 7 AND 4)

Here we are comparing the national technocrat with the leader whose orientation to change is more associated with his commitment to economic equality than to nation. These types of leaders are similar in their low concern for participation. Thus, their crucial difference is an attachment to nation for one group and economic equality for the other.

Examination of Table 11 again reveals that education provides the one probable four-country association. The equalizing innovator, like the general innovator, is clearly less educated than the national technocrat in every country. And, as with the general innovators in both Poland and Yugoslavia, the equalizing innovators have been local residents for a longer time. The similarity in these findings adds further support to the conclusion that education operates on the social component of change (economic equality) rather than on the political one (nationalism).

For the Indian equalizer, however, a new pair of informal role variables appear. These leaders are more likely to select their local political party as a primary reference group, whereas the national technocrat selects the nation.[12] And in Yugoslavia, leaders who are primarily elected, rather than appointed, are more likely to be equalizing innovators than national technocrats.

Table 11—Differences Between Equalizing Innovators and National Technocrats (profile types 7 and 4)

	India			Poland			U.S.			Yugoslavia	
var.	8	L #	var.	8	L	var.	7	H	var.	8	L
	24	H		11	H		8	L		11	H
	25	L								21	H

H indicates that the mean for social progressives on the given variable is significantly higher (at .05 level) except where indicated by #, than the mean for national technocrats. L indicates that it is lower.

LOCAL PARTICIPANT INNOVATOR AND NATIONAL TECHNOCRAT
(TYPES 6 AND 4)

The distinction between these groups centers on commitment to political participation and nation. Their position on the value of economic equality is held constant, as both groups score low. To sharpen the contrast, locally oriented participationists were selected for comparison with nationally oriented innovators who are relatively *un*enthusiastic about broad participation in decision-making.

There are absolutely no cross-country associations, and indeed very few distinguishing characteristics at all. (See Table 12). The Indian local participationist is younger than the national technocrat; the Polish tends to have been longer in office, is less likely to have been elected and is less likely to view the nation as primary reference group; the American is more likely to favor a broad range of local government responsibility; the Yugoslav is likely to be in a less active commune than the national technocrat. Thus a distinction between a "democratic" and a "national" basis for orientation to change cannot be sustained for any of the four countries. Leaders differing in most other ways, are as likely to be in one group as the other.

Table 12—Differences Between Local Participant Innovators and National Technocrats (profile types 6 and 4)

	India			*Poland*			*U.S.*			*Yugoslavia*	
var.	7	L	var.	10	H	var.	18	H	var.	3	H
				21	L		29	L			
				25	L						

H indicates that the mean for local progressive democrats on the given variable is significantly higher (at .05 level) than the mean for national technocrats; L indicates that it is lower.

LOCAL POPULIST AND NATIONAL TECHNOCRAT (TYPES 5 AND 4)

This comparison pits the national "technocrat" (scoring low on both the values of Participation and Economic Equality) against the locally oriented leader who is highly committed to both Participation and Economic Equality. In other words these groups of leaders are as starkly opposed to each other in their motivations for change as possible. There is no overlap of their value commitments except their common disposition toward change.

Table 13 indicates a broader set of associated characteristics than in the previous comparison, but there are still no powerful consistent relationships across all four countries. However, in three countries, education again sets apart leaders who have a high commitment to economic equality from those who do not, despite other value differences in their profiles. Why this is not also true for American leaders is not apparent.

A pair of two-country similarities is present here. In India and in Poland, local populists believe they have less local autonomy than the national technocrats, a rather paradoxical finding in that it implies that the locally oriented innovators see less prospect of their local government solving its problems. Perhaps because this kind of leader desires change in order to enhance local control, he is sensitive to the constraints of political realities.

In both Poland and the United States, local populists see more conflict in their communities than national technocrats do. This may imply a kind of "self-fulfilling prophecy," on their part. The local populist sees what he thinks desirable: local conflict leading to change and greater economic equality at the local level. This conjecture gets additional support in Poland, where such leaders also see more divisions based upon income disparities, while in the United States it is, instead, political differences that are perceived. But why something similar is not true for the other systems as well is not readily understandable.

A profile of the Polish local populist can be rounded out to include a relatively long political career based on appointive office. In contrast, the Yugoslav local innovators is more likely to be elected and to have lived in his commune for a longer time than the national technocrat is.

Table 13—Differences Between Local Populists and National Technocrats (profile types 5 and 4)

India			Poland			U.S.			Yugoslavia		
var.	8	L	var.	8	L	var.	12	H	var.	8	L
	19	H		10	H		16	H		11	H
				12	H					21	H
				15	H					23	H
				19	H						
				20	H						

H indicates that the mean for the local populist on the given variable is significantly higher (at .05 level) than the mean for the national technocrat. L indicates that it is lower.

PARTICIPATIONISTS AND EQUALIZERS (TYPE 2 VS. 3) (NATIONALLY ORIENTED) (TYPE 6 VS. 7) (LOCALLY ORIENTED)

A final comparison focuses on the distinction between a political concern—popular participation; and a social concern—economic equality. Relative commitment to nation or local community is held constant.[13]

Again, education emerges as the most consistent cross-national distinguishing characteristic (See Table 14). The fact that in seven out of eight possible correlations, the participant-oriented innovator is significantly more educated than the "equalizer" seems to clinch the case for the powerful effect of schooling *per se* in reducing social motivation for change.[14]

In India, the United States and Yugoslavia, this finding is supported by the age factor, the older leaders being the equalizing innovators.

No other consistent cross-national or even single country relationship appears, however, to explain what seems to be the most important motivational distinction among leaders desiring change—the distinction between those who see progress primarily in terms of political opportunity and those who nurse a feeling of social injustice arising out of the gap between the economically deprived and the privileged. In these countries, education and youth seem to *politicize* the motivation of leaders for change, while defusing egalitarian impulses at least as applied to the material rewards of life.

Table 14—Differences Between Participant and Equalizing Innovators
(profile type 2 vs. 3 = nationally oriented)
(profile type 6 vs. 7 = locally oriented)

		India			Poland			U.S.			Yugoslavia	
Type 2 vs.	var.	3	H	var.	4	H	var.	7	L	var.	7	L #
Type 3		7	L		7	L		8	H		8	H
(national)		8	H		8	H #		11	L		9	H
					22	H					20	L
					23	H						
Type 6 vs.		7	L		8	H		6	H		3	H
Type 7		24	L		10	H		7	L		7	L #
(local)		29	L		14	L		8	H		8	H
								18	H		21	L
											22	L

H indicates that the mean for progressive democrats on the given variable is significantly higher (at .05 level) except

Imperatives of Leadership
for Innovation

It is evident that the disposition toward change does not grow from the same roots in all countries. There is virtually no cross-national similarity among the personal characteristics and environmental conditions of leaders who profess the greatest eagerness to support "new solutions" for the problems of their countries and communities. As a matter of fact the evidence strongly suggests that the customary distinction between radical and conservative is not in itself sufficient to form the basis of a clear classification of local leadership types in four countries. The innovator—regardless of what he is innovative about—cannot be identified by a coherent set of characteristics except possibly in Yugoslavia. This was demonstrated in the analysis in the first part of this section. So scattered are the explanatory variables among different types of innovators and conservors, that it is virtually impossible to pick one from the other unless one had full knowledge of the leader's value profile. What this analysis decisively implies is that the radical-conservative dimension is not an intrinsic or fundamental characteristic for distinguishing between political leaders. It is only when the leader is motivated by some substantive concern that he emerges as "change-oriented"; he is still quite as likely to be a pusher for change on one front, and a custodian of the status quo on another. A change-oriented leader can only be talked about therefore in terms of the specific character of the goals he seeks to achieve.

There *are* some "multiple radicals"—in varying numbers in different countries—who link up the urge to change in several areas simultaneously. (See Chapter 3, Tables 6A and 6B.) But the genesis of such all-out radicalism is not at all clear (see Table 9) and varies from country to country. In the less economically developed countries (India and Yugoslavia), education, or rather the *lack* of education, seems to influence the breadth of radical commitment. However, on close inspection, this association is almost entirely due to the fact that the less educated are committed to lessening *economic* inequality; whenever economic egalitarianism is a part of the value profile of change-oriented leaders, limited educational background is one of the significant imperatives.

The connection between educational deprivation and economic radicalism is the most consistent cue in all four of the countries. The economic radical tends to be less educated than the man committed to broadening the base of political participation. He is also likely to be less educated than the leader who is nationally oriented but unconcerned with the issue of economic inequality. However, education has little effect on the general disposition to seek change. (Bivariate correlations between education and commitment on the change-orientation value scale approach significance at the .05 level only in Yugoslavia.) What this adds up to is that low education may trigger demands for change of a *particular* character—improving the lot of the poor and narrowing the gap between haves and have-nots. But as education advances, interest in economic equality recedes, and so does a general radical disposition. Education appears as a conservative force socially, although viewed from the perspective of a competitive market economy it might be heralded as an incentive to economic development because it works against subsidized egalitarianism. The more highly educated leader may tend to oppose change if it means moving toward a welfare state; he will support change or at least not frustrate it, if it does not affect the existing system of economic distribution.

Environment has surprisingly little to do with shaping the value profile of the change-oriented leader. While the disposition to seek new approaches to community problems is greater among leaders of the more affluent communities in Yugoslavia (but just the reverse in India),[15] economic and other community distinctions do not explain the *direction* of change sought by the leaders. One cannot expect to find economic radicals nesting in poor communities, or those torn by social conflict, any more than in rich and harmonious ones. Spokesmen for popular democracy are as likely to appear in communities where influence is concentrated as in those where it is dispersed, or in those that are socially homogeneous as in those where cleavages are many and deep. In Yugoslavia, as we have seen, there is a tendency for the change-oriented leader with a high sense of national consciousness to come from the larger and more affluent communes, but this situation is not found elsewhere.

These findings obviously contradict much of the theoretical speculation designed to explain political motivation, particularly motivation for social and political change in terms of environmental conditioning. Perhaps any explanation of change orientation must come from the context of other values with which the value of Change is associated; in other words, it must come from the nature of the value *profile*. For most leaders, change is not an end in itself; it is a *means* to secure the implementation of certain other values. The values that justify change for some leaders are strikingly different from those that impel other leaders to accept and to seek change. What ulterior factors bring leaders to these different postures remain largely unaccounted for, with the noted exception of the effect of education in lowering the inclination to egalitarian economic reform. It must be apparent however that for the most part the determinants of a radical or progressive disposition are not the same everywhere. These differences are to be found in the make-up of the human personality rather than in the impact of structural and systemic anatomy of the society.

Conflict: Intensity, Tolerance
and Avoidance

The transformation of leaders' disposition toward change into the social development of communities appears to depend upon another critical element—the extent to which conflict is viewed as a danger to be avoided, or an evil to be accepted as a necessary concomitant of change. In a later section of this volume it is shown that the value of Conflict Avoidance is clearly the most cross-nationally relevant influence accounting for community activeness. Communities whose leadership is less committed to avoiding conflict are the more active, and vice versa.[16]

This fact calls for in-depth examination of the sources of this value dimension, especially on the part of those leaders whose commitment is intense, one way or the other.

We will examine the value of Conflict Avoidance from two perspectives. First, what kinds of leaders are sensitive to conflict, either in avoiding it or in accepting it? A comparison will be made between those

leaders who hold an extreme position on the value of conflict avoidance
—either pro or con—and those who are moderate—in the middle—in
their concern. By disregarding the direction of commitment, we can
examine intensity *per se.*

Secondly, what characteristics demarcate those leaders who are
most concerned with avoiding conflict from those who are least concerned? Can we find some general syndrome of characteristics that cross-
nationally differentiate conflict tolerators from conflict avoiders?

INTENSITY

Intensely committed leaders in each country were identified as the
10% to 15% whose scale scores at either end of the scale placed them
apart from the main body of respondents. Leaders whose scores fell
near the national mean were selected as the moderate group.[17]

This procedure resulted in the following distributions in each
country:

Table 15—Intensity of Commitment on Conflict

	India (n = 945)	Poland (n = 888)	United States (n = 905)	Yugoslavia (n = 1174)
Intensely committed:				
Tolerators	36	71	50	92
Avoiders	82	44	63	61
Total	118	115	113	153
Moderately committed	101	177	160	244

The first question considered was whether the intensely committed
were essentially the same kind of persons, regardless of the fact that
some were strongly disposed to avoid conflict and others were prepared
to live with it and perhaps even welcomed it. In other words, is extremism on this value, whether *high* or *low* the result of similar influences,
which are different from those affecting leaders who are moderate? Is
intensity of commitment itself a distinguishing behavioral phenomenon,
more so than the direction of the commitment?

Our evidence indicates that extremism *per se* is not a viable distinction for the local political leaders, at least in regard to the value of
Conflict Avoidance. Extreme conflict avoiders differ from extreme
conflict tolerators far more than either set of extremists differs from the
moderates.[18] This finding is in contrast to the familiar observation in
studies of political psychology that there are dimensions of personality
"style," for instance, an authoritarianism that characterizes individual
dispositions, quite apart from the substance and direction of the dis-

Table 16—Comparison of the Intense and Moderate Leaders

	India		Poland		U.S.		Yugoslavia	
	Avoid	Tol.	Avoid	Tol.	Avoid	Tol.	Avoid	Tol.
Community Characteristics								
1 Economic level					L			
2 Size		H	L					
3 Activeness					H			
4 Community conflict			L					
5 Variation in leader influence			L					
6 Value congruence				H				
Demographic Characteristics								
7 Age	H		H		H		#	
8 Education	L		L	H	L	H	#	H
9 Occupational mobility			L	L				
10 Duration of career				L	H		H	
11 Years in community	H				H		H	L
Perceptions								
12 Conflicts: total								H
13 Conflicts: political								
14 Divisions: total								
15 Divisions: income			L			H	H	
16 Divisions: political			H					
17 Divisions: change			H					
18 Local government responsibility			L				L	
19 Local government autonomy			L				H	
Political Role								
20 Appointed (proportion)	L							
21 Elected (proportion)	H							L
22 Activity: total	H			H				
23 Influence: total areas	H							
24 Support extended: party				L				
25 Support extended: nation					H			
26 Support sought: total	H				L		H	
27 Support sought: party						L		L
28 Support sought: elected								
29 Support sought: administrative	H							

H indicates significantly higher than the moderates; L indicates significantly lower than the moderates.
\# indicates relationship in the same direction as other countries but just below the .05 level of significance.

position. The authoritarian individual is considered independent of *what* he is authoritarian about.[19] This is not so with regard to intensity of commitment on the value of Conflict Avoidance.

The finding that there is no distinctive corps of local political leaders who can be identified as extremists *per se* regardless of the nature of their value commitment on the conflict issue is complemented by evidence that few leaders who are extreme on one value are also extreme on others.[20] There appears to be no "syndrome" of extremism among our respondents in any of the countries. Local political leaders, at least those in our sample, discriminate among the values on which they feel strongly. Either because of the moderating influences of their political roles and responsibilities, their generally higher education (compared to the general population), or the cross pressures emanating from the people with whom they deal, local political leaders holding formal positions in their communities are not consistently extreme in their values.

CONFLICT TOLERATORS—CONFLICT AVOIDERS

The value of Conflict Avoidance is perhaps the single most important universal variable linking local leadership to what happens in their communities. What we find (see Table 17) is that in all countries those leaders with a greater stake in the system as it exists value

Table 17—Conflict Avoiders vs. Conflict Tolerators

	India Tol.	India Avoid	Poland Tol.	Poland Avoid	U.S. Tol.	U.S. Avoid	Yugoslavia Tol.	Yugoslavia Avoid
Community Characteristics								
1 Economic level	L	H						
2 Size	H	L						
3 Activeness	H	L						
4 Community conflict	L	H						
5 Variation in leader influence	L	H						
6 Value congruence								
Demographic Characteristics								
7 Age	L	H	L	H	L	H	#	#
8 Education	H	L	H	L	H	L	H	L
9 Occupational mobility								
10 Duration of career					L	H		
11 Years in community	L	H	#	#	L	H	L	H
Perceptions								
12 Conflicts: total								
13 Conflicts: political								
14 Divisions: total					H	L		
15 Divisions: income					H	L		
16 Divisions: political			H	L				
17 Divisions: change			H	L				
18 Local government responsibility								
19 Local government autonomy			L	H				
Political Role								
20 Appointed (proportion)								
21 Elected (proportion)	L	H					L	H
22 Activity: total areas			L	H			L	H
23 Influence: total areas								
24 Support extended: party	L	H	L	H	L	H	L	H
25 Support extended: nation	H	L						
26 Support sought: total	L	H					L	H
27 Support sought: party					L	H		
28 Support sought: elected			H	L				
29 Support sought: administrative								

"H" indicates high and "L" low on the variable. # indicates relationship in the same direction as other countries but just below the .05 level of significance.

avoiding conflict; those with less of a stake, value community peace less.[21]

How well this general conclusion can be supported from these data depends on the interpretation of the indicators of the leaders' stake in the existing "system." But consider, for example, these striking findings for all four countries: older, long-time local residents, and those committed to the political party, the wielders of political power within the system, are more committed to the value of avoiding conflict.[22]

This is probably the greatest number of significant findings of cross-national similarity reported anywhere in this study. Further, some two-country and nation-specific findings reinforce this general conclusion.

In India and Yugoslavia, elected officials are conflict avoiders rather than conflict tolerators. If we can assume that elected officials are more dependent on the existing structure of relationships within their communities than appointed officials, who are covered either by some formal or informal tenure arrangements and look to some central governmental agency, then this is further support for the general importance of a stake in the system and the leader's position on conflict.[23]

In both Poland and Yugoslavia, those leaders who have a broad range of areas of policy activity again consider the avoidance of conflict desirable. If it is possible to assume that a large network of contacts with the existing social and political structure of influence is a concomitant of a leader who ranges widely, rather than specifically, across questions of local governmental functions, then this relationship between a large area of activity and conflict avoidance may add evidence to the general connection between the leader's investment in the existing social structure and his concern to avoid conflict.

The connection between a leader's investment in the existing social and political network and his commitment to avoid conflict can be seen in the relationship between the number of support groups sought when making a decision and the value of conflict avoidance. In both India and Yugoslavia, the conflict avoiders turn to more groups for support than the conflict tolerators; this indicates again that a stake in the continuation of existing community structure is associated with a concern to avoid conflict.

As very indirect evidence, we find that leaders who see divisions prevalent in their communities are more accepting of conflict; those whose cognitive structure reflects less community divisions, also find conflict less desirable. In Poland and the United States, perception of divisions is a characteristic of conflict tolerators. The content of these divisions is nation-specific. In Poland it is perceived as political divisions and divisions arising from those desiring change and those wanting to avoid it, which significantly distinguishes the conflict tolerators from the conflict avoiders. In the United States, conflict tolerators see divisions in general (sum total of divisions) and particularly those arising from differences in income.

Additionally, there are some nation-specific differences between the conflict avoiders and tolerators that might further support the connection between interest in the existing social and political structure and commitment to avoid conflicts that might disturb it. In India, the smaller, economically more developed but less active community (committing fewer resources to collective purposes and engaging less of the population in community affairs) is characterized by a leadership dedicated to the avoidance of conflict. We have argued that the active communities contain seeds of change, whereas, the *level* of economic development reflects a relatively rewarding situation and one in which the leadership has an interest.

Further, the conflict avoiders are linked to more support groups than the tolerators.

In Poland, the conflict avoiders see that they have less autonomy to act locally than the conflict tolerators. Again, this may reflect the interest of local leaders who, to a greater extent than in any other country in this study, are part of a centralized political system, on which the local leadership is dependent. In the United States, we find that the conflict avoiders turn to local elected officials significantly more than the conflict tolerators and have had a longer career tenure in the local system. Local leaders in the United States are indeed subject to the pressures of locally elected officials in the system of American local government. If the local elected officials indeed represent the local "establishment," then again we find that the conflict avoiders are interested in their support. The fact that length of tenure is generally recognized, indeed justified, as insuring an interest in the existing institutions, is further evidence to what might be a general feature of local political leaders everywhere: a stake in the system enhances their value of social harmony—the avoidance of conflict.

Conclusion

This analysis points first to the diversity of the sources of leaders values in different countries; and, consequently, to the inadequacy of most theories of the socialization of political leaders to alone provide a general explanation of the genesis of values relevant to developmental change. Regrettably, the evidence so far available from this study is too thin to permit the presentation of any convincing comprehensive alternatives to prevailing notions, even for particular countries. One is led tentatively to a view that places more confidence in hypotheses that emphasize the personal demography of leaders, rather than environmental conditions, as a determinant of their values, and to look more to role theory than to conflict theory for cross-national explanation. But the particularities, rather than the uniformities, predominate in our data and suggest that values are made in many different ways.

The most powerful imperatives of value choices among the leaders in our sample are: (1) the amount of education, which goes a long way toward dictating adoption of profiles built around a core position opposed to economic egalitarianism; and (2) the breadth of a leader's political role, which tends to generate profiles oriented to change and national commitment.

Notes

1. Variables were chosen if it had been demonstrated that they correlated significantly with at least two of the value scales composing the profile in any one country, or with one scale in at least two countries. For example, community economic level correlated significantly (.01 level) with both Change and National Commitment in India and thus qualified. Education correlated with only Economic Equality in India, but it correlated with this value in the other three countries and was thus included.

2. Significance levels for t-tests reported throughout this chapter are for two-tailed tests. Variables compared were each checked for homogeneity-of-variances, in line with the assumptions of the test used.

3. In these analyses, position on a value refers to whether the respondent stood above or below the national mean in his score on the relevant value scale: "High" includes everyone above, and "Low" everyone below the mean. See Chapter 3, for detailed description of the profiling procedure.

4. Pearson's r for India is $-.102$, Poland $-.191$, U.S. $-.202$ and Yugoslavia $-.326$ with p greater than .01 for all countries. Correlations of education with the value scale of Participation are not as consistently powerful.

5. This finding is also confirmed by consistent bivariate correlations between the various background characteristics and the values respectively of Economic Equality and Participation. Each of the five background variables correlates above .02 level of confidence with these two values, but in each case the relationship to Economic Equality is the inverse of that to Participation.

With respect to the influence of age on values, Michael Mau has examined the implications of some ISVIP data for a range of propositions emerging from geriatric studies. See "Values and Aged Leadership," a report to the Seminar on Values and Motivation in Political Behavior, Department of Political Science, University of Pennsylvania, 1968. Unpublished.

6. A searching comparison of the values of appointed and elected officials in the ISVIP Indian sample confirms the finding that differences between these groups of leaders are not sufficient to support the hypothesis of a basic role distinction. In particular, there is no evidence to sustain the often expressed view that bureaucrats hold "modern" values while politicians are committed to "traditional" ones. See Marshall M. Bouton, "Role and Politics in India: A Study of Elected and Appointed Officials in Panchayati-Raj," M.A. Thesis in South Asian Regional Studies, University of Pennsylvania, 1968. Unpublished.

7. The impact of perceptions of conflicts and cleavage on the commitments of U.S. and Indian leaders has been explored in some depth by Leo A. Hazlewood, "Community Cleavage and Action for Change," paper presented to the Seminar on Values and Motivation in Political Behavior, Department of Political Science, University of Pennsylvania, 1967. Unpublished.

8. See Table 1. These are comparisons of relative differences, it should be repeated, between groups of leaders, who are classified according to whether their scores on the four value scales of Change, National Commitment, Participation and Economic Equality are above or below the mean of the sample of leaders interviewed in their country. There is therefore no necessary cross-national comparability in the *degree* of commitment of those falling in the same category. A leader classified as change-oriented with "high" national commitment in one country may actually be much more committed to the status quo and locally directed than a similarly classified leader in another country. But *relative to others in his own country* the man would tend to be a "national innovator."

9. The pairs of profiles chosen for comparison held all values constant except the particular one under analysis.

10. See Chapter 3.

11. A parallel situation prevails in the tendency of national innovators to seek support from local administrative officials. This factor distinguishes national innovators from local conservors for those committed to participation, but not for those who reject participation.

12. The way this question was administered in India calls for caution on this finding, but the direction of the association seems reasonable.

13. "Participationists" high on nation are compared with "equalizing innovators" who are similarly high on national commitment; correspondingly, locally oriented leaders who are high on participation (and low on equality) are compared with the locally oriented who are high on economic equality and low on participation.

14. The eighth possible correlation (in India) is in the same direction as the others, but not significant at the .05 level of probability.

The variable termed "education" is strictly limited to the amount of schooling completed, regardless of location, character of institution attended, or type of curriculum. See Table of Variables in Appendix for specification of the educational code used.

15. Correlation of Economic Level with Commitment to Change Scale: $r = -.143$ (India), $+.168$ (Yugoslavia), $p < .01$.

16. See Chapter 9. It also appears that the amount of conflict perceived in a community is among the more powerful cross-national explanatory variables related to activeness.

17. The cutoff points of the extremist groups varied from country to country depending on the different distributions of scores on the Conflict Avoidance scale. On the basis of histograms, points were chosen where there was a clear break between a relatively small body of leaders scoring high or low on the scale, and the rest of the respondents.

18. See Table 16.

The procedure followed in this analysis was to compare the differences of means on 29 variables between the two extremist groups on the one hand and each extremist group and the moderates on the other. There was only one variable in one country—occupational mobility in Poland—where the conflict avoiders and conflict tolerators both differed significantly from the moderates on the same variable. (Both groups of extremists, more than the moderates, tended to have moved from the manual occupation of their fathers to nonmanual work.) By contrast, there were 11 of the 29 variables in Poland that discriminated between the intensely committed avoider and the extreme tolerator. In the other countries, while there were fewer factors that differentiated the avoider and the tolerator, there were none that commonly distinguished them from the moderates.

19. See H. J. Eysenck, *The Psychology of Politics*, London: Routledge, Kegan Paul, Ltd., 1953.

20. An analysis of Indian and U.S. leaders comparing the extremes on conflict avoidance with instances where these extremes fall on similar types of cutoff points on the value scales used for the value profiles conducted by Sheila Babbie at the University of Hawaii, indicates no consistent pattern of extremism. There were a few combinations of extremism—those who were conflict avoiders and extreme on the economic equality scale (11 out of 63) in the United States, and the 18 (out of 82) Indian leaders who are committed strongly both to avoiding conflict and to wide-scale popular participation.

21. There is some evidence that people everywhere, despite economic class or social role, who have some "stake" in the existing system are active politically (vote) and tend to support existing institutions. See S. M. Lipset, *Political Man*, Garden City, N.Y.: Doubleday, 1960, for a review of some of the evidence.

22. It is also true that the conflict avoiders are less educated than the conflict tolerators, but as we have seen, the more highly educated are also less committed to the desirability of reducing the gap between the rich and poor. This correlation, thus, is probably spurious, as the younger political leaders everywhere had a better chance of getting more education than their older colleagues.

23. In the first pre-test, the U.S. elected and appointed leaders also differed significantly on their value of "social harmony," as this value was called then. (See ISVIP Doc. USA/52.)

CHAPTER 5

Consensus and Diversity

This chapter was written by Puric and Jacob, following a plan of analysis designed with the collaboration of A. Przeworski. Puric is primarily responsible for the section on Determinants of Diversity; Jacob for the others and general editing.

The purpose of this chapter is to analyze to what extent leaders in the four countries share the same values, and whether congruence of values among leaders is a factor in the social and political development of their communities. This is an exploration of the implications of consensus, or the lack thereof.

One reason for such an examination is the possibility that the behavior of leaders may be influenced by the degree to which they are united in their value commitments. Does the fact of wide consensus itself generate pressures upon leaders to adopt settled modes of action, and to develop their own value orientations to conform even more closely to the consensus? Does diversity of values open the way to the consideration of more alternatives, and hence lead to greater innovation in the public life of the community? Diversity, on the other hand, could be expected to block action if the difference of values were fundamental and leaders devoted themselves to frustrating one another. These questions obviously bear directly on the primary concern of this study, the determinants of community activeness.

There are also important theoretical implications. To understand the bases of social and political solidarity, the validity of alternative concepts of integration and the extent to which different forms of integration are interrelated need to be assessed. Is "integration" a single unidimensional state of affairs, or is it a many-faceted phenomenon, in which a certain threshold must be crossed on each facet before a society may be considered integrated? Or may integration occur at different levels and in different areas of association, quite independently of what goes on at the other levels and areas?

The data available from the International Studies of Values in Politics permit analysis of these questions with reference to two of the major concepts of integration: (1) integration conceived as shared, or at least mutually compatible values; and (2) integration conceived as corporate social activity directed toward the accomplishment of social goals.[1]

In considering the first, we are of course limited by the data to leaders' values, and we must leave unanswered the critical question of whether leaders do indeed lead or merely represent their constituencies, and whether a leader's consensus necessarily indicates consensus within the whole community. We are however, by virtue of the composition of the sample, in the fortunate position of being able to explain the levels of social influence from which the value consensus of leaders is derived. Are differences in leaders' values greater within nations or between them, within their local communities or between communities within the same nation?

At the local level we can push further and answer the question of whether integration conceived as shared values (of leaders) is closely related to integration conceived as community activeness. If the value consensus is great, is the community also integrated in the sense of putting out social effort?[2]

What this adds up to is a test of the proposition that the foundations of social solidarity rest on ideological unity, and of the further widely held proposition that integration in the sense of shared values is a basic condition of dynamic social development.[3] Will a community whose leaders, at least, are committed to common values demonstrate its cohesiveness by mobilizing its resources for social purposes? Does lack of such consensus impede its development? Positive findings to this effect would sustain the second of the propositions. The accomplishment of substantial community development with a minimum of friction or compulsion would tend to support the first contention.

There is a further line of theoretical import to which the analysis of value consensus will contribute. In the consideration of the processes of socialization, particularly of political socialization, there has long been need for cross-cultural and cross-systemic empirical measures of the degree or stage of socialization achieved. If one conceives of political values as a product of the many elements in socialization, then the consensus or deviation among political leaders in the values they profess would be an apt overall index of the efficiency of the process. Homogeneity of leaders' values would mark successful political socialization (granted that one would wish for other indices based on activity and performance). With such an index, it is then possible, as will be shown later in this study, to analyze the relationship to socialization of a series of national, community and personal characteristics, and to determine which social unit has the greatest effect in socializing the leaders within it—the community they belong to, the country they live in or something else. Different levels of social aggregation, or group affiliations, are in effect competing to instill different values in leaders. Which one is the most successful?[4]

Measuring
Consensus

The raw material for determining the value consensus of local leaders was the responses to 98 items in the interview survey conducted with 3930 elected, administrative and party officials in 30 localities each in India, Poland, U.S. and Yugoslavia. As described previously, it was possible on the basis of these responses to scale leaders on their professed commitments to nine values.

The congruence of the scores on each of these nine values (i.e., as measured by the standard deviation) indicates to what extent these leaders or any group of them share that particular value.

To secure a more general view of the degree of consensus, however, a composite index was needed. Two approaches were used. First, the average deviation from the mean on all nine values was computed. Secondly, intercorrelations of the standard deviations within communities on all values were examined, and a "best international set" of three values was selected on the basis that the degree of community deviation on these values correlated positively and strongly in all four countries. The standard deviations on these three values (National Commitment, Change and Economic Equality) were averaged to constitute another composite index. Analysis was performed with both measures, but we shall report here only the results for the inclusive nine-value congruence index, representing as it does a fuller spectrum of the area of consensus, or variation.[5]

Through the use of both the composite index and the deviation of each value separately, the degree of variation or congruence has been determined at four levels: the nation, the community, among all 30 communities in each nation, and among the four nations. (1) At the national level, the amount of deviation was computed for each national sample treated as a separate population (deviation calculated from each national mean). (2) At the community level, deviation was computed from the mean for the leaders in each community treated as a separate population. (3) Intercommunity variation was determined by calculating the deviation of all 30 communities in each country from the mean value scores of those 30 communities. (4) For purposes of international comparison, and analysis of the extent to which differences in congruence could be attributed to a "national factor" as opposed to intranational variables, a fourth statistic was developed—the deviation of each national sample from the mean for all four nations.

In the ensuing discussion, the following terms will be used to describe findings at these levels, respectively:

(1) *national* variance
(2) *intracommunity* variance (within community)
(3) *intercommunity* variance (among communities)
(4) *international* variance

The analytical procedures adopted were intended to test the significance, first, of cross-national differences in congruence, and secondly, of intranational differences among communities. In a one-way analysis of variance, using the F-test, country was paired with country, and community with community. Thus, it is possible to demonstrate how significant the difference is on each measure of congruence between each pair of countries and each pair of communities.

Next, an analysis of variance at different political levels has been performed in order to discover how much of the variation in leaders' values is accounted for by (1) national differences, (2) intercommunity differences within each country, or (3) differences within each community. This makes it possible to determine how far one can predict a leader's values by knowing the country he belongs to or the community he lives in, or whether one must look to personal characteristics, reference groups within the community or other influences to explain why leaders do or do not share the same values.

Third, in an attempt to pinpoint further the sources of consensus or dis-sensus, an analysis was made of correlations between the measures of value congruence and approximately 150 leadership and community characteristics for which data were available.

Finally, the possible effects of leaders' consensus or diversity of values upon community activeness were assessed by bivariate correlation.

The Uniform Level of
Consensus Among Nations

We are concerned first with whether the amount of consensus on values among leaders differs from country to country. The answer to this question must be given in cross-national comparative terms, as no neat conceptual or operational dividing line has been discovered to distinguish countries that have consensus from those that do not.

From Table 1, it would appear that in the United States and Yugoslavia, local leadership is somewhat more homogeneous in their values than in India and Poland (note the smaller standard deviation on the full spectrum of nine values).

But what is remarkable is that the countries *differ so little* in the degree of their leaders' overall value consensus. From a statistical standpoint only the differences between the total Indian sample and the other national samples taken as a whole are significant [Table 2 column (a)]. None of the others are.

Table 1—General Congruence of Leaders' Values—International Comparison

		Mean Standard Deviation on Nine Value Scales	
		(a)	(b)
		Within Total National Sample of Leaders around the National Mean	Within 30 Communities around the Respective Community Means
India	n = 945	0.454	0.431
Poland	n = 889	0.410	0.459
U.S.	n = 905	0.389	0.371
Yugoslavia	n = 1178	0.389	0.354

Table 2—Significance of International Differences in Congruence of Leaders' Values

(As measured by Mean Variances on Nine Value Scales)

	Difference in Variance of Total National Sample	F = Ratio	Difference in Mean of Variance within 30 Communities for each Country	F = Ratio
India/U.S.	0.061	1.40	0.055	1.39
India/Yugoslavia	0.059	1.38	0.067	1.51
India/Poland	0.043	1.25	0.017	1.09
Poland/U.S.	0.018	1.12	0.072	1.51
Poland/Yugoslavia	0.016	1.10	0.084	1.65
U.S./Yugoslavia	0.002	1.01	0.012	1.09
F-Ratio at .02 level		1.15		2.38

When one compares cross-nationally the average amount of variation among leaders *within* their respective communities [Table 2 column
(b)], there are *no* significant differences. This means that, in general,
Indian communities (or Polish communities whose leaders, it will be
noted, appear to disagree among themselves even more than Indians,
when the Polish communities are observed at the community level)
are in fact no more heterogeneous in terms of their leader's values than
those in the United States or Yugoslavia. The differences can easily be
accounted for by chance.

These findings are presented graphically in Chart A.

The degree of national consensus does differ more markedly
country-to-country on particular values. Several of the differences
reported on Table 3 (see lines B and C) are statistically significant,
notably:

The Indian leaders are much more divided than those of other countries
on the extent to which they are committed to (1) *national* as against
local interests (SD = 0.604), (2) the value of *avoiding conflict*
(SD = 0.566), (3) *action* propensity (SD = 0.469), and (4) *honesty*, i.e.,
truthfulness, as a principle in public conduct (SD = 0.466).
Yugoslav leaders are significantly more divided on the issue of *economic
equality* than leaders in the other three countries (SD = 0.496).

On the other hand, most of these differences cease to be significant
when the amount of consensus or diversity *within communities* is compared cross-nationally (Table 3, lines G and H). The major contrast that
remains is again between India and the others, specifically on the issue
of *national commitment*. The dissensus among Indians on this value is
almost as pronounced within their communities (SD = 0.570) as in the
sample of leaders taken as a whole, and is vastly greater than elsewhere.
Concern for nation thus emerges as a core of division, distinctive for
Indian leadership, though, as will be recalled from the previous chapter
on Leaders' Values, the stand of Indian leaders, averaged out, is not
unlike that of the other countries.

This emphasizes that what is being compared here is the *extent to
which leaders agree or disagree* with each other on their values—not
what values they hold. We have already reported extensive international
differences in the actual positions taken on the average by leaders on

Chart A—Deviation and Congruence of Leaders' Values

(Graph indicates distribution of 30 communities in each country according to the composite congruence index, i.e., mean standard deviation on 9 value scales)

Code: Number of communities listed vertically, n = 30 for each country

  Amount of congruence listed horizontally, S.D. 0.220–0.580

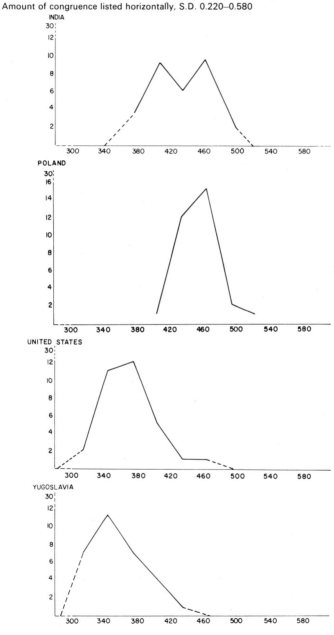

Table 3—Congruence of Leaders' Values—International and Interlevel Comparisons

	Chan	Apro	Ecde	Equa	Part	Core	Lana	Self	Hone	
A National sample mean										
India *N* = 946	1.53	3.40	1.36	1.50	2.87	1.87	2.57	1.59	1.62	
Poland *N* = 889	1.67	2.85	1.89	2.26	2.74	2.58	2.70	1.77	1.87	
U.S. *N* = 905	2.17	2.52	2.17	3.28	2.26	2.87	2.29	1.85	1.72	
Yugoslavia *N* = 1178	1.73	2.94	1.55	1.97	2.26	2.15	2.66	1.79	1.52	
B Standard deviation around A										National Variation
India	.420	.469	.367	.429	.457	.566	.604	.307	.466	
Poland	.386	.393	.437	.463	.390	.468	.382	.422	.351	
U.S.	.388	.407	.417	.428	.417	.351	.346	.374	.374	
Yugoslavia	.375	.357	.354	.496	.435	.392	.383	.386	.322	
C Variance around A										
India	.176	.220	.135	.184	.209	.320	.365	.094	.217	
Poland	.149	.154	.191	.214	.152	.219	.146	.178	.123	
U.S.	.151	.166	.174	.183	.174	.123	.120	.140	.140	
Yugoslavia	.141	.127	.125	.246	.189	.154	.147	.149	.104	
D Mean of community means										
India	1.53	3.39	1.29	1.50	3.17	1.84	2.57	1.43	1.68	
Poland	1.67	2.85	1.89	2.26	2.74	2.58	2.70	1.77	1.87	
U.S.	2.17	2.52	2.18	3.28	2.26	2.87	2.29	1.86	1.72	
Yugoslavia	1.73	2.94	1.55	1.97	2.26	2.15	2.65	1.78	1.52	Among Community Variation
E Standard deviation of community $\bar{X}$ around D										
India	.125	.147	.084	.094	.219	.181	.153	.103	.191	
Poland	.105	.102	.130	.128	.077	.106	.071	.108	.076	
U.S.	.088	.112	.099	.128	.103	.087	.098	.073	.077	
Yugoslavia	.174	.089	.165	.201	.195	.109	.183	.120	.138	
F Variance of community $\bar{X}$ around D										
India	.016	.022	.007	.009	.048	.033	.023	.011	.036	
Poland	.012	.010	.017	.016	.006	.011	.005	.012	.006	
U.S.	.008	.013	.010	.016	.011	.008	.010	.005	.006	
Yugoslavia	.030	.008	.027	.040	.038	.012	.033	.014	.019	
G Mean standard deviation in 30 communities										Within Community Variation
India	.393	.440	.319	.412	.461	.515	.570	.323	.443	
Poland	.446	.452	.473	.490	.453	.495	.448	.469	.429	
U.S.	.368	.387	.400	.401	.397	.336	.326	.363	.363	
Yugoslavia	.330	.341	.313	.450	.388	.375	.334	.364	.289	
H Mean variance 30 communities										
India	.159	.198	.106	.174	.217	.271	.336	.107	.201	
Poland	.199	.203	.224	.240	.205	.245	.260	.220	.184	
U.S.	.142	.153	.164	.166	.162	.116	.110	.135	.134	
Yugoslavia	.111	.120	.099	.208	.153	.143	.116	.135	.085	
I Mean of 4 national means Σ line A ÷ 4	1.77	2.92	1.74	2.25	2.53	2.36	2.55	1.75	1.68	
J Standard deviation of 4 nations around I	.239	.314	.311	.652	.276	.385	.160	.097	.129	International
K Variance of 4 nations around I	.057	.099	.097	.425	.076	.148	.026	.009	.017	
L Mean variance within 4 nations Σ line C ÷ 4	.154	.167	.156	.207	.181	.204	.194	.140	.146	

Value Code

Chan:	Commitment to Innovative Change	Core:	Conflict Avoidance
Apro:	Action Propensity		
Ecde:	Economic Development	Self:	Selflessness
Equa:	Economic Equality	Hone:	Honesty
Part:	Participation		

particular values, that is, their mean scores. What is now shown is that, regardless of the substance of the values they profess, community leadership groups are in general no more, and no less, united in one country than in another. The *degree* of consensus, or dis-sensus, among the local leaders in these four countries is essentially the same, though *what* they agree about and the direction of their value commitments may differ.

The great contrasts of national political system, cultural background, historical development, economic well-being and ideological profession have *not* brought about a state of notably greater unity, or diversity in the basic value commitments of the infra-structure of political leadership. Whatever the operative forces in consensus formation or deformation, they do *not* include the differentiating national characteristics of these four countries.

In a word, national solidarity is shown not to be a national characteristic, insofar as consensus of values among leaders is concerned. The secret of the integration of values is hardly to be found in the attributes of nationality or a peculiar national heritage.

Two caveats need to be entered. First, the Indian leaders, as noted, were sufficiently more divided to differ significantly from the others when pooled as a national group without reference to their communities. Second, the leadership sample in all countries was loaded on the side of "establishment." Strong opposition to the prevailing political mode, actual or potential, was little represented. Hence the extremes of divergence and dis-sensus were not tapped.

The Uniform Level of
Consensus Within Nations

The more or less common inter-national level of consensus among the sampled leaders decided, the next point to determine is whether the amount of consensus is similar throughout each country, or whether the leaders of some communities are notably more united than others. Are the differences in leaders' values greater among communities within the same country than between one country and another?

In terms of the overall measure of congruence, the answer appears unequivocal. The similarity of communities in the degree to which their leaders agree or disagree on the nine scaled values is, with one exception, complete for all countries. If one compares the community with the most heterogeneous leadership and the one with the least (using the overall congruence measure) only in the United States is there a statistically significant difference (see Table 4); this difference results from just one community where the leaders are exceptionally at odds with each other. Note that when one compares this community of maximum heterogeneity with the average, even this one difference ceases to have significance.

This would mean that community leaders differ with each other on their values just about as much in one community as another, just as they do in one country or another.

This finding that the amount of consensus does not vary community to community within countries is corroborated by comparing the amount of variation within communities to the variation within the total national sample of leaders (disregarding the community location of the leader). No significant difference emerges in any country between the amount of national variation and either the maximum or minimum amount of heterogeneity in a community (see Table 5).

Furthermore, the evidence clearly shows that the differences among leaders' values *within* communities far outweigh the differences

Table 4—Significance of Inter-Community Differences in Value Consensus

	Community Congruence Index			F = Ratio	
				(1)	(2)
			Mean for 30	Communities	Community with
	Max.	Min.	Communities	with Max. vs.	Max. Variance
				Min. Variance	vs. Mean Variance
					for 30 Communities
India	489	360	431	1.78	1.26
Poland	529	431	459	1.51	1.33
U.S.	479	300	371	2.71	1.80
Yugoslavia	427	304	354	1.93	1.48

F-Ratio = 2.38 at .02 level of confidence (n = 30/30).

Table 5—Significance of Intranational Differences in Value Consensus

F-Ratios Based on Composite Congruence Index (nine values) for Total National Sample Compared with:

(1) Community with maximum variance
(2) Community with minimum variance

		Nation vs.	
		Max.	Min.
		(1)	(2)
	India	1.16 (2)	1.58 (1)
	Poland	1.66 (2)	1.11 (2)
	U.S.	1.65 (2)	1.64 (1)
	Yugoslavia	1.23 (2)	1.57 (1)

F-Ratio = 2.02 at .02 level of confidence for items marked (1) n = 1000/30, F-Ratio = 1.71 for items marked (2) n = 30/1000.

among communities on each of the nine values in each of the four countries (compare lines F and H, Table 3 and note that all of the relevant F-ratios are significant at the .02 level of confidence). Thus it is *inside* the communities that one finds the maximum amount of dissensus. Individual leaders are often wide apart in their value commitments; but these differences tend to cancel out when one groups all 30 to 35 leaders in a community together. As a result, one community's leadership looks about as united or split as another's. The lines of cleavage are not much more pronounced in one place or another, and it is difficult to identify particular communities, particular types of communities, or communities situated in a particular section of the country, as having any peculiar potency for consensus formation on the one hand, or proneness to dissension on the other.

Account must be taken, however, of some significant intercommunity differences in the amount of consensus on *particular* values; as will be demonstrated, a few of these differences in the degree of agreement among leaders on peculiarly sensitive questions correspond to the kind and amount of community activity and change.

Table 6 summarizes the values on which there is most division among leaders *within* communities and *between* communities. The correspondence of the issues that divide leaders within and among their communities is striking.

In fact, one can say that the values on which leaders split most sharply within their communities are also the ones that tend to generate maximum divergence among community leaders across the same country. If there is wide disagreement on a value within most communities, the chances are that on *that* value the leadership group in some

Table 6—Diversity Within and Among Communities

	SD within Communities		SD among Communities	
India	Local/National	0.570	Local/National	0.153
	Conflict Resolution	0.515	Conflict Resolution	0.181
	Participation	0.461	Participation	0.219
	Honesty	0.443	Honesty	0.191
Poland	Conflict Resolution	0.495	Conflict Resolution	0.106
	Equality	0.490	Equality	0.128
	Economic Development	0.473	Economic Development	0.130
	Selflessness	0.469	Selflessness	0.108
U.S.	Equality	0.401	Equality	0.161
	Economic Development	0.400	Economic Development	0.169
	Participation	0.397	Participation	0.158
Yugoslavia	Equality	0.450	Equality	0.288
	Participation	0.388	Participation	0.253
	Conflict Resolution	0.375	——	
	——		Economic Development	0.203

communities will end up leaning, *on the average*, in a direction markedly different from leaders in others. This difference or distinctiveness in what may be called the general "posture" of a community's leaders on one of these divisive values—often a weathervane of the community's pattern of social performance or activeness—finds its source in the cutting power of the value at the very base of the political pyramid. Dis-sensus in the community is the seedbed of differentiation of values among communities.

This finding runs counter to the widely held view that intergroup differences and conflict originate in (and often reinforce) the solidarity of different "in-groups." Within the context of these studies, i.e., local political leadership in four countries, the reverse is true. In-group divisions in community leadership spill over into intercommunity divisions on identical issues, though on a considerably reduced scale.

Taking inventory of the values that are most divisive (see Table 7), it is apparent that no one value has equivalent cutting power in all four countries.

1. With regard to the desirability of *Innovative Change*, disagreement is greatest in India, least in U.S. and relatively strong in Poland and Yugoslavia.

2. *Economic Values* (commitments to national development goals and economic equality) stir up a surprising amount of disagreement in the two socialist countries, Poland and Yugoslavia, paradoxically, much more disagreement than in capitalist U.S. But it is in India, the least developed and poorest of the countries, that leaders appear most sharply divided in regard to these values.

3. The value of *Conflict Avoidance* also divides Indian leaders most sharply, in contrast to the U.S., where leaders tend to agree that avoiding conflict should *not* be a critical factor in decision-making. Yugoslav and Polish leaders are only modestly split on this issue.

4. The issue of *National Commitment* is far more divisive in India than in any of the other countries, even Yugoslavia with its wide range of ethnic and linguistic difference.

Table 7—Divisive Values (Coefficients of Variation)

	India	Poland	U.S.	Yugoslavia
Innovative Change	0.278	0.231	0.179	0.217
Action Propensity	0.137	0.137	0.161	0.121
Economic Development	0.269	0.231	0.192	0.228
Economic Equality	0.286	0.205	0.131	0.252
Participation	0.159	0.142	0.185	0.193
Conflict Avoidance	0.303	0.181	0.122	0.182
National Commitment	0.235	0.142	0.151	0.144
Selflessness	0.193	0.238	0.202	0.215
Honesty	0.287	0.187	0.217	0.211

5. The *participation* issue, i.e., how far to involve the people in decision-making, is on the other hand, not particularly a bone of contention in any country.

6. The relevance of *moral principles* to public conduct is evidently a hot issue among Indian leaders, but it is an issue that also divides leaders in the other countries.

The fact that consensus tends to form only around certain values, and leaves other areas open to serious disagreement among community leaders, is borne out by the correlations between the amount of deviation within communities on each of the nine values (see Table 8). These show that there are "bellwether" values. Knowing that leaders are broadly in agreement on these values, one can predict with high probability that they will be in agreement on others—but only certain others. Further, these bellwether values tend to interlock, creating consensus "syndromes" in which each of several values is correlated significantly with each of the others. The composition of these syndromes differs considerably country-to-country.

Yugoslavia: Action Propensity is the key bellwether; high deviation or high consensus on this disposition is associated correspondingly with deviation or consensus on six others—Conflict Avoidance, Participation, Selflessness, National Commitment, Change and Economic Equality. Of these, four also intercorrelate significantly with at least three—Participation, Selflessness, Change and Economic Equality. Thus one can conclude that if Yugoslav leaders in one community tend to be divided on their commitment to economic equality, they will also be divided on the other four values in the syndrome. If they are broadly in agreement on the issue of wide popular participation in decision-making, they are likely also to be united on the need for change, their propensity to act, their commitment to economic equality and their profession to the subordination of self-interest to public goals.[6]

United States: The bellwether values, pointing to the scope of consensus, are Economic Equality and Change. Deviation on each of these values correlates significantly with deviation on three others, as well as with each other. Deviation on two of these others—Economic Development and Selflessness—is mutually intercorrelated and hence they qualify for the syndrome. This means that if American leaders in a community are badly split on the issue of economic equality, they are also likely to be split on the need for change, commitment to economic welfare and the extent to which they believe self-interest should be sacrificed in favor of community or national interests.

Three of these values are the same as in Yugoslavia; but notably there is no similar association in the United States between deviation on participation and action propensity. Unity or the lack of it on these issues bears no relationship to consensus or diversity on the others.

Table 8—Intercorrelations of Community Deviation on Nine Value Scales

India

	CHAN	APRO	ECDE	EQUAL	PART	CORE	NATL	SELF	HON
Change		-0.163	0.169	0.235	0.314	0.008	0.506	0.036	-0.025
Action Propensity			0.073	0.407	0.255	0.157	0.041	0.286	0.052
Economic Development				.286	-0.116	-0.293	-0.156	0.134	-0.225
Economic Equality					0.414	0.204	0.063	0.053	-0.182
Participation						0.440	0.467	-0.703	0.107
Conflict Avoidance							0.328	-0.093	0.193
National Commitment								-0.306	0.094
Selflessness									0.161
Honesty									

Poland

	CHAN	APRO	ECDE	EQUAL	PART	CORE	NATL	SELF	HON
Change		0.185	0.425	0.150	0.296	0.059	0.372	0.289	0.253
Action Propensity			-0.018	0.243	0.162	0.146	-0.103	0.312	0.327
Economic Development				0.270	0.165	-0.086	0.348	0.079	-0.003
Economic Equality					0.052	0.304	0.399	0.186	0.043
Participation						0.288	0.285	-0.010	0.328
Conflict Avoidance							0.453	0.176	0.194
National Commitment								0.353	0.212
Selflessness									0.393
Honesty									

United States

	CHAN	APRO	ECDE	EQUAL	PART	CORE	NATL	SELF	HON
Change		-0.278	0.451	0.692	0.366	0.151	0.315	0.389	-0.141
Action Propensity			-0.198	-0.117	0.052	0.434	-0.187	-0.083	0.603
Economic Development				0.626	0.113	0.229	0.299	0.360	-0.076
Economic Equality					0.302	0.322	0.565	0.428	-0.040
Participation						0.130	0.264	0.030	0.177
Conflict Avoidance							0.185	0.177	0.213
National Commitment								0.220	-0.017
Selflessness								0.258	0.113
Honesty									

Yugoslavia

	CHAN	APRO	ECDE	EQUAL	PART	CORE	NATL	SELF	HON
Change		0.425	0.240	0.554	0.365	0.328	0.336	0.241	0.269
Action Propensity			0.108	0.439	0.417	0.503	0.461	0.399	0.177
Economic Development				0.146	-0.305	0.050	-0.026	0.174	0.214
Economic Equality					0.365	0.328	0.349	0.412	-0.051
Participation						0.154	0.283	0.534	0.198
Conflict Avoidance							0.205	-0.055	0.136
National Commitment								0.350	-0.018
Selflessness									0.308

India: Low deviation on Participation is the bellwether of consensus in India, predicting consensus on Conflict Avoidance, National Commitment and Economic Equality and being close to significance in its correlation with diversity of position on Change.

However, there is no tight syndrome as in the United States and Yugoslavia; the amount of deviation on the other values does not mutually intercorrelate (except between national commitment and change). This means that the pattern of consensus in India is not consistent across the country. Leaders in one community will split along certain lines and those in another along others. Or, they will tend to be united on one set of values in one place, and on another set elsewhere.

This probably reflects the somewhat greater amount of international heterogeneity in India that was noted above. The lines of cleavage are more fluid and the basis of consensus are not so firmly or uniformly fixed.

Poland: The bellwether of consensus and diversity is the degree of congruence on Commitment to Nation. Congruence on this value intercorrelates significantly with congruence on the values of Change, Conflict Avoidance and Economic Equality, and somewhat less significantly with congruence on Economic Development and Selflessness.

But there is little relationship in the degree of diversity among the other values; hence no real "consensus syndrome" emerges in Poland.

Only the national issue emerges as an important predictor of value consensus or dis-sensus—a curious finding in view of the fact that leaders in Poland are on the average more strongly committed to nation than in any other country, and are about as united on this issue as leaders in the United States and Yugoslavia, and much more so than the Indians. Nevertheless, the facts seem to be that, should Polish leaders *not* be in substantial agreement on the supremacy of national over local interest, they are then likely to disagree on most other values. Put the other way around, the commitment to nation is the tie that binds leaders together around the issues of change, economic equality and development, and their approach to conflict.

When these sets of observations are balanced, the dominant conclusion is that it is within local communities that the major differences of values among leaders in these four countries appear; the differences among individuals within the same community are far greater than any sectional or other differences that would set some community leadership groups apart from the leadership of other communities.

Variations in consensus among communities, even to the degree evident in India, are not of the nature to pinpoint pockets of "integrated" communities, whose leaders are so much more alike in their *overall* value commitments that one can clearly distinguish them from "disintegrated" communities.

Communities are sufficiently alike in the degree to which the values of their leaders differ so that any community is, in effect, a microcosm of the consensus, or dis-sensus in the country at large. Put the other way around, the leadership of a country as a whole, as represented by the sample of roughly one thousand local leaders, is as integrated or dis-integrated, as unified or divided as the leadership of any particular community.

Determinants of
Diversity

In previous sections we have reported that (1) local political leaders in all countries differ significantly in many of the values they profess; (2) the greatest range of difference exists among leaders *within the same community*; (3) variation is least when comparing leadership *among* communities in the same country; and (4) even differences among countries are not sufficient to conclude which country as a whole is clearly more or less homogeneous, or "integrated" (in the sense of leaders sharing the same values). It is at the local level that the confrontation of divergent values is clearly most acute and where the implications of a *lack* of political cohesion can therefore be most readily observed.

How far consensus is actually required for effective developmental action, as illustrated by the ISVIP community sample, will be analyzed in the next section on "Effects of Diversity." In this section we shall try to explain *why* the leaders of some communities are more united than those of others, or conversely, why there is greater diversity of values among the leaders of one community than another. In other words, what are the "determinants" of diversity, so far as can be judged by examining correlates of the amount of variation within communities in the values expressed by their leaders?[7]

In this analysis of the determinants of diversity, the level of observation is the community. What we seek to explain is differences *among* communities in the amount of consensus among leaders within communities. This implies a group-institutional model of explanation in which every community is considered an independent unit of the national sample, and the sample in each country consists of 30 communities.[8]

We should stress again that what we are concerned with here is the *degree* to which leaders share or do not share the same values. This is not a question of *which* values they accept or which they reject, but whether they *all* tend to reject the same values. Thus, one community's leaders could exhibit a high degree of consensus or "congruence," if most of them said they agreed or strongly agreed with statements expressing the values of Conflict Avoidance, Participation, Economic

Development and Economic Equality, while disagreeing on the five other values scaled. Another community would be considered just as congruent, if about the same proportion of its leaders took the reverse positions. The measures of congruence we are using, as previously stated, are (1) the standard deviation of the scores of the respective leadership groups on each of the nine value scales, and (2) the average standard deviation on all of the nine scales combined.[9]

Differences in the amount of consensus or diversity may be explained in two ways. They can be considered as consequences of the personal characteristics of local leaders (such as age, education, occupational mobility, political affiliation), or the result of social conditions under which leaders live and work, that is, characteristics of the local communities to which leaders belong. The latter may include ecological characteristics (degree of local economic development, urbanization, etc.) or characteristics of the socio-political structure of the community (support groups, cleavages, autonomy). In every instance we are concerned with aggregated characteristics, that is, the *average* age of education of a community's leaders or the *general* community level of resources.

Eighteen possible explanatory factors have been examined, as reported in Table 9.

EXPLAINING OVERALL DIVERSITY

The search for a systematic explanation of why leaders of some communities are more divided in the values they profess than leaders in other communities frankly ran into a blind alley, at least in the matter of finding a set of factors, common to all countries, that related to our overall measure of consensus and diversity. As is evident from Table 8, none of the 18 possible "determinants" correlated uniformly in all four countries with the composite index of diversity, at even a modest level of significance. As a matter of fact, not a single factor correlated in the same direction in any *two* countries.

In India and Yugoslavia, some of the *personal characteristics* of leaders appear to explain, in part, whether they will share values or not, though the pattern of association is entirely different in the two countries.

Age: Age in India tends to produce consensus; youth stimulates diversity.

Homogeneity of age in India tends to produce consensus, and vice versa—the more diversified the age of the leaders, the more likely they are to disagree on their values, which seems consistent with the finding just reported.

But the opposite is true in Yugoslavia for some reason; if community leaders *vary* widely in age, they are likely to *agree* more on their values than if they are closer to being of the same generation. Ideological homogeneity, in the sense of shared values, does *not* follow from biological homogeneity.

Whether this contrast reflects differences in the culture of the two societies or the dynamics of their development, and just how, is not immediately apparent to us, though it is obvious that more substantial and rapid social and political changes have been occurring in Yugoslavia, and perhaps have tended to break up generational pockets of consensus and have substituted economic or other bases of ideological homogeneity that cut across age differences.

Education: Education emerges as a significant factor *only in India*— the more highly educated the leaders, the more likely they are to differ in their values.

Homogeneity of education has no effect on the diversification of values in any of the four countries.

Mobility: Intergenerational mobility (a change from manual to non-manual work from father to son, or vice versa) affects diversity of values *only in Yugoslavia*; leaders whose occupations differ from their fathers' in this respect tend to differ more widely in their values.

Party membership: Only in Yugoslavia, membership in the dominant party is related to congruence of values, but in a manner the reverse of what some might expect—the greater the number of local leaders who are members of the League of Communists, the more likely are their values to *differ*!

This has been explained as the result of the distinctive character and purpose of the League of Communists in Yugoslavia; rather than forcing strict conformity to a single party line on its members, it is constituted to represent the varied ideological and political forces emerging in a self-managed community of producers.[10] Differences in viewpoint among local leaders at a time of intensive economic and political development in the society are to be expected; the fact that these differences are particularly expressed among members of the League of Communists would suggest that the League is functioning as a sensitive barometer of the political climate.

In the consideration of the character of the community as a determinant of diversity, it is obvious from Table 9 that neither its *social and political structure* as perceived by its leaders, nor its *ecological earmarks* have much to do with the amount of consensus or disagreement among leaders' values. In India and the United States the number of support groups to whom leaders turn does seem to have some bearing on congruence, though in opposite directions; in India, the broader the base of support, the more homogeneous are the leaders' values, whereas in the United States homogeneity follows upon the selection of a few (and presumably sharply focused) interest groups as the leaders' guideposts. Then in India, there is a tendency toward greater uniformity of values in poorer, less developed communities. There is notably no

Table 9—Determinants of Diversity of Values[1]

Variables[2]	Change	Parti- cipation	Conflict Avoidance	National Commit- ment	Overall (Nine Values)[3]
I *Personal Characteristics of Leaders*					
1 Age—average			IND – US + YU +		IND –
2 Age—variance	YU –		IND –		IND + YU –
3 Education—average length			IND +	YU –	IND +
4 Education—variance in length	IND + POL –	IND +	US +	IND +	
5 Residence in community— average stay			US +		
6 Intergenerational mobility (re manual occupation)		YU +	YU +		YU +
7 Party affiliation (% of leaders members of dominant party in the community)			IND +	US + YU +	YU +
II *Socio-political Structure of Community (as perceived by Leaders)*					
(a) Support structure:					
8 Groups to which leader turns for support— average number		US +	POL –		IND –* US +
9 Support groups—variance in number mentioned				YU +	
10 Support sought from: local party leaders (% leaders so indicating)				YU +	
11 Support sought from: elected representatives to local government bodies					
12 Support sought from: local administrative officials			IND –		
(b) Cleavages					
13 Differences that divide the community—average number of issues noted by leaders			IND – US +	YU –	
14 Differences that divide— variance in number of issues noted	IND +		IND – POL + US +		
(c) Lack of autonomy					
15 Areas where local govern- ment lacks autonomy— average number mentioned				IND – YU –	

Table 9—Determinants of Diversity of Values[1] —continued

Variables[2]	Change	Parti-cipation	Conflict Avoidance	National Commit-ment	Overall (Nine Values)[3]
16 Areas where local govern- ment lacks autonomy— variance in number mentioned		US –		YU –	
III *Ecological Characteristics of* *the Community*					
17 Level of economic development	IND +	POL +	IND – * US –	YU –	IND +
18 Percentage of urban population					

Note 1: This table reports that variables correlate with the standard deviation of leaders' scores on the indicated value scale in the 30 communities in each country. Correlations are significant at .05 level or above, except where indicated by asterisk when they are slightly below.

    Direction: a positive sign indicates that the variable is associated with diversity, i.e., the larger the variable the larger the standard deviation. A negative sign indicates that the variable is associated with consensus, i.e., a low standard deviation.

Note 2: All variables are community aggregates.

Note 3: Variables are correlated with the composite index of diversity, i.e., the average standard deviation in communities of scores on all nine value scales. See text, p. 141.

observable link in *any* of the countries between the amount of consensus on values and:

(1) whether support of local leadership is based primarily on party, the elected bodies of the local government, or the local administrative bureaucracy;

(2) the issues that divide the community;

(3) the amount of local autonomy that the leaders feel exists;

(4) the extent of urbanization.

On an overall basis, one can only conclude that many of the purported environmental forces of political socialization are not operative in these countries, at least in inducing a general consensus of values among leaders at the community level. It may also be concluded that personal characteristics, while partially explanatory in two countries, operate in such entirely different ways that they indicate that the pattern of socialization, such as it is, is not nation-specific.[11]

Possible reasons for this remarkable vacuum of adequate explanation for diversity or consensus of values among leaders are the following:

(1) The composite measure of diversity, being an average of deviation on nine values, minimizes to some extent the amount of diversity observed within communities. On the other hand, there is no reason to suppose that this would greatly affect differences *among* communities in their degree of internal diversity. In any case, analysis was undertaken, looking at each value separately, of possible determinants of diversity, and this is reported below.

(2) Differences among communities in the diversity of their leaders values are, it will be recalled, much smaller than either cross-national differences or variation within each community. It may be that such differences are insufficient for significant correlations with other community characteristics. This would be the implication of the findings reported in Table 4 (see above).

On the other hand, in India and Yugoslavia, some modestly significant correlations actually were found, so that, in these two countries at least, this reason would not, by itself, seem to be adequate.

(3) We may not have hit upon the right set of variables to explain diversity of values adequately, although our set was chosen to tap quite a wide range of possibilities.

(4) Each country may *in fact* have its own distinctive pattern of forging consensus or precipitating diversity of values among the leaders of its communities. What is determinative in one may not be at all applicable in the others. Thus the role of party in Yugoslavia is not to enforce conformity to a single set of values but to encourage active consideration of the best means of realizing the goals of the society. The support group base of leaders may work in opposite directions in India and the United States because of substantive differences in the character of interest groups in the two countries and in the nature of their political influence.

This interpretation would be compatible with many of the other ISVIP findings, which emphasize dissimilarities rather than similarities among nations in their patterns of values and, most particularly, in the factors influencing community activeness.

We should not lose sight of the power of the negative findings to challenge some of the theories of consensus formation that have been advocated. First, certainly any *general* theory, involving indiscriminate cross-national application of the variables included in our analysis, should be suspect. Secondly, the presumption must be strong that consensus (or diversity) of values among leaders does not depend *anywhere* on the extent of cleavages within the community; note that in none of these four very different countries, does the number of issues that are seen to divide a community relate to the amount of variation of values among the leaders. There is no way of predicting whether a socially, economically and politically homogeneous community will have leaders who share the same values, or that a community that is divided along many lines will necessarily have leadership that is disunited. Integration in the sense of shared values (at least among leaders) is thus neither a condition nor a consequence of integration in the sense of social uniformity.

The conclusion is strengthened by the number of other characteristics in which homogeneity of the community or of the leaders is shown to have no significant relationship to consensus of leaders' values in most, if not all, of the four countries: the percentage of the urban/rural population, homogeneity of leaders' education, party affiliation (except Yugoslavia), and a similar specific base of political support for the leaders.

This means that the formation of value consensus among leaders is largely *independent* of pre-existing institutions and forces of socialization (or, more accurately, that the institutions and forces to which socialization power has been widely attributed, do not or may not have such power when it comes to determining the congruence of leaders' values as the leaders grapple with the problems of change and development in their communities). While we do not know very clearly what actually does produce a broad consensus among the leaders, especially in some countries, we are reasonably convinced that such a consensus is not barred either by personal demographic differences of the leaders, or by socio-political heterogeneity in their communities. People can share values even if they are not the same kind of people, or their values may differ, even if they are the same kind of people.

EXPLAINING CONGRUENCE ON PARTICULAR VALUES

The previous section examined the diversity of leaders' values on an overall basis, and found, for whatever reasons, no clear pattern of explanation for differences among communities in the degree to which leaders were generally divided or united on all of the nine scaled values. One of the possible reasons for this inconclusive result was, as suggested, the possibility that averaging out the amount of disagreement on the nine values, as was done in the composite index of congruence, may have artificially concealed a much more substantial amount of disagreement on certain specific values. Consequently, parallel analyses were undertaken of community differences in the degree of consensus (or dis-sensus) on four values that were found to have particular relevance to the processes of social change and development in at least some countries; the values involved were Conflict Avoidance, Participation, National Commitment and Concern for Change.

While there is evidence of some factors conceivably influencing consensus in certain countries on some values (see Table 9), there is still no common pattern that applies to all four countries, or even there countries—for *any* of the four values. Not a single supposed "determinant" correlates in the same direction with consensus or diversity on a given value in more than *two* countries. And even two-country uniformities are scarce; there are five, to be exact:

On Conflict Avoidance:

(a) consensus is associated with *youth* in United States and Yugoslavia; younger leaders tend to agree in their stand, the older leaders are more split on this value. (Age is also a factor in India but it works in the opposite direction.)

(b) leaders in United States and Poland (but not Yugoslavia) are influenced by their *perception of divisions* in their communities—the more they *vary* in their estimates of cleavage, the more likely they are to be split in regard to the desirability of avoiding conflict. (In India, again, the reverse is true.)

(c) consensus on Conflict Avoidance is associated with a *high level of economic development* in the two countries that differ most in their level of affluence, India and United States. The rich in each country tend to agree on avoiding conflict; the poor are more divided on this value.

On National Commitment:

(a) *party affiliation* is associated with *dissension* in United States and Yugoslavia—the greater the number of leaders who belong to the dominant party in the community, the more divided they are in the extent of their commitment to national interests. This occurs despite the great difference in political systems and, particularly, the structure and role of the party in these two countries.

(b) further, in regard to National Commitment, between leaders in Yugoslavia and India there is a similar relationship between consensus and the leaders' estimate of local autonomy—the *less* autonomy they feel their community has, the more likely they are to share the *same* outlook toward nation.

This set of two-country uniformities is so scattered that we are forced to conclude that the determination of consensus or diversity of values, either in general or with regard to particular values, is not cross-nationally comparable, in even a limited sense. Consensus formation is a national phenomenon to the extent that any consensus does arise, and each country has its own special formula. What may contribute to consensus on Conflict Avoidance in India, will not affect consensus on that value in the other countries; if there is a pretty clear indication of factors responsible for consensus on National Commitment in Yugoslavia, this does not hold true for India, Poland or the United States.

On a distinctively national basis, something approaching a pattern of explanation does emerge in India and the United States with regard to the value of Conflict Avoidance, and in Yugoslavia on National Commitment. On the values of Participation and Change, not one of the countries has produced evidence to explain why leaders of one community are more united than those of another.

In the three cases mentioned, the motivation of consensus can be summarized as follows:

Consensus on Conflict Avoidance—India   Consensus on the value of avoiding conflict in India is likely to be greater among leaders in a community if they are older on the average (r = .445), and if at the same time, there is considerable variation in the age range (r = .408); if they perceive that their community is divided along many lines (r = .403); if they tend in general to look for support to the local administrative officials (r = .601); and, interestingly enough, if they tend *not* to belong to the Congress Party (r = − .427).[12] (In other words, if a large number belong to Congress, the chances are they will *not* be united on the value of avoiding conflict, perhaps because they feel rather confident that party unity will enable them to override community conflicts). There is a possibly significant tendency for leaders to be more united on this value if they govern in communities that are relatively higher than others in economic development (r = .351).

Consensus on Conflict Avoidance—U.S.   Consensus on this value in the United States is likely to be greater if the leaders are *younger* (r = − .388), and if they perceive relatively *few* divisions in their communities (r = − .420) (just the reverse of India in these two respects); in addition, leaders who have been in the community only a short time, and who have had about the same amount of education, are likely to be in agreement on the value of avoiding conflict (r = − .490 and − .458 respectively). Consensus is more likely to be found on this value in communities that are relatively affluent (r = .595) (in this respect, U.S. experience is similar to India's).

Consensus on National Commitment—Yugoslavia   This can be explained in part by party affiliation, in reverse; as previously noted, the higher the percentage of leaders who are members of the Communist Party, the more likely they are to *differ* on the value of national commitment (r = − .391). Similarly, the more they tend to rely on local party leaders for support, the more likely they are to be *disunited* on Commitment to Nation (r = − .497).

Factors *conducive to consensus* are as follows: (1) a higher degree of economic development of the commune (r = .512); (2) higher average education of leaders (r = .582); (3) perception of a *large* number of divisions in the commune (r = .622); (4) perception of a *lack* of local autonomy in many areas (r = .442); and (5) a common range of support (leaders differing little in the number of groups to whom they turn) (r = .392).

Were these factors influential in regard to consensus or dis-sensus on the other values, one might be tempted to formulate tentative conclusions about a motivational pattern of social and political integration peculiar to Yugoslavia, when one notes, for instance, the curious *dis*-conformity role of party, the fact that community divisions lead to *con*-sensus rather than dis-sensus, and that values tend to be shared when leaders feel they *lack* power rather than when they have it. All these observations rouse interest, as they challenge so sharply some of the neat theories of what produces social unity. But it must be stressed that the focus of explanations here is *solely* on the sense of national commitment, though it is granted that this value is of great importance when the integrity of the country as a political-social community is concerned.

But let us return to highlight the principal finding. *None* of the variables posited to explain consensus or diversity of values—whether personal characteristics of the leaders or characteristics of their communities—turns out to explain consistently community differences in leaders' consensus on *any* given value in all countries, or on all values in any one country.

The implication is clearly to disprove, or at least to cast serious doubt upon theories that attribute consensus formation to political solidarity, homogeneity of reference groups, or perceived social diversification; nor does mobility (either geographical or in terms of status) seem systematically to relate to diversification of values.

The *particularity* of the processes of socialization as they affect the value dispositions of local political leaders again gains prominence in this four-nation comparative study. Particular values come to be more widely shared as a result of particular factors working to influence leaders in particular community and national environments. This is not to suggest confirmation of the extreme position of the uniqueness of all human historical development. It does strongly challenge most single-cause, or dominant-cause, theories of ideological integration, at least to the extent that it is unlikely that such causes are to be found along any of the dimensions indicated by our selection of variables.

What is of perhaps greater significance, is the probability that consensus of values has been exaggerated as an important distinguishing element in social development and political integration. In *no* communities in our sample has leadership come to the point of a real consensus of values. Typically, there are major confrontations of divergent values, or different priorities of values. Pluralism seems to be the prevailing condition in the value orientations of leaders, regardless of the country or kind of community in which they live. And the degree of pluralism is not that much different, at least between communities within the same country, to be systematically accounted for by the other kinds of differences between communities and among leaders.

The conclusions of these studies indicate that whether community leaders generally do or do not share the same values makes little difference in the social outputs of their communities or in community responsiveness to initiatives for social change.

In none of the four countries does the degree of overall consensus among leaders on the values they hold correlate with the most general and comparable measure of community activeness we were able to develop.[13] And only in India does the amount of consensus on any of the values we assessed seem to bear on the generation of this kind of activeness: here *dis-sensus*, on the issue of conflict avoidance, is a significant correlate of innovative community development (r = .442).

These negative findings undercut each of the two major but contradictory theories that link social dynamics to social consensus, i.e., (1) that commonality of aspirations is conducive to social mobilization, and conversely (2) that social progress has its roots in ideological pluralism and an open market of competing values. Our evidence demonstrates that it is the specific content of values held by leaders, rather than their general homogeneity, that is a determinant of social action, when leaders' values have a social impact at all. Neither overall diversity, nor overall consensus, in the broad spectrum of political values professed by leaders, appears to affect the basic thrust of public life at the community level.

The implication of these findings is that neither community nor nation has demonstrated a peculiar homogenizing influence upon its leaders. Nor has the leadership of a particular community or country demonstrated that it has a special penchant for sharing values. Leaders in one country, or one type of community, are no more likely to share values than those in another. The socializing of leadership in this sense (or its opposite, the splintering and fracturing of leadership) does not reflect either the kind of community where leaders function or the nation to which they belong.

From the standpoint of nation building and development, this conclusion points to the importance of personal factors, and a range of influences inside or outside the community that affect the leader *individually* in his choice of values, and his consequent choice of actions. Evidently the common social forces, operating from either national or community level, do *not* produce a common set of values among local leaders, at least in the areas considered in this study. The powers that differentiate individuals are greater than the powers that press them toward a common mold. The forces of diversification seem stronger than those of social conformity.

If values must be widely shared to sustain national solidarity or progressive social change, then the evidence from these studies suggests that none of these four countries has succeeded better than the others in the welding of values at the local base. No claim can therefore be made that a particular political heritage, be it long or short, more or less authoritarian, with or without a colonial background, capitalist or socialist, has given a country a greater capacity for integration, if one considers that integration can be measured by, or is necessarily dependent upon, a consensus of values among its leaders. The same must be said about influences associated with the type or location of community within the country. However rich or highly developed the community or area, for instance, or whether it is more or less industrialized, seems to make no difference in the degree to which its leaders are united in their values.

From a different perspective, these findings appear to justify some confidence that nation building and development are *not* dependent upon the achievement of ideological conformity. These four countries, despite their different social conditions, stages of growth and paths of political action, have all been able to tolerate (or have had to tolerate) a basic level of dis-sensus right at the foundation of the structure of political authority. The fact that this level is just about the same in all these countries means that the dire prophecies of doom if a country has failed to get its leadership to stand together in pledged allegiance to the same political standards are suspect. Unless, of course, all four countries go down the drain together.

A more optimistic expectation is likely to be more valid in terms of the data and the analysis emanating from these studies. Different commitments among leaders in regard to principles of public conduct and the social good may be the mark of a dynamic polity, rather than of a society on the brink of disintegration. A goodly potion of dis-sensus among the leadership may stoke the fires for continued social health, economic growth and political vitality in their respective countries. The fact that the dis-sensus is widely and quite evenly distributed throughout these countries should be reassuring to those who fear disintegration along sectional or other lines of cleavage; it is only reassuring provided there can be sufficient give-and-take between the various levels and segments of leadership to prevent their differences from hardening into irreconcilable ideological blocs.

Notes

1. In developing the design of the ISVIP, cognizance was taken of many other concepts of integration. See Chapter 1, and the Reports of the First and Second International Roundtables. But the problems of securing reliable empirical indicators that would be comparable for all four countries involved in the study were so great that only these two could be effectively operationalized with the time and resources available. See Philip E. Jacob and James Toscano (eds.), *The Integration of Political Communities*, Philadelphia: J. B. Lippincott, 1964, Chapters 1 and 8, for a resume of concepts of integration and discussion of the implications of value consensus for social and political change.

The concept of integration as shared values is advanced *inter alia* by Karl Deutsch *et al.*, *Political Community and the North Atlantic Area*, Princeton, N.J.: Princeton University Press, 1957; and the *Polish Encyclopedia*.

2. Theoretically, this question should be raised at the national level also. But the operational indices of community activeness are so different for the four countries (despite rigorous attempts to have them conform to a common conceptual definition) that cross-national comparisons are hazardous on this variable.

3. See, for instance, the development theories advanced by W. W. Rostow, Myron Weiner, Karl W. Deutsch and others. On the other hand, the classic democratic view, as expounded by John Stuart Mill for instance, maintains that in diversity of values is the seedbed of social change and growth.

4. This formulation, and the analytical design to derive from ISVIP data empirical evidence concerning the effectiveness of alternative forces of political

socialization was conceived by Adam Przeworski, a former participant in the project.

It was further elaborated and tentatively applied to U.S. and Indian data in a research paper by Richard Brandon, "Values, Congruence and Support-Group Selection: Indicators of Socialization in the United States and India," presented to the Seminar on Values and Motivation in Political Behavior, Department of Political Science, University of Pennsylvania, January, 1968. Unpublished.

5. The principal reason for constructing the second index was to take account of the fact that leaders often differed substantially on one value and agreed on another. In some instances, these variations were so great that the amount of deviation on one value correlated *inversely* with the deviation on another. (See Table 8, Intercorrelations of Community Deviation on Nine Value Scales.)

The supplementary index thus measured congruence in that area of values where deviation was maximum and the pattern of deviation was most consistent cross-nationally.

Curiously, however, the two composite measures themselves intercorrelated highly for each national sample, as follows: India 0.796, Poland 0.850, U.S. 0.841, Yugoslavia 0.875. Hence the two measures are relatively comparable, even though the second naturally registers a higher amount of deviation than the nine-value index.

6. We must stress once again that the analysis here concerns the amount of *consensus*, not the nature of the position taken on the various values. For the latter, one must refer to the correlations of *mean scores* (see Chapter 3) rather than to the standard deviations. The form in which the consensus syndrome has been stated here implies a certain position on each value in line with the national mean; but it is entirely possible that in some communities leaders are united around the reverse of these positions on one or more of the values. The question we are exploring is strictly whether one can predict that there will be substantial unity around one value (whether it is unity to accept or to reject the value) from knowing that leaders are largely united in their position on another value. Or, if there is much disagreement in the positions taken on one value, are the leaders also likely to be at odds over another value?

7. Strictly speaking, our data do not make possible findings that certain factors *cause* differences in the degree of value consensus; we can only demonstrate whether there is a statistically significant correlation, at a given level of probability. As a matter of fact, it will be apparent that negative conclusions are far more impressive than positive ones. It is possible to assert with considerable confidence that very few of the factors examined are likely to have affected the extent to which community leaders were united or disunited on the values they expressed. This finding of "no-cause" is much firmer than a causal claim. Details and possible explanations will be presented later in this section.

8. Alternative levels could have been chosen: for instance, country could be compared with country, if all leaders in a country were taken as a single sample and their deviation around the national mean used as the measure of congruence or diversity. Then the explanatory variables would be national aggregates, characteristics of the national sample of leaders, or of the country as a whole. Because the central purpose of this project was to study social change and integration at the local level, however, *intercommunity* differences in congruence seemed to be the most appropriate object of analysis.

9. See Section above, "Measuring Consensus."

10. See the constituent Acts and major policy declarations of the League,

viz. VII Congress of the League of Communists of Yugoslavia, Belgrade, *Kultura*, 1958, pp. 1106–1107 and IX Congress of the League, Belgrade, *Kultura*, 1969, pp. 204–213.

Since 1953, this principle has been consistently reaffirmed and elaborated at all Congresses of the League.

The term "producer" encompasses all who are integrated in whatever production processes of social means of production, either as manual or nonmanual workers.

11. Even the limited amount of positive evidence must be treated with caution, because the level of significance is not high (close to .05) and the coefficients of determination (amount of variance explained) is low ($r^2 = 0.185$ for the strongest correlation).

Further analysis of the implications of these data for the processes of political socialization is reported by R. Brandon, *op. cit.*

12. Signs of the correlation reported in these paragraphs have been adjusted to indicate association with consensus, i.e., a low standard deviation, rather than diversity.

13. See Chapter 9. It should be noted however, that diversity or consensus especially in regard to the value of Conflict Avoidance, does correlate with an alternative measure of activeness in the other countries as well as in India. For an interpretation and evaluation of this second set of activeness indicators, see Appendix C. The relevant correlations are for India 0.572, U.S. − 0.560 and Yugoslavia −0.438 with $r = 0.361$ at .05 level, with a positive correlation indicating that a high standard deviation, i.e., dis-sensus, on Conflict Avoidance is associated with activeness.

PART TWO

The Ecology of Local Politics

This part describes the political and economic conditions that form part of the environmental context within which local leaders function.

The autonomy of local government—legal and perceived—and the organization of decision-making in the local political units in each of the four countries are among system variables often held to be determinative of patterns of social change. These are discussed in Chapter 6.

In Chapter 7, the resource base of the sample of communities is compared, using measures demonstrated to be equivalent. The data presented are the basis for subsequent analysis in which the influence of economic level is controlled in the process of isolating the impact of leaders' values on community activeness.

Political Structure: The Institutional Basis of Local Responsibility

The four sections of this chapter were written respectively by Sirsikar, Wiatr, Watts and Vratusa. Wiatr also wrote the introduction and conclusions, and was responsible for assembling and editing the chapter.

The purpose of this chapter is to analyze differences in the institutions of local government that might affect community activeness in the four countries. Three main areas of diversity appear.

First, the countries differ in the nature of their ideological rationale for local government, and in the degree to which it is deliberately institutionalized to accomplish specific national purposes of political or social development.

Second, the amount of autonomy exercised by local institutions varies greatly, depending mainly on the extent to which powers have been formally decentralized, but also on the prevailing sense of political efficacy among local leaders.

Third, the structure of decision-making in the governance of the community is very different—concentrated in some cases, highly dispersed in others; reflecting major differences in the relationships of administration to representative organs; expressive of quite diverse forms of political participation, depending on the nature of the party system and the roles of other interest groups in the political process.

Obvious as these cross-national differences in local political structure seem to be, we encountered considerable difficulty in developing a basis for systematic comparison, especially in devising measures that would enable such institutional differences to be assessed as behavioral determinants. We could turn as a starting point neither to general theoretical treatment of the structure of politics at the local level,[1] nor to systematic comparative analysis of the political systems of India, Poland, U.S. and Yugoslavia at any level.

Consequently, the approach we have taken, by necessity, has relied heavily on formal documentation concerning, first, the historical development of local political institutions in each country, second, major policy formulations regarding the role and functions of local government within the overall system, and third, the legal bases of local authority and governmental organization including the scope of local autonomy. Evidence concerning the *practice* of government and politics in the community has come mainly from direct field investigation, through the leadership survey and through subsequent intensive case studies of decision-making in some of the ISVIP samples of political units.[2] The survey also casts light on how much autonomy leaders felt they had, and how much they thought desirable.[3]

Before we present the results of this study of the nature and functioning of local government in the four countries, we ought to explain the distinction between the concepts of "local community" and "local political system" used in this chapter and other parts of the book.

Local community, as understood in social-anthropology and in a part of sociology, differs from the concept currently used in political science. Whereas in the former disciplines, local community is identified with a certain ecological structure within which individuals remain in direct, personal relationships, in political science and, under its influence, in a part of sociology, one tends to treat local community as a functionally autonomous social unit. Adopting precisely such an approach, we may distinguish, as Terry N. Clark does, two aspects of this functional autonomy: "first, following the more traditional usage, as a relatively autonomous *political* system; but second, and generally encompassing a larger geographical unit, as a relatively autonomous *social* system."[4]

On the other hand, one of our colleagues has contended that local communities do *not* have absolute autonomy within modern political systems:

(1) In a modern society the local community is basically a non-autonomous system and it is economically, socially, and politically interwoven into the more complex setting of the broader systems; and

(2) the local political system constitutes one of the levels of the political organization of the state, and as such it comprises several elements

common to all levels of political organization and is typical for the functioning of the national political system as a whole.[5]

The basic difficulty remains to find a valid cross-nationally applicable definition of "local community." The degree to which particular, territorially separate units within states actually enjoy political and social autonomy differs from country to country, depending on the character of the national political system. We cannot therefore adopt a hard and fast yardstick or threshold of autonomy as a basis for distinguishing "local communities." That is why we chose instead, as the criterion for selecting local units of observation in this study, whether the *level* they occupied in the overall political system was comparable. This could roughly be described as the third level of power, with the nation as the first, and a state, republic or wojwodship as the second. The degree of local autonomy, i.e., the amount of formal or actual power that a community had to act, then became one of the important variables distinguishing one community from another (just as the communities are distinguished by size or population), rather than a basic element in the definition of a community, i.e., in the determination of whether a territorial unit was, or was not a "community."

We use the concept "political system" in a double sense. First, we speak about the *national political system*, meaning all institutions whose role is to exercise power, aspire to power, or exert influence over the way in which power is exercised, as well as all established patterns of interactions existing between such institutions. Second, we speak also of the *local political system*, meaning all institutions of the above mentioned type and all patterns of interactions existing between them within local communities, i.e., administrative units that we adopted as basic observation units in our study. Differentiating in this way between the national and local political systems, we do not assume that the local system constitutes an entity separate from the national system; on the contrary, we realize that between the national and the local system there is always considerable intertwining and that the extent to which the local political system is integrated with the national one is different in particular countries, depending on the degree of autonomy of local political bodies. In this chapter we shall make clear the differences in this respect that exist between India, Poland, the United States and Yugoslavia. In a later chapter the consequences of these differences for community activeness will be examined.

Local Government in
Rural India

Ten years after securing independence in 1949, India launched an experiment to increase popular participation in social and economic development by establishing a system of rural local government, in which considerable powers could be exercised by locally elected bodies, known as *panchayats*. Although this system of *Panchayati Raj* was heralded as a return to traditional, indigenous institutions, it was in fact a deliberate attempt to implement a process of democratic decentralization that broke with the longstanding practices of centralized authority that characterized the governance of India even before British rule. It was also a step away from the predilection for concentration of power that lingered on in India's contemporary constitutional system—nominally federal and parliamentary, but effectively managed in its first decade by a dominant single party with socialist orientation, and a centralized professional civil service.

The general political background of this move was the enfranchisement of the peasant masses, who, with universal adult suffrage, suddenly became a significant determinant of Indian politics, local and national. But the immediate impetus to the new structure of local government was the failure to secure adequate popular response for centrally initiated efforts to promote economic and social development in village India, where 80% of the population lives. An investigation of the lagging Community Development programs and National Extension Services led to the Balwantrai Mehta Committee Report in 1958[6] and the adoption of legislation authorizing the introduction of Panchayati Raj in the various states.

Implementation, left as it was to the states, varied in timing (see Table 1) and, to some extent, in substance (for instance, the powers granted to different levels of panchayats were not uniform). However, Panchayati Raj institutions have now been established in most of the 17 states and form an integral part of the total political structure through which Indian democracy functions.

Table 1—Progress of Panchayati Raj Legislation and its Implementation

Year	States where Panchayati Raj Acts were passed	States where Panchayati Raj Acts were implemented
1959	Rajasthan, Andhra Pradesh, Assam, Madras and Mysore.	Rajasthan, Andhra Pradesh and Madras.
1960	Orissa.	Assam and Mysore.
1961	Punjab and Uttar Pradesh.	Orissa, Punjab and Uttar Pradesh.
1962	Bihar, Gujarat, Madhya Pradesh and Maharashtra.	Maharashtra.
1963	West Bengal.	Gujarat.
1964	—	West Bengal and Bihar.

Note 1: Kerela Panchayati Raj Bill lapsed with the dissolution of the state legislature.
Note 2: Jammu and Kashmir state have set up a committee to work out a pattern of Panchayati Raj for the state.
Note 3: Implementation of Panchayati Raj is in progress in Madhya Pradesh.
(Source: Kurukshetra, October, 1966.)

There are three tiers of panchayats. At the lowest level, villagers directly elect members of a *gram panchayat* or village council. These bodies are then represented on the *panchayat samiti* or *kshetra samiti* covering a *taluka,* or development "block" comprising 50–100 villages. At the third tier, the *zilla parishad* functions for an area coterminous with the administrative *district.* The immense scope of the system is indicated in Table 2, for India as a whole, and for the three states in which this project was conducted.

Table 2—Panchayat Samitis and Zilla Parishads

(As on 31-3-1967)

Parti-culars	No. of Dist-ricts	No. of Taluka-Tehsils	No. of Blocks into which Delim-ited	No. of Zilla Pari-shads	No. of Pancha-yat Samitis	No. of Pancha-yats	Average No. of Pancha-yat Samitis per Zilla Parishad	Average No. of Pancha-yats per Pancha-yat Samiti
India	322	1873	5192	253	3494	211,764	13.8	60.6
Gujarat	18	186	250	17	182	11,755	10.6	64.6
Maharashtra	26	232	425	25	295	20,287	11.7	68.8
Uttar Pradesh	54	231	899	51	854	72,333	16.7	84.7

(Source: Kurukshetra, October, 1966.)

Table 2A—Gram Panchayats

(As on 31-3-1967)

Particulars	No. of Pancha-yats	No. of Villages Covered	Rural popula-tion Covered (in 100,000)[*]	Percent-age of Villages Covered	Percent-age of Rural Popula-tion Covered	Average No. of Villages per Panchayat	Average Popula-tion per Panchayat
India	212,986	557,264	3496.9	99	97	2.6	1642
Gujarat	11,755	18,247	153	100	100	6.8	3125
Maharashtra	20.787	35,492	281	99	99	1.7	1385
Uttar Pradesh	72,333	112,624	643	100	100	1.6	889

[*] According to 1961 census.
(Source: Kurukshetra, October, 1967.)

The tiers of Panchayati Raj roughly parallel the structure of local administration, continued virtually intact from the days of British rule. The district is the major administrative unit under the state. Responsibility for law and order, and collection of revenue is concentrated in the hands of the Collector, a civil service official appointed from above by the state government. For a decade after independence, he was also saddled with the execution of the community development and national extension programs, but now development activity is administered by a separate officer. This functionally divided but centrally directed system of administrative responsibility extends downward to the taluka or block, and ultimately to the village. At each level, two sets of officials appointed by and accountable to the next rung in their respective hierarchies, discharge the duties of general administration (including revenue) on the one hand, and development on the other. The latter, but not the former, are also accountable to the panchayat at the corresponding level. The introduction of the Panchayati Raj thus had the effect of establishing an entirely separate line of administration for development, reaching down from the state to the village, as well as creating a set of elective institutions pushing up from the village to the higher levels of government.

It should be noted that the panchayat system is also functionally separated from the general legislative process, and the corresponding electoral process. The legislative assemblies of each state and the Parliament of the Union are directly elected from constituencies that usually, but not always, conform to the talukas previously mentioned. In any case, there is no formal connection between the panchayats and the legislatures, except that the MLA's (members of legislative assemblies) are sometimes *ex officio* members of the panchayats in their constituencies.

Furthermore, the purview of the panchayat is strictly rural. They do not function in urban areas, which have a separate system of municipal government within their respective districts.

From the standpoint of political organization, the major parties were quick to realize that the panchayats represented a base of considerable potential influence and power. Hence they adapted their activities and structure to compete for control in the panchayats as well as in the general electoral process. This has tended to make rural politics a more continuous occupation, as local political leaders not only become responsible for mobilizing voters for an occasional election to a far removed legislative body, but must also take a hand day-to-day in panchayat decisions immediately affecting their constituents. This in turn has had the effect of institutionalizing local party units as a basic component of the Congress and other major parties.

Thus, in this study, we have been concerned with a segment of the Indian political system designed and introduced deliberately to engage the rural population in political responsibility for social and economic development. Despite its recent origin, and many difficulties in implementation, it has been adopted throughout most of the country and now forms the principal vehicle of governmental action concerned with development, both administrative and political. In intent and, increasingly, in practice, it breaks with the tradition of centralized authority in two respects: first and foremost, in creating units of local government that at least have some authority to act; secondarily, in separating out the development functions of government as a special sphere of responsibility apart from the customary tasks of maintaining public order.

FROM DEVELOPMENT TO POLITICS: THE EVOLVING
RATIONALE OF PANCHAYATI RAJ

Panchayati Raj started as a bold experiment in democratization as a spur to modernization. By giving local institutions the power to make decisions, it was assumed that a revolution would occur in the mental makeup of the rural masses, which would bring them into the mainstream of civic life and assure their support for basic social and economic changes needed in the development of rural India. "The Panchayati Raj system was conceived and set up as an instrument of change, of transformation," frankly declared Ashok Mehta, former Deputy Chairman of the Planning Commission and one of the original architects of the proposal. "It was, as it were, going into the very bowels of our system and trying to change it."[7]

Voluntary popular participation in the processes of development administration was established not just to satisfy ideals of democracy, but very pragmatically as a way of energizing the Indian people and pulling them in to fulfill planned development programs. The panchayat institutions were set up as an integrated system of political socialization, communication and mobilization that, it was hoped, would result in massive involvement in the efforts both to increase agricultural output and to better the social conditions of life.

But while the Panchayati Raj was conceived as an institution for development, in practice it has tended to become an arena for power politics and oligarchic control by the rural elite, under the garb of party struggle. As a result, friction has developed between the elected leaders and the appointed civil servants, friction reflecting their different objectives and expectations. The elected look to the Panchayati Raj as a mechanism of power, while the bureaucrats continue to feel that the task of these institutions is to carry out the development activities of the state government. As decision-making power has shifted from the state to the local level, and from administrators to elected leaders, the original development objectives have often become adulterated by the bargaining and patronage of politics. Thus, paradoxically, as

Panchayati Raj has moved ahead in its democratizing mission, it has been somewhat diverted from its developmental purpose.

Nevertheless, there seems no doubt that the Panchayati Raj institutions have indeed succeeded in accelerating the pace of the "green revolution" by inducing the peasants to use new fertilizers, improved seeds of high yielding varieties and new techniques of agriculture; villages have been opened up to the process of modernization through improved roads, better communication, community radios and farm forums.

AUTONOMY: (1) THE SCOPE OF LOCAL POWERS

The system of Panchayati Raj rests, as we have indicated, on both a functional and a territorial division of governmental powers.

Functionally, the panchayats were expected to take on considerable responsibility for the allocation of resources for social and economic development, including education, health and the improvement of agricultural production. This involved decisions affecting the distribution both of local resources and of grants made available by the state or central governments, though in the case of the latter there was often little actual discretion left to the panchayats. The amount of local responsibility for the *mobilization* of resources, in contrast to their allocation, varies. In some states, panchayats have been given the power to tax for local purposes. But the main job of raising revenue is customarily carried on from above and the panchayats are largely dependent on the grants-in-aid made from above, plus whatever voluntary contributions and investments they can encourage, either of funds or of work.[8] The conduct of other functions, such as police and, indeed, much of the actual administration of such public services and utilities as irrigation projects, the training and assignment of teachers, and the development of medical facilities is also still carried out directly by agencies of the state or federal governments.

Territorially, the amount of power exercised by the panchayats at different levels—village, block (taluka) and district—varies from state to state, as demonstrated in Table 3.

In Maharashtra, for instance, the Zilla Parishad, operating at the district level, occupies the key position in the whole Panchayati Raj setup. All the powers and most of the money to implement development programs have been concentrated in its hands. It receives substantial grants from the state government and also 70% of the land revenue collected in the district (as opposed to 30% distributed to the village panchayats). It may also levy a tax of its own on land revenue. In

Table 3—Classification of Zilla Parishads According to Resource Position

Zilla Parishads with Powers to Levy Taxes, Cess or Fees and receive Government Grants or Assistance	Zilla Parishads with No Power to Levy Taxes, Cess or Fees but receive Government Grants, etc.	Zilla Parishads with no Independent Funds and Whose Expenses are met by Government
Bihar	Orissa	Madras
Andhra Pradesh	Punjab	Mysore
Gujarat	Rajasthan	Assam
Maharashtra		Himachal Pradesh
Uttar Pradesh		

Uttar Pradesh and Gujarat, the center of gravity was intended to be placed more at the village level. Though the Zilla Parishad also has revenue powers, it acts mainly as a supervisory administrative agency.

Despite the formal allocation of powers, however, there has been a general tendency for the *middle level Panchayat Samiti* to grow in effective influence, especially in U.P. and Gujarat. This was one of the reasons why the block or taluka was chosen as the principal unit for observation in this project.[9]

It should be emphasized that the entire Panchayati Raj system does not function in isolation, but in unison with the state and federal systems. The Zilla Parishads and other panchayati institutions are responsible to the Minister of Rural Development at the state level and are also related to the federal Ministry of Food and Agriculture. Thus, the autonomy exercised at the local levels is qualified, partly by the formal delineation of the powers of the panchayats, partly by their heavy dependence on the state and central governments for financial resources, and partly by the fact that, in effect, the panchayats are not independent legislative entities grouped in local authority, but instruments for decentralizing *administration*. They serve, in most of their functions, to carry out programs conceived and supported at the higher levels, although the format attempts to distribute much of the day-to-day responsibility for local implementation to local elected bodies rather than to centrally appointed officials.

The fact that the Panchayati Raj institutions operate within a federal structure also has certain political implications that affect their functioning. There is a close relationship between the local power structure and the power structure at the state and the national level. Thus the state level leadership is deeply interested in the district level power groupings and its configurations. Secondly, there is a two-way traffic from the Panchayati Raj institutions to the state legislature and from the legislature back to Zilla Parishad. The second trend is not as strong as the first one, but it exists. The district level power-pool could be considered the crucial stratum of leadership. For example, in the 1967 elections, as many as 40% of the members of the Panchayati Raj in Maharashtra aspired to run for the state legislature.[10] The story in Gujarat and Uttar Pradesh is similar. However, the oligarchic tendencies of the leadership, friction between the elected and the appointed, and the inherent contradiction between centralized planning and decentralized implementation have adversely affected the functioning of the Panchayati Raj as a system of autonomous local government. In the context of centrally determined plan priorities, schematic budgets and a rigid administrative framework, the scope of local autonomy is in practice severely restricted.

AUTONOMY: (2) PERCEPTIONS OF EFFICACY[11]

Local leaders participating in the system are shrewdly aware of the sharp limits to their practical authority, in contrast to the vaunted objectives of Panchayati Raj.

In response to the survey conducted by the International Studies of Values in Politics, Indian leaders, as compared with those in other countries, considered that their local government had far less autonomy (see Table 4). That is, fewer Indian leaders believed that local government had the power to act effectively in regard to any of the seven areas suggested. It is in regard to housing, jobs, electrification and youth problems that the greatest deficiency is felt. Schools are the area where they see the most likelihood of effective local action. But the bare figures hardly convey the immense gulf between Indian leaders and their counterparts, especially in the United States and Yugoslavia, in their sense of the area of the possible.

There is a significant *regional* difference within India, in the degree of felt autonomy, despite the similarity of actual powers in the three states studied.

Table 4—Perceived Lack of Autonomy

Country	Housing Problems	Jobs	Schools	Clinics	Art and Culture	Electri- city	Youth Problems	Mean for all Area
India	.72	.76	.31	.46	.38	.76	.55	.55
Gujarat	.54	.48	.41	.43	.22	.50	.23	.39
Maharashtra	.86	.92	.30	.52	.50	.89	.83	.69
Uttar Pradesh	.77	.89	.21	.43	.44	.91	.59	.61
Poland	.59	.50	.65	.45	.29	.55	.15	.45
U.S.	.39	.51	.16	.23	.20	.26	.24	.28
Yugoslavia	.16	.25	.15	.24	.16	.15	.13	.18

This table reports the mean response in each country, or state, to the question: "In which of these areas does the local government here lack enough power and autonomy to act effectively?" The maximum score of 1.00 would indicate that all leaders stated that the local government *lacked* sufficient autonomy in a given area.

Leaders in Gujarat express a markedly stronger sense of local efficacy than those in Maharashtra and U.P. In many communities in the latter two states, leaders are virtually unanimous in *denying* that the local government has adequate powers to cope with such matters as housing, jobs or the problems of youth.

Parallel to this finding, Indian leaders, when asked who *should* undertake major responsibility for action in these areas, turned more to the central or state government than to local institutions (See Table 5). In other words, they tend to accept a lack of local autonomy not only as a fact, but as desirable. They are content to function within the tradition of centralized initiative and direction, rather than to champion the new order of democratic self-management propounded by the ideology of Panchayati Raj.

What is even more discomfitting to the advocates of autonomy is the finding that the leadership of the more active blocks (in terms of adopting new techniques of social and economic development) tends to feel more strongly than others that their local government *lacks* power and that they should depend on the *higher* levels of government to do the development jobs.[12]

Table 5—Aspiration for Autonomy: Who Should Do What?

Country	(1) Central or State Government	(2) Local Government	(3) Local non-Governmental Institutions	(4) Leave to People
India	3.32	2.44	.57	.62
Gujarat	2.85	2.78	.55	.76
Maharashtra	3.80	2.24	.66	.25
Uttar Pradesh	3.30	2.32	.50	.85
Poland	1.47	4.83	.50	.18
U.S.	1.33	2.96	1.84	.77
Yugoslavia	2.29	3.27	.88	.46

This table reports the mean number of functions (out of seven specified) for which respondents considered that primary responsibility should be (1) undertaken by the central or state government, (2) undertaken by local government, (3) undertaken by local nongovernmental institutions (cooperatives, etc.), or (4) left to the people to work out personally. Maximum score: 7.00.

The conclusion seems inescapable that Panchayati Raj has yet to "catch on" with the very leaders who must make it work if this experiment in using democratic political processes as a mobilizer of development effort is to succeed.

THE STRUCTURE OF DECISION-MAKING

Formally, the structures of Panchayati Raj roots developmental decision-making in the hands of villagers through their elected representatives.

At the base, the Gram Panchayat, or village council, consists of five to thirty members elected directly for four years. It acts as an executive committee of the Gram Sabha, a general meeting of adult villagers held at least twice a year, but whose attendance often suffers from apathy.[13] The Sarpanch, or chairman, of the Grampanchayat is elected by the other members in Gujarat and Maharashtra, but in Uttar Pradesh he is directly elected at the Gram Sabha.

The composition of the next tier of panchayats, at the block level, varies from state to state. In Gujarat and Uttar Pradesh, the Panchayat Samiti is automatically made up of all Sarpanches in the block; but in Maharashtra representatives are elected by groups of Grampanchayats, to whom are added *ex officio* the members of the Zilla Parishad who have been elected from the concerned block. Representation of women and the scheduled castes is secured by cooption if not by election.

Most members of the Zilla Parishad, or district council, which is at the apex of the Panchayati Raj, are in the three states under study directly elected on the basis of adult franchise. In addition, chairmen of the Panchayat Samitis are *ex officio* members. In Gujarat and Uttar Pradesh the Panchayat Samitis also elect additional representatives from among their number. In these two states, but not in Maharashtra, district members of the Union Parliament and the state legislatures are *ex officio* members of the Zilla Parishad. In all three states, members are coopted from or elected by the cooperatives, as institutions intimately concerned with development; women and persons belong to scheduled Castes and Tribes are also coopted, as much to stimulate a greater sense of self-respect and community recognition on their part as to give them an active voice. The Zilla Parishad is thus ingeniously contrived to be independently responsive to the general population, while assuring that the regular political leadership of the district will not be bypassed in its decision-making.

While the system, on the surface, decentralizes developmental decision-making, the structure is so designed that administrative and fiscal control at every level coordinates local action with centrally determined objectives. The Panchayati Raj Administration in the district is headed by a senior civil servant appointed by the state government. At the block level, the Block Development Officer, a civil servant, serves as executive secretary of the Panchayat Samiti. Budgetary control is effected by having the budget for each level subject to approval by the organ at the next higher level. Ultimately, it is, of course, largely dependent on funds allocated by the state government through the District Development Officer.

In practice, developmental decision-making insofar as it does operate through the Panchayati Raj, is strongly influenced by the political parties. It had been hoped that parties would abstain from participating in these institutions.[14] But the compulsions of political power led them instead to compete for their control. Without strengthening their position at the grass roots, party leaders feared they would be unable to capture positions at the state and national levels. Also, they saw in the Panchayati Raj institutions a new source of patronage.

Consequently, first the Congress Party, then others, proceeded to organize new units at the district level, deliberately designed to manipulate the Zilla Parishad. These units, usually consisting of all party members in the Zilla Parishad plus the president and secretary of the district Party committee, function as a caucus, determining in advance of the formal meeting what decisions shall be put forward. This has also occurred at the block level in regard to the Panchayat Samiti. When a single party dominates, as usual, the net effect is to transfer the decision-making power out of the Panchayati Raj into the hands of the local party leaders; this explains in part why decisions in the panchayat institutions are generally unanimous.

Party control also extends to the cooperatives that are the source of much of the economic initiative in the community—distributing credit, seeds and fertilizers and managing the sale and purchase of agricultural produce. Thus, what might have been an independent influence in developmental decisions also fell under political domination, and resulted in further, almost monolithic concentration of decisional power, especially whenever and wherever one party ruled virtually unchallenged.

The intrusion of party into Panchayati Raj reinforced the built-in elements of administrative centralization, and seriously undercut the intended broadening of the decision-making process. At its best, such a system may in time feed back up through its various organs and parallel administrative structure, the ideas, initiatives—and remonstrances—of an increasingly responsible and capable citizenry, even to the point of influencing development policy at the top. But for the interim, the most to be expected is probably an increased identification of local leadership with the programs they are offered from above, as they secure political recognition for their part in implementing them. In short, with Panchayati Raj, the *power* of decision remains concentrated and centralized in the political and administrative hierarchies, though in form it seems dispersed through the various organs of local self-government.

The Polish Local
Political System

The Polish People's Republic has a centralized system of local administration, linking together relatively autonomous local authorities by a vertical subordination to higher levels of government. The structure of local governments is based on the Constitution of 1952 and the People's Council Act of 1958 with subsequent amendments. The legislative acts eliminated the division of local authorities into self-government (elected) and administrative (nominated-appointed), and introduced a uniform system of governmental authority.

At the end of 1965, there were 17 woiwodships and 5 city territories with the powers of a woiwodship; 391 powiats of which 74 were separate city territories; 789 towns within the powiats; 102 settlements; and 5,238 gromadas, or administrative units comprising several villages and functioning as the lowest link of state authority in rural areas.

The units included in this study were powiats with a mixed urban-rural population (town-village), excluding the city territories. The units studied have a majority of rural population, not dominated by either a rural or urban character, and reflect the general social structure of Poland.

There is great diversity in size, numbers of people, economic development, and industrialization across the 317 mixed urban-rural powiats.[15] Six percent of the powiats had less than 500 square kilometers, and seven percent had over 1500 square kilometers, with slightly over half in the range of 500–1000 square kilometers. Although over 80% of all powiats had a population between 30,000 and 100,000, the range varied from 17,300 to 193,400. Wide differences in density also prevail. The national average was 101 per square kilometer, but 45% of the powiats had less than 50 persons per square kilometer, and 7 of them exceed 250 people. About two-thirds of the powiats had from 10–40% urban population and 47 powiats have a majority of urban population. In industrial employment, again about two-thirds had less than 60 persons per 1000 people, but in 42 powiats there were over 120 per 1000, the national average being 119.

AUTONOMY

The autonomy of the powiats was increased in 1963 with the amendments to the People's Councils Act widening the financial powers of the powiat councils. The powiat people's councils have the income from payments from profits by establishments subordinate to the council, turnover tax on operations not involving transfer of goods, income tax on cooperatives, turnover and income tax from private sectors, land tax, tax on acquisition of property rights, income from the State Soil Fund, fees for transport facilities in the gromadas, income from electrification, and taxes on alcohol fixed by the councils. The budget of the powiat includes direct grants and equalizing subsidies from the central government. In recent years the proportion of all funds raised locally has increased relatively to that from the central government.

There are uniform provisions for all local subordinate units in Poland. This is defined in Article 19 of the People's Council Act: "Powiat people's councils and the city councils in cities constituting city territories are competent in all matters within the competences of the people's councils with the exclusion of matters reserved for the competences of the people's councils at a higher level." The powiats, thus, have residual powers, or all powers to act in areas not given to another level. Within these restrictions, the powiat can opt for their own programs.

Despite the extension of formal autonomy in 1963, the local leaders sampled in this study did not see that they had wide latitude in many areas of local decision-making. Half or more felt that the organs of powiat government lacked sufficient powers to deal adequately with housing, jobs, schools, and the provision of electric power. Nearly half considered local autonomy insufficient in the area of health. Only in regard to youth affairs and cultural matters did a substantial number of leaders consider the local powers adequate for effective action. Of course, these perceptions in large part reflect the distribution of powers in the Polish political system. Comparatively, Polish powiat leaders perceive almost as little autonomy as their counterparts in India and significantly less than those in the United States and, especially, Yugoslavia.

The uniformity of local powers and the vertical relationships between the levels consist of several components. First the highest institution of governmental power in a defined territory is the People's Council, whose members are elected by direct ballot. Secondly, the People's Council elects the chief administrative officials in a Praesidium. Thirdly, the local administrative agencies are subject not only to the People's Council and the Praesidium, but also to the relevant administrative departments of the People's Council at a higher level. Finally, the People's Councils at a higher level have the right to veto the decisions of the People's Councils at a lower level; in the case of powiats, this power rests with the woiwodship, and for the woiwodship, the Council of State of the Polish People's Republic.

How they carry out their responsibilities can be seen by an examination of their structures and functions.

STRUCTURE AND FUNCTIONS

The major components of the formal structure of powiats are the People's Council; the Praesidium of the People's Council; Departments of the People's Council and Praesidium; and Commissions of the People's Council.

The People's Council holds a plenary session usually once every two months, with allowance for special sessions at the request of 25% of the members. In plenary session, the Council adopts economic plans and the budget, establishes or recalls its agencies, reviews the work of agencies charged with administration, issues administrative directives, assesses the work of institutions not subordinate to the powiat but operating in the powiat area, and hears petitions from the electors. The People's Council performs these tasks as the highest authority within its territory.

The Praesidium of the Council is an executive organ of the Council. It is elected by the Council in secret ballot from members of the council or others. The structure of the Praesidium includes a chairman, a deputy chairman (in some cases a second deputy chairman is allowed), a secretary, and not more than three members. The chairman, deputy chairman, and secretary automatically become full time officers of the Council; the other members remain part-time. The responsibilities of the Praesidium include the preparation of the plenary sessions of the Council, the designing of draft economic plans and budgets, the overseeing of the work of institutions under control of the Council, and the issuance of regulations based on existing laws.

The Praesidium can set up the following departments: (1) building, architecture, and town planning; (2) budget; (3) finances; (4) communal services and housing; (5) transportation; (6) legal and organizational affairs; (7) education and culture; (8) industry and trade; (9) agriculture and forestry; (10) farm produce purchasing; (11) internal affairs; (12) employment; (13) health and welfare; and (14) water, pollution, physical culture, tourism, and roads. For these departments, the praesidium appoints the heads and deputies, who meet the qualifications set by the Council, such as education. The department heads are responsible to the chairman of the Praesidium, who is the chief of all of the heads of the departments. In addition, the departments are subordinated vertically to the appropriate departments of the woiwodship councils, which can give directives and change the decisions of the powiat departments.

Commissions are composed of a minimum of seven persons elected by the Council from its own membership and from the outside, at least half of whom must be councilors. Commissions may be set up in the following areas: (1) budget and economic planning; (2) law enforcement and security; (3) agriculture and forestry; (4) building and communal services; (5) public facilities; (6) health, employment and welfare; (7) culture and education; and (8) transportation. During 1965–1969,

28,059 people were active as members of the Commissions, 16,360 of whom were councilors. The chairmen of the Commissions are appointed by the People's Councils, while other officials are selected by the Commissions themselves.

The responsibilities of the Commissions include establishing liaison with the population and organizations in the powiat, initiation of projects to be considered by the Council, examination of matters proposed by the Council or the Praesidium, supervision of the operations of departments under the jurisdiction of the Council, factories, and other institutions, and maintenance of "civic" control over institutions outside of the jurisdiction of the Council.

The role of political parties and social organizations is much more complex than the formal structure. Political parties have a central place among all social and political organizations. The Polish party system is characterized by three parties, the Polish United Workers Party, the United Peasant Party, and the Democratic Party (with memberhips in 1965 of 1,894,895; 367,032; and 74,445 respectively); a stable pattern of cooperation between them; and the hegemony, within that alliance, of the Marxist-Leninist Polish United Workers Party.

The leading role of the PUWP in the tripartite alliance is based on its strong social position nationally and across all social milieus (the United Peasant party is based on peasants and the Democratic Party on an urban intermediary strata), its ideology that defines the goals for the whole system, and whose preeminence is recognized by the other two parties, and its control of the majority of governmental positions, including the national Parliament and the People's Councils, with party activists exerting decisive influence over the general policies of social organizations. The PUWP, however, works in consultation and cooperation with other parties within the interparty commissions and with both the other parties and social organizations within the Committees of the National Unity Front. Although the PUWP is the leader and hegemonist within this broad alliance, it recognizes the independence of the other parties and the autonomy of social organizations.

The political party system is manifest at the powiat level. Studies of local authorities in Poland point to the key role of the powiat committee of the PUWP in shaping policy in the powiat. Its crucial role at the local level stems from the fact that the powiat party organizations are directing the implementation of development programs of the country at the powiat level. Further, the PUWP is influential, often decisive, in policy matters, and particularly in the selection of people to important positions. It has a large number of activists who act to reconcile multiple and often conflicting interests of groups, and forms the most important local link with the national party hierarchy and thus with the higher echelons of the central government. Again, although the PUWP has a leading role at the local level, the significance of other parties and social organizations remains. Together they take part in managing local affairs, nominating candidates to the People's Council on joint lists of the National Unity Front, and presenting resolutions to the appropriate authorities.

A number of organizations, active both nationally and in powiats, are part of the political system at the local level. Articulation of interests takes place in the following kinds of organizations: trade unions (8,070,300); Union of Socialist Youth (994,243); Union of Peasant Youth (813,685); Polish Student Association (144,194); Polish Scouts Union (1,752,215); Women's League (169,665); Union of Fighters for Freedom and Democracy (veterans, 204,852); Voluntary People's Militia Reserve (260,932); and Voluntary Fire Brigades Union (444,078).

The People's Councils themselves provide platforms for obtaining expression of concerns from a broad base of citizens. At the end of 1966, there were 171,101 people elected to People's Councils, composed of 2346 for the woiwodships, 22,218 for the powiats and the city territories constituting powiats, and 146,447 for the gromada, town, borough and settlement councils.

The local leadership is composed of leaders holding key posts in the following three institutional circles: (1) the formal structure of power, the institutions discussed above and other state organs at the local level, such as the prosecutor's office; (2) voluntary structures, most importantly the Polish United Workers Party, but including other parties and organizations active in the powiat; and (3) the structure of economic activity, particularly in the management of large industrial and economic organizations. The structure of power and influence throughout Poland is highly institutionalized. A leader popular by force of his own personal virtues may add to the importance of an institutional role, but this is the exception. The position of an individual is generally and almost entirely derived from his position in the institutionalized and formal power system. Narojek, in his study of power in a small town, for example, started with "not individuals, distinguished because of their influence over local matters, but organizations."[16] The way in which leaders were defined and selected in this study on the basis of formal positions is especially well suited to Poland, for the circles of formal and actual power closely coincide.

The three institutionalized circles of power are closely intertwined, particularly by the same individual holding more than one position in the powiat. The secretary of the PUWP is usually a member of the Praesidium, while the chairman of the Praesidium holds a similar post in the structure of the party of which he is a member. In another way of linkage, the director of a large industrial establishment will almost certainly be a member of the People's Council and a party committee. Because of this structural cohesion of the collectivity of the powiat leaders, a higher degree of similarity in their values can be expected.

THE POLISH POWIAT: A CONCLUSION

The political system of Poland is highly centralized, clearly substantially more centralized than any other country in this study. If we were to ask to what extent does the powiat form a local community— what does it imply for social relationships—we would have to conclude that the powiat is too large and too populous to meet the definition of a community as a territorial unit within which individuals can and do have face-to-face interaction. Taking the powiat as a political unit, however, we can say that, on the one hand, it is large enough to have extensive administrative and political functions as well as the institutions for implementing social policy and a substantial enough group of leaders to study as a single entity, and, on the other hand, it is sufficiently small so that it is possible for local leaders to have direct, close contacts not only among themselves but with the population as well. The leaders can have a direct impact on the character of the powiat.

Governing U.S.
Municipalities

Local government in the United States is composed of 50 separate types of local governments. Although each of the 50 states retains the right to design its own pattern of local government, there are great similarities in the structure of local governments throughout the country.

THE INSTITUTIONS OF LOCAL GOVERNMENT

The basic pattern of local government was set at the time of the founding of the country. When states were admitted to the Federal Union, they submitted a constitution to Congress. The state constitutions provide for the basic structure of local government, which is further defined by legislation, court rulings, and practice. Of all of the countries in this study, the United States probably has the most institutionalized form of local government, which has retained a basic pattern in existence for several decades. Whatever changes have occurred have taken place largely at the instigation of local reform movements to increase popular control and to improve the administrative capability of local governments. These reforms continue to this day.

Local government is a "creature" of the state. Forty-seven of the fifty states are broken down in 3043 counties, approximately 18,000 municipalities, 38,000 school districts and 18,000 special districts, devoted to one or a limited number of functions. Townships generally are concentrated in the eastern and middle western sections of the country, and in many states their importance has declined with the urbanization of the United States. School districts, like special districts, have restricted functions and their importance varies from state to state.

The American system of local government, like some other countries, is based on an urban and rural pattern where the county, and in some cases the township, is basically rural, and the municipality is urban—the focus of this study. In some cases the city and county overlap much the same area, such as Cook County and the city of Chicago.

Although there is some uniformity in the structure and functions of counties within a state, the municipalities (including in some states, urban places and boroughs) vary widely not only in the nature of their socio-economic infra-structure, but also in their legal powers. Most states have passed legislation for classes of cities. Indeed, in some cases, the legislation pertains to a single city in the state. The powers to tax, provide services, and borrow money are proscribed for these classes of cities. One speaks of a city charter, which generally is a composite of state constitutional provisions, state legislation, court rulings, and administrative practice that defines the governing role of the cities. In several states there are home rule provisions providing a city with the right to design its own "constitution," while in principle the state reserves sovereign power.

Most Americans live in cities. These, however, vary from several million to less than five thousand in population. According to the 1965 census of the some 18,000 cities reported, 27 had over 500,000 population, but altogether only about 3000 had over 5000 people. Many cities are a part of a conglomerate of cities, counties, townships, and special districts in what is officially called metropolitan areas. But size is only one major difference. The problems that cities face are another. On the one hand, there is New York City, with more people on welfare than the entire populations of several other major cities; on the other hand, there are well-administered cities of 30,000 with no welfare cases.

Although the counties retain their paramount position as local administrators of state responsibilities, when they function in urban areas they share the problems of municipalities. The county is the effective unit of local government in the rural, less populated area, but with less than 5% of the United States working force engaged in agriculture, the county in rural areas accounts for a small part of the local governmental mosaic in the United States.

Each citizen lives under a set of layers of government. For example, a person in the eastern part of the United States may be subject to, in addition to the federal government, his state, county, city, school district, a water district, a township, and perhaps even a general transportation authority. Each of the units of government, in order to be called a government, has to have some autonomy to raise its own revenue and to select some of its own officials, in ways independent of superior authorities. The power to raise revenue, usually through some form of taxation, to some extent defines the authority and autonomy of the local political unit. In addition to the usual view of autonomy as the allocation of powers to a subordinate unit, there is also the possibility that powers may be divided between units at the same level of government, such as, city and county, or city and school district.

Several levels of government are interlaced in a particular locality. For example, in a city there will be not only federal offices and federal programs staffed with federal appointees, but also state officials, the county building with its personnel and then, of course, city hall itself. Generally there is an overlap of functions, such as, for example, in narcotics control, a matter of concern for the city police, the county sheriff, the state police, the U.S. Department of Treasury and the Federal Bureau of Investigation. Where there is a variety of levels of government involved in a policy area, there is both friendly cooperation and sometimes outright and damaging competition. Within their respective spheres of activity, each of these units has some autonomy.

Although in principle the local governmental units below the state level are agents of the states, in practice, especially during recent years, there are a variety of other constraints. The limits of what a city can do depends first of all on the state provisions, secondly, on competition or even formal contracts with neighboring units of government, such as an intergovernmental compact to share facilities or exchange services, and thirdly, on certain federal programs. Many local units, especially cities but traditionally counties, share in the operation of federal programs such as the job retraining centers, poverty programs, sewerage construction, and, of course, the traditional agricultural agents assigned to counties. These federal programs, although usually based on voluntary participation, do restrict the discretion of local units in return for the benefit of federal revenues.

In governing urban America, the federal government has access to revenues, the states have the formal responsibility, and the municipalities have the job. Although in most cases counties can raise most of the necessary money for their jobs, the cities and school districts are increasingly dependent on direct or indirect assistance from the state and federal governments. In part this is due to the exhaustion of the taxation capacity of local governments, which rely heavily on property taxes when most of the wealth is centered in industry and personal incomes. Particularly in the large cities of the northeast, there is a feeling that the cities are in great need of additional revenue. Although there has been a rapid increase in the use of state and local income taxes and increases in local sales taxes, centers of industrial wealth and upper income people continue to shift out of the reach of the central cities into suburbs.

The local governments bear the brunt of supplying services to the population. In 1960, for example, of all governmental revenue, the federal government spent approximately 30%, the states 24%, and all other local units 46%. In recent years, state and local expenditures have been increasing over federal nondefense related expenditures at a three to two ratio.

Despite the formal dependency on the state and the increasing financial dependency on the state and federal governments, local political units in the United States have a great deal of autonomy in what they can do and how they can do it. Many of them, in addition to traditional service functions of water, sewerage, roads, education and the like, have taken to subsidizing museums and theatres, owning and operating, often indirectly, public utilities (especially electricity), administering massive recreation programs, and researching their own operations. Within some broad limits, local governments, particularly municipalities, have a wide range of options open, if not the capacity to select them. Even if some option is not open, it is possible for the cities to lobby in the state legislatures or in Congress for legislation authorizing or financing what they feel necessary.

There is great diversity not only across the states but also within states in the actual autonomy of local governments. In general the larger the city, the greater the autonomy to select its own course. Furthermore, many of the political leaders of major cities have become formidable political forces within the country since many have more people under their jurisdiction than some of the state governors.

What probably prevails in most local governments is a feeling that they have the legal power to deal with problems, but not the capacity to raise the resources in the face of mounting demands. These problems stem largely from migration from the farms during the last two decades, particularly from the South to major urban areas, the increased demands for services, and the consequences of industrialization. One of the older problems of local government in the United States is that the problems have spilled over their legal boundaries; these problems include air and water pollution, transportation systems, and employment. All of these problems are larger than any single local government (indeed, than many states) can cope with in terms of the geographical limitations on their authority.

Despite these growing difficulties, most U.S. leaders interviewed in this study expressed confidence that the various units of local government did have sufficient power to provide effectively for schools, public utilities and social services, and to meet the problems of youth. They were less confident about the ability to handle housing and, especially, employment needs. Overall, the sense of local efficacy is much stronger in the United States than in India, but considerably weaker than in Yugoslavia.

In respect to who *should* take on responsibility for such activities, U.S. leaders are overwhelmingly committed to local initiative—governmental and nongovernmental. Less than 20% of the possible choices called on the national government to assume the primary role in coping with these needs.[17]

Thus local autonomy is deeply grounded in American political consciousness and obviously conditions the basic disposition of the American toward governmental action.

STRUCTURE

The structure of local governments is quite diverse within a set of general parameters. Most counties and townships in a state have set structures, such as a county commission (elected), and administrators (several appointed). In American cities certain common structures have diffused throughout the country.

The most dominant form of municipal structure in the United States is the mayor-council form, in which councilmen elected either from various constituencies or "at large" (by the entire population) form a legislative body, and the mayor, independently elected, functions both as a chief legislator and as the city's executive. The two types of mayor-council forms are the weak and strong mayor, the distinguishing factor being the relative power of the mayor vis-a-vis the council. The strong mayor usually has extensive powers of appointment and removal of administrative heads of various agencies, as well as the power to veto ordinances passed by the council. This form is usually found in large cities. The weak mayor is usually confronted by a set of administrative officials—auditor, city attorney, water commissioner, etc., chosen in election—and lacks, or is seriously constrained in his power to veto municipal ordinances. Of course, in keeping with the general structure of American government, there is an independent judiciary.

The second most frequent structure that is dominant in cities of middle size, 25,000–250,000 (the size range that constituted the universe in this study) is the council manager. There is an elected council, and the council appoints a manager, who meets certain professional standards and has the job of chief administrator. The manager can be, within certain contractual limits, hired and fired by the council. The council also appoints, usually upon recommendation of the manager, the administrative officials of the city.

Finally, there is the commission form, where certain administrative heads—auditor, water commissioner, city clerk, etc.—are directly elected, and not only perform administrative functions but also sit together as a municipal council. This type of government is found in only about 8% of all the cities.

County governments have a set of commissioners, usually about five, and some directly elected administrators, such as sheriffs, and appointed officials. The number of elected officials varies a great deal from state to state. Townships, in a similar manner, have elected and appointed people, as do the school districts and special districts.

What characterizes local government in the United States is a division between elected officials who perform legislative policy-making functions and others, both elected and appointed, who act as administrators. But over 90% of the local officials are appointed to office. What defines local government is the independent nature of the selection of officials, and their powers to decide on revenues and expenditures independently of other levels of government.

The structure of political parties follows the basic structure of the U.S. government. State political parties federate for national elections; local political parties, particularly at the county level, are the basic components of the state party system. Most cities have Democratic and Republican competition for office, although several cities have developed their own local parties; these, however, are usually identified with one of the two major parties. Some cities have non-partisan elections; again, contestants can usually be identified with one of the major parties. The election process has two formal stages: nomination and the election proper. In cities with party contests, the officials of the local party organization are important. However, during this century there is at least formal popular control through the direct primary, in which all members of the political party can participate in choosing the nominees of the party.

At the local level, one or another political party is usually dominant. They will often be active in the appointment of local officials. In most states the key party unit is the county, with a chairman and vice-chairman, who often have the primary responsibility for the conduct of the party in the county and, in some cases, are considered "bosses." The party organization is broken down into precincts (or sometimes wards), which are generally coterminous with election units (of approximately 500–1000 people) and are managed by a chairman and chairwoman who are often elected in the party primaries.

Local governments, especially in cities, contain many civic and other organizations with an interest in the conduct of government. Unions, business organizations, civic clubs, veterans and the like may be active not only in the electoral process but also in the day-to-day affairs as representatives on special boards or as purveyors of special policies. There are also city or county wide charitable efforts, as represented by the United Fund (a form of behavior used in this research to assess activeness), which plays an important role in providing financial support for hundreds of organizations committed, at least officially, to improving the city or some segment of it.

During the last few years there has been substantial growth in research on who runs local government and what differences this makes. This research is often conducted on one or a very few local governing units; consequently it is difficult to generalize about the "informal" or "real" power structures. The research does seem to indicate, however, that people holding formal decision-making positions are also influential and sometimes decisive in what happens, but that a variety of other groups and individuals are also involved, in a way that appears not consistent across local units, indicating many cases of highly fragmented effective power.

AMERICAN LOCAL GOVERNMENT: A CONCLUSION

There are over 90,000 units recognized by the U.S. Bureau of Census as local governments. Although these vary in detail from state to state, there are several uniformities of powers, problems faced, and formal structure. Their powers, especially in municipalities, are often broad in range, but effective over only a limited geographical area, and hampered by actual and legal constraints on revenues; the constraints on revenue create severe limitations on what a local government can realistically attempt to achieve. As a result, municipal leaders, often acting together at one of their regularly scheduled meetings, are trying to work out new relationships with both the state and the federal government.

Within the bounds of these similarities, however, there is great diversity of programs, successes, and prospects for the future. In any event it is no secret that the United States has a problem governing its urban population. One factor in this is the municipal governments, one stratum of whose behavior is examined in this research.

Self-Government in the
Yugoslav Commune

Local government in Yugoslavia has undergone deep changes, both structural and other, during the last 20 years, a process reflecting a general change in the social structure in Yugoslavia prompted by speedy industrialization of the country, and the progressive implementation of the principle of social self-management as the socio-political basis for the whole political system.

In the initial post-war phase of centralized state administration, local government was directed from above through administrative units that corresponded more or less to inherited muncipalities and people's committees of national liberation created during the national liberation war (1941–1945). The main characteristic of these elected bodies of the revolutionary local government was their autonomy and all embracing activity during the war. They existed both in liberated territory and occupied areas. Owing to the need for a centralization of resources and power, the people's committees lost much of their autonomy immediately after the war, as they were above all local representatives of the central government. However, after the introduction of workers' self-management in economic enterprises and other institutions (1950), this principle (self-management) was extended to local communities in order to develop their self-governing autonomy. At the same time a territorial enlargement and economic strengthening of the commune took place.

Consequently, the 7866 municipalities and 427 administrative districts that existed in the country in 1947 gave way, by 1963, to 548 communes that became the pivotal units of local self-government throughout the country. The present Yugoslav commune averages 33,000 inhabitants and covers an approximate area of 44 square kilometers. But size varies greatly, some urban communes having as many as 100,000 inhabitants, whereas some rural communes have less than 10,000.

As a rule, a commune is developed around an urbanized center with economic potential and a hub of schools, hospitals, social welfare facilities, and business organizations. Large cities, such as Beograd, Zagreb and Ljubljana, are divided into several communes, with a city council to coordinate action on issues of common interest to the city as a whole. Groups of small communes in economically integrated areas also may have their joint council to facilitate activities of common interest. The district has been practically abolished as an administrative unit. However, commune assemblies of neighboring communes are used to create joint councils or other organs to coordinate matters of common interest.

THE BASES OF AUTONOMY

The commune is an autonomous and self-governing community within the integral socio-political system of Yugoslavia. As such it is neither an organ of the central government, as was the municipality in the first phase of Yugoslav socialist development, nor does it receive its rights from the central authority.

Basic principles concerning the structure of self-government in a commune were set forth by the Law on Workers' Councils in 1950 and the Law on Organization of Communes and Districts in 1955. These were later sanctioned by the Constitution of 1963. But the actual application of these provisions comes from a statute adopted autonomously by each commune; this is its basic law of self-government.

The statute of the Commune is a specific kind of constitutional law. Through provisions concerning concrete relationships in the commune, and especially the self-governing rights of man, the statute brings about an ever closer participation of the individual citizen in the management of social affairs. This process provides and safeguards, every member of the local community, his real position in every social relation.

The statute elaborates in a detailed form the mechanism of self-government in the commune. It specifies the relations among different self-governing bodies, the place and role of commune administration, the organs of control and supervision, the procedures to be used in exercising authority and realization of rights, and the relationship of the commune to the larger territorial units, such as district and republic.

But the commune is not only a framework of citizens' self-government; it also discharges certain functions of the state. It has to guarantee material conditions for work and assure the participation of all in social self-management, as well as protect other rights and freedoms guaranteed by the Constitution. Furthermore, the commune has to protect the socially owned property and private property of individual citizens, and see to their personal security and the maintenance of public order. And finally, the commune has to ensure the role of law and provide legal assistance to citizens.

To carry out its manifold responsibilities, the commune has assumed major fiscal powers. Besides raising revenue to meet administrative expenses, it played a large role in mobilizing and managing investment for economic and social development. The commune assembly could decide investment priorities, supervise the utilization of resources by enterprises, set up equalization funds, and undertake other measures to solve problems relating to the local economy and the performance of other activities. However, the practice of investment in economic undertakings by the commune has now been almost completely abandoned, the funding of these activities being left to enterprises and their associations within a unified crediting system.

The recent abandonment of specific commune investment funds has been a most decisive factor in eliminating autarchic practices within the commune proper, and in the stimulation of free integration founded on individual incentive, common interest, and autonomy of enterprises. This has served progressively to eliminate state-administrative elements from the running of economic and other activities, and has transferred direct responsibility for efficient unification of social savings to the work organizations that actually created them. The Commune Assembly may, however, still exercise its influence to promote efficient utilization of its accumulated resources through corresponding decisions by its bodies, as well as through control within the framework of competence conferred on it by the Constitution.

If a commune cannot meet expenses for elementary schooling, essential health services and social welfare, the government of the republic is constitutionally obligated to provide subsidies. The higher level of government may also grant credit on favorable terms to speed the economic development of the commune. But this assistance is definitely supplementary to what the commune itself, and enterprises within the area of the commune, do independently.

Social self-government rests not only on a territorial basis, i.e., within the framework of the mechanism of the commune, but also on a functional basis. As a matter of fact, self-government on a territorial basis and the self-management in enterprises, and all other work organizations represent two parts of a unique system of participation of the people in the decision-making process, a system that is as direct as possible.

It would be inconceivable to develop genuine local self-government without a provision for workers' self-management in enterprises and institutions. This represents the material basis for political rights of the individual. In other words, the working man can realize, through the system of functional self-management, his right to dispose of the results of his work. At the same time, this imposes upon him the responsibility not only for the sound performance of his factory or institution, but also for the development of schools, hospitals, social welfare, and other facilities to improve social and individual standards of living. Therefore, self-government in local communities is a natural extension of self-management in enterprises and institutions. Every factory and institution has its own autonomously elected bodies of self-management—workers councils, managing boards, commissions, workers' assemblies, etc.

In keeping with general regulations and norms delineated by the Constitution and laws, as well as on the basis of its own statute, every work organization autonomously makes decisions on the following matters: production plans, prices and marketing, organization of work, promotion of the material basis of its activity, including expansion and modernization of enterprise, new investments, cooperation and merging with other work organizations or cessation, distribution of income, employment of new labor or cessation of this relationship, labor safety and general protection of the health of workers and office employees, vocational training, rest and recreation, general development of social and personal standards of living of all members of its collective, etc.

Work organizations are linked to the territorial framework of commune mechanism of self-government through the election of a special self-management chamber of the assembly of the commune.

THE STRUCTURE OF DECISION-MAKING

In the commune citizens participate in decision-making through diverse forms of self-government: directly, through voting, assemblies, the referendum, meetings of the Socialist Alliance (the all embracing social-political organization) neighborhood communities, and other media; indirectly, through representation on the assembly of the commune and its organs.

(1) THE COMMUNE ASSEMBLY

The most important organ of self-government is the Commune Assembly. As a legislative and executive organ, its decisions are vital for the creation of adequate conditions and appropriate socio-economic development on one hand, and to safeguard the right of each citizen to exercise that right on the other.

The structure of the Commune Assembly reflects the interdependence of the individual's interests as a worker on the one hand and as a resident of the community on the other, by linking self-management in work communities with self-government in the territorial community. It is a bicameral body with legislative and executive power and has two chambers that enjoy equal rights; the commune chamber represents the whole population of the community, the chamber of self-management represents the people in their various occupations and specific fields of activity. The first chamber is elected by all citizens in the commune over 18 years of age; the other is elected by all working people in the enterprises and institutions in which they work, regardless of age. More developed communes, where economic and social life is ramified and complex, have special chambers of self-management, concerned with economic, educational and cultural, social welfare and health matters. In such cases, these chambers, functioning together, are the counterparts to the first chamber, each one acting as a partner in matters coming under its specific competence. It means that all legislation, as well as any decision, has to be adopted in identical texts.

The Commune Assembly elects commissions and councils. Commissions are composed only of members of the assembly and act as auxiliary bodies concerned with internal matters of the assembly, e.g., a commission for elections and appointments, a commission for grievances and proposals. Councils serve as executive organs of the assembly within their respective sphere of activity, e.g., a council for planning and financial affairs, a council for communal services, a council for education, culture and science, and a council for health and welfare. The membership of a council is mixed, consisting of members of the assembly and other citizens appointed by the assembly on the basis of proposals and recommendations of the voters' assemblies. This mixed composition facilitates direct participation of a larger number of citizens in the running of the affairs of the commune.

The Commune Assembly elects its president, its vice-president and chairmen of the chambers. The assembly also elects and dismisses judges of the commune court.

The president represents the assembly vis-à-vis other bodies and organisations. He is responsible for the functioning of the assembly and for coordinating the work of the council and the commissions of the assembly. He convenes the assembly and presides over joint sessions. The president also supervises the performance of the assembly's administration.

The Commune Assembly elects deputies to all four chambers of the assembly of the constituent republic, as well as to the Federal Assembly (with the exception of members of the chamber of nationalities, who are nominated by the assemblies of constituent republics), from among the candidates nominated at voters' meetings. Candidates for the first chamber (social-political chamber, also called chamber of communes), elected by the Commune Assembly, are in turn subject to the approval of general elections through secret ballot. The elections of candidates for the three chambers of self-management is final.

The term of office of members of the Commune Assembly is four years. According to the 1963 Constitution 50% of the membership is replaced by new members every two years (rotation). No one may be elected twice in succession to the same chamber of the same assembly (limitation of reelection). The purpose of the outlined principles is to ensure continuity in the performance of the assembly and to keep permanently open access to this representative body. By amendments to the Constitution that were adopted by the Federal Assembly in December 1968, instead of the principle of rigid rotation, the possibility of an election twice in succession has been allowed, and the whole membership may be renewed every four years.

In order to carry out its tasks, the Commune Assembly has important powers at its disposal. It adopts autonomously the statute of the commune. It passes a plan of development in conformity with the plans of wider territorial communities—the constituent republic and the Federation. Every year it adopts a budget and a social plan, encompassing all activities in the commune.

The Commune Assembly may found enterprises and institutions in its territory, make recommendations concerning their work, and place them under official receivership should they fail to function efficiently (i.e., should they be unable to ensure at least the conservation of the basic capital of their enterprise). Once affairs improve and the enterprise regains its stability and effectiveness, the autonomy guaranteed by law and the rights of self-management are restored to it. A special procedure has been provided by law in order to avoid any arbitrary interference with the self-managing rights of work organizations. But, pending the conclusive decision of the Constitutional Court, the Commune Assembly may stay the execution of any decision taken by organs of self-management of a work organization, if the decision obviously violates the provisions formulated by the Constitution and the law.

The assembly autonomously organizes and develops its own administration and different services of supervision, control, planning, accounting, public safety, etc. The secretary of the assembly heads the administration. All the staff of the commune administration are appointed by the authorities of the commune on the basis of the law and criteria adopted by the Commune Assembly.

Within the territory of a commune, there are no central government agencies or services. However, organs of central inspectorates have the right to supervise directly the implementation of central legislation and to undertake actions in case the commune organs of supervision fail to discharge their duties satisfactorily. Only by a decree of law may the assembly be requested to establish, on behalf of the central bodies, special organs to engage in particular activities, e.g., national defense.

The assembly is an open institution, and all citizens are entitled to be informed about its work. It must report to voters' assemblies; also, it may invite citizens and representatives of various institutions and social organizations to participate in a consultative capacity at its sessions. The Commune Assembly may convene a general session at which the representatives of social-political organizations (League of Communists, Socialist Alliance, Youth and Trade Unions) participate in a total capacity, if issues of cardinal importance are discussed.

(2) VOTERS' ASSEMBLY AND REFERENDUM

The Voters' Assembly is an independent general meeting of all citizens in a section of the commune; this section consists of one or more villages in rural areas or one or more blocks in a city. At such a rally, citizens consider matters of special concern to them, as well as problems of general interest; they initiate problems to be examined, advance proposals for their resolution, and discuss the performance of their representatives. These rights are ensured by federal laws and the statute of the commune.

The assembly of the commune and other self-governing organs are bound to consider grievances, proposals and demands raised at Voters' Assemblies, to take a position, and to inform citizens of their decision when the assemblies meet again.

Under the statute of a commune and in conformity with the law, the draft of a social plan and the budget, including other proposals directly affecting the living standard of citizens and the socio-economic position of the individual, must be discussed at the Voters' Assembly before being submitted to the Commune Assembly for adoption.

The Voters' Assembly is convened by the president of the Commune Assembly. The convening of a meeting may also be initiated by a group of citizens, the Socialist Alliance, the council of a neighborhood community, the council of a commune or any other body of self-government interested in discussing a particular matter with citizens. The meeting is presided over by a president elected from among the participants at the meeting. The president makes sure that the decisions are brought to the attention of the corresponding bodies. The Voters' Assembly has a special responsibility for conducting elections to all legislative bodies from the commune to the Federation within electoral procedures prescribed by law, in order to ensure a continued influence of citizens in the creation of these bodies. The Voters' Assembly nominates candidates to the assembly of the commune, the constituent republic and to the Federal Assembly.

The functions of the referendum are twofold: first, it is used to consult public opinion on matters before the assembly; second, it enables citizens to decide directly through secret ballot on questions of major importance. The statute of the commune decrees what issues must be decided by referendum. The assembly is free to submit additional issues to referendum. Also, a given number of Voters' Assemblies may request that a certain matter be decided through a referendum. A decision made by referendum is mandatory and final. The same practice has been used in neighbourhood communities as well as in enterprises and institutions.

(3) THE NEIGHBORHOOD COMMUNITY

The neighborhood community is a self-governing territorial unit consisting of citizens living in the countryside or in cities. The assembly of the neighborhood community constitutes a specific form of direct socialist democracy organized on a territorial-residential basis. The executive body of the assembly is a council elected for a term of two years. Its duty is to prepare and convene meeting of the assembly. Membership and activities in this council and its commissions are voluntary and nonremunerative.

A neighborhood community assembly may sit as a reconciliation council—as a self-governing nonjudicial body—functioning as a specific form of a collective ombudsman. Its main functions are the settlement of grievances and disputes through reconciliation, the promotion of good-neighbor relations, and the elimination of sources of conflicts and disagreements.

In the framework of a neighborhood community, the citizens deal with their daily needs and other day-to-day business, develop social standard facilities and housekeeping services, organize nurseries and creches, maintain playgrounds, set up laundries, see to milk, bread and fuel deliveries, food supply, social welfare, training, education and culture programs, public libraries, and as a rule, building and maintenance of streets, local roads, etc. These activities are self-financing; some of them, especially those concerning educational, cultural, and social welfare, are mostly financed or subsidized by the commune.

The statute of the commune may specify activities to be performed by neighborhood communities. A neighborhood community adopts its own statute at the Community Assembly, which, in more detail, delineates its scope of activity.

Social-political organizations, such as the League of Communists, the Socialist Alliance of Working People, trade unions, youth organizations, Union of Veterans, etc., are important instruments of self-government in the commune as well as on the national level. Membership is voluntary. Their authority is functional to their capacity to understand and reflect socio-political realities, including the needs and aspirations of the people. They exercise their influence above all by force of political argument. The Constitution prohibits their interference in the competence of the formal organs of self-government. Actually, their primary aim is to teach the citizen how to use the organs of self-management in order to realize his rights and aspirations.

These associations are organized on the commune level and have branches at lower levels, too. Their influence is present in everyday life in all fields of social activity.

The League of Communists is an association of ideologically homogeneous people, who accept the Marxist ideology as their world outlook. Membership in the League is the major factor promoting ideological and political unity throughout the country. Its program sets the strategy and long-term aims for the building of socialism; the League has been the pioneer in furthering humanization of Yugoslav society through a democratic socialist evolution on the basis of self-government.

The Socialist Alliance is more broadly constituted. Every citizen who accepts the socialist orientation of the country is entitled to be a member. On the average, more than 75% of the voting population joins. Within the Alliance, citizens discuss the whole range of social and political questions concerning the community, exchange and reconcile opinions, and make decisions relating to the protection and implementation of the freedoms and rights of man in all spheres of social life.

The Federation of Trade Unions, with units in each work organization, acts to safeguard the right of self-management of workers, to encourage their professional and managerial education, to protect the individual against the arbitrariness of state or other authority, as well as to protect the interest of the community against individual or collective selfishness or narrow-mindedness. The trade unions also have an important role in the field of professional and general education of workers; they founded and manage Workers' Universities, spread all over the country.

The Federation of Youth Organization, with branches operating on both a territorial and work basis, introduces youth to civic responsibilities through the advancement of encouragement of their active participation in bodies of self-government in all fields.

The Association of Veterans, as a mass organization of war veterans, works to protect their specific interests. At the same time, it plays an important role in mobilizing people to promote socialist relations in the country, and bases its activity on ideals and traditions of the National Liberation War. It also takes care of the specific problems of war veterans in cooperation with the governmental and other agencies, as well as through different forms of solidarity and mutual assistance.

CONCLUSIONS

It is thus apparent that participation is the central motive in the structure of local self-government in Yugoslavia. The citizen is given different channels through which to express his needs, and to influence public policy. The most important channels are the following: as a general citizen, he acts mainly through processes of representation in the autonomous communal assembly (with an occasional ultimate power of decision by referendum). As a worker, he acts through the self-management organs of his place of employment. As a resident of a particular neighborhood community, various media of direct democracy are open to him. And finally, he can influence decision by his activity through social-political organizations and through professional or other interest groups with which he wishes voluntarily to associate himself.

Decision-making thus has a large basis, not only in terms of the sheer number of people who can become involved, but also in the multiplicity of roles that each individual can undertake in the political process, roles that utilize a multitude of decision-making centers. As the same person can, in effect, participate in many different capacities, his behavior may not be altogether consistent. On the same issues, positions may differ in different bodies. He may vote one way on an issue in the perspective of his closer interests as a worker in a particular enterprise, and another way when considering his interests as a consumer or a resident of a neighborhood community. However, he has to reconcile in himself his interest as worker and citizen; the existing mechanism of self-government is there only to help him realize better his own interest and to implement it.

The existence of a multitude of autonomous centres of decision-making in the commune underlines the importance of coordination among organs representing differing interests, coordination among different levels of government, and, from the overall standpoint of national unity, coordination among self-governing communes in different parts of the country.

The experience has shown that the possibility of a free expression of individual incentive represents by itself an important force of a democratic integration. However, in a relatively underdeveloped community with limited resources, a permanent political activity in this direction is needed, too, as well as the corresponding role of the state administration.

The major factors of the political activity, on the country-wide scale, are political associations, and especially, the League of Communists, the Socialist Alliance and the Federation of Trade Unions. Not less important as integrative factors are the assemblies from the commune to the federation; owing to their structure, they represent a solid link binding the governing and self-governing bodies from the commune to the Federation and ensure a corresponding popular participation in decision-making on all levels.

Systems of Local Power:
A Comparison

In comparing the systems of local power in India, Poland, U.S. and Yugoslavia, the differences that emerge are far deeper than ones of form or terminology. Even without benefit of strict comparative indices, it must be apparent that contrasts in the extent of local autonomy, the structure of decision-making, and the relationship of politics to administration are great enough to indicate a profound divergence in political "culture," especially in assumptions regarding the genesis of political responsibility for developmental change.

The main differences are these:

The autonomy of local authorities   In practice, decentralization of powers has gone much farther in Yugoslavia and the United States than in India and Poland; it seems to lead to a greater awareness and acceptance of autonomy on the part of local leaders in Yugoslavia and the United States. This can be attributed in part to their federal structure, but India of course is also federal, with strong centrifugal tendencies. However, a long tradition of centralized administrative authority in India, now matched by oligarchical party rule (although increasingly fragmented), militates against the successful devolution of political responsibility propagated through the structure of the Panchayati Raj.

Poland continues to retain the uniform, centralized structure to which it has been historically accustomed, so that decentralization has never really been construed to mean the independent local exercise of substantial political authority.

In Yugoslavia, unlike the United States, the practice of autonomy extends, it will be recalled, to the self-management of economic and social enterprise, as well as the self-government of territorial entities. Local responsibility thus has a much broader base, and is becoming the underlying principle of socio-political structure of the entire society.

On the other hand, the system of local power in the United States is much older, and rooted, as a matter of fact, in the highly independent institutions of town government in colonial America. After a period of decline, the extent of local autonomy has markedly increased in recent years as more cities have acquired "home rule." In Yugoslavia and the other countries, the present system only developed in the last quarter century. This raises the question of how quickly alterations in formal political structure can take hold, especially if they are initiated from the top, and whether they can transform the basic political habits and dispositions of leadership and population into forms that are compatible with the assumption of local responsibility.

Political and social objectives of local government In India, Poland and Yugoslavia, the system of local government is purposefully directed to the accomplishment of basic developmental goals. To some extent these reflect the dominant ideological commitments of these countries' leadership, especially in regard to the necessity and character of socio-economic change.

The socio-economic systems of Poland and Yugoslavia are determined by the fact that both countries since World War II have entered upon the road of building socialism, while admitting the possibility of different approaches to socialist construction, as in the relationship between economic decentralization and central planning. In this perspective, the functions of local government in both countries are geared to the development of socialist enterprise. In Poland this takes the form of fulfillment of goals set by the national plan; in Yugoslavia the goals emerge from the processes of local self-government operating within the individual commune or enterprise, but they are expected to lead to coordinated action at higher levels. This difference reflects the distinctive Yugoslav ideological commitment to voluntary participation as the base for both political and social development.

In India, also nominally socialist, though with a large private sector of the economy, planning for economic and social development has been initiated from the center and executed primarily through the various state governments. The whole rationale of the new system of local government is oriented to the problem of mobilizing popular support for the massive rural developmental efforts called for by the higher levels of government; these efforts are designed to pull India up by its own bootstraps from poverty and social injustice. From this point of view, local self-government is not an end in itself, but a political instrument to energize the human resources for economic and social development.

Nothing of this broad national purposefulness infuses the functioning of local government in the United States. With the socio-economic system based on privately owned enterprise, and a wide aversion to state interference of any kind, the objectives are for the most part parochial and limited to public services of immediate benefit to the local citizenry—police, fire protection, water, sewage, streets, recreational facilities, some social welfare, and, occasionally, certain efforts at urban renewal and public housing when encouraged and assisted by state and federal governments.

These basic differences in the expectations of local governments obviously affect their performance, the pattern of activeness in their communities and the motivations of their leaders.

The party system and the structure of local decision-making   Different types of party systems significantly affect the way in which the institutions of local government function in the four countries, and how they are linked to government at other levels.

In the United States, with its lasting two-party system, local government in most communities is the subject of interparty rivalry. This competition, however, does not necessarily result in the rotation of ruling groups, because of the continued power that one party is often able to gain at the local level through organization and patronage. Nevertheless, some opposition is almost always present within the elected organs; cities in close proximity are likely to be controlled by different parties (typically, suburbs under one party and inner city under the other), and, of course, power at the local level will as likely as not be in the hands of a different party than the one holding power at the national level.

The same is coming to be true in India. Despite the long tenure of its so-called party of consensus, interparty rivalry has grown, and now the Congress Party has lost control over local authorities in many areas.

Poland and Yugoslavia have party systems that exclude the possibility of organizing opposition political parties, and that concentrate political leadership—both at the national and the local levels—in the hands of one party. In Yugoslavia, however, there is only one political party (the League of Communists) besides the Socialist Alliance, an all-embracing social-political organization. In Poland the Polish United Workers Party cooperates with two other parties; in both these countries, the parties are closely linked with a number of social organizations. In

Yugoslavia, however, the League of Communists has been progressively losing the attributes of a traditional political party, especially after having detached itself from the structure of state administration.

Political parties in India and the United States have the character of rather loose agglomerations of groups and factions; political parties in Poland and Yugoslavia have a more cohesive character. Ideological programs of American parties are not very expanded. Parties in India have more elaborate ideologies than the American parties, but even they constitute conglomerates of diverse ideological tendencies. In Poland and Yugoslavia political parties—especially the two main ones—have a clear-cut political doctrine (Marxism-Leninism) and do not admit factions within party.

The above are the most important differences between the four local political systems in our study. We could also mention others. Polish laws define the structure and rights of local authorities in a uniform way throughout the country, while in India and especially in the United States there are, in this respect, considerable differences between particular states and regions. The same has been more and more true for Yugoslavia, as the Constitution, as well as the federal laws, are built on the premise of a large autonomous legal activity of the commune as well. The size and social structure of local communities are also different, with the American communities being of an urban character, Polish and Yugoslav ones being of a mixed composition, and Indian communities being of a basically rural character. Among local leaders in India and, in particular, in the United States, a relatively important role is being played by representatives of private business; in Poland and Yugoslavia this social group is in practice deprived of influence over local political systems. On the other hand, in Poland, Yugoslavia, and to some extent, India, professional work in the apparatus of political parties or social organizations plays a more important role in the selection of local political leaders.

These differences suggest that in our study the set of variables, which stem from the fact that a given community forms part of India or Poland, United States or Yugoslavia, will be of considerable importance. On the basis of the analysis of local political systems, we may hypothetically assume that:

(1) On matters where the degree of autonomy has particularly great influence, Poland will differ from India, the United States and Yugoslavia, while the latter three should show many similarities.

(2) On matters connected more closely with the economic system, party system and ideology, Poland and Yugoslavia will show institutionally large formal similarities, although in political practice constitutional,

institutions, and conceptual premises, there are important differences; similarities between India and the United States will not be too far reaching.

(3) Ideological differences will influence differences both in the hierarchy of values within particular countries and in the degree of concurrence of those values; the concurrence of values should be the greatest in Yugoslavia and also in Poland, but smaller in India and the United States.

(4) Traditions of self-government and dominant ideologies should influence the attitudes of local leaders toward national initiatives (particularly favorable in Poland), toward participation by the public in decision-making processes (particularly favorable in the United States and Yugoslavia), toward self-government (particularly favorable in Yugoslavia), and toward moral values of leaders in the eyes of the public (particularly strictly defined in India).

Our empirical findings will demonstrate to what extent these hypotheses concerning the effect of differences between local political systems do in fact explain differences in community activeness and the values of leaders. This in turn will allow us to perceive more fully the role of the local political systems within the entire body politic of India, Poland, the United States and Yugoslavia.

Notes

1. Morris Janowitz concluded at the beginning of the 1960s that "despite the number of community studies in the literature of social anthropology and sociology, few make explicit reference to political institutions and few relate community organization to the larger political systems in which they operate." Morris Janowitz (ed.), *Community Political Systems*, Glencoe, Ill.: Free Press, 1969, p. 13.

For a beginning at comparative political analysis between two of our four countries, focused on the party system, see Rajni Kothari and Jerzy J. Wiatr, "Party Systems and Political Pluralism: Comparisons between India and Poland," paper presented to the VIth World Congress of Sociology, Evian, France, Sept. 1966, mimeo. This paper has been published in Polish in the journal *Studia Socjologiczno-Polityczne*, No. 25, 1968, pp. 177–188.

2. The program and procedures for the decisional case studies were set forth at the Third International Roundtable, Warsaw, Poland (Doc. RT/III/3 and 3A); reviewed in the light of pre-tests at the Fourth Roundtable, Kanpur, India (Docs. RT/IV/15 and 16); and the structure of analysis to insure comparability completed at the Fifth Roundtable, Bellagio, Italy and Budva, Yugoslavia (Docs. RT/V/4, 9 and 11). For the original reports of the investigators, see, for India, ISVIP Docs. IND/107 and IND/137 (T. K. Attarde) and IND/108 (H. R. Chaturvedi); for Poland, Docs. PO/25, PO/26 and PO/29 (J. Tarkowski, M. Kesy, A. Ostrowska and E. Rylko, with the collaboration of R. Marinkovic from

Yugoslavia; for U.S.; Docs. USA/83 ard USA/84 (Terry N. Clark with the assistance of William Kornblum and J. W. Wagner Jr.); for Yugoslavia; Docs. YU/77, YU/79 and YU/93 (R. Marinkovic with the collaboration of J. Tarkowski from Poland) and YU/94 (Eugen Pusic).

3. Cf. Leadership Survey Questionnaire, Part IV, questions 6 and 7. Appendix A.

4. Terry N. Clark (ed.), *Community Structure and Decision-Making: Comparative Analyses*, San Francisco: Chandler 1968, p. 84.

5. Winicjusz Narojek, *System wladzy w miescie*, Wroclaw, 1967, p. 18.

6. The Committee concluded that "So long as we do not discover or create representative and democratic institutions which will supply the local interest, supervision and care necessary to ensure that expenditure of money upon local objects conforms with the needs and wishes of the locality, invest it with adequate power and assign to it appropriate finances, we will never be able to evoke local interest and excite local initiative in the field of development." Government of India, *Report of the Team for the Study of Community Development Projects and National Extension Services*, Vol. I, New Delhi, 1957, p. 5.

7. Inaugural Address, Panchayat Raj Seminar, 1964. Quoted in M. V. Mathur and Iqbal Narayan (eds.), *Panchayati Raj Planning and Democracy*, Bombay: Asia Publishing House, 1969, p. 3.

8. Broadly speaking, the resources of the Panchayati Raj institutions in the three states under study can be classified into four groups: (1) assigned revenues, (2) matching assistance, (3) equalization fund, and (4) tax efforts.

9. See Appendix B. For a more detailed description of the structure of Panchayati Raj in Gujarat, Maharashtra and Uttar Pradesh, see the Report of G. R. Lakshman and D. L. Sheth, Centre for the Study of Developing Societies, New Delhi, ISVIP Doc. Ind/62.

10. See the unpublished records of the Maharashtra Pradesh Congress Committee regarding nominations to the 1967 general elections.

11. This section is mainly based on the final report by Philip E. Jacob to the A.I.D. Science Director, on a study of "The Interaction of Social Values and Political Responsibility in Developing Countries," Philadelphia: University of Pennsylvania, October 20, 1967, pp. 88–92.

12. This finding is reported and analyzed in Chapter 10.

13. J. S. Jadeja, "Villagers View Their Grampanchayat," *Quarterly Journal of Local Self-Government Institute*, Bombay, Vol. 35, No. 2, October–December, 1964, pp. 214–215.

14. See Jaya Prakash Narayan, *A Plea for Reconstruction of Indian Polity*, 1959 and, by the same author, *Swaraj for the People*, 1961. Akhil Bharatiya Sarva Seva Sangh Publication, Ras Ghat, Kashi.

15. The data described throughout is for 1965, the year most appropriate for this study, unless otherwise indicated.

16. Winicjusz Narojek, *System Wladzy W Miescie*, Wroclaw: 1967, p. 18.

17. The data on which these findings are based are summarized in Tables 4 and 5 above.

CHAPTER 7

The Resource Base of Community Activeness: Economic Measures of Capability

This chapter was written by Bosnic.

In social theory and research there is broad consensus on the interdependence of economic and political factors. Economic factors are usually viewed as either independent or intervening variables in the explanation of political structures or behavior.[1]

In line with this perspective, our study has assumed that the economic situation of a local community may profoundly affect both the amount and kind of institutional and citizen behavior that we have identified as community "activeness." Economic factors are treated essentially as intervening, or "control," variables, whose influence, direct or indirect, on what the local government and the people in the community do, must be taken into account in exploring the relationship of leaders' values to activeness.

Actually, the "economic situation" of a community reflects a multitude of separate factors, whose impact may not be uniform, either in strength or direction. We have, however, sought a general measure that would express a synthesis of these varied impacts; this synthesis would represent their *net effect* upon the resource base of the community.

Two such measures have been secured. The first, defined as the *level* of local economic development, represents the situation at one point in time, and is thus a static appraisal. The second, economic growth, is a dynamic measure expressing the trend and *rate* of change in economic activity and resources over a period of time.[2]

The logical and empirical connection between these two measures of the economic situation is obvious. For instance, level of economic development can always be defined as a moment in the process of economic growth. But these two aspects of economic situation should not be equated. Concrete differences between communities in the level of development may not correspond to their differences in the rate of growth. One community may have a higher growth rate than another, but may possess fewer resources.[3]

This research aimed to assess both the static and dynamic aspects of the local economic situation. That is, in addition to assuming that the political behavior of citizens and local leaders might be affected by the local level of development, it was hypothesized that some phenomena, such as the leaders' perceptions of the political situation, of conflicts or of the social structure of their communities, might be influenced by the dynamic of economic change, i.e., the rate of economic growth during an interval preceding 1966, when the ISVIP survey was conducted.

Measuring Economic Development

The theoretical necessity of incorporating economic dimensions in our analysis was complicated by problems of assessment stemming from the nature of the data; we had to decide how to evaluate variation in economic dimensions at the level of local political units, when economic development is customarily envisioned as a macro-phenomenon, either of the nation-state or a region, and how to obtain, in each country, a measure of local economic development that would be comparable across countries, when economic activity is so tightly enmeshed in the peculiarities of the national political and social systems. This is largely a report of the solutions to these questions, and represents only a part of the experimental analysis undertaken and the lessons learned.

National differences in the economic development of the four countries are extreme. Compared in terms of two frequently used indicators, the United States has approximately 40 times the per capita income and 55 times the per capita consumption of power of India. Poland and Yugoslavia stand between, in that order. (See Table 1.)

Table 1—National Wealth

Country	National Income Per Capita $ U.S. (1966)[1]	Per Capita Consumption of Power in Kilograms of Coal (1966)
India	79.1	171
Poland	745.3	3608
U.S.	3153.0	9595
Yugoslavia	371.3	1202

Source: *Statistical Yearbook UN 1968*, pp. 176–177
[1] Calculated by the following exchange rate: 1 U.S. $ = 7,541 Rupees; 12.5 New dinars; 24 Zlotys.

However, differences are not only great in regard to the achieved level of economic development; the countries also differ in the changes their economies have undergone during the last several decades, as shown in Table 2. These great differences, all of which are ultimately manifest in the economic makeup of local communities, create complex

Table 2—National Economic Change

Country	Annual Growth GNP Per Capita in %	Percentage of Labor Force Employed in Agriculture Average Annual Change
India	1.0 (1948–1959)	+.17 (1931–1961)
Poland	5.8 (1953–1960)	−.37 (1931–1950)
U.S.	1.8 (1948–1960)	−.51 (1940–1957)
Yugoslavia	7.2 (1953–1960)	−.50 (1931–1953)

Source: Bruce M. Russett et al., *World Handbook of Political and Social Indicators*, New Haven and London, 1964, pp. 158–160, 175–176.

problems in establishing any common measures, applicable in all four countries, for assessing the local economic situation. These problems are compounded by the structural differences in the economies of the four countries—from primarily agrarian India on one hand, to industrially developed United States on the other. What would be the usefulness of a "common measure" that merely confirmed the enormous differences already obvious?[4]

Consequently, it was decided early in the design of the research to construct measures that were not absolute, but relative to the economy of the particular countries. It was considered inappropriate to measure either the level or the rate of socio-economic development of local communities by any single indicator, or any set of indicators that were identical for all countries. Instead, separate lists of indicators were chosen, specific to each country, on which to base general indices of the economic level and growth of communities. This obviated the possibility of making direct cross-national comparisons of the economic position of communities or countries in terms of common continuous scales; however, it was agreed this was not necessary, given the nature of the research problem that confronted us.[5]

Our immediate task was to assess the impact of the local economic situation as an intervening variable in the explanation of relationships *within* countries. Only when these intracountry patterns were established, could cross-country comparison be undertaken to compare the relative strength demonstrated of the association between economic and political community variables within each country.

With this in mind, effort centered on finding indicators of development that were highly relevant to the particular situation of a specific country;[6] attention was also focused on the methodological problems involved in making cross-country comparisons of patterns of inter-variable relationships, rather than of aggregated data directly.[7]

A special problem in this research arose from the fact that economic phenomena were being measured in small territorial units, namely local communities. Measuring economic factors in so-called micro-frame-works cannot be carried out in the same way as in macro-frameworks, which have a relatively close area of validity, such as a unitary economic system, a unitary market, etc. (usually limited by a state frontier). In the case of local communities, from an economic point of view, they are only conditional relative entities of a broader institutional whole, the unitary economic system of a state. The market, and other macro-economic mechanisms, cannot be "restricted" or "measured" within local frameworks. Therefore certain generally accepted indicators for measuring economic phenomena, such as GNP, may have a significant comparative importance, but, when calculated for small areas, they are only approximations of reality.[8]

Indicators of the Level of Local
Economic Development

Table 3 lists the indicators that were finally chosen to measure the economic development level of local communities in each country.

It is apparent that there is considerable cross-national comparability; this occurs, despite the decision not to seek identical items in the various countries. By careful comparison of the meaning of the selected indicators, one discovers a number of *common dimensions* of local economic development, even though the specific indicators may be different.

(a) Income—India, U.S., Yugoslavia
(b) Employment—India, Poland, U.S.

Table 3—Indicators of Level of Local Economic Development

India	Poland	United States	Yugoslavia
(a) *Income* Value of agricultural production per acre Value of agricultural production per capita	(a) *Retail trade* Trade turnover per capita	(a) *Income* Income per capita Median family income Percentage families under $3000 income Percentage families over $10,000 income	(a) *Income* Income per capita Gross personal receipts per capita Gross personal receipts as percentage to total income Income in social sector in percentage to total income
(b) *Agriculture* Coefficient of irrigated area[1] Coefficient of sown area[2] Coefficient of cropped area[3]	(b) *Employment* Employment in industry per 1000 inhabitants Employment in industry per 1 km² Percentage of nonagricultural employment	(b) *Retail trade* Retail trade establishments per capita	(b) *Retail trade* Turnover in retail trade per capita
(c) *Employment* Proportion of workers in the tertiary sector to total working population	(c) *Agriculture* Percentage of arable land under cultivation of wheat Agricultural population per 100 hectares of arable land Men in agriculture per 100 hectares of arable land Cattle heads per 100 hectares	(c) *Employment* Percentage employed in white collar occupations	(c) *Investments* Investments in percentage of income Investments per capita Share of funds for investments in percentage to income Basic assets per capita
(d) *Urbanization* Percentage of urban population to total population	(d) *Urbanization* Percentage of urban population to total population Density of population Percentage of nonagricultural population to total population	(d) *Housing* Percentage housing units sound with all plumbing facilities Median gross monthly rent of renter-occupied units	(d) *Institutional Expenditures* Total institutional expenditure in percentage of total budgetary revenue Institutional expenditure per capita Total institutional expenditures as percentage of total income
(e) *Housing* Households with three or more rooms as percentage of total number of households Percentage of household living in puca houses to total number of households	(e) *Housing* Persons per room in cities Persons per room in country-side Percentage of farms with electricity to total number of farms	(e) *Traffic* Percentage housing units with two or more automobiles	(e) *Traffic* Number of inhabitants per one passenger car Number of inhabitants per one truck lorry
(f) *Schools* Villages with schools as a percentage of total number of villages	(f) *Schools* School room area per one pupil in rural areas		

[1] Net area irrigated/Net area sown.
[2] Net area sown/total geographical area—Net area sown
[3] Gross cropped area—Net cropped area/Net cropped area

  (c) Agriculture—India, Poland
  (d) Urbanization—India, Poland
  (e) Housing—India, Poland, U.S.
  (f) Retail Trade—Poland, U.S., Yugoslavia
  (g) Traffic—U.S., Yugoslavia
  (h) Schools—India, Poland

INDIA

The indicators selected in India reflect the fact that agriculture is the dominant area of economic activity: five out of a total of ten relate to agricultural production. Their content is positive in that the greater the score on these indicators, the higher the community's level of development is considered.

The other items, though more social than economic in substance, are closely enough associated to qualify as indirect indicators of economic development; the number of workers in tertiary activities, for instance, demonstrates the development of public services and utilities; housing and schools point to social wealth.

A particular problem in the use of socio-economic indicators of local development in India is that the "meaning" of such indicators, as well as their reliability, is not stable throughout the country, but varies regionally. We cannot deal here in detail with these regional differences, but the following considerations should be borne in mind in assessing the validity of any attempts to construct and apply a general, common index of economic development for the whole of India:[9]

(1) Economic variations are so great in India that single national measures are not likely to be meaningful at the local level. At least, one cannot assess that a particular measure of resources or productivity would be equally applicable to all localities. For instance, national measures of wealth, such as per capita income, are based largely on market transactions. In poor areas, little enters the market and such measures could not discriminate effectively *among* poor communities, to indicate those relatively better, or worse off. Further, as will be demonstrated later, measures which relate to areas where there is some industrialization simply do not apply to largely agricultural localities.

(2) There is great variation between Indian regions. Following the point made above, just because a measure would be valid in one region does not mean much in terms of another. The empirical approach makes a measure meaningful in the *context of the system*; in the case of this study, in the context of three particular Indian states.

(3) India is basically agricultural. Agricultural indicators are heavily influenced by geography, whereas industrial type indicators tend to be meaningful almost anywhere. One state in India produces sugar cane, a cash

crop; another produces no sugar cane. Sugar cane, therefore, cannot be used as an equally valid measure of agricultural wealth. One state relies on wells for irrigation and another, because of terrain, can use canals. Economic assets, therefore, cannot be validly used for comparisons across states using either water wells or canals. Agricultural type economies have *systematic* rather than *random* error in their phenomena—in the data that can be used to assess economic level.

(4) Indian data contain error. While most data are subject to some error, in countries such as India, especially at the local level, inaccuracies pose a very serious problem. However, these inaccuracies can be viewed as random, not systematic, at least with regard to a single region or a local community. Hence, if several indicators, relevant to the region or type of community, are incorporated in a particular measure, the impact of inaccuracy in any one indicator is reduced or, hopefully, cancelled out by other indicators.

(5) Indian data are not uniformly available across the country. Even if some measure or indicator could be agreed upon as valid, the fact is that the data are not likely to exist in all regions. One reason for the lack of data was pointed out above. This is the case where phenomena of a particular kind do not occur, such as sugar cane. Another reason, and this is especially true in countries such as India, is absence of administrative uniformity in collecting and reporting data. In Uttar Pradesh, this was particularly a problem.

POLAND

The 15 indicators chosen for Poland related to six dimensions of economic development. The dominant focus was on the degree of industrialization and urbanization, which were both considered positive, and interrelated aspects of development. By contrast, agricultural output, which correlated inversely with indicators of industrialization and urbanization, was held to be a negative measure of development. Consequently, most rural communities, which would naturally score low on urbanization and industrialization, would be ranked low on level of economic development, even though their agricultural productivity might be very high.

This orientation then determined the developmental significance of other indicators. Retail trade and employment, correlating positively with industrialization and urbanization, were treated as signs of a higher level of economic development. The situation of housing and schools, however, was confused; from one standpoint they would appear to indicate aptly the social welfare aspect of development, but in fact they tended to be inversely related to urbanization (reflecting a situation in Poland where housing in urban areas is scarce, and people must therefore live in more crowded quarters than those in the country-side). The percentage of rural population, a good indicator of agricultural manpower, naturally has a low correlation with industrialization, and becomes an indicator of a low level of economic development.

Per capita income was not available at the powiat level; but as trade turnover is customarily closely related to the standard of living of the population, this could be substituted for income as a positive indicator of development.

UNITED STATES

The U.S. indicators cover five dimensions of economic develop-ment: "Income," "Retail Trade," "Employment," "Traffic" and "Housing." While the indicators of the first group can be directly interpreted economically, the indicators of housing and traffic are, above all, indicators of a living standard. Of course, a higher standard of living correlates, as a rule, with a higher level of economic develop-ment. The percentage of those employed in white-collar occupations is an indicator insufficiently differentiated with regard to its economic nature. However, the fact that a larger proportion of white-collar occupations correlates with a higher level of industrialization, of urbanization, and of public utilities and services (all a consequence of better economic opportunities in a community) can be assumed to be relevant to the level of economic development.[10]

YUGOSLAVIA

The indicators chosen for Yugoslavia differ considerably from those selected in other countries. Two dimensions—*investments* and *institu-tional expenditures* (expressed by several indicators of budgetary expenses)—were added to reflect the wealth and assets available to a local community. In addition to their economic significance, these indicators are relevant to general social development.[1]

Indicators of employment, housing, urbanization and schools were omitted in Yugoslavia, because they seemed to measure economic development less directly than the other data available.

Validity of the Indicators

Indicators of the level of local economic development were de-liberately chosen, as noted, to take into account the specific features of each country's economic system and structure. Their validity depends therefore on the extent to which they reflect the processes of economic activity actually in effect in local communities in the particular countries involved in this study, rather than on some general concept of development held to describe activities of nations as a whole, and to apply commonly to all nations. From this standpoint, validity has been demonstrated by the homogeneity of the indicators. To the extent that they intercorrelated, positively or negatively, they identified a concrete phenomenon, a reality in the units being studied, in the country where they were located. Whether this was the same phenomenon as that described by the indicators used in other countries, i.e., the question of cross-national validity, is less certain. A case in point is the pivotal role of agricultural production in defining the developmental level in India, as opposed to industrialization in Poland (with agriculture cast as a negative or antidevelopment indicator in the latter). However, the presence of cross-links in the batteries of indicators—where, as noted, the indicators relate to dimensions similar in two or more countries— provides some reassurance that what is being described as local economic development in one country is indeed the appropriate counterpart of what has been measured as such in the others. Thus, it is entirely possible that, given the kinds of communities surveyed in India (blocks), agriculture rather than industry would indeed provide a more accurate basis for estimating the level of resources available, whereas the opposite would be true in Polish powiats, where industrialization has been a key factor in expanding output and income over areas that remained largely agricultural. In general, the use of multiple indicators in each country (following the principle of "better more than less") made possible a considerable matching of indicators across countries, perhaps sufficient to establish the correspondence of the phenomena, if not their exact comparability.

One particular problem is the different degree of economic "purity" in the indicators chosen for different countries. There is more of a mix of social with economic indicators in India and Poland, for instance, than in Yugoslavia. In the United States, inclusion of the percentage of persons employed in white-collar occupations also gives a social, rather than a purely economic, twist to the measure. However, we have carefully tried to avoid redundancy in the use of indicators; those chosen for assessing economic development, directly or indirectly, have *not* been used to indicate activeness or political behavior in the local community.[12] Furthermore, as will be seen in the next section, we constructed alternative measures differing in the socio-economic composition of indicators, and the interrelationship of these measures was statistically determined. When the measures were not strongly congruent (as in India), communities were scored on more than one measure, so that the effect of stressing social, as opposed to economic, components of "development" could be observed.

Measures of the Level of Economic Development

With the data available, the following measures of the level of economic resources of local communities were constructed:

INDIA

AGRICULTURAL UTILIZATION. This measure is the mean Z-score of the following variables: (a) irrigated area; (b) cropped area; and (c) area sown. Their intercorrelations (see below) demonstrate that these indicators are not tautological; instead, they express various dimensions of agricultural utilization, and, taken together, provide a general measure of economic development appropriate to the predominantly rural Indian communities that were the object of study.

Variance of Indicators of Agricultural
Utilization—India[13]

	B	C
A Irrigated area	.266	0.194
B Cropped area		0.003
C Net area sown		

SOCIO-ECONOMIC DEVELOPMENT. While the six indicators included in this measure are more socio-economic than strictly economic in nature, they point indirectly to the level of economic development, as demonstrated by the fact that the index (derived from the mean Z-scores) correlates moderately with Measure I ($r = .579$). The indicators are: (a) urban population (% of total); (b) workers in the tertiary, i.e., services, sector (% of total population); (c) percentage of households having three or more rooms; (d) percentage of households living in pucca houses; (e) percentage of villages in the block having schools; and (f) amount of irrigated area.[14]

AGRICULTURAL PRODUCTIVITY. This measure is composed of the following indicators: (a) irrigated area; (b) per capita value of agricultural production; and (c) per acre value of agricultural production. In view of the similarity of these indicators to those in Measure I [indicator (a) is actually identical] it is not surprising that these two measures are highly correlated ($r = .748$), which means that 56% of the variance is common. The reason for keeping these two similar measures was that data for indicators (b) and (c) were available for only two states, Uttar Pradesh and Maharashtra. Hence, the figures for the local communities in Gujarat had to be estimated.[15] Further, the amount of sown area, which is one of the basic indicators for Measure I, does not correlate significantly with the *value* of agricultural production, which forms the core of Measure III. It is evident that to some extent the dimensions of development measured by these two sets of indicators are different.

POLAND

The construction of the index of economic development for Polish powiats was based on previous studies, with the 15 indicators for all 391 powiats in Poland taken into account. The data related to 1960.

Factor analysis was used to develop the index. Principal components were first extracted from a product-moment correlation matrix with unities on the principal diagonal. Five dimensions were identified as the result of the analysis.[16] Three are reported here.

The first factor, explaining 36.9% of total variance and 48.4% of common variance, depicts the *dimension of urbanization and industrialization*. The following indicators are loaded higher than $\mp$ .50 on this factor:

Percentage of nonagricultural employment	.944
Percentage of urban population	.931
Percentage of nonagricultural population	.930
Employment in industry per 1000	.899
Density of population	.849
Trade turnover per capita	.837
Employment in industry per square kilometer	.824
Percentage of farms with electricity	.646

The second factor explains 19.2% of total and 25.2% of common variance. It can be regarded as the *dimension of overpopulation* in the countryside, and, as such, is a negative expression of economic development. The indicators and loadings are:

Persons per room in rural areas	.935
Men in agriculture per 100 hectares	.900
Agricultural population per 100 hectares	.837
Schoolroom area per one pupil in rural areas	.729
Persons per room in cities	.637

The third dimension can be treated as the *development of traditional agricultural production*—mainly wheat and cattle. Only two indicators are highly loaded. This factor still explains 9.0% of total and 11.8% of common variance:

Percentage of arable land under cultivation of wheat   .865
Cattle per 100 hectares   .724

The common index was comprised of the following components: industrialization and urbanization *minus* rural overpopulation and *plus* output of traditional agriculture.[17] The level of economic development was aggregated in factor scores. Factor scores for these three factors were calculated by an approximation method: those variables that were loaded higher than .50 on the given factor and not higher than .40 on any other factor contributed to the scores. The index is a linear function of those scores:

$$ED_i = a_iF_1 - a_iF_2 + a_iF_3$$

UNITED STATES

The results of a factor analysis for 65 socio-economic indicators for all cities of more than 25,000 population (i.e. 644 towns) were used for the general index of economic development in the United States. Thirteen indicators of an economic nature with a factor loading greater than ± .5 were chosen, and two slightly different measures were constructed. These indicators have mutually strong correlative relationships.

ECONOMIC LEVEL. The following indicators compose this measure:

A   Median family income
B   Percentage families under $3000 income
C   Percentage families over $10,000 income
D   Percentage employed in white-collar occupations
E   Percentage housing units found with all plumbing facilities
F   Median gross monthly rent of renter occupied units
G   Percentage housing units with 2 or more automobiles
H   Income per capita

This is in effect a measure of the general economic power of the *population* of a community and the conditions of life therein. Only "Percentage employed in white-collar occupations" relates to the social structure of the community.

The common measure of the level of economic development for each municipality was the average T-score value of each of the mentioned (8) indicators.

SOCIO-ECONOMIC LEVEL. This measure differs from the first only by an additional indicator: Retail trade establishments per capita.

This indicator was included in the common index in order to put more emphasis on social aspects of the living standard.

The same procedure for calculating a general index was applied as for measure I. Therefore, these two measures do not essentially differ, but show a mutually high correlation (r = .98). The result of this is that the position of communities on both measures is almost identical.

YUGOSLAVIA

Fourteen indicators were selected from a total of 33 indicators of economic development by repeated factor analyses. Therefore the majority of these indicators show mutually high correlations.

Two different procedures were used for working out the general index. Thus the two measures for this country differ only in the procedural sense, not in content.

Economic Development Level I is the factor score on the first factor. Out of 14 indicators only three have a factor loading smaller than $\pm$ .50. This factor covered most of the important indicators from a broad spectrum of the economic situation and economic activity of a commune, and is characterized by a mutual positive relationship between all 14 indicators.

Since the analysis was carried out on the basis of data from all 516 communes, the factor score for the 30 communes in the ISVIP sample places these communes in the continuum of the entire universe of Yugoslav communes.

Economic Development Level II is based on the same 14 indicators as measure I, but the index was based on T-scores of the indicators.

Therefore, the coefficient of correlation between these two measures is very high (r = .991) and the analysis is confined to Measure I.

Distribution of Communities According to
Level of Economic Development

The preceding expositions have shown the variety of methods of measuring the level of economic development in each of the four countries. One way of evaluating the validity of cross-national comparison is to compare the distribution of the units sample that resulted from applying these different national measures of the level of economic development. In this way it will be possible to answer the following questions:

—Are the distributions of samples of communities in the four countries similar, in spite of different indicators and procedures for determining the measures?

—In the sample of 30 communities, were those with low, medium and high
degrees of economic development equally represented?

—Are the positions of the 30 communities in the distribution affected by the
measures that were used?

Since all the measures were based on standard values (Z-scores),
there were no great technical or procedural difficulties in comparing
the positions of local communities, both across communities in the same
country and across communities in different countries.

It can be seen from Table 2 that the largest number of communities is concentrated around the middle of the scale. The distribution of
communities in the median range of T-scores (from 46.0 to 55.9) is as
follows:

Table 4—Level of Economic Development: Communities in the Median Range (T = 46.0 to 55.9)

		Communities	
Country	Measure	Number	Percentage of Total (30)
India	I	15	50.0
	II	18	60.0
	III	14	46.0
Poland		15	50.0
U.S.	I	16	53.4
	II	19	63.4
Yugoslavia	I	17	56.7
	II	14	46.6

The common tendency is a very similar distribution as a concentration around the median range of the scale, regardless of which measure
of economic development is used. For a more precise comparison, a
criterion was worked out to distinguish low, medium and highly developed communities. Because measures of the level of economic
development in each country were constructed on the basis of nation-
specific indicators, it is impossible to compare the position of local
communities on the basis of the *same* substantive criterion. However,
comparison can be made on the basis of an empirical criterion, such as
the standard deviation interval. Communities within one standard
deviation of the mean can be considered as *medium developed*; those
that fall above some cutoff point as *highly developed*; those that are
located below a chosen cutoff point below the mean as *underdeveloped*.

This criterion certainly has shortcomings. But when the common
index of the level of economic development is based on *different indicators* and on *different procedures* for each country, the suggested solution

for distributing the communities into low, medium and highly developed ones is a useful illustration of *relative* comparisons.

In view of the distributions and concentrations that are seen in each country, the communities will be distributed in all the four countries according to the following criterion:[18]

—low developed: T-score 45.99 or lower,
—medium developed: T-score between 46.00 to 55.99,
—highly developed: T-score 56.00 or greater.

Using these limits, the communities in the four countries are distributed as follows:

INDIA

Table 5—Distribution of Indian Blocks According to Three Measures of Economic Development

Measure of the Level of Economic Development	Level of Development			
	Low	Medium	High	Total
Agricultural Utilization (Measure I)	11	15	4	30
Socio-economic Development (Measure II)	6	18	6	30
Agricultural Productivity (Measure III)	10	14	6	30

As expected, the distribution of local communities by the measure "Agricultural utilization" and "Agricultural productivity" are very close. More significant deviations are found between these two measures and the distribution provided by the socio-economic development scale (Measure II). In this case there is a symmetrical concentration of a smaller, equal number of communities in the low and high categories of development and a larger number in the medium category. By contrast, both agricultural measures of economic development show that communities of low and medium levels of development are far more numerous than highly developed ones. This could be expected because of the nature of these indicators and the agrarian situation in this country.

The obvious differences between the measures suggest the possibility of using all three measures to express different aspects of economic development level; also, these differences suggest that they will be differently relevant to situations in different communities.

Table 6—Distribution of Polish Powiats According to the Measure of Economic Development

Low	Medium	High	Total
12	15	3	30

The sample of Polish powiats is skewed in the less developed category: 40% are in the less developed category and 10% in the highly developed category. This distribution is due to the scoring and sampling procedures. The economic development scores were based on all 391 powiats, but the sample was drawn from the universe of 317 mixed urban-rural powiats. The exclusion of the wealthier urban powiats resulted in a sample with an economic development score below the national mean.

THE UNITED STATES

In the preceding section it was pointed out that the differences existing between the two measures of the level of economic development in the United States exist only in terms of broadening the social emphasis. Therefore a significant shift in the distribution of local municipalities does not occur in the second measure. This can be seen from the following table:

Table 7—Distribution of U.S. Municipalities (3 levels)

Measures of the Level of Economic Development	Low	Medium	High	Total
Measure I	8	16	6	30
Measure II	7	19	4	30

It is obvious that both U.S. measures lead to a concentration in the medium level of development (this is even more pronounced in regard to Measure II).

It seems that applying a scale with an even number of modalities would correspond better for the United States, since such a scale would produce a more symmetrical distribution. (For this country as well as others, however, it is characteristic that a larger number of communities is below the median T score, i.e., T = 50.99.) A more even distribution is shown in the following table, in which the cutoff points are altered.

Table 8—Distribution of U.S. Municipalities (4 levels)

Level of Development

Measure of Economic Development	Low (to 45)	Medium–Lower (46.0 to 59.9)	Medium–Higher (51.0 to 55.9)	High (56.0 and above)	Total
Measure I	8	9	7	6	30
Measure II	7	10	9	4	30

Of course, in this case too, the smallest number of communities is in the highest category—the high development level.

YUGOSLAVIA

As noted, there are no substantive differences in content and meaning between the two measures of economic development in Yugoslavia. In both cases, 14 identical indicators are involved. The difference is only in computational procedure. However, a difference can still be found in the distribution of the communes.

Table 9—Distribution of Yugoslav Communes According to Level of Economic Development

Level of Development

Measure of Economic Development	Low	Medium	High	Total
Measure I	9	17	4	30
Measure II	11	14	5	30

The differences resulting from the different ways of calculating indices point to a serious methodological question. In Measure I the value of each of the indicators is weighted by the value of the factor loading. The values for the factor loading for the 14 indicators are different. In Measure II the index was calculated without weighting, and was derived simply from the mean value of all 14 indicators. Therefore, significant shifts occur between the low and medium level of development.

It is difficult to say which way of computation is more adequate. Both have the following tendencies:

—a larger part of the sample is below the mean;
—the communes at a medium level of development are most represented, next, the communes at a low level, while the communes at a high level of development are least represented.

Economic Development as a Cross-National
Local Phenomenon

From all that has been said so far about each country separately,
the following conclusions emerge:

There is very great similarity in the distribution of communities in
all the countries, regardless of the measure of level of economic development. The largest number of communities in all the countries is concentrated around the mean value. Further, highly developed communities are the smallest in number. This may be a consequence of the
following:

(a) It is possible that *in fact* the number of medium and low developed communities in each country is much larger, and the number of highly developed communities is very small. The reason for having a normal
distribution in our samples of communes may be the procedure of matching units of the samples. Particularly in Poland, the United States and
Yugoslavia, the measures of the level of economic development are
based on data from a majority of communities of a particular type in
those countries.

(b) It is possible that the indicators chosen for assessing the level of economic
development are biased in favor of medium and low levels of economic
development in each country.

(c) Finally, the techniques applied for calculating the index based on the
standard scores may have contributed to the leveling of differences
between the communities, which resulted in a concentration around the
median values.

Because the countries have carried out the measurement of economic development in different ways, it is difficult to prove that the
*same phenomenon was being measured with different indicators and pro-
cedures*. Preceding considerations show that in all four countries,
irrespective of the way of measuring, similarities exist in the distribution of communities; these similarities are expressed in a standard
continuum across the four countries. These similarities permit the
assumption that though different methods were used, the same phenomenon—theoretically defined as economic development—was indeed
being measured in each country. If this is so, it is an example of *how,
with the same theoretical content, it was possible to achieve operational
determination that adequately took account of differing specific realities in
each country*.

If this strategic idea of cross-national research has been realized,
the interrelationship between the level of economic development and
political activity can be reliably tested across widely different national
systems.

Notes

1. The view that the conditions of social and political behavior lie in the economic reality of life was first emphasized by Marx in *Das Elend der Philosophie*, 1847, and again in his *Zur Kritik der Politischen Ekonomie*, 1859. This position, interpreted within the framework of Marx's entire theoretical work, is expressed succinctly by Joseph Schumpeter as follows: "The economic interpretation of history *does not* mean that people, consciously or unconsciously, are completely or predominantly guided by economic motives . . . Marx did not support the view that religion, metaphysics, schools, ethical ideas and political aspirations could be reduced to *economic motives* or that they are not of importance. He only wanted to discover economic *conditions* which shape them and explain their rise or fall." And, further: "What the theory really says may be put into two propositions: (1) The forms or conditions of production are the fundamental determinant of social structures which in turn breed attitudes, actions and civilizations. . . . We may say that it is our daily work which forms our minds, and that it is our location within the productive process which determines our outlook on things—or the sides of things we see—and the social elbowroom at the command of each of us. (2) The forms of production themselves have a logic of their own; that is to say, they change according to necessities inherent in them so as to produce their successors merely by their own working." See *Capitalism, Socialism and Democracy*, Part II, New York: 1950, pp. 11–12. See also his *The Theory of Economic Development*, Cambridge, Mass.: Harvard University Press, 1934, trans. by R. Opie.

There are still disputes about "economic determinism." See, for instance, the opinions of several Marxist sociologists expounded in *Social Research*, vol. 34, No. 3, Autumn, 1967. For empirical research on this relationship, see I. Adelman and C. Morris, *Political and Economic Development*, Baltimore, Md.: Johns Hopkins University Press, 1968.

Two recent works that closely relate to our study, in that they report major cross-national studies of political motivation, are also deeply concerned with the explanatory functions of economic variables: Hadley Cantril, *The Pattern of Human Concerns*, New Brunswick, N.J.: Rutgers University Press, 1965, and David C. McClelland, *The Achieving Society*, Princeton, N.J.: Van Nostrand, 1961.

2. The level of local economic development has been used in three ways in our research: first, as a criterion for selecting the sample of local communities (see Appendix B); second, as an explanatory factor of community activeness (see Chapters 9, *The Processes of Activeness*, and 10, *Patterns of Activeness*, and third, as an intervening variable in explaining the value systems of political leaders (see Chapter 4, *The Shaping of Values*).

For an overall exposition of the place of economic variables in the research design, see Chapter 1, pp. 20–22.

3. The way in which the concepts of "economic development" and "economic growth" are defined here differ from the positions prevalent in the terminology of economists who, most often, consider that: "Economic development and *economic progress* are widely used synonymously with *economic* growth. . . ." [A. Hazlewood, "Economic Growth," in *Dictionary of the Social Sciences*, J. Gould, W. L. Kolb, (eds.) New York: Free Press, 1964.]

Of course, in an operational sense, there are even greater differences among authors in determining the indicators for these two concepts. See, for instance, Gerald M. Meier and Robert E. Baldwin, *Economic Development*, (New York: John Wiley, 1957; W. W. Rostow, *The Process of Economic Growth*, New York: Norton, 1952.

4. The problem of a "common measure" for assessing the level of economic development has been considered against the background of such proposed solutions as those reported in: United Nations, *Measures for the Economic Development of Underdeveloped Countries*, New York: United Nations, 1951, Doc. ST/ECA/10; Colin Clark, *Conditions of Economic Progress*, London: Macmillan, 1957; W. S. and E. S. Woytinsky, *World Population and Production*, New York: Twentieth Century Fund, 1953.

The effort to compare and classify countries according to common economic-social indicators, when they differ greatly in level of economic development and in social system, is particularly criticized by such European authors as Jean Weiler. See "The Path From Analysis to Economic Sociology," in Georges Gurvitch (ed.) *Traite de Sociologie, I*, Paris: Presses universitaires de France, 1958–1960.

An empirical classification of states by economic indicators is attempted in Bruce M. Russett *et al.*, *World Handbook of Political and Social Indicators*, New Haven; Yale University Press, 1964, pp. 293 ff.

The four countries in the ISVIP are not categorized according to this or any other particular socio-economic classification, but their selection was determined in part by a desire to insure that they would differ substantially in level of economic development and in social system.

5. This position was adopted early at the joint meetings of the national teams and it has been continuously maintained. See the conclusions of Round tables I, II and III and especially J. Wiatr, "Indicators of Socio-Economic Development," ISVIP Doc. RT/II/10.

This procedure did not exclude the selection of indicators that were designated by identical labels in two or more countries. But in these instances "identity" was only nominal. The common label concealed basic differences in the methodology of collecting data and establishing indicators. For example, GNP for Poland and Yugoslavia is calculated as a "net material product"; for India as a "net domestic product at factor cost"; for the United States it is the "gross national product." More details can be found about these differences in the *Statistical Yearbook* of the United Nations. The problems of different approaches to calculating and presenting particular social and economic indicators can also be found in Russett, *op. cit.*

6. In India, preliminary research was carried out on 27 taluks in the 3 states of Maharashtra, Gujarat and Uttar Pradesh; in this research, 23 sets of data from the Census of India, 1961 were used. On this basis, 18 indicators were selected to calculate the economic development of blocks. For elaboration of the procedures followed, see University of Pennsylvania, *Third Report to A.I.D. Science Director* on *A Study of Social Values and Political Responsibility in Developing Countries*, Philadelphia: October, 1967, and the memorandum by A. Nadkarni on *Indicators of Economic Development of Blocks in India*, reproduced therein. (ISVIP Doc. IND/90). An important contribution to the solution of the problem of establishing synthetic measures of local economic development was made by M. N. Pal and C. Subramaniam, who factor-analyzed data for all districts in India (one level higher than the blocks with which ISVIP was concerned). See *Regional Disparities in the Level of Development in India*, New Delhi: Indian Statistical Institute, mimeo, 1965; also reproduced as ISVIP Doc. IND/54.

In Poland, 25 economic characteristics, on all 319 powiats derived from 1960 census data, were factor-analyzed in working out the synthetic index of economic development. See Institute of Philosophy and Sociology, *A Preliminary Report of the Polish Study*, ISVIP Doc. PO/28.

Relevant indicators in the United States were derived by factor analysis of the 65 economic and social characteristics originally collected for all American cities by J. K. Hadden and E. F. Borgatta, *American Cities: Their Social Characteristics*, Chicago: Rand McNally, 1965. The choice was tested on the data for cities having a population of more than 25,000. This suggested that 17 indicators would be adequate. See Henry Teune, *A Factor Analysis of Characteristics of American Cities*, ISVIP Doc. USA/61.

The selection of indicators in Yugoslavia was based initially on a bivariate correlation of 32 characteristics of all Yugoslav communes, derived from 1961 census data. Those having highest mutual correlations were chosen and the index was calculated as the mean T-score. See S. Bosnic and H. Teune, *Index of Economic Development for Yugoslav Communes*, ISVIP Doc. YU/33. The final determination of a synthetic index of the level of development was based upon a factor analysis of 1965 statistics for all communes. The index was expressed both by a factor score and the mean T-score, based on national means and standard deviations. The position of the 30 communes in the ISVIP sample could thus be fixed in relationship to the entire universe of communes in the country, as was the case also in Poland and the United States.

7. See, for example: A. Przeworski and H. Teune, "Equivalence in Cross-National Research," in *Public Opinion Quarterly*, vol. 30, 1967, pp. 551–568; H. Teune, *Measurement in Comparative Research*, ISVIP Doc. USA/106; Slobodan Bosnic, *Problems of Cross-National Comparison of Communes According to Level of Socio-Economic Development*, ISVIP Doc. YU/72.

8. Studies on measuring economic development of micro-communities are rare. For various approaches to the problem, see: United Nations, *Bibliographie des Ouvrages Relatifs aux Methodes et Problèmes de L'Industrialization dans les Pays Sous-Developpés*, New York: United Nations, 1956. Doc. ST/ECA/37; also, Institut de Science Economique Appliquee, *Niveaux de Developement et Politiques de Croissance*, Paris: Presses universitaires de France, 1955.

9. For further consideration, see University of Pennsylvania, Final Report to *A.I.D. Science Director*, op. cit., pp. 95ff, from which the statement quoted immediately hereafter is excerpted.

10. The selection of data for socio-economic indicators in the United States are further explained in the document previously cited, *A Factor Analysis of Characteristics of American Cities*, ISVIP Doc. No. USA/61.

11. In Yugoslavia, the Federal Institute of Statistics publishes current data relating to activities in the communes every year. Of special significance is the detailed survey contained in *Komuna u statistickom sistemu Jugoslavije*, 1960 and 1961, 2 vols., Boegrad: Federal Institute of Statistics, 1963.

Regrettably, similar data relevant to these dimensions were not available for local communities in the other countries.

12. The problem of overlap between indicators of activeness and economic development is examined in Chapter 8, *Activeness: Concept and Assessment*.

13. The figures presented are the coefficient of determination (r^2) and indicate the amount of common variance among the variables.

14. The intercorrelation matrix for all the indicators of economic development and the intercorrelation among all three measures of economic development in India is presented in Appendix D.

There is some question as to the logical coherence of this measure because of differences in the degree to which the indicators mutually intercorrelate. "Irrigated area" correlates significantly with "households with 3 or more rooms" and with the "percentage of villages having schools." This certainly suggests that these 2 indicators have economic significance. In contrast, "workers in the tertiary sector" has a low correlation with other indicators in this measure, except with the "proportion of the population that is urban." The homogeneity of indicators is thus not as strong as in the first measure.

15. The missing data were estimated according to the following regression formula:

$$a = \overline{X}_1 - x_2 b$$
$$b = r_{12}[S_1/S_2]$$
$$x_1 = x_{12}b + a$$

16. The number of factors extracted was on the basis of Kaiser's criterion: eigenvalues larger than 1.00 were taken into account. The original factor matrix was then rotated orthogonally to the varimax criterion. In this fashion the basic of 25 indicators was reduced to a smaller number of independent dimensions (factors)—with decreasing generality. The intercorrelation matrix for all 15 indicators, including the final measures, is given in Appendix D(2).

17. The basic problem in constructing the index of economic development concerned the relation of the second factor (the development of agriculture) to

other factors. Therefore, the yield of four grains per hectare (the standard indicator of agricultural production) was correlated with the factor scores. These correlations indicated that yield per hectare is inversely related to the second factor and positively to the third factor.

18. As is known, this division corresponds to percentile ranks as follows: *low developed* to 34.45 percentiles, *medium developed* between 34.46 and 72.56 percentiles and *highly developed* from 72.57 percentiles. This measure corresponds to standard values in the so-called normal distribution (Z-values) as follows: low developed — .399 and less; medium developed from — .400 to + .599, and highly developed + .600 and more.

PART 3

The Active Community

Chapter 8 introduces the concept of activeness, and links it to the literature on political development in a local context. It gives a model for the cross-national measurement of activeness and discusses the results of factor analysis of the data gathered in each country. A common measure of community activeness for the four countries is established.

Chapter 9 presents the general model of analysis used to explain activeness, a model that gives the rationale for the particular ordering of explanatory variables and states the specific procedures followed. This is followed by the core of the findings. The relative influence on activeness of major categories of variables, such as values, economic level and social structure, is emphasized. The broad conclusion is that explanatory patterns of activeness are quite different in the four countries.

The final chapter attempts to explain the striking cross-national differences by shifting analysis to systemic differences among the four countries.

CHAPTER 8

Activeness: Concept
and Assessment

The section on Concept was written by Sheth; the section on Assessment
by Ostrowski and Teune.

Obvious differences among localities and nations
are often summarily expressed. General characterizations, however,
either blanket a variety of differences or assume that most of these
converge into a single direction, such as developed or underdeveloped,
modern or traditional, growing or stagnant. Social scientists, especially
those engaged in comparative research, have specified some dimensions
on which differences can be observed, if not precisely assessed. These
dimensions include consolidation of political authority; the gap between
political authorities and the population; the barriers between social
groups; linkages of individuals or groups into the mainstream of
national life; the individual's orientations to his role in communities
larger than his immediate locality; values and attitudes considered
supportive of urban industrial life; participation of individuals and
groups in political life; individual loyalty, allegiance or identification
with a political system; the capacity and effectiveness of institutions,
particularly governmental ones, in formulating and implementing
policy; the extensiveness of social and political structures in linking

individuals and groups together; the capacity of the system to respond to change; and, perhaps the most general of all, the extent of role differentiation and functional interdependence within the total society. These dimensions have been conceptualized in a variety of terms. Some of the more common of these dimensions are "mobilization," "modernization," "political development," "integration," "civic culture," "democratization," "institutionalization," "legitimacy," and "governmental effectiveness." The referents of these terms can be viewed as constituting a universe of all possible dimensions on which local communities could be differentiated. Taken together, these dimensions may reflect a general underlying phenomenon. One term that perhaps has evolved as the most inclusive of all these concepts, and is often used to refer to a general underlying phenomenon, is political development.[1]

Activeness and Political
Development

General social phenomena, such as political development, can be examined from two standpoints: the aggregative and the collective. In order to derive an aggregate characteristic of some unit, characteristics of individuals belonging to some group are combined, with the use of some composition rule. Although aggregate characteristics are a characteristic of a group, they must be interpreted as a composite of individual characteristics. Collective characteristics, in contrast, are properties of the *structure* of a unit and include, therefore, something other than simple individual characteristics. They must be interpreted as properties of a collectivity, and not as characteristics of any individuals within a collectivity. The median age of the population of a city is an aggregate characteristic of individuals who are defined as members of the city. A decision to allocate resources is a characteristic of a structure of the local political unit (the political decision-making structure), and not a property of any individuals.[2]

In this study, the properties of structures and processes are of primary importance. Indeed, the very notion of a local community implies the presence and relevance of structure and process. Aggregate concepts do not incorporate structural characteristics; rather, they require an arbitrary structuring of individual characteristics through the use of a summarizing composition rule.

The collective dimensions of a general concept of political development represents diverse components. These components may reflect some underlying general patterns. This research conceived of two such patterns or dimensions. One is the extent to which social and political institutions (particularly governmental institutions) mobilize resources and accomplish collective goals; the other is the extent to which individuals relate to social and political structures, and particularly individual engagement in the decision-making structures of national or local collectivities. These two dimensions, both confined to the structure and process of collectivities, constitute the definition of *activeness*.[3]

Although the phenomenon designated by the term "activeness" has counterparts in many of the phenomena referred to by such terms as "social mobilization," "political development," "modernization," and "institutionalization," the context of this research made it difficult to use these terms without substantially distorting their current meanings. The decision to use a new term was prompted by several considerations. First, it is important to express clearly that the phenomenon assessed in this research is at a single point in time, and any explanation is, therefore, of differences among several units at one point in time rather than over several points in time. In contrast, many of the concepts, that refer to similar phenomena, particularly such terms as political development and modernization, connote a process. Secondly, this research was confined to comparisons of local units within countries, whereas most of the referents of these terms are at a national level. Third, although most of these concepts call for assessment of collective level characteristics, in fact many of their measures are at the individual level. Activeness, however, is restricted to collective behavior or manifestations of individual involvement at a collective level. Fourth, many of these contemporary concepts either refer to a single dimension of social or political behavior or are inclusive of almost all of them. It turns out that there is no term in usage that refers to specific combinations of discrete dimensions, such as a combination of institutionalization and popular participation. The concept of activeness, as defined for purposes of this research, refers to a combination of two types of social and political behavior—resource mobilization and popular involvement. The term activeness is a name for these two specific phenomena.

The theoretical relevance of activeness depends in part on the extent to which it represents the domain of concerns covered by political development. Insofar as political development refers to the effectiveness of political systems at the local level in mobilizing resources for collective purposes and in involving the local population in public affairs, activeness refers to two syndromes of the multidimensional referents of political development that are structural rather than individual. Insofar as social science research is focused on the structural and process aspects of development, the concept of activeness could serve as a means of specifying some components of what is now a very general concept. Insofar as this research provides an empirically verified explanation of activeness, these findings can enter the growing body of empirical knowledge about political development.

The Definition of
Activeness

Activeness is the combination of individual and collective behavior directed to, or having consequences for, an increase in community facilities and the extent of individual involvement in solving problems at a collective or community level. There are two kinds of behavior in the general concept; (1) *collective behavior*, which refers to actions of community institutions (particularly the local government) in generating community facilities and in increasing the opportunities for individual involvement, and (2) *individual behavior*, which refers to the involvement of individuals in broader community relations through participation in socio-political institutions and in responding to community programs. The general definition of activeness incorporates both types of behavior. They will be respectively called *resource mobilization* and *popular involvement*. Resource mobilization refers to the actual performance of the local institutions in providing facilities and services when the acceptance or involvement of individuals is not necessarily required. Popular involvement is the sum total of individual behavior in articulating preferences or demands and responding to collective initiatives. The latter need not have a direct impact on the level of community facilities and services.

The structural content of the resource mobilization dimension of activeness is evident in that it refers to the behavior of institutions. The collective nature of the popular involvement dimension, however, is less obvious. The individual behavior referred to in the popular involvement dimension is restricted to role behavior in local social and political structures. This behavior, therefore, can be observed at the collective, rather than individual level. Although it may be difficult to distinguish sharply between individual and collective behavior in actual observations, it should be possible to separate behavior that is primarily institutional, or role related, and behavior that is primarily individual. If the goal of the research is to explain characteristics of collectivities, as is the case here, then observations should be made at the collective level, rather than transforming individual observations into collective characteristics. The referents of the definition of activeness call for observations of what is going on in local organizations, political processes, or government programs, rather than observations based on individuals' reports of their own behavior. For example, instead of asking a sample of the population about their affiliation and activity in organizations, what is observed is institutional performance in eliciting participation of individuals.

The definition of activeness was influenced not only by consideration of data available at the collective level, but also by investigation of the kinds of behavior appropriate for local governmental units. The components of the definition of activeness were continuously shaped by information gathered at the local level in the four countries. Consequently, the definition of activeness, although intended to be applicable to a wide variety of social and political units, is particularly appropriate for local political units. The components of the definition include most of the important social and political functions performed at the local level. The specific indicators of activeness are derived from the kinds of decisions that are taken at the local level in these four countries.

Although these two dimensions can be distinguished conceptually, in fact they may not be independent. Some discussions of political development have pointed to the independence of institutional capacity to act, and the involvement of the population in decision-making. It has even been argued that involving the population in decision-making may impair the institutional capacity to mobilize resources. Another view holds that mobilization of resources is dependent upon the extent to which the population can be involved in collective activities. The definition of activeness allows for either of these two views—the independence or interdependence of these two dimensions.

The question of the empirical distinctiveness of these dimensions can be treated as a hypothesis. This hypothesis is that popular involvement and resource mobilization are to some extent related and to some extent independent. In order to construct a measure of activeness that expresses the actual interdependence of these two dimensions, this hypothesis must be assessed. If the hypothesis is found to be true, then local political units can be differentiated on a measure that incorporates both dimensions composing the underlying phenomenon—the measure of activeness.

A Model and Language for
Measuring Activeness

The definition of activeness requires that assessment procedures meet three criteria: (1) independent assessment of both popular involvement and resource mobilization; (2) accurate expression of their interdependence; and (3) comparability across the four political systems. To meet these criteria, the inferred model of measurement was chosen and factor analysis was used as the language of measurement.

The inferred model of measurement is based on observations of several specific phenomena that are treated as indicators of some more general underlying phenomenon.[4] Activeness is so assessed. The intercorrelation of specific observations is an estimate of the validity of the measure based on all indicators. Use of an inferred indicator model of measurement was necessary, first, because activeness is defined as an underlying phenomenon, and, therefore, could not be directly observed, and secondly, because activeness is a collective characteristic, and collectivities cannot be directly observed.

Factor analysis (with orthogonal rotation) was selected as the language of measurement because it first tests the assumption of interdependence of popular involvement and resource mobilization, and if they are interdependent, it then provides weights or coefficients for each indicator that precisely expresses the extent of this interdependence. Factor analysis approximates an ideal language of measurement for activeness as it has been defined. If a factor analysis of the indicators results in factors that are isomorphic with activeness and its separate dimensions, then the factor loadings can be interpreted as weights expressing the relationship of each indicator to activeness, popular involvement, and resource mobilization. The indicators and their factor loadings then can function as the measurement instrument of activeness.

Initially, every indicator is considered of equal importance in reflecting activeness. Therefore, the total variance of all indicators (the total test space) must be analyzed. A type of factor analysis that treats the total variance of all observations is principal component analysis.[5] By rotating the principal components, it is possible to reduce the dimensions to a number that is more likely to correspond with the hypothesized dimensions. If, after rotation, it is found that the factors correspond to the hypothesized dimensions, then these loadings can be used as the weights or coefficients for the indicators.

One alternative to factor analysis as a language for the measurement of activeness is the one used in the assessment of values. Here each value item was treated as an indicator of a single value. Those items that were hypothesized to be related to a value, and were in fact interdependent with other items, were each given a weight of "1" in the value scale score. This language in effect places each item into one of two categories; each item is interdependent with other hypothesized indicators of this value or it is not. If it is interdependent, the item is weighted "1"; if it is not, it is weighted "0" (excluded). The interdependence of any specific item with items of other scales is not taken into account, nor are items differentiated within a scale according to the degree of their interdependence. Either of these languages of measurement are not inherently superior. The critical question is which of these or other languages will best meet the theoretical definitions of the variables in terms of the nature of the data.

The Indicators of
Activeness

The indicators actually used to measure activeness are viewed as a sample of the universe of all indicators of the phenomenon. The universe of verbal indicators of authoritarianism would, for example, be every verbal statement that validly differentiated individuals on authoritarianism, anywhere in the world. For a particular study, the question is whether the indicators identified in any particular system constitute a random sample of the universe of all indicators. One procedure for answering this question is to compare the total variance of the sample of indicators with the total variance of the universe of indicators; if these variances are approximately equal, then the sample of indicators can be treated as a random sample of the universe.

An alternative procedure, and one that was followed in the assessment of activeness, is to hypothesize the relevant indicators for each system separately (in this case, for four countries). Instead of stating that membership in civic organizations is an indicator of activeness everywhere, the statement takes the form: "In India an indicator of activeness is . . .; in Poland an indicator of activeness is. . . ." This approach to the identification of indicators allows historical, cultural, and other systemic characteristics to be taken into account. Then the variances for each country are compared with each other. If they are approximately equal, then each is assumed to be a sample of the universe of indicators. The measure of activeness assumes that the indicators for each country constitute such a sample.

The problem of comparability of measures is of special importance because of the great differences between the political systems under study. Although it is highly probable that comparable social and political structures for participation, such as elections, organizations, and public forms for discussing civic problems, exist in every system, the particular political system determines whether and in what ways these similar structures validly differentiate communities as active or inactive. Even though civic organizations exist in India, the small number of people who participate in them and the limited role they

Table 1—Indicators of Activeness in Four Countries

Popular Involvement

India	Poland	United States	Yugoslavia
1 Average number of adults made literate per year, 1962–1965	1 Membership in Polish United Workers' Party, 1965, per capita	1 YMCA: total number board and committee members, 1965, total population	1 Membership in League of Communists, 1965, per capita
2 Average increment in school enrollment 1962–1965 (base year 1961–1962)	2 Membership in Peasant Party, 1965 rural population	2 Mean turnout of voters local 1959–1966, population 21 and over	2 Membership in Socialist Alliance, 1965, per capita
3 Average increase in the proportion of members of cooperative societies, 1962–1963/1965–1966 (base year 1961–1962)	3 Change in membership of the Polish United Workers' Party, 1963–1965	3 Mean turnout of voters on referenda, 1960–1966, population 21 and over	3 Voters in Communal Assembly elections, 1967, registered voters
4 Average increment in the proportion of paid-up share capital of cooperative societies, 1962–1963/ 1965–1966 (base year 1961–1962)	4 Change in membership of the Peasant Party, 1963–1965	4 Membership in League of Women Voters: 1965, population 21 and over	4 Citizens attending candidacy meetings of voters, 1967, registered voters
5 Average number of steriliza-tions (male and female) per year, 1962–1965	5 Membership in Union of Socialist Youth, 1965, per capita	5 Change in Boy Scout members.1960–1965	5 Voters' meetings held, 1965, per electoral constituency
6 Average number of smallpox vaccinations per year, 1962–1965	6 Membership in the Union of Rural Youth, 1965, rural population	6 Boy Scout adult volunteers, 1965, population 21 and over	6 Voters' meetings initiated by the Communal Assembly, 1965, total meetings held
7 Number of loops inserted, 1965–1966	7 Membership in the Union for Freedom and Democracy, 1965, per capita	7 Mean turnout of voters for President, 1960–1964, population 21 and over	7 Membership in Cultural and Educational Association members, 1965, population 18 and over
8 Average number of drinking wells constructed per year, 1962–1965	8 Membership in Voluntary Fire Brigades, rural popula-tion	8 United Fund contributions raised.1965, per capita	8 Cinema attendance, 1965, per capita
9 Average number of manure pits dug per year, 1962–1965	9 Membership in Agricultura Circles, 1965, per farms	9 Change in United Fund contributions raised, 1960–1965, per capita	
10 Average number of latrines built per year, 1962–1965	10 Pathfinder organizations in rural areas, 1965, rural population	10 YMCA contributions, 1965, per capita	
11 Average number of innoculations of cattle per year, 1962–1965	11 Proposals for organizational changes in electoral cam-paign, 1964, per capita	11 YWCA contributions, 1965, per capita	
12 Average number of artificial inseminations per year, 1962–1965	12 Proposals for investment programs in electoral campaign, 1964, per capita	12 Change in the number of YMCA volunteer group leaders, 1960–1965	
	13 Donations to the school construction fund, 1965, per capita		
	14 Typhoid vaccinations, 1965, per capita		

Resource Mobilization

India

1 Average supply of chemical fertilizer per year, 1962–1965
2 Average number of improved ploughs distributed per year, 1962–1965
3 Average increment in proportion of the supply of improved seeds, 1962–1963/1965–1966 (base year 1961–1962)
4 Average increment of area irrigated per year, 1962–1965 (base year 1961–1962)
5 Average increment of motor-run pumping sets per year, 1962–1965 (base year 1961–1962)
6 Average number of new schools opened per year, 1962–1965
7 Average increment of village radios per year, 1962–1965 (base year 1961–1962)

Poland

1 Local expenditures, 1965, per capita
2 Local investments, 1965, total investment
3 Local investments, 1965, per capita
4 Change in local investments, 1961–1965, per capita, 1961–1965
5 Local investments in industry and agriculture, 1965, total local investments
6 Change in pupils, 1961–1965, per school rooms, 1961–1965
7 Change in inhabitants, 1961–1965, per shop, 1961–1965
8 Change in physicians, 1961–1965, per capita, 1961–1965

United States

1 Total general expenditure, 1964
2 Expenditure: public health, and hospitals, 1965, per capita
3 Change in expenditure: public health and hospitals, 1960–1965, per capita
4 Expenditure: law and order, 1965, per capita
5 Change in expenditure: law and order, 1960–1965, per capita
6 Expenditure: parks and recreation, 1965, population, 21 and over
7 Change in expenditure: parks and recreation, 1960–1965, per capita
8 Expenditure: libraries, 1965, per capita
9 Change in expenditure: libraries, 1960–1965, per capita
10 Per pupil expenditure: 1965
11 Increase in per pupil expenditure, 1960–1965
12 Change in revenue from property taxes, 1959–1964, per capita
13 Change in intergovernmental revenue, 1959–1964, per capita
14 Nonpublic hospital, revenue, 1965, per capita
15 Value poverty program, 1965, per capita

Yugoslavia

1 Change in total budget expenditures, 1964–1966
2 Change in school budget expenditures, 1964–1966
3 Investments from local sources, 1965, per capita
4 Proportion of investments derived from local sources, 1965, national income per capita
5 Unpaid taxes, 1965, levied
6 Change in primary school teachers, 1964–1966
7 Classroom space, 1965, per pupil
8 Public library books, per capita, 1965
9 Change in buildings completed, 1964–1966
10 Change in inhabitants, 1964–1966, per physician

247

have in local communities make organizational participation a weak basis for evaluation of popular involvement. Even though elections are held regularly in Poland, the fact that turnout is close to 100% of those eligible indicates that differences between local communities are so small that it is not possible to discriminate effectively between them. Because political party affiliation in the United States is so heavily influenced by the municipalities and counties, and because political parties are not a common focal point of political activity for all local communities, party affiliation is an inadequate basis for comparison across communities. Although participation in self-management bodies in Yugoslavia has been initiated as an important form of popular involvement, the role of these bodies in the local communities was not clearly defined during the period in which observations of activeness were made.

In order to differentiate communities reliably within each country, knowledge of each political system was used to identify the important manifestations of activeness. In India, the adoption of development programs, such as sterilization and sanitary latrine construction programs, is a structure by which individuals become involved in broader networks of social and economic relationships within the local community. Various political organizations in Poland are the primary forms of the political life of the community and nation. Campaigns for charitable contributions to local organizations are a means for expressing support for the community in the United States. In Yugoslavia, individual participation is focused on local governmental organs and dominant political organizations.

Resource mobilization is defined as the community's efforts to maintain and increase community facilities. In Indian blocks, these efforts will be directed to agricultural development. Services, financed by the local government, are the major responsibility of municipalities in the United States. The municipality's efforts to provide these services can be appraised by its revenues and expenditures. The ability of Polish powiats to finance investments for development from local sources differentiates those communities capable of mobilizing resources from those subsidized from central sources. In Yugoslavia, communal investments, directed to the improvement of local facilities, reflect ability to mobilize resources. These different structures of behavior, although specific to each country, were focal points for the identification of sets of indicators.

Table 1 presents the indicators of activeness that were used in each country. These were selected from a larger number of indicators initially hypothesized to be significant in each country. The criteria that were used to discard indicators were overall correlations with other indicators, the amount of variance or discrimination between communities, and the proportion of missing data.

The Structure of Activeness in
Four Countries

The indicators presented in Table 1 were factor analyzed, using principal component analysis with the varimax criterion for rotation.[6] This type of factor analysis was used because of the definition of activeness. What was desired was an expression of the interdependence of two types of indicators. Orthogonal rotation with the varimax criterion produces uncorrelated or independent factors, and expresses interdependence among indicators on single factors. The principal components were rotated in an iterative manner, and up to eight separate factor matrices—alternative expressions of the relationships among indicators—for each country were produced.

The rotation of four components was the most easily interpreted, structure in India, the United States, and Yugoslavia, while in Poland the first four factors from the rotation of eight components were chosen as the best fit of the indicators with activeness and its dimensions.

The criteria for interpreting the various factor matrices in each country were: (1) the correspondence of the factors produced by each rotation with the definitions of activeness, resource mobilization, and popular involvement; and (2) the total amount of variance accounted for by the rotation. Although additional factors were found for different rotations, the selection of a particular rotation was based on how well it fit with the definition. The purpose of the factor analysis was to scale indicators of a theoretically defined phenomenon, rather than to describe and explain the relationships between particular indicators, and to determine the interdependency between resource mobilization and popular involvement—the basis for the assessment of activeness.

The results of this analysis were a general measure of activeness in all four countries. The analysis demonstrated the existence of a common phenomenon of activeness underlying diverse indicators of popular involvement and resource mobilization. Activeness, although manifest in quite different forms of social and political behavior in different political systems, is a general social and political process.

The assumption of this measurement procedure, in contrast to attempts to measure such concepts as development, change, mobilization and integration, is that the measure is based on phenomena embedded in the political and social processes of each country, rather than on phenomena assumed to be identical in all systems. If these phenomena can be shown to have a common structure or pattern, the criterion of comparability in part has been met. The specific criterion of a common structure of the phenomena of activeness was a common factor structure in all four countries, or, in other words, the pattern of interaction between indicators. The question is: to what extent do diverse indicators behave in an equivalent fashion? If they do behave in a similar way, the measures of activeness can be said to be equivalent and comparable.

Table 2 shows those indicators that loaded highly on a factor composed of a mixture of popular involvement and resource mobilization indicators. This is the factor that we have identified as "activeness." The percentage of the total variance accounted for by this factor is presented, as well as the proportion of popular involvement and resource mobilization loadings to the total loadings on the factor. Poland has the largest number of highly loaded indicators, the United States the smallest. The loadings for India are weighted in favor of popular involvement, and, for the United States, in favor of resource mobilization. The proportions of popular involvement and resource mobilization loadings for Poland and Yugoslavia, however, are about equal. The bias of popular involvement indicators in India and resource mobilization indicators in the United States is to some extent a result of the number of indicators (of each dimension) that were initially entered into the factor analysis. An imbalance in the number of indicators of the two dimensions, however, can only partially explain the relative proportions of highly loaded indicators, as the number of popular involvement indicators used in Poland substantially exceeds those of resource mobilization, and yet the proportions contributed by both dimensions to activeness are about equal.

The mixed factor is an agglomeration of indicators. In India and Poland there is a pattern. Four of the Indian indicators concern general agricultural improvement—fertilizer, cattle inoculations, pumping sets, and artificial inseminations; three of them represent individual decisions to participate in governmental programs in literacy, birth control and health. In Poland the pattern is a combination of local investments and membership in political organizations. It is more difficult to ascertain some common characteristics of the high loading items in the United States and Yugoslavia. One general characteristic of the indicators in the United States, however, seems to be a willingness to spend for education and to provide libraries and recreational facilities, services that are generally held to be less essential than basic governmental services such as police protection. In Yugoslavia, local investment is a major component of activeness in the local community.

Popular involvement emerged as a separate factor in India and Poland, and a separate resource mobilization factor appeared in the

Table 2—The Structure of Activeness in Four Countries

Indicators loading above .35 on the Mixed Factor, in Order of Magnitude

India		Poland		United States		Yugoslavia	
1 Chemical fertilizer	RM	1 Local investment	RM	1 Pupil expenditure	RM	1 League of Communists	PI
2 Adults made literate	PI	2 Percentage investment raised locally	RM	2 League of Women Voters	PI	2 Cinema attendance	PI
3 Cattle inoculations	PI	3 Proposals for investment	PI	3 Park and recreation expenditure	RM	3 Library books	RM
4 Sterilizations	PI	4 Local expenditures	RM	4 Library expenditure	RM	4 Percentage investment raised locally	RM
5 Village radios	RM	5 Pathfinder organizations	PI	5 Presidental voting	PI	5 Local investment	RM
6 Smallpox vaccinations	PI	6 Local investments in development	RM			6 Voters in communal assembly elections	PI
7 Pumping sets	RM	7 Peasant Party	PI				
8 Artificial insemination	PI	8 Polish United Workers Party	PI				
		9 Union of Rural Youth	PI				
Percentage of total variance explained	23%		29%		12%		18%
Percentage of resource mobilization loadings to total	38.2%		51.9%		63.1%		46.7%
Percentage of popular involvement loadings to total	61.8%		48.1%		36.9%		53.3%

United States. The criterion for identifying these factors was the fact that a preponderant proportion of the consistent loadings on the factor had to be found for one set of indicators. Bipolarity, where the positive and negative direction of the loadings cannot be interpreted in terms of the hypothesized dimensions, dominated the other Yugoslav factors and one factor in both India and the United States.[7] Although it was possible to attain a general factor—activeness—in each country, the two dimensions of activeness, resource mobilization and popular involvement, are not independent phenomena. The fact that popular involvement is separable in India and Poland, and resource mobilization is separable in the United States, is evidence that these processes are somewhat independent.

The hypothesized interdependence of popular involvement and resource mobilization has been sustained. The degree of interdependence, however, varies from country to country, depending both on the kind of indicators that were used and on the peculiarities of the political systems.

These results can be treated as findings for each of the four countries. An evaluation of how well a particular factor can serve as a measure of activeness is another question, one which depends on the total factor structure—the configuration of loadings for all of the indicators on each of the interpreted factors.

The Measures of
Activeness

The factor loadings for the factor interpreted as activeness were used as weights or coefficients in the assessment of activeness. In scoring, the standard score for each community on each indicator was multiplied by its factor loading. An average was then taken of all of the weighted indicators for a score. These are not factor scores, which would take into account the magnitude and direction of the correlations between indicators.[8]

The validity and comparability of this instrument depends first of all on whether the loadings for each indicator is consistent with the hypothesized dimensions. Secondly, the comparability of the measurement instrument depends on whether there is a similar kind and degree of consistency in each country. The hypothesized dimension is assumed to be represented by the pattern of intercorrelations between all indicators. The factor loadings themselves can be treated as reflecting how well specific indicators fit into an overall pattern. Thus, if every indicator of popular involvement and resource mobilization loaded positively on one factor, every indicator could be assumed to fit with the overall pattern, or underlying dimension, called activeness here. To the extent that items that were predicted to have a consistent loading among themselves, in fact, are inconsistent is the extent to which error has entered into the factor, and has contaminated the factor as a measurement instrument. Specifically, the predictions were that: (1) all items would have a consistent (positive or negative) loading on one factor; (2) all popular involvement items would have consistent loadings on another factor, and resource mobilization indicators loading near "zero"; and (3) in a separate factor, all resource mobilization items would be consistent with each other and popular involvement indicators would load near "zero."

These three predictions, if empirically true, would result in an ideal measurement instrument for activeness; validity would have been established, insofar as it could be measured by the consistency of the behavior of hypothesized indicators (internal validity); all of the hypotheses contained in the definition of activeness would have been vindicated; and comparability would have been assured, in that the measure would have had maximum validity for each system, and would have exhibited a common structure of interaction in all systems. This is the rationale for calculating how close the predicted measurement instrument came to what in fact was obtained. A proportion of the "true" and the "error" (error defined as departure from the direction predicted) in the activeness factor was calculated. The results of these calculations are: India 87%; Poland 94%; United States 78%; and Yugoslavia 83%.[9]

Regionalism: Intra-country Differences

After scoring was completed, one obvious bias in the measure was checked—the bias of regionalism. Regionalism has a different kind of impact on the four countries under study. Although regionalism was not formally introduced into the analysis of activeness, the regional bias in the measure of activeness is an important part of an evaluation of the activeness measure. Table 3 is a comparison of the most obvious regional configurations in each of the four countries, by the proportion of communities above and below the median on activeness.

It is evident that there are substantial regional differences in each country. These differences conform to impressionistic knowledge of the countries. Two implications can be drawn from these differences: one, that the activeness measure does validly incorporate known regional differences within countries; and two, that further studies on activeness

Table 3—Regional Influence on Activeness

Percentage of Cases Falling Above and Below the Median
on Activeness

		% above N	% below N
India			
Uttar Pradesh	*N* = 10	10 (1)	90 (9)
Maharashtra	*N* = 10	80 (8)	20 (2)
Gujarat	*N* = 10	60 (6)	40 (4)
Poland			
Western Region	*N* = 11	55 (6)	45 (5)
Northwestern Region	*N* = 7	100 (7)	0
	N = 7	0	100 (7)
Eastern Region	*N* = 5	40 (2)	60 (3)
United States			
East	*N* = 7	43 (3)	67 (4)
Midwest	*N* = 12	75 (8)	25 (4)
South	*N* = 7	14 (1)	86 (6)
West	*N* = 4	75 (3)	25 (1)
Yugoslavia			
Slovenia	*N* = 10	70 (7)	30 (3)
Serbia	*N* = 10	50 (5)	50 (5)
Bosnia	*N* = 10	30 (3)	70 (7)

ought to take into account not only the local community but also the regional environment of those communities. Some discussion of the influence of region on activeness will be presented in the last chapter of this section.

*A Summary of
Procedures*

Table 4 is a summary of the major procedures followed to arrive at the final measure of activeness. The table indicates not only that the concept of activeness was comparable but also that similar procedures were followed in order to insure comparability of measurement instruments for activeness. By following similar procedures, the vast heterogeneity of the indicators were cast into a common form. These procedures resulted in a comparable measure of activeness and, in certain countries, measures of specific dimensions of activeness.

The results, themselves, of the operations used to measure activeness contribute to an explanation of the nature and interdependencies of social and political processes at the local level. The most important of these is that what happens in a local community with respect to a specific aspect of social, political, or economic behavior is a part of a general process, which has been described here as activeness.

Table 4—Summary of Activeness Measurement Operations

	India	Poland	United States	Yugoslavia
Indicators				
1 Number of items analyzed	25	45	52	29
2 Number of items selected	19	23	27	18
Factor Analysis				
1 Type of factor analysis	Principal component	Principal component	Principal component	Principal component
2 Type of rotation and rotation criterion	Orthogonal varimax	Orthogonal varimax	Orthogonal varimax	Orthogonal varimax
3 Number of rotations	4	8	4	4
4 Estimate of commonality	1	1	1	1
Interpretation				
1 Activeness				
(a) Factor and percentage of variance explained	First, 23%	First, 29%	Third, 12%	First, 18%
(b) Percentage of "true" coefficients	87%	94%	78%	83%
2 Popular Involvement Dimension				
(a) Factor and percentage of variance explained	Third, 14%	Second, 15%	Fourth, 11%	None
(b) Percentage of "true" coefficients	76%	81%	56%	—
3 Resource Mobilization Dimension				
(a) Factor and Percentage of variance explained	None	Fourth, 7%	Second, 14%	None
(b) Percentage of "true" coefficients	—	58%	78%	—
4 Bipolar, factors (Approximately 50% of loadings negative and positive on the same dimension)	Second	None, Third interpreted as growth	First	Second, Third Fourth

255

Notes

1. For a review of some of the definitions of political development, see L. W. Pye, *Aspects of Political Development*, Boston: Little Brown and Company, 1966, Chapter 2.

2. Collective characteristics, in addition to individual properties, include properties of relationships and interaction. These are "put together" by use of a set of composition rules, which do more than summarize.

3. This definition is similar to that discussed by Amatai Etzioni, *The Active Society*, New York: The Free Press, 1968. Etzioni's concept is more general. This book came to our attention after the data had been gathered and most of the analysis was completed.

4. See Chapter 2 for a general discussion of the assumptions and procedures.

5. See H. H. Harmon, *Modern Factor Analysis*, Chicago: University of Chicago Press, 1967, Rev. Ed.

6. The estimate of commonality was "1." The results of this analysis are given in Appendix D.

7. These factors are interpreted and discussed in some detail in Appendix D.

8. Harmon, *op. cit.*

9. The sum of all factor loadings was computed for each interpreted factor. This was the basis for computing a proportion of consistently loading items. For example, if the total loadings for the resource mobilization factor was 1,000 and

all of the resource mobilization items loaded positively except one, which was loaded 100 negatively, and one popular involvement item also loaded positively at 200, then two items loading 100 and 200 respectively were inconsistent. The total inconsistent loadings would be 300, which is 30% of the total loadings of 1000. However, 700 or 70% of the total loadings were consistent. Thus the factor can be said to have 70% "true loadings."

CHAPTER 9

Processes of Activeness

The first section of this chapter, The Model of Analysis, was written by Mlinar. The second section, Testing the Model, was co-authored by Bosnic, Mlinar, Ostrowski, Sheth and Teune. This section was assembled and edited by Ostrowski and Teune.

The general design presented in Chapter 1 has set the parameters for the explanation of activeness. The central questions are, first, how much of the variance in the activeness of local political units can be explained by the economic level of the community, its socio-political structure, and the values of its leadership, and, second, to what extent is the pattern of explanation either common across all countries or determined by system differences among the countries?

The Model of
Analysis

This model includes: (1) an ordering of the explanatory variables; (2) a statement of expected relationships between these variables and activeness; and (3) a structure for examining the interaction among the variables that explain activeness. Accordingly, the model will present the sequence of the variables to be examined, spell out reasons for their presumed importance, and present a logic for the ordering and grouping of the variables. The model of analysis will be multivariate, noncausal, common for all countries, and largely confined to the characteristics and behavior of collectivities.

Although the general design is causal by implication, the observations are cross-sectional, that is, at one point in time. Thus the language of the model must be noncausal, or a language of covariance which states functional relationships between the variables. However, insofar as the relative importance of the variables in the explanation of activeness can be determined through multivariate analysis, causal relationships may be suggested. The design also aims at a level of generality applicable to all local communities, regardless of the socio-political systems to which they belong. The same model of analysis is used for all countries. The relationships between variables for each country are examined separately. Finally, since the dependent variable, activeness, is a collective characteristic of a local political unit, it is assumed that collective explanatory variables are of primary importance. This means that the model of explanation will be sociological, or at the group level; consequently, the model does not consider the role of specific individuals.

The Nature of Explanatory
Variables

The pivotal point around which this model for the explanation of activeness is built is the values of local political leaders. Although values have been recognized or assumed to be crucial determinants of individual behavior, the case is not all clear at the collective level. Even though the values of individual leaders may determine their own behavior directly, their values may not have the same degree of freedom to determine the behavior of a collectivity.

The degree to which the values of leaders can influence the collectivity through the leaders' individual and joint behavior may be constrained by the ecological and systemic context in which the leaders operate. A major consideration in this model for explaining activeness, therefore, was the specification of contextual factors as control variables, to insure that their influence upon the behavior of the community could be weighed along with leaders' values. The principal contextual factors chosen for analysis are ecological factors (primarily the resource base of the community) and the socio-political structure of the community, including conflict and cleavage patterns, the way in which the leadership is tied to the community, and the general level of local governmental competence as seen by the leadership. The model provides for comparison of the relationships of these variables to activeness with the relationships of leaders' values to activeness.

ECONOMIC LEVEL. Economic level represents the accumulated resources of a community, which may in part be a legacy of previous activity of the local population, but which also may be the result of inputs from outside the community and of the indigenous natural endowments of the area.[1] Regardless of the actual direct relationship between the economic resource base and activeness, the material capabilities for action must be considered as one of the potential limitations on the interaction between leaders' values and activeness. For this reason, the economic level must be treated as a critical variable by itself, as well as an interacting variable in the explanation of activeness.

A wealthy community will have a substantial tax base, enabling the community, if it so desires, to build schools, hospitals, and recreational facilities. The individuals in a wealthy community will be able to pay for transportation and will have time beyond that necessary to make a living to participate in social activities. In addition, as individual wealth increases, aspirations for greater and improved services should also increase; this leads to demands for the improvement of existing community facilities and perhaps results in a response from the community to provide them.

OTHER ECOLOGICAL FACTORS: STRUCTURAL INTERDEPENDENCE. Other general community characteristics that may affect the ways in which the values of leaders influence the community's activeness include size, urbanization and density. Although these variables are often included in social analysis as a matter of convention, they are justified in the context of this research by the fact that they may represent an underlying property of community environment, such as interdependence. The cost to both individuals and the community to mobilize local resources may be affected by the amount and kind of interdependence in the community. Density, for instance, is a rough measure of population concentration. The closer together the population is physically, the greater its interdependence is, and the smaller, presumably, the cost of interaction.

Interdependence is, furthermore, a consequence of the nature of the social system, and particularly of the degree of specialization of functions. One rough indicator of functional specialization is urban population or its converse, nonagricultural labor. Size, the third indirect indicator of interdependence, is related to the diversity of opportunities for individual participation and the potentiality of the community to provide, for a number of people, facilities sufficient to guarantee their effective utilization.

If a high level of structural interdependence reduces individual costs of involvement and provides a range of interests wide enough for viable collective facilities, it can be expected that structural interdependence will be positively related to activeness. Although high functional interdependence may offer an environment that enables leaders to influence their communities, it may turn out that a high level of interdependence may so determine the nature of community behavior that the leaders, and their values, are perhaps irrelevant to the character of collective behavior of the community. The latter may be true if high structural interdependence within the community is accompanied by interdependence with the general society. Furthermore, high structural interdependence is based on structural complexity that insures the presence of alternative decision-making bodies within the community and, potentially, a relatively less important role for the local leadership.

SOCIO-POLITICAL STRUCTURE I: CONFLICTS AND CLEAVAGES. Although the general level of interdependence in a community may be important in explaining activeness, there are several specific features of the socio-political structure that have a direct bearing on what leaders of a community can do. It is the leaders' decisions, not their values, that have an immediate impact on the community. But additional constraints on the kind of decisions that can be made are imposed both within and outside the community. The most obvious of the internal constraints are conflicts among the people and the cleavages dividing them.

Cleavages in a community should seriously inhibit the local leadership from bringing together the population for corporate action. Substantial gaps between groups in the population will reduce the likelihood that individuals will participate in common community structures or institutions. As a result, opportunities in the community for participation in community organizations will not appeal equally to all segments of the population, and the full potential of the community will not be utilized by its citizens. Cleavages can be expected to have an adverse effect on community activeness.

The relationship between community conflicts and activeness is more complex than that of cleavages. Absence of conflicts, on the one hand, might reveal a stagnant community; issues will not be put forward and different interests will not be articulated. On the other hand, pervasive conflict in the community may lock both the leadership and the population in the management of differences, and absorb their energies in maintaining a semblance of harmony. Conflicts may indeed become so intense that they will fragment the population and preclude collective action necessary for development. Conflict, thus, must be considered from both of these standpoints, and the relationship of the leaders' values to activeness must be examined independently of the conflict in their communities.

SOCIO-POLITICAL STRUCTURE II: THE LEADERSHIP AND THE COMMUNITY. The leadership is a collective component of the socio-political structure of the community.[2] Five characteristics of the leadership's tie with the community behavior were observed: the scope of leaders' activity, the range and nature of their influence, the groups to which the leaders turn for support, the obstacles they see to their rule as leaders, and their party membership.[3]

The fact that leaders are active, influential, and have extensive contacts with significant groups in the community may, in itself, influence the activeness of the community, quite apart from any programmatic values. The leadership, however, instead of initiating policies, may act largely as brokers between various interests, and as facilitators for the activities of others. It is expected that a high level of leadership activity and influence, and extensive contacts, will be positively related to activeness.

In addition to the general level of leadership influence, the extent to which influence was spread out among the leadership groups rather than concentrated in a few, was assessed. It is anticipated that the greater the distribution of leadership influence among the leadership, the more likely it will be able to stimulate the population to allocate their efforts to community purposes and to involve the people in community affairs.

As activeness is concerned with the involvement of the population in community problems, the extent to which a leadership that reaches out into the community for support in making decisions should be a characteristic of the active community. The extent to which leaders touched base with groups in their community should be related to the activeness of the community.

Leadership faces obstacles in the performance of its role. Some of these are seen to be locally oriented, others are imposed from outside, and still others are part of the human condition. As the connection between leaders' values and activeness presupposes that leaders are able to do something and are able to have an impact, the extent to which the leadership sees obstacles in its way should reflect, on one hand, the extent to which it is possible to engage the resources and energies of the population, and, on the other, the efforts put forth by the leadership.

SOCIO-POLITICAL STRUCTURE III: LOCAL GOVERNMENTAL COMPETENCE. Despite resources, conflicts and cleavages, and the ties of the leadership to the community, the powers of the local governments are of obvious importance. Both what the leadership considers ought to be the scope of its responsibilities and what it sees as possible were assessed. The local leadership that is in favor of assuming responsibility for solving a large number of problems rather than letting central or regional governmental bodies or individuals within the communities do the job, should reach out into a broad range of community affairs. Thus, the more responsibility desired by the leadership of a community, the greater the activeness of the community should be.

In two countries in this study, Poland and Yugoslavia, there are no basic differences in the degree of formally defined local autonomy. However, perhaps even more important than the formal rules of autonomy are the leaders' perceptions of limits on their decision powers. Differences in perceptions of autonomy are a function not only of differences in formal legal structure but also of the leaders' general sense of competence in handling the problems of their local communities. A positive relationship between perceived autonomy and activeness is expected.

LEADERS' VALUES. As the focus of this study is whether, and in what ways, leaders' values influence the activeness of the community, the model of explanation will, as far as possible, remove the influence of the community environment in order to examine the relevance of the values of leaders to community activeness.

As discussed in Chapter 3 the nine values selected were: Economic Development, Conflict Avoidance, Participation, Selflessness, National Commitment, Action Propensity, Honesty, Change and Economic Equality. Values such as Economic Development, Popular Participation, Economic Equality and Change have been formulated into programmatic appeals for corporate action, and have been associated with major social and political revolutions. These appeals have engendered a new motivational structure on which the modern nation-state stands or aspires to be built. These motivations find expression in aspirations for economic well-being, democracy, equality, and progress (often undifferentiated change). Since activeness is a measure of the extent to which local communities have collectively achieved certain goals expressed by the values of Change, Economic Development, Participation, and Economic Equality, those communities whose leaders are committed to these values should be more active than those whose leaders are less committed. Further, those communities whose leaders espouse these values are likely to be in the mainstream of national development, and consequently, are likely to be in a position to communicate with higher level officials and are likely to obtain resources and support for local programs.

The leader's propensity to link the community to the nation and its policies is expressed in the value of National Commitment. One dimension of a leader's valued decision-making style that is assessed is called Action Propensity, which refers to how much the leader thinks he is entitled to risk community resources in the name of the future well-being of the community, and how much he values expeditious resolution of community issues. Conflict Avoidance refers to the unwillingness of the leaders to accept conflict to achieve community goals.

Although it should be expected that a position at either extreme— too much or too little concern for avoiding conflict, over-commitment or no commitment to the nation, unwillingness to take risks or disregard for the consequences of decisions—would be negatively related to the level of community activeness, the relationship between these values and activeness will be tested in the explanatory model in a linear fashion. A linear relationship is assumed because the measures of these values, the value scales, do not assess the extreme positions in an absolute sense, and because the value score for a community is the result of the averaging of the individual leader's scores. The data, therefore, can be expected to show a positive relationship between Action Propensity and Activeness, and a negative correlationship with Conflict Avoidance, and, because of the importance of the national programs for community activeness, a positive relationship with Commitment to Nation.[4]

The degree to which the local leadership adheres to universal moral values, such as honesty and sacrifice for others, and behaves accordingly, could be a major factor in the trust accorded to it by the population. Insofar as trust contributes to the willingness of the population to give their support to the leadership, the commitment of the leadership to the principles of honesty should be related to activeness. Trust is also, of course, an essential condition of corporate activity. This interpretation of the relationship between the values of Selflessness and Honesty, and community activeness is perhaps overdrawn in a world of managerially oriented, professional politicians. In this context, political leaders are judged and supported for their capacity to get things done, rather than on their personal moral qualities.

The degree to which leaders in a community share similar value orientations was assessed by a general measure of value congruence. The relationship of value congruence to activeness is perhaps not a linear one. On the one hand, it could be argued that the more similar leaders are in their values (that is, the more their values are shared by their colleagues), the greater the activeness of the community should be. On the other hand, some dispersion of values, and even active disagreement among leaders, may stimulate public discussion and action. In addition, differences in values may be complementary and thus a positive force in generating community activeness.[5]

BACKGROUND CHARACTERISTICS OF LEADERS. A limited number of background characteristics of leaders were included. Many conventional background characteristics, such as age, education, and occupation, are known to differentiate individuals in meaningful ways. At an aggregate level, their relevance is not as clear. Years of residence in the community in political life was included as a possible indicator of the knowledge and the stake of leaders in getting things done in the local community, particularly in countries where many of the local leaders are recruited nationally. The predictions that can be made from demographic information about leaders in relation to community activeness are problematic. However, by including these variables, it is possible to see if they can contribute to the explanation of community activeness in all four countries.

The Structure of Activeness—The Interplay
of Variables

Up to this point, the relationship of particular types of variables to activeness has been discussed. The remaining task is the specification of the interplay of the sets of variables. The overall strategy for examining this interplay aims, first, to see how much of the variance in activeness can be explained by the values of leaders after the variance explained by relevant structural variables of the community is removed. The structural variables that were selected are the resource base, the amount of community conflict, and the leadership influence in the community. Secondly, the interaction of all the major explanatory variables will be examined in a manner that will first remove all of the activeness variance accounted for by major community characteristics, so that the variance contributed by values can be examined without the constraints imposed by the community environment. Thirdly, the importance of each major variable will be considered in a hierarchy defined by its relative contribution to the explanation of activeness. This will be provided by a multiple regression analysis that will take the importance of the variables into account, without regard to their hypothesized importance for the explanation of activeness.

The general model of explanation seeks to determine: (1) the influence of each variable, independently, on activeness; (2) the influence of certain variables after removing the influence of the resource base, conflicts and leadership influence; (3) the influence of values on activeness, after the influence of a set of environmental and structural variables is removed; and (4) the importance of each explanatory variable, where any variable has an equal, rather than a predetermined, chance of accounting for variance in activeness. The design of this analytical model will include bivariate, first-order partial correlations, and forced and stepwise regressions.[6]

For the partial order correlational analysis, the design was the primary basis for selecting controlling variables. The design, for example, states that economic level is a general environmental condition for the play of the leaders' values on activeness. Also, the general design states that conflict in the community will affect the leaders' behavior. Finally, the influence of leaders in various areas of activity is considered a condition of the way in which leaders' values may interact with community activeness. Three general types of partial correlations were analyzed: one, for the most general and pervasive environmental variable, economic level, for all other relationships; another, for a salient socio-political characteristic of the community, conflict, for leadership role behavior and values; and finally, leadership influence, for the relationship between values and activeness.[7]

Since any choice of inclusion would affect the general pattern, the two criteria for selection were strictly applied for the multiple regressions. The most precisely measured and most general variables were selected and ordered according to their hypothesized importance in the explanation of activeness. These variables were ordered in the sequence defined in the general design: economic level, conflict, leadership activity, etc. The characteristics of the community precede the values of leaders in the analysis so that the total amount of variance explained by these variables can be examined, and their relative importance can be compared with leaders' values.

The design itself, however, should be tested or evaluated. Although the design requires that the influence of major community characteristics be removed in order to see whether, and in what ways, leaders' values influence community activeness, the data may indicate something quite different. Most of the variance in community activeness can perhaps be explained by the values alone. How the overall configuration of the data fits with the general design will be evaluated in terms of a stepwise regression, which will order variables according to how much of the variance in activeness they account for in comparison to other variables.

The general structure of the explanation of activeness is presented in Table 1 below. In this table the variables are ordered according to their hypothesized interaction with other explanatory variables. This is not a list of the variables entered into the bivariate analysis, but only those that, because of their hypothesized general importance and their role in the design, were examined in a multivariate analysis.

Table 1—Structure of Activeness

Variable	Economic Level Partial	Conflict Partial	Influence Partial	Inclusion in Stepwise Regression	Order in Forced Regression
1 Economic level				×	1
2 Perceived community conflicts	×			×	2
3 Total perceived divisions	×			×	
4 Division on education	×				
5 Division on income	×				
6 Division on religion	×				
7 Division on political views	×			×	
8 Division between city and country	×				
9 Division between superiors and subordinates	×				
10 Divisions over change	×			×	
11 Conflict between political groups and interests				×	
12 Total leadership influence	×	×			
13 Variance on leadership influence	×	×		×	5
14 Influence in agriculture	×	×			
15 Influence in public improvements and services	×	×			
16 Influence in culture	×	×			
17 Influence in welfare	×	×			
18 Influence in political organization	×	×			
19 Total leadership activity	×	×	×	×	4
20 Activity in agriculture	×	×	×		
21 Activity in public improvements and services	×	×	×	×	
22 Activity in welfare	×	×	×		
23 Activity in political organization	×	×	×	×	
24 Perceived autonomy	×	×	×	×	3
25 Total number of support groups sought	×	×	×	×	6
26–41 Support of specific groups (16 groups)	×	×	×		
42 No obstacles to leadership action	×	×	×	×	
43–51 Values: nine values	×	×	×	×	9–17
52–59 Importance of values: eight values	×	×	×		
60 Local government should do	×	×	×		
61 Local institutions should do	×	×	×		
62 Supports interest of nation	×	×	×		
63 Support interests of party	×	×	×		
64 Support interests of friends	×	×	×		
65 Support interests of people	×	×	×		
66 Leaders belonging to dominant party	×	×	×	×	7
67 Value congruence	×	×	×	×	8
68 Education	×	×	×		
69 Years in the community	×	×	×		

To determine the general applicability of this model, the following questions were addressed in analyzing the data: (1) Are relationships found in one country also found in others? If so, there is a strong presumption that the relationship may be universal, in view of the great differences among the four countries in the study. (2) If the structures of explanation are different, what features of these countries could account for these differences?

The unavoidable overall conclusion is that the explanation of activeness is not universal, and that country differences are determinative of the ways in which variables are related to activeness.

Out of the approximately 170 bivariate relationships examined in all four countries, no single variable is significantly related to activeness in all four countries ("p" at the .05 level is r = .361). There is only one variable—the value of Conflict Avoidance—that is significant or nearly significant in all four countries, but in Poland the direction of even this relationship is different. On only eight variables are there significant correlations in the same direction in two countries. The same kind of diversity prevails, when the influence of the intervening variables is examined.

Even the categories of variables—the resource base, ecological factors, socio-political structures, and leaders' values—have substantially different positions in the structure of explanation in each country. Although each of the general categories of variables has some relevance, the economic factors seem to dominate in the United States, the ecology in Yugoslavia, the socio-political variables in Poland, and values in India.

The Resource Base and Ecological
Characteristics

Table 2 provides the correlations between economic level and ecological characteristics and activeness. In the United States there is a high correlation between economic development and activeness—the highest correlation among all the variables. In Yugoslavia, economic level is relatively highly correlated with activeness—the second strongest correlation. The highest correlation in Yugoslavia, however, is between nonagricultural labor (an indicator of urbanization) and activeness, and, to a great extent, the correlation between economic development and activeness is a result of the relationship between nonagricultural labor and economic development.[8] In India and Poland the correlations between economic level and activeness are not significant. However, ecological characteristics are important. The active Polish powiats are small, less densely populated, and have younger people. By contrast, the active Indian blocks are associated with population agglomeration—size and density.

Table 2—Correlations Between Economic and Ecological Characteristics and Activeness

(Variables correlated at .05 level of significance in at least one country)

	India	Poland	U.S.	Yugoslavia
1 Economic level	−.113	−.011	.847	.658
2 Population: size	.382	−.750	−.161	.227
3 Population: growth	Not determined	−.267	−.062	.373
4 Population: density	.452	−.707	−.111	.646
5 Population: nonagricultural labor	.239[1]	−.312	Not applicable	.838
6 Population: median age	Not determined	−.514	.183	.340

[1] This variable is percent urban population.

The importance of economic level varies widely in the four countries. It is of almost no significance in India and Poland. In the United States it is preeminent—the wealthier the municipality the more it is active. In Yugoslavia the correlation is positive and moderate, but this correlation is exceeded by the proportion of nonagricultural labor in the commune, and almost equaled by the density of the population; this indicates that it is structural interdependence of the population, as expressed by nonagricultural labor and density that perhaps is the critical factor.[9]

One of the problems in analyzing the relationship between the economic level of a political unit and its activeness is the question of overlapping indicators, or the similarity of readings taken from the indicators. An attempt to reduce this difficulty was made first by taking indicators from a period prior to the indicators of activeness. For the most part, the date of the economic level indicators is 1960 and the activeness indicators are between 1960–1965. Second, the indicators, as far as possible, are related to different levels within the unit— the holding of wealth at other than the collective level. This is especially true of the American indicators where wealth was measured for individuals or family units. In Yugoslavia, the dates of most of the indicators were for a period closer to the indicators of activeness— 1964–1965; some of the measures reflect collective rather than individual wealth.

What we find across the four countries is that the macro-structure and processes of local political units as expressed in the measure of economic level and some ecological characteristics provide some of the highest correlations with activeness. The exception to this statement is India, where the highest correlations are found among the values of the local leaderships. But in every country a substantial segment of the variance in activeness can be accounted for by the economic level or some other ecological characteristics (72% in the United States; 70% in Yugoslavia; 59% in Poland; 20% in India). As activeness was intended to represent a general underlying process at the macro-level, these kinds of relationships confirm the general model that underlines the macro-socio-economic processes for activeness and calls for consideration of their influence before interpreting other relationships.

But despite the general relevance of these socio-economic processes to activeness, the specific nature of the relationships are quite different. In India, the greater the population aggregation, the higher the activeness is. In Poland the less the population aggregation, and the younger the population, the higher the activeness is. Although in Yugoslavia economic level is related to activeness, this relationship to a great extent appears to be the result of the structural interdependence among the individuals in the commune; wealthier communes have fewer agricultural workers, are more densely populated, and are more active. In the United States the economic level stands out as an independent and highly determinative factor in the explanation of activeness. Other ecological variables matter little. Thus, although the place of this category of variables in a general model that places initial emphasis on the importance of macro-economic and social processes seems vindicated by the findings, in terms of specific relationships, diversity dominates.

Socio-Political
Characteristics

The socio-political characteristics of the community are of three types: conflicts and cleavages within the community; the relationship of the local *leadership* and the community; and the views of the leaders concerning their capacity to act in their roles. Although the data for these three types of characteristics are all derived from the responses of the local leaders, they represent different kinds of variables. The first is an assessment based on the leaders' *perceptions* of the state of affairs. The leaders interviewed in each community are in effect used as a panel of judges where the average or mean judgment is treated as a characteristic of the community. The second, the relationship of the leadership to the community, is an aggregation of the *behavior* of the individual leaders into the collective characteristic of the leadership and how it is tied into the community. The sum of individual behavior occurring in a set of leadership roles is interpreted as a collective characteristic of that set—the leadership. The third is a *self-evaluation* of the leadership roles—the view of the leaders of their role, what it is and what it ought to be.

SOCIO-POLITICAL STRUCTURE I: CONFLICTS AND CLEAVAGES. Table 3 indicates that the relationship between conflicts and cleavages and activeness is quite different in the four countries. Active blocks in India have political conflicts. By contrast, conflict is clearly *not* perceived as a component of active powiats in Poland; nor are political cleavages seen as present. The opposite seems to prevail in Yugoslavia; the greater the conflict and the sharper the divisions between managers and employees, the more active the commune is. In the United States there is a difference between the conflicts and divisions. Although conflicts, particularly social conflicts, are positively associated with activeness, divisions between managers and employees are negatively related.

Table 3—Correlations Between Conflicts, Cleavages and Activeness

(Variables correlated at the .05 level in at least one country, r = .361)

	India	Poland	U.S.	Yugoslavia
1 Intensity of perceived conflicts	.236	− .564	− .003	.208
2 Conflicts between social groups[1]	.276	.087	.411	.036
3 Conflicts between political groups[1]	.466	− .303	.125	.126
4 Conflicts perceived as a community problem[1]	− .020	.171	.363	.445
5 Divisions on political views	.252	− .460	− .122	.145
6 Divisions between managers and employees	.164	.072	− .458	.377

[1] Open-ended question.

At this point, the model, which states the importance of general categories of variables, is still viable for Poland, the United States, and Yugoslavia, but somewhat less so for India. In Poland, the United States and Yugoslavia the macro-socio-economic structure and the socio-political structure have an important role in the explanation of activeness, although in Poland the socio-political structure appears more relevant than in the United States and Yugoslavia. In India, there is some departure from the general design. However, in terms of specific variables, the diversity between countries has grown substantially. The socio-political structural variables are operating in different ways in the four countries.

The socio-political structure and macro-socio-economic structures are intertwined. The general model, therefore, requires that the influence of the socio-economic structure should be removed in order to clarify the nature of the relationships between the socio-political structure of the community and activeness. Since the general model is cast in the language of universality, both generally and specifically, the influence of the same macro-economic variable—economic level—was examined in all four countries. In Table 4, the changes in relationships between socio-political structures and activeness that result from partialling out the influence of economic level are presented.

Table 4—The Influence of Economic Level on the Relationship Between Conflict-Cleavages of the Community and Activeness

(First order partials which remove or add to correlations at the .05 level)

	India		Poland		U.S.		Yugoslavia	
	Bivar.	Partial	Bivar.	Partial	Bivar.	Partial	Bivar.	Partial
1 Perceived conflicts	—	—	—	—	− .003	.437	—	—
2 Divisions between managers and employees	—	—	—	—	− .458	− .142	.377	− .011
3 Divisions on change	—	—	—	—	.337	.368	—	—

Some major changes occur in the United States. The intensity of perceived conflicts becomes a strong correlate of activeness. A new variable is added: the greater the divisions over change in a community, the more active the community. Even though the correlations of divisions between managers and employees were related in an opposite manner in the United States and Yugoslavia, the process of controlling for economic level minimizes the significance of this variable in the explanation of activeness for both countries. In Poland the lack of perceived conflict remains a predictor of activeness. Hence, by controlling for economic level, the diversity of the explanations of activeness in the four countries is, if anything, increased.

Socio-Political Structure II: The Leadership and the Community. The second type of socio-political characteristic of the local political communities is the role of the local leadership in the community. This characteristic has three aspects (based on the behavior of the leaders), which were examined: leadership activity in certain areas of local policy, leadership influence in those same areas, and the number and types of support groups sought by the leadership in decision-making.[10] There is, as expected, high correlation between leadership activity and leadership influence. Table 5 presents the correlations between these leadership characteristics and activeness for all variables correlating significantly in at least one country. Because the type of support

Table 5—Correlations Between Characteristics of Local Political Leadership and Activeness

(Variables correlated at the .05 level of significance in at least one country)

	India	Poland	U.S.	Yugoslavia
Leadership Activity				
1 Economic development	.525	−.112	−.192	.086
2 Agriculture	−.092	.184	not applicable	−.637
3 Public improvements, services and utilities	−.002	−.298	.290	−.498
4 Political organizations	.277	.231	−.459	−.246
Leadership Influence				
1 Economic development	.600	−.131	−.253	−.299
2 Agriculture	−.282	−.076	not applicable	−.657
3 Public improvements, services and utilities	−.105	−.386	.222	−.509
4 Health services	−.207	.078	−.206	−.401
5 Education	−.201	.173	−.250	−.373
6 Political organization	.209	.017	−.596	−.232
7 Sum of Areas of Influence	−.077	.233	−.236	−.430

Support Groups

India	
1 Appointed officials in the community	−.398
2 Respected and influential people	−.477

Poland	
1 Local elective officials (Praesidium of powiat Peoples' Council)	.446
2 Appointed officials in the community (top officials of powiat)	.370

U.S.	
1 Local civic, professional or reform groups concerned with local politics	.519

Yugoslavia	
1 Committee of League of Communists in commune	−.460
2 Communal Committee of Socialist Alliance	−.584
3 Professional groups	.498
4 Farmers	−.569

groups sought were specific to each country, these variables are presented country by country.

In India there is a high correlation between the activeness of the block and both leadership activity and influence in economic development. What the leaders do in that general area of policy, which is perhaps the most directly relevant political activity for activeness, seems to have impact. It is only in India, in fact, that there is a positive correlation between either leadership's activity or its perceived influence and activeness. In all other countries activity and influence in specific spheres of local programs are negatively correlated or not correlated at all with activeness.

For all practical purposes there is no correlation between what the leadership in the Polish powiat does or, its perceived influence, and activeness. There is one significant negative correlation between influence in public improvement, services and utilities, and activeness. This correlation, however, is not corroborated by a similarly significant negative correlation between reported activity in that area and activeness.

There is one consistent correlation between activity and influence of the American local leadership and activeness; this is activity and influence in political organizations. Where the local leadership is tied up in the local political organizations, there is less activeness. Cities of low economic development, with conflict between labor and management, lack of overt conflict at the community level, but with a leadership that is active in political organizations, are less active. The tie between a unionized working class population, low levels of economic wealth, and a leadership involved in the local political organizations is important in the explanation of activeness.

The Yugoslav pattern of leadership activity and influence and activeness fits with what has already been presented. The importance of the economic-urban nexus again appears with the strong negative correlations between leadership activity and influence in agriculture and activeness. The negative correlation between leadership activity and influence in public improvements, services and utilities perhaps can be accounted for by the fact that active communes have adequate levels of services and utilities, requiring less attention from the leadership than in the less active communes.

With regard to support groups, the leadership of active Indian blocks does not seek support from what could be considered the "more traditional" sector—appointed officials in the blocks and respected and influential people. On the other hand, active powiats in Poland are associated with a leadership that turns to the major elected and appointed officials—the formal structure. The single support group that is positively related to activeness in the United States substantiates the finding of leadership activity and influence. The leadership in active cities in the United States seeks support from local civic, professional and reform groups. The leadership in less active cities is active and influential in party organizations and perhaps draws its support from the party organizations.

In Yugoslavia the negative correlations between those seeking the support of farmers and activeness is at this point redundant. But what is interesting, if not explainable, is that the leadership in active communes does not seek support from the two major national political organizations, the League of Communists and the Socialist Alliance, but does seek support from professional groups. We know that professional groups are found in urban, wealthy and structurally interdependent communes, not in poor, agricultural ones. But why the leaders do not seek the support of the political organizations is less clear.[11]

The way in which the leadership characteristics are related to activeness is expected to be influenced both by the macro-economic structure of the local unit as well as by the socio-political structure, particularly conflict. These relationships are presented in Table 6, where economic level and conflict are controlled.

In Poland, in keeping with the earlier findings, economic level does not in the least affect the absence of relationships found between the leadership role characteristics and activeness, and clarifies the important, independent role of the socio-political structure. Conflict is associated with activeness independently of the macro-socio-economic structure and only in minor ways affects the behavior of the leadership.

In Yugoslavia almost all of the correlations between the socio-political structure variables and activeness are dependent on the economic level of the commune. The correlations of these variables with activeness—the influence of the leadership and the support groups sought—drops with one or two minor additions (influence in welfare and support sought from the intelligentsia). This again shows that the importance of the socio-political structure is largely a function of the macro-socio-economic structure of the commune, and by itself has a small role in the process of understanding the process of activeness.

The importance of the activity and influence of Indian leaders in economic development is independent of the macro-socio-economic structure of the blocks. However, whether the activity and influence of the leaders in economic development is related to activeness seems to be entirely dependent on the amount of conflict in the community. Further, when controlling for conflict, leaders influential in agriculture tend to be associated with less active blocks.

In Poland, conflict influences the relationship between seeking support from the formal structure of the powiat and activeness. If there were no conflict in the powiat, the formal structure would be less important and the informal structure (support from colleagues) more important in the explanation of activeness.

The American pattern of leadership structure and activeness remains uninfluenced by the level of economic development and conflict, with one exception. Whether or not there is a positive relationship between seeking support from local civic and reform groups and activeness is definitely a function of the wealth level of the city. The wealth level of a city explains the relationship between the leadership and those civic and reform groups and activeness.

The leadership structure has some importance for the explanation of activeness in all countries. Its relevance, however, is very dependent

Table 6—The Influence of Economic Level and Conflict on the Relationships Between Leadership Characteristics and Activeness

(First-order partial correlations that remove or add to correlations at the .05 level of significance)

	India Bivar.	India Partial	Poland Bivar.	Poland Partial	U.S. Bivar.	U.S. Partial	Yugoslavia Bivar.	Yugoslavia Partial
Leadership Influence								
A *Economic Level Partials*								
1 Public improvements, services and utilities	—	—	—	—	—	—	−.509	−.338
2 Health services	—	—	—	—	—	—	−.401	−.089
3 Culture	—	—	—	—	—	—	—	—
4 Education	—	—	—	—	—	—	−.373	−.308
5 Welfare	—	—	—	—	—	—	−.225	−.378
6 Sum of areas of influence	—	—	—	—	—	—	−.430	−.214
7 Variance on sum of areas of influence	—	—	—	—	—	—	−.419	−.258
B *Conflict Partials*								
1 Economic development	.600	.052	—	—	—	—	—	—
2 Agriculture	−.282	−.456	—	—	—	—	—	—
Support Groups								
A *Economic Level Partials*								
India								
1 Rich people	−.356	−.373	—	—	—	—	—	—
U.S.								
1 Local civic professional or reform groups concerned with local politics	—	—	—	—	.519	.202	—	
Yugoslavia								
1 Committee of League of Communists in commune	—	—	—	—	—	—	−.460	−.107
2 Communal Committee of Socialist Alliance	—	—	—	—	—	—	−.584	−.205
3 Different professional groups	—	—	—	—	—	—	.498	.114
4 Farmers	—	—	—	—	—	—	−.569	−.301
5 Intelligentsia	—	—	—	—	—	—	−.309	−.431
B *Conflict Partials*								
Poland								
1 Praesidium of Peoples' Council	—	—	.446	.354	—	—	—	—
2 Top administrative officials	—	—	.370	.347	—	—	—	—
3 Support of colleagues	—	—	.281	.373	—	—	—	—

on the macro-economic structure in Yugoslavia and on conflict in Poland and India. In India, even though the macro-economic structure of the block is of little importance, the leadership structure is relevant, but to some extent dependent upon the amount of conflict in the community.

Knowledge of the socio-political structure of the communities substantially increases the explanation of activeness in all countries. The ways in which political structure contributes to the explanation of activeness is specific to each country. Despite the general relevance of socio-political structural factors, the way in which they influence activeness must be interpreted in the context of a specific political system. Although conflicts are relevant in the explanation of activeness in both Poland and the United States, they operate in opposite ways. Although conflicts in general are not highly relevant in India, political conflicts have a substantial impact on the general community development. Activeness in Yugoslavia is primarily a product of macro-economic processes and the impact of the socio-political structure is indirect, dependent on the macro-economic structure.

SOCIO-POLITICAL STRUCTURE III: LOCAL GOVERNMENTAL COMPETENCE. There were four variables that expressed the views of the leaders concerning their governing responsibilities: their perceived power and autonomy; the obstacles that the leaders felt limited their effectiveness; the level of responsibility they valued at the local level; and the extent to which they felt their primary responsibility was to the nation, the party, friends or the local population.[12]

In no country was the leader's view of their powers and autonomy related to activeness. Indeed, judgments about the capacity of a local government to act and the activeness of a local unit are independent. Further, in no country was there any relationship between the reference of responsibility—nation *vs.* party *vs.* friends, *vs.* the local people—and activeness. In Yugoslavia, there is a significant correlation ($r = .40$) between the leader's view that responsibility for local nongovernmental institutions should be greater, and activeness. But this relationship disappears when controlling for the macro-socio-economic structure of the commune. It appears that in those communes with greater structural interdependence, as expressed in the level of economic development, there are more nongovernmental institutions capable of taking on more responsibility. This again affirms the importance of the macro-socio-economic structure in Yugoslavia in understanding the processes related to activeness.

Whereas the leadership's perception of the powers of local government is relatively unimportant, their assessment of *obstacles* to their own effective performance as leaders has much to do in three countries with whether the community is active. However, the relationship is very different in the three countries. In Poland, the leadership of active communities generally sees no obstacles: activeness and the proportion of leaders mentioning any obstacles is negative (r = − .42). In the United States the opposite is the case: the proportion of leaders conscious of obstacles correlates positively (r = .36), just below the .05 level of significance. India is similar to the United States, but in a very distinctive way: it is *political conflict* that besets the leadership (r = .70, the strongest of all the correlates of activeness in India). Such conflicts, although they may trouble the leadership, evidently do not interfere with the processes of activeness in the community.

The relationships between the variables pertaining to local governmental competence and activeness are generally consonant with the findings for the other types of socio-political characteristics. They are generally unimportant in India, related, but largely as a reflection of the socio-economic characteristics of the community in the United States and Yugoslavia, and of critical importance in Poland, especially if one considers that the leaders' evaluation of the obstacles in their way to some extent reflects the state of affairs in the powiats.

Leaders'
Values

The general model for the explanation of activeness anticipated that a substantial amount of the variance in activeness would be explained by the characteristics of leaders in the community. The model assumed that the way in which the characteristics of leaders would be related to activeness would be influenced by both the macro-economic and the socio-political structure of the local units.[13]

Table 7 gives the correlations between the nine value scales and activeness in the four countries. There is no correlation between any of the values and activeness in Poland, two correlations in India and Yugoslavia, and three in the United States. There is not a single correlation for Honesty and Selflessness.

Table 7—Correlations Between Leaders' Values and Activeness: The Value Scales

Values	India	Poland	U.S.	Yugoslavia
1 Economic development	− .052	.124	− .371	− .141
2 Conflict avoidance	− .357	.330	− .373	− .375
3 Participation	− .089	.023	.418	− .259
4 Selflessness	.173	− .185	− .086	− .151
5 National commitment	.503	− .209	.027	− .076
6 Action propensity	.044	− .154	.245	.093
7 Honesty	.054	−.041	.187	− .262
8 Change orientation	.361	.022	− .072	− .136
9 Economic equality	.055	− .094	− .033	− .433

Of all the correlations between values and activeness, Conflict Avoidance has the most predictive power across all four countries, but the direction of the correlation is reversed in Poland. Of all the values, this one is perhaps the most clearly tied to the socio-political structure of the community. It happens that the direction of the Conflict Avoidance value parallels the relationships found between activeness and perceived conflicts in every country. In India, the United States, and Yugoslavia the active community had more conflict and the leaders considered Conflict Avoidance of less importance. In Poland where the active powiats have less conflicts, the leaders value the avoidance of conflict.

In general, the relationships between the values of leaders and activeness is consistent with the relationships found between the macro-economic and socio-political structures and activeness in each country. In the United States the active cities are highly developed economically and their leaders are less concerned with the value of economic development. Leaders in active cities turn more frequently for support to local civic and reform groups, and also value participation. Indian leaders in active blocks tend to avoid seeking support from the "more traditional" sectors in their communities—appointed officials and respected and influential people—but are committed to the nation and to change. In Yugoslavia the less active communes are less economically developed, and their leaders value economic equality.

Another way of assessing the interaction of the macro-structural variables with the relationship between values and activeness is through partial order correlations. By examining the interaction of economic level, conflict, and also the extent to which leaders in the community are influential across a broad set of policies, the interdependence of values, the macro-structural variables, and activeness can be appraised. The partial order correlations are shown in Table 8.

In the United States and Yugoslavia the level of economic development is decisive. All significant correlations become insignificant. Thus, whether and in what ways the values of leaders are part of the process of activeness is entirely dependent on the macro-economic structure of the community. In India, the importance of the value of conflict avoidance for activeness is sharpened when the actual level of conflict is controlled: the greater the concern for conflict avoidance, the less active the community. The extent to which Indian leaders value conflict avoidance appears to be a result of the amount of conflict they see in their communities. In Poland, values of leaders remain unimportant, even after controlling for socio-political characteristics.

Because the relationships between values and activeness corroborate some of the relationships between the macro-socio-economic and

Table 8—The Influence of Economic Level, Conflict, and Leadership Influence on the Relationship between Values and Activeness

(First-order partial correlations that remove or add to correlations at the .05 level)

	India Bivar.	Partial	Poland Bivar.	Partial	U.S. Bivar.	Partial	Yugoslavia Bivar.	Partial
Economic Level Partials								
1 Economic development	—	—	—	—	−.371	−.244	—	—
2 Conflict avoidance	—	—	—	—	−.373	−.077	−.375	−.011
3 Participation	—	—	—	—	.418	.058	—	—
4 Change	.361	.355	—	—	—	—	—	—
5 Economic equality	—	—	—	—	—	—	−.433	.014
Conflict Partials								
1 Conflict avoidance	−.357	−.544	—	—	—	—	−.375	−.338
Influence Partials								
1 Economic development	—	—	—	—	−.371	−.316	—	—
2 Economic equality	—	—	—	—	—	—	−.433	−.276
3 Change	.361	.348	—	—	—	—	—	—

socio-political structures of local communities and activeness, the diversity of the explanations is intensified. Poland and India stand in sharp contrast. There is no single significant relationship in Poland, while in India one of the strongest correlations found up to this point is the one between the value of National Commitment and activeness. In the United States and Yugoslavia, the values that are important for activeness are different, although in both countries the macro-economic structures depress these correlations to insignificance. In India the correlations between values and activeness are only slightly affected by other variables.

The amount of variance any value explains in activeness in the four countries also differs: 25% in India with the value of National Commitment; 18% in Yugoslavia with the value of Economic Equality; 17% in the United States with the value of Participation; 10% in Poland with the value of Conflict Avoidance.

In addition to the value scales, a variety of other dimensions of leaders' values were assessed in a question on value priorities and responses to two open-ended questions on aspirations and desirable characteristics of leaders. The analysis of the three most important values selected in each country and over 20 categories of values coded from the open-ended questions reinforces the findings from the nine value scales, but adds an important dimension to the value-activeness association in India.[14] In Poland there is not a single significant correlation between activeness and either the three most important value priorities or any of the open coded categories of values. In the United States the leaders in active municipalities rank change as one of the important priorities (r = .55) while leaders in inactive cities rank economic development as important ($r = -.49$) a finding consistent with that found for the value scale of economic development. Both of these relationships, however, drop in significance when controlling for the economic level of the cities, again confirming the decisive role of the macro-economic structure in explaining the interaction between leaders' values and activeness in the United States. In Yugoslavia, there is a negative correlation ($r = -.37$) between activeness and the valued leadership trait of impartiality.

In India, it is significant that the leaders of active rural communities do *not* put their hopes for the future development of the nation in industrialization. Aspiration for industrialization correlates *negatively* ($r = -.43$) with community activeness, indicating that the leadership of the most active communities in the Indian countryside is not committed to industrialization as the target of economic development. These same leaders do not place high priority on the value of avoiding conflict ($r = -.44$), even though the Indian leaders in general consider it one of the three most important values. This relationship is unaffected when controlling for any of the macro-economic and socio-political structural variables; this reinforces the independent role of leaders' values for explaining activeness in India.

By examining the influence of the economic and socio-political structures of the local political units on the relationship between values and activeness, we can support the following conclusions: *the economic and socio-political structures are entirely independent of the relationship between values and activeness in Poland, almost entirely independent in India, and almost entirely determinative in both the United States and Yugoslavia.*

Leaders' Background
Characteristics

In order to determine what kinds of leaders are associated with active communities, a few background characteristics of the leaders were examined. Table 9 presents the bivariate correlations.

Table 9—Correlation between Background Characteristics of Leaders and Activeness

(Variable correlated at .05 level of significance or higher in at least one country)

		India	Poland	U.S.	Yugoslavia
1	Age	−.466	.061	−.222	.338
2	Education	.357	−.162	.293	.625
3	Length of residence in community	.012	−.437	−.374	−.269
4	Intergenerational mobility	−.067	.251	−.389	−.037

In India young leaders with higher education (reflecting perhaps the greater educational opportunities for the younger generation) are found in active blocks. In Yugoslavia, education, available in the more urbanized and structurally interdependent communes, is a characteristic of the active communes. This is one of the three highest correlations found in Yugoslavia. In Poland and the United States, education is not an important characteristic of leaders in active communities. Whereas education was found to be one of the more "universal" factors at the individual level, at the collective level its relevance is less uniform.

In Poland and the United States, the leaders in active communities are relative newcomers to their communities, indicating that in both countries the active communities are open to infusion from the outside. In the United States, the leaders in the active cities are upwardly mobile. (Do not have the same occupation as their father.)

Correlates of Activeness in
Four Countries

Table 10 is a summary of the relationships found in the four countries, and provides an overview of the general model for the explanation of activeness. In each country there were significant correlations with activeness for all categories of variables described in the general model, with the noteworthy exception of any of the measures of values in Poland. Although the correlation of the value of conflict avoidance and activeness is nearly significant, this correlation reinforces the importance of actual conflict in Poland in understanding the processes of activeness. In Poland, the combination of macro-social characteristics and socio-political structure by themselves provide an adequate explanation of activeness. The active Polish powiat is small, with a young population and leaders drawn from outside, and has a low level of conflict, a stable set of leaders who are oriented to the formal elected and appointed officials of local government.

The active Indian block has a high level of population aggregation (density, size) and can be described largely in terms of the characteristics of the leadership structure and individual leaders. The leaders are young, well educated, highly conscious of political conflicts and how they affect leadership behavior, but unconcerned with avoiding conflicts, are committed to the nation, are oriented to change, feel they have influence on development, and shun support from the traditional and formal structures of influence in their blocks.

In the United States, the economic level of the city is the dominant explanatory factor. In addition, however, the nature of conflicts and divisions are important, especially if the influence of economic factors is discounted. The role of leaders' characteristics, although correlated with activeness in several ways, seems to be a product of the general economic environment. The leadership in the active city seems to avoid political organizational activities, but seeks out the support of local civic and reform groups.

As in the United States, activeness in Yugoslavia is closely linked to wealth, but, more importantly, also to the structural inter-dependence within the commune. All relationships depend on these factors. When the urban-wealth factors are accounted for, all other important relationships disappear. To understand activeness is to understand the economic development processes in the communes. The inactive commune is economically underdeveloped, with an elaborate leadership structure; the leaders feel influential in a variety of areas, seek support from several social and political sectors, and value economic equality, if not development, and the avoidance of conflict.

Table 10 clearly shows that the patterns of explanation in the four countries are different. However, the relevance of the three general categories of variables described in the general model is sustained, except for leader characteristics in Poland. The relevance of the three general categories of variables clearly reflects country differences: in India, the characteristics of leaders, especially their values, are of primary importance; in Poland, the socio-political structure, especially conflict, predominates; in the United States, the macro-economic structure and, to a lesser extent, the socio-political structure is important; in Yugoslavia, the variable that tends to absorb all others in explanation is economic development.

Table 10—Summary of Relationships: Bivariate and Partials

Variables	India	Poland	U.S.	Yugoslavia
Community Characteristics: Economic-Demographic	1. Density .45 2. Population size .38	1. Population -.75 2. Density -.71 3. Age -.51	1. Economic level .85	1. Nonagricultural labor .84 2. Economic level .66 3. Density .65 4. Population growth .37
Socio-Political Structure I: Conflicts and Cleavages	1. Conflicts: Political groups .47	1. Conflict intensity -.56 2. Divisions: Political views -.46	1. Divisions: Managers and employees -.46 RE 2. Conflict intensity .44 AE 3. Conflicts: Social groups .41 4. Divisions: Change .37 AE 5. Conflicts viewed as community problem .36	1. Conflicts viewed as community problem .45 2. Divisions: Managers and employees .38 RE
Socio-Political Structure II: Leadership Role	1. Influence: Economic develop. .60 RC 2. Activity: Economic develop. .53 3. Support: Respected and influential people -.48 4. Influence: Agricult. -.46 AC 5. Support: Appointed officials -.40 6. Support: Rich people -.37 AE	1. Support Praesidium Peoples' Council .45 RC 2. Influence: Services -.39 3. Support: Colleagues .37 AC 4. Support: Appointed officials .37 RC	1. Influence: Political organization -.60 2. Support: Civic groups .52 3. Activity: Political organization -.46	1. Influence: Agriculture -.66 2. Activity: Agriculture -.64 3. Support: Socialist Alliance -.58 RE 4. Support: Farmers -.57 RE 5. Influence: Public improvements -.51 RE 6. Activity: Public improvements -.50 7. Support: Professions .50 RE

Socio-Political Structure III: Government Competence	1. Obstacles: Political conflicts .70	1. Obstacles: Total −.42	1. Obstacles: Total .36	8. Support. League of Communists −.46 RE 9. Support: Intelligentsia −.43 AE 10. Influence: Total −.43 RE 11. Influence: Health −.40 RE 12. Influence: Welfare −.38 AE 13. Influence: Education −.37 RE 1. Preferred locus of responsibility: Local non-govt. institutions .40
Leaders' Characteristics: —Values	1. Conflict Avoidance −.54 AC 2. National Commitment .50 3. Change .36 RE		1. Participation .42 RE 2. Conflict Avoidance −.37 RE 3. Economic Development −.37 RE	1. Economic Equality −.43 RE 2. Conflict Avoidance −.38 RE
—Aspirations and Value Priorities	1. Aspiration: Industrialization −.43 2. Priorities: Conflict Avoidance −.44		1. Priorities: Change .55 RE 2. Priorities: Economic Development −.49 RE	
—Background	1. Age −.47 2. Education .36	1. Years in Position .50 2. Length of Residence −.44	1. Mobility −.39 2. Length of Residence −.37	1. Education .63

RC = Removed in conflict partial
RE = Removed in economic partial
AC = Added in conflict partial
AE = Added in economic partial

285

Notes

1. Data for economic level were gathered for 1960 in India, Poland and the United States and for 1964–1965 in Yugoslavia (see Chapter 7). Activeness data in all countries but Yugoslavia were for the years 1960–1966.

2. Although leadership is conceived as a collective characteristic, it is assessed in this study as an aggregate characteristic.

3. As the extent of the local leadership's affiliation with the dominant national party in India (Congress), Poland (Polish United Workers Party), and Yugoslavia (League of Communists) and the dominant local party in the United States (either Democrat or Republican, whichever had the most members among the city council) did not correlate with activeness, it is not further considered in this part. It is doubtful whether this characteristic of the leadership—relationship to party organization—expresses a relationship with the community. Party affiliation, however, did matter for individual leader characteristics. See Chapter 4.

4. If the data were to be examined for curvilinear relationships, it would be necessary to score each community on the basis of the non-normal distribution of individual values *within* the community itself. It is within the community that the curvilinear distribution of scores would be expected to make a difference. The community scores on the values, however, are measures of central tendencies within the community under the assumption of a normal distribution of the leadership within the community.

5. See Chapter 5 for a discussion of value congruence and activeness.

6. Although the partial correlation assumes no error in the dependent variable, among other things, it is used in this analysis. Results based on controlling, however, must be taken with skepticism.

7. These variables were selected both for their presumed theoretical importance and their actual behavior in explaining activeness. Although perceived autonomy represents one of the categories of variables, and thus should have been included in the partials, in no country did it approximate a significant correlation with activeness.

8. The correlation between nonagricultural labor and economic level is .74; between density and economic level .68.

9. Following the three-category breakdown on economic level suggested in Chapter 7 and comparing this with a similar breakdown on activeness, we find the following for Yugoslavia. If these scales can be taken as representing more than rankings, this table shows that a low degree of economic development correlates with a moderate amount of activeness. This table should be read with the caution that there are no "high activeness" communes and only five "low" ones. In the United States, there are only five exceptions of a high economic level municipality being below the median on activeness or a low economically developed city being above the median. This can be expected from the high correlation. The other countries, of course, can be expected to have almost no pattern.

	Economic Level			
Activeness	Low	Medium	High	Total
Low				
T = less than 46.99	0	2	3	5
Moderate				
T = 46.00–55.99	9	15	1	25
High				
T = greater than 56.00	0	0	0	0
Total	9	17	4	30

10. The proportion of leaders belonging to a dominant political party was an additional variable in this category. However, only in the United States was this variable specifically related to party dominance in a particular community; in the other three countries it was the dominant national party.

11. The support group variables were scored in one way in India and the United States and in another in Poland and Yugoslavia. In India and the United States, a score of "1" was assigned to an individual if he selected a group as one to which he turns for support, and a score of "2" to that same group if the individual chose it as one of the three most important. Thus the scores reflect both selection and importance. In Poland and Yugoslavia, selecting a group was scored "1" and a different "variable" was used to designate whether the individual considered the group one of the three most important. As this analysis is restricted to within-country correlations, the results should not seriously affect the significance of the correlations, as has been shown in various experimental analyses.

12. This variable was coded differently in India and thus its comparability must be treated with caution. Further, this variable is perhaps more properly conceived of as a characteristic of individual leaders, rather than as a collective characteristic of the leadership (with reference to local roles).

13. The values of leaders are an aggregated characteristic of the leaders in the community. As these are aggregated characteristics, it is possible to group the

leaders without regard to the community to which they belong; this is done in Chapters 3 and 4. These aggregated characteristics should be distinguished from the collective characteristics described as socio-political characteristics. In this case, in order to obtain a measure of community conflict or of leadership influence in the community, the particular community sets the bounds of aggregation. The questions ask about the state of affairs, behavior, or evaluation of roles in that community rather than about individual characteristics. See Chapter 2 for further elaboration of this distinction. (This is not true for the individual leader's views of the groups to which he owes primary responsibility.)

14. See Appendices A and C for a discussion of these questions, which include the coding categories for the open-ended questions. Because leaders were asked to select three of eight values, this discussion is limited to the three most important value priorities in each country.

CHAPTER 10

Patterns of Activeness: The Influence of Country and System

This chapter was written by Teune.

One purpose of this research is to test the generality of a hypothesized explanation of activeness in different political systems. What was found is diversity. The great differences in the variables that explain activeness in the four countries can perhaps be dismissed by the possibility that those variables that would explain activeness in all four countries were not examined. This is something about which we can only speculate. What we do know is that the study included a large "sample" of political, social, and psychological variables, and of that large set of variables, those which explain activeness are different for each of the four countries.

As most of the variables examined are not related to activeness anywhere, the absence of relationships, of course, is the most generalizable finding of the study. The basis, however, for including variables in the general model is that they are related to activeness, rather than the specific manner of the relationship. Thus the focus of the comparative analysis must be on those relationships that were found. The central question is: why does one relationship, or type of relationship, exist in one country but not in the others? This question, which in part can be answered by reference to the differences among the countries, is the core question for comparative research.

Strategies of
Explanation

Differences in relationships within countries, or a relationship in one or more systems but not in all, can be explained by characteristics of the countries themselves. What is to be explained by these country characteristics are differences in relationships. If there is (or is not) a relationship between a variable and activeness in all four systems, it can be assumed that the systems are all the same in this regard. As there is no "variance," little else can be said. Three general types of system characteristics will be used to explain differences found in relationships between certain variables and activeness: (1) the peculiarities of the units, the local political systems, under study; (2) certain general differences between the four countries; and (3) certain contextual differences in the nature of the phenomena being explained in the four countries—activeness and, in some instances, known differences in the error in the variables.

Peculiarities of the Local
Political System

Perhaps the most critical difference is the degree of homogeneity on dimensions bearing on activeness among the local units within each country. In Poland, there is similarity in the urban-rural mixtures of population among the units. The Indian blocks are almost entirely rural. Although the communes in Yugoslavia contain both urban and rural population, there is substantial variation among communes in the degree of their urbanization. Of all countries, however, the United States perhaps has the most differentiated local political units. Municipalities in the United States tend to serve specialized functions both for their citizens and for the regions of which they are a part. There are manufacturing cities, suburbs, and regional centers. The fact that there are vast differences in the degree of diversity of the local political units within the four countries will obviously influence the explanatory patterns of activeness.

The second peculiarity of most national systems is regional differentiation. The units in this study were political units, which are only infrequently homogeneous and autonomous social and economic units. In every country in this study most of the local units are a part of a larger economic and cultural area. As demonstrated in the discussion of the assessment of activeness, these regional influences are important in each country, and their role in the explanation of activeness needs to be emphasized. Nine out of ten blocks in Uttar Pradesh, all seven powiats from the Central Region in Poland, six out of seven southern American cities, and seven out of ten Bosnian communes are below the median activeness score. The highly active local units are concentrated in Maharashtra in India, in the northwestern region in Poland, in the Midwest and West in the United States, and in Slovenia in Yugoslavia.

The importance of regionalism can be interpreted in one of two ways. On the one hand, a region can be viewed as a self-contained subsystem, and, consequently, any attempt to extract a local unit from the region of which it is a part is misleading. This position would argue for a measure of activeness specific to each region; this measure should differentiate units within each region separately.[1] On the other hand, it is possible to take the position that regional differentiation itself is a manifestation of some general processes, which are reflected in units within regions. This position holds that the distribution of local units by region can be explained by such facts, as, for instance, Maharashtra having a large number of urban places, the northwestern region in Poland receiving a great deal of development funds from the central government, midwestern and western cities in the United States being unencumbered by unalterable settlement patterns, and Slovenia being the most developed Yugoslav republic. The second position will be taken here except, of course, where regionalization cannot be interpreted in terms of some general processes.

Finally, each local unit is part of a nation-state system with policies that directly affect the development of local political units. National policies will, of course, be most important in highly centralized political systems, such as Poland, which has adopted a policy of developing the western territories. There has been an infusion of funds and efforts to mobilize the population. In highly decentralized systems, such as the United States, national policies are often not decisive, but, in default of national policies, there are the policies of the fifty states.

*System
Differences*

The four countries are different on a conceptually infinite number of dimensions. Of all of the possible dimensions of differences, a few ought to make a critical difference for the behavior of local political units. Because of the small number of systems in this study, it is not possible, of course, to be conclusive about the importance of any of these system differences in explaining the different patterns of activeness in the four countries. We can, however, suggest what role some of these system differences play, in order to explain the different structures of activeness within each country.

Three such system characteristics will be used. First, there is the general economic level of the country, as indicated by estimates of gross national product per capita. The United States, Poland, Yugoslavia, and India—this is the rank order of general national wealth.[2] General wealth is considered important for two reasons. First, there is the amount of resources at the disposal of local governments. It is assumed that the higher the level of general wealth, the more able any local government is to mobilize resources for specific purposes. Secondly, if the country is generally poor or developing, then the local political leadership (as a matter of fact almost all of the political leadership) will be heavily involved in matters of economic development and the problems related thereto. Where the leadership is involved in development, its characteristics should make a difference in the development of local units.

The second major dimension is the general autonomy of the local political units. It should be recalled that in this research the important factor is that local political units *differ*. Differences between local political units *within* a country provide the basis for seeing whether and to what extent variables covary. All four countries differ in the amount of decisional latitude allowed their local political units. Structurally defined, decisional latitude is distinguished from the autonomy perceived by the local political leadership, which was assessed. In considering differences in relationships within countries, what is important is whether the legal or actual structural latitude is constant for all local political units, or whether it can vary. In fact, only in the United States are there substantial differences in legal autonomy between political units. The relevance of autonomy is that the greater the degree of structural latitude, the greater the possible impact of the differences of local political leaders on their communities. This proposition, if true, should be manifest both for the units within the United States and for the importance of leader characteristics in the explanation of activeness across countries. The four political systems can be ranked on the relevance of autonomy to activeness: the United States, Yugoslavia India, Poland.

The third major characteristic of political systems that will be considered is the institutionalization of local governmental behavior— the degree to which structures of local government have become settled. The indicator used to rank the political systems on the degree of local governmental institutionalization is the amount of time the present local structure has been in effect. Although it is dangerous to equate time with institutionalization, the vast differences between the countries in this study may obviate the danger. The ranking of the four political systems is: the United States (although there are great variations depending on the area of the country), Poland, India, Yugoslavia. The link between institutionalization of the local political system and activeness is based on the proposition that to the extent that there are established ways of handling problems, the less important particular characteristics of individual leaders will be for the character of the local community.

*Context of the
Variables*

One of the methodological perspectives of this research has been the recognition of the importance of the contexts, the systems in which the observations are made.[3] These contexts determine not only the "meaning" of specific variables but also how they interact.

One of the assumptions ordinarily made when comparing processes or comparing relationships between variables within systems is that the amount of error contained in each variable is approximately equal for all systems. This assumption is particularly open to question in a cross-national study. There is some information about the possible error contained in a particular variable for a specific country. For example, on perceived divisions in the community, racial divisions were used in the United States and caste divisions in India. Where appropriate, this kind of consideration will be brought into the discussion to help understand similarities and differences found across countries.

What is perhaps of a more critical nature in the explanation of activeness than actual error are the biases inherent in the measure of activeness in the four countries. Some of these have been discussed in the section on the assessment of activeness. The biases in the measure of activeness hopefully reflect the social and political process to which the concept refers in each country. But some specific biases remain, will emerge in the relationships found, and will exaggerate the differences in the explanation of activeness found in each country, although the bias in the measure of activeness is treated as the same for all units within a country. As a result, one competing hypothesis to explain any difference among countries is that there are specific country biases in the measure of activeness.

In India many of the measures of activeness relate to individual participation in programs that are more likely to be available where there is some urban population or urbanized center; these are programs such as vaccinations, sterilizations, and literacy. There is a correlation between population aggregation and activeness, despite long-held views that density hinders social development. It appears that the kind of behavior contained in the measure of activeness requires some degree of population concentration.

In Poland there are several measures of organizational participation, especially of organizations that are likely to attract younger people. The bias is in favor of areas with a large number of young people. This factor has contributed to the finding that the highly active powiats are those that have recently been settled by younger Poles.

The United States, with its indicators of participation in organizations, such as the League of Women Voters and the Boy Scouts, favors communities with a large middle class as active communities. If middle-class participation structures are scored high on activeness, then those same areas will score high on the measure of economic wealth that is based on individual family income and consumption.

Yugoslavia is a country undergoing urbanization. The activeness measure is weighted in favor of those communes with large memberships in the League of Communists and the Socialist Alliance. It turns out that in urban areas the proportion of people who are members of these organizations is higher than in rural areas. There are several reasons for this, among them higher educational levels in urban areas and the general propensity for urban populations to join organizations of various types. Urban areas score high in activeness, reflecting an urban bias in the measure of activeness. Further, it turns out that many of the political participation measures are, as in so many countries, designed for the face-to-face contact characteristic of rural areas. Participation in voters' meetings tends to be high in rural and discounted in urban areas. The structure of the activeness measure is highly fragmented in Yugoslavia. The reason for this fragmentation is that the structure of political participation, based on face-to-face participation in meetings of neighbors, is a rural phenomenon, whereas the political structure based on secondary association, such as the League of Communists and the Socialist Alliance, is an urban participation structure.[4] Combining these two structures of participation into a single measure of activeness tended to fragment the overall structure of the activeness measure.

Interaction Between
System Factors

The system level factors will interact to push the explanation of activeness in a particular direction. Three major kinds of variables were considered in this study: the macro-economic and social characteristics of the community; the social and political structure of the community; and the characteristics of an aggregation of local leaders—in particular their values. The implication of the foregoing discussion is that in systems with developing economies, high levels of local autonomy, and low levels of institutionalization of the local political system, the play of leaders' characteristics should be important in explaining the levels of activeness. Conversely, in systems where there is a developed economy, a low level of local autonomy, and a substantial degree of institutionalization, the local leadership should be less relevant to what happens in those communities. For the four countries under study, India and especially Yugoslavia approximate the case where leaders are important, although the level of autonomy in India is lower than in Yugoslavia. Poland fits the second case. The United States has a developed economy, a large amount of local autonomy and high levels of institutionalization, especially in older, more settled parts of the country.

The basic question is to what extent does any kind of local variation make any difference for activeness? This question concerns not only the variables included in this study, but the importance of *any* variables reflecting differences in local political units for explaining variation in activeness. Here, the peculiarities of the local political units are crucial. To the extent that there is general homogeneity among the units, some regionalization, in which differences between units within the region would be absorbed, and to the extent that there are national policies of local development, any kind of local political unit variation, should make little difference. Poland has the greatest amount of homogeneity between units, a great deal of regionalization, particularly as reflected in the western territories, and strong national policies for local development. Yugoslavia was experiencing, at the time of this study, the effects of national policy toward local government; the country has strong regionalization, and some homogeneity among units, particularly with respect to size. India obviously has strong regionalization, state as well as national policies of development, and heterogeneity among units. The United States has regionalization but few decisive national policies and a great deal of heterogeneity among units, perhaps more than any other country included in this study.

Local and National Political Systems:
Patterns of Interdependence

The relevance of three sets of variables for activeness and specific variables for the explanation of activeness was established and compared across countries in the previous chapter. To some extent, the independent contribution of specific variables to the explanation of activeness was determined by examining their interdependence with the macro-economic structure (economic level), and with the socio-political structure (conflicts). When system level characteristics are used to explain differences in relationships found, the question is: to what extent are general political, economic, and social processes of the nation-state taking place at the local level? To what extent can the processes observed at the local level be accounted for by some more general, macro-level processes?

The importance of the Polish political system to the understanding of the explanation of activeness is clearer than for the other countries. First, there is a national plan of development with emphasis on regional equality. Secondly, the structure of the system that emphasizes unity in various institutions, such as the national unity front, treats conflict as detrimental to social development. Thirdly, there is the program of development, settlement, and incorporation of the western territories. Furthermore, there is a relatively high level of economic development, little local autonomy, and a reasonably well-institutionalized structure of local government. If some consideration is given to the "organizational" and "youth" biases in the measure of activeness, then the overall constellation of variables relevant to the explanation of activeness in Poland is interpretable in terms of what is happening within the country generally.

For Poland, economic level does not matter, but small size, low density, and the youth of the population of the powiat does. These correlations reflect the "new territory" nature of active powiats. If the national policies toward the new territories are discounted, conflict seems to enter the picture and stays. Conflict generally, but also political conflict in particular, has a role that is more or less independent of other factors. As there are mechanisms for resolving conflict throughout the political system, general conflict, and often perhaps political conflict, is associated with less active powiats, perhaps where those mechanisms are not working. When conflict does appear, the role of the formal political structure emerges. Where conflict is part of the local scene, leaders turn to the formal leaders for support; if there were no conflicts, leaders in active powiats would be more likely to turn to their colleagues. To some extent, the formal leadership is engaged where conflict is part of the processes associated with less activeness.

The leader characteristics of importance in Poland appear to be a result of these other processes; the leaders in active powiats come from other areas, but tend to have held their positions relatively longer than leaders in less active powiats.

But despite these and other relationships found in Poland, national policies dominate the character of the explanatory variables. Conflict adds to the understanding of activeness. But when national policies in a centralized political system are combined with the homogeneity among the powiats, few community differences and, for all practical purposes, none of the differences among the leaders across powiats are important. For activeness, then, the between-powiat differences, emanating at the national level or as part of the general social and economic processes of the country, will provide a set of variables sufficient for an understanding of the processes of activeness at the local level.

One of the most salient features of Yugoslav national life in recent years is its relatively rapid rate of economic growth, which is often accompanied by urbanization. This general characteristic of the Yugoslav political system by itself explains a great deal of the variation found in activeness at the local level. Among all of the variables examined, the two that are among the strongest are nonagricultural labor and economic level. Furthermore, economic level influences practically every other relationship found. Although there is a set of variables related to activeness, they are all overshadowed by general development—the urban-wealth nexus—of the Yugoslav commune. The characteristics of the commune's socio-political structure and the leaders that are associated with activeness (and indeed some of these correlations are quite strong and more numerous than for any other country), and the variation in activeness that they account for are overwhelmed by the basic process taking place within the general economic and social system.

But economic factors are not the complete picture. There is also the structural interdependence of the commune reflected in urbanization. The economic factor helps to interpret an urban conflict component of active communes: conflict, and in particular, conflict between managers and workers, presumably within economic organizations. The urban component of activeness in Yugoslavia is further highlighted by the fact that leaders in active communes are better educated, do not value the avoidance of conflict that seems to be characteristic of rural communes, and do not value economic equality, an equality for which they would presumably have to pay.

The ideology of the political system is relevant. First, there is the ideology that economic inequality is an acceptable short-term means to increase productivity for equality in the long run. Second, ideology helps explain what, at first glance, seems to be a strange set of relationships: leaders in active communes in general see themselves as less influential and active in a variety of policy areas than do leaders in less active communes; the former tend to turn not to the League of Communists and the Socialist Alliance for support, but rather to professional groups in the commune. These relationships between leadership activity, influence, and support generally fits an "expected" pattern of Yugoslav social development. It is anticipated that, as the country develops economically, the formal political leadership will recede in importance, and political organizations, having fulfilled their leadership role in development, will give way to the basic associations of social and economic life. As the active communes can be considered the more developed, both socially and, as discussed, almost surely economically, then this shift from the formal political roles to the emerging social and economic institutions can already be seen.

Although Yugoslavia has a high level of local autonomy, a great deal of variation among political units, and some of the least institutionalized structures of local government in this study, the process of activeness appears so much a part of the general social and economic development of the country that the role the leaders can play, at least at present, seems to be marginal. If wealth and urbanization, especially as reflected in regional differentiation, and perhaps a general development ideology of the country, are understood, the basic processes of activeness at the local level are, to a great extent, described.

Although the United States, with great heterogeneity among its local governments, a high level of local autonomy, and a high level of economic development, should give room for local leaders to interact in the process of activeness, it appears that the general character of urban America is the pivotal factor for the set of variables associated with activeness. In some ways, the institutionalization of local government and the problems that face the American city submerge the importance of leaders into the general urban environment they confront.

There are few urban policies of the national government in the United States; neither development programs nor pervasive ideological positions exist. There has been, however, a substantial and growing differentiation of the economic base of the cities.[5] What appears to differentiate the municipalities most is the nature of the citizens, and particularly the citizens' economic status. Differences in types of population seems to be the dominant factor in the set of variables that correlate with activeness.

The leadership of active cities turns to local civic organizations for support, but it is not particularly active or influential in party organizations. In active cities, there is some conflict, particularly between social groups, and, importantly, there is an absence of divisions between labor and management. To some extent, conflict is manifest in the processes of active cities. Leaders in active cities do not value economic development, which they already have, or the avoidance of conflict, which they see as present. They do value participation. The values of Participation and Conflict Avoidance are negatively related ($-$ .61), indicating that in cities that can afford it, conflict and participation are seen as necessary or desirable aspects of collective life. But what is critical is that every relationship between the characteristics of leaders and activeness becomes insignificant when the level of economic development is taken into account. This indicates that what the leaders value is more a function of the nature of the macro-economic structure of the city than a component of the process of activeness.

Economic level, reflecting the proportion of middle-class people living in a city, affects most relationships, except the negative relationship between influence in the political party organization and activeness. Despite the level of economic well-being, a city characterized by a leadership influential in party organizations is less active. The independence of this relationship may reflect a characteristic of the national system, the nature of the party organization not being as relevant to the local community as to the national political system.

India is the clearest case where local leaders make a difference. India has a low level of economic development, some local autonomy, and, at the local level at least, low institutionalization of governmental structure. There are substantial differences between local units, and these can be seen in the characteristics of the leaders. The relationships between population aggregation and activeness is perhaps a function of the "urban bias" in the measure of activeness. Neither population aggregation, nor the macro-economic structure, however, plays an important role in explaining activeness.

The strongest correlations in India involve the leadership characteristics: leaders in active blocks are influential and active in economic development, shun support from "traditional" groups (appointed officials, and "respected and influential people") and tend to look for support from among their colleagues. In comparison with leaders in less active blocks, they do not aspire for industrialization, are aware of political conflicts, are more committed to the nation, are less concerned with avoiding conflict, and find collective solutions at the local level desirable.

Conflicts in India are an aspect of the relationship between the nature of the leadership and activeness. When the effects of conflict are removed, the correlation between leadership influence in economic development and activeness disappears. Despite the fact that so many of the indicators of activeness pertain to agriculture, when the effects of conflict are removed, the relationship between a leadership that sees itself as influential in agriculture and activeness is negative. Conflict by itself appears to have little direct impact on activeness. Rather, it seems to accompany a leadership involved in economic development; this type of leadership, in turn, seems to be an important ingredient of the active block.

Leaders associated with active communities almost fit some kind of image of a developmental cadre: they value change, the nation, and do not care about conflict; they are young, educated, and oriented toward the political party (mostly the national Congress Party); they do not aspire for industrialization; they do not value individual initiative, but rather find collective solutions in local nongovernmental institutions desirable. There is one exception to the image, and that is the fact that some indifference about economic development as a value exists.

Although it may be argued that activeness of local political units in India can be understood as a local process, *per se*, and not a national one, it is nonetheless possible to interpret the variables related to activeness as a part of a national developmental ideology that perhaps must be followed in a political system the size and complexity of India. Activeness is related to a particular kind of leader holding a position at the local level. The active local unit has a set of leaders with political sensitivity and commitment to the nation. The importance of national commitment indicates a link to the ideology of the national political system. The nature of the development of the local political system should be put into the perspective of the national political system; this is particularly true of the manner in which the national ideology has affected the local political system, and the kinds of people who man it.

In all four countries, many of the findings can be accounted for by some dominant processes of the political system to which the local systems are inextricably linked. The lack of independence of the process of activeness at the local level—the general dependence of local units' activeness on the political system—is an important finding of the research. The local political units are not autonomous; activeness is not independent of what is happening in the nation. Some variation in activeness, of course, can be explained by specific differences among the local units. But these differences must be understood against the background of what is happening within the general system: the national development policies in Poland; economic development and urbanization in Yugoslavia; urban differentiation and the urban problem in the United States; the general development problems in India, particularly as they affect the character of leaders at the local level.

These processes form a more complex pattern than that of the syndrome of relationships discussed. The set of relevant variables themselves have a structure. Further, the variables relevant for an explanation of activeness in a country are not equally relevant for all local units.

The Structure of
Explanation

Up to this point, the explanation of activeness has proceeded by examining the relationships between sets of variables and activeness. Another central question is: what kind of causal linkages between the variables can be detected; which variables are of primary importance and which are of secondary importance; which relationships are concomitant but not critical? The direction of these linkages has already been suggested.

Is a relationship between, for example, the value of economic development and activeness better understood as a relationship between economic level and activeness, and, consequently, can the relationship between the value of economic development and activeness be accounted for in terms of the relationships between economic level and activeness?[6] The goal is to discover which variables are critically related to activeness and which are merely associated with the critical variables but are not necessarily related to the dependent variable—activeness. This, of course, can only be suggested. The assumption of this discussion is the major assumption of this research: the social, economic and political structure, the leadership structure, and the values of leaders are antecedent conditions of activeness, or, conversely, activeness is not the antecedent condition of the other variables.

The following chart summarizes the major relationships found for India. The completed arrows show the direction of the relationships as indicated by the influence of intervening variables and relationships between variables found to be directly related to activeness. The broken arrows are used to display those relationships that perhaps are better explained by other variables.

The active blocks in India are those with young, educated leaders who are nationally oriented, change-oriented, and indifferent about conflict avoidance. They generally are committed to the nation and oriented toward party politics. Where they turn for support, how they respond to conflict, and in what sectors of local political life they are influential (economic development)—these seem to be more or less a by-product of their primary value commitments. Desirous of change, they avoid traditional support structures; aware of political conflict, they do *not* consider avoiding conflict of primary importance; not aspiring to industrialization, they are nonetheless busy in economic development, broadly conceived. It appears that the relationships

Chart A—The Structure of Explanation: India

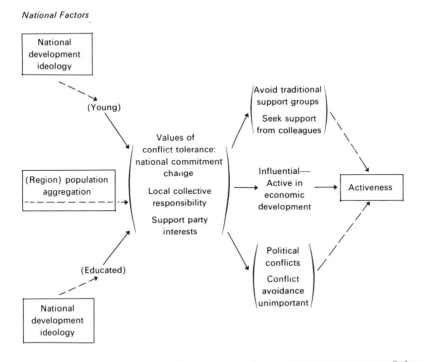

óther than the prımary commıtments to values, are consequences of the leaders' values themselves.

The prior question, of course, is how the Indian leaders in the active blocks acquired those values and how they achieved their positions of leadership. Two factors that have been discussed stand out, and they both appear very ordinary. The leaders in active blocks are from the younger generation and are well-educated. The socialization of the younger leaders, especially in educational institutions, is in part responsible for their values and their espousal of a developmental ideology. Perhaps national and state policies have helped them attain positions of leadership within the blocks.

Although the leaders in India are an important factor, the system in which the local leaders operate sets the stage for their importance. India is not developed economically; it has national policies of development. The leaders are, consequently, in an environment in which change, economic development and national policies are important. Also, in many areas of India, the local political structure is not highly institutionalized, and perhaps allows certain leaders to have a greater degree of maneuverability now than they will have as time progresses. In addition, there is a degree of autonomy allowed the local leadership. The political system in which the Indian local leaders must operate is in many ways conducive to their having an impact on the local political units, particularly in development.

The path of relationships in Poland is the simplest of all the countries. The explanatory structure is also obvious. National policy on development (mainly economic, but also social—involving people in organizations, improving educational facilities and stimulating investment) appears to have an overwhelming impact on the powiats. Poland is a centralized government with carefully prescribed functions for the powiat and little variation in autonomy. Further, the local political structures are institutionalized. The nature of the local leadership matters less than the national policy.

Chart B—The Structure of Explanation: Poland

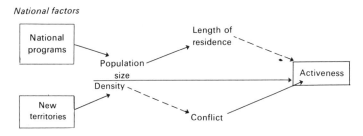

There is one type of relationship that remains independent of national policies—conflict. Whereas in the three other countries, conflict seems in some way to accompany activeness, in Poland it is a definite hindrance. Where there is conflict, there is less activeness. Where the leaders perceive little conflict and few obstacles (assuming that some of these obstacles are conflict), the community is active. Even here, however, the importance of the absence of conflict in explaining activeness may be due to the fact that the new territories have active powiats. New migrants, who are often young people, and are committed to the development of this region, may be more homogeneous in outlook and less prone to conflict.[7]

The structure of explanation in the United States is strong and consistent. Wealthy cities, with a middle-class population, are active; poor cities, often with a working-class population, are not active. The leaders in active cities value participation, whereas leaders in the less active cities value economic development and the avoidance of conflict. In the poorer cities there are active party organizations in which the leaders perceive themselves as influential. In the less active cities there

Chart C—The Structure of Explanation: United States

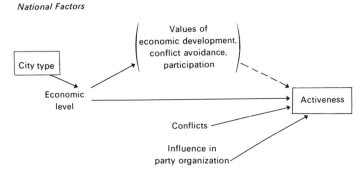

are divisions between labor and management. The most salient finding about the American cities is that almost all of the relationships between characteristics of the socio-political structure and individual leaders and activeness disappear when the economic level of the city is removed from consideration. There is one exception to this—influence in the party organization. Even if there were no differences in the wealth of the cities, a leadership involved and influential in party organization appears to be less concerned, and thus perhaps less directly influential in the affairs of the city.

The immediate local environment of the American local leader seems to determine the impact he can have on his city. American cities are in a period of transition, and at present seem to have problems over which their leadership has perhaps only marginal control.

Chart D—The Structure of Explanation: Yugoslavia

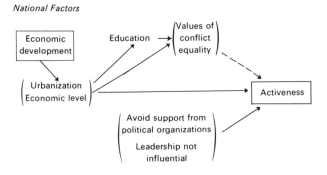

The political system in Yugoslavia provides an environment on which the local leadership could have a significant impact; there is a great deal of local autonomy, a need for economic development, and the absence of numerous mandatory national policies for local development. There is regional differentiation in activeness; Slovenia has the more active communes, and Bosnia the less active. What is a little surprising is that there are so few relationships between the characteristics of individual leaders and the activeness of the commune. Two values distinguish leaders in active communes: they value neither the avoidance of conflict nor the promotion of economic equality. Also, the leaders in active communes do not see themselves as influential, and avoid seeking support from the major political organizations in the commune, the League of Communists and the Socialist Alliance.

The critical factor in Yugoslavia, as in the United States, is the economic level of the commune, which reflects the structural differentiation of the commune. Most of the relationships between leader characteristics and activeness disappear when the influence of economic level is removed from consideration. It further turns out that even the regional influence on activeness is related to this developmental factor. Slovenia is wealthier than Bosnia; it is also more urban.

The path of correlational "causation" in Yugoslavia is largely a direct one between the economic level and activeness. The other relationships are, to a large extent, incidental to this basic relationship. The development of the communes colors not only the other structural features of the communes, but also the way in which the leaders are associated with activeness.

The Explanatory Power
of the Design

How well do the variables included in the design explain activeness in the four political systems? In order to answer this question, a multiple stepwise regression was run according to the structure provided in the design; the economic level of the community, its social and political structure, and the structure of the local political leadership would all be important factors in explaining how the values of the leaders are related to activeness. To this end, some of the major variables (17) were included in this analysis.[8]

Table 1 presents the results of this analysis. It gives the total amount of variance explained (regardless of the direction of the relationship), for each step in the multiple regression. The total amount of the variance explained should provide us with some basis for evaluating how well the design of the research fits each of the countries.

A first impression of this table is that the design, as represented by these 17 variables, explains almost all of the variance in India—90%;

Table 1—The Major Variables of the Research Design: A Forced Regression on Activeness

Step	Variable	India	Poland	U.S.	Yugoslavia
			Multiple R^2		
1	Economic level	.013	.001	.717	.374
2	Conflicts	.338	.313	.771	.374
3	Autonomy	.398	.336	.772	.378
4	Leadership activity	.398	.360	.787	.388
5	Variance in leadership influence[1]	.520	.396	.806	.433
6	Support (number of groups)	.528	.449	.815	.448
7	Percentage dominant party	.577	.449	.816	.451
8	Congruence of values	.580	.462	.816	.461
9	Change	.630	.476	.816	.461
10	Economic equality	.631	.490	.821	.463
11	National commitment	.852	.504	.825	.486
12	Conflict avoidance	.853	.533	.827	.502
13	Honesty	.856	.533	.827	.504
14	Participation	.863	.722	.830	.513
15	Economic development	.864	.756	.833	.528
16	Selflessness	.894	.792	.837	.557
17	Action propensity	.895	.792	.850	.593

[1] A measure of the spread of influence in the community.

85% in the United States; 79% in Poland; and 59% in Yugoslavia. More important, however, than the total amount of variance explained, is the type of variables that account for the variance.[9]

After the structural variables have been controlled, the extent to which the remaining variance is explained by the values of leaders can be seen. What has been suggested is reinforced in this analysis: the structural variables—the first eight variables in the table—account for 58% of the variance in India; 46% in Poland; 82% in the United States; and 46% in Yugoslavia. After this, there are striking differences between the countries. In India 32% of the remaining variance is accounted for by the values of leaders; 33% in Poland; 3% in the United States and 13% in Yugoslavia. What can be concluded is that, setting aside the importance of other variables, the values of leaders are of critical importance in explaining activeness (particularly the value of national commitment) in India, of marginal importance in Yugoslavia, and of almost no importance in the United States. However, this analysis, for the first time, introduces the role of values in Poland; this is perhaps due to the character of regression analysis.

We speculated that in economically developing systems with some autonomy and low levels of local political institutionalization, the values of the leaders would be an important determinant of activeness in the community. India fits this pattern, and, to some degree, so does Yugoslavia. The overall minor role of values, except for the value of participation after many other factors are controlled, in Poland fits the conjecture that a somewhat economically developed system with low autonomy and institutionalized political structures would allow for little play of the leaders on the nature of their communities. In the United States, with a highly developed economic system and firm local political institutions, the values of leaders, despite local autonomy, seem to be of little importance.

The sequence in which the variables contribute to explaining a significant amount of the variance in activeness further details the patterns. In India, perceived community conflicts, the second variable in the sequence, contributes a great deal—an increase in variance explained of 23%. One possible reason for this is that leaders in active communities not only do not value the avoidance of conflict, but they may to some degree be willing to create conflict in their pursuit of economic development. The importance of conflict in the community is in large measure a result of the kind of leaders that operate in those communities. The critical importance of the value of nation can be seen. The value of nation by itself contributes 25% in the variance explained.

In Poland there are two substantial increases in the variance explained. The first is the intensity of conflict in the community—an increase of 31%. The second is the value of participation—an increase of 23%. Here Poland deviates from the pattern of explanation that has been so far emphasized—the pattern of the socio-political structure being crucial and the values of leaders insignificant. Now, to some extent consistent with the bivariate correlation between the priority of participation and activeness, which was not confirmed by the value scale, we find that if the influence of several structural variables, particularly those related to conflict, are removed, the more the leaders value participation, the higher the activeness is. The activeness measure in Poland was heavily composed of organizational participation indicators; this relationship may be a consequence of these participation indicators.

The American pattern is clear. Most of the variance is explained by the economic level of the city. Perception of conflicts increases the total variance explained by 6%. No other variables of the 17 adds more than 2% of the variance explained. This pattern again proves the importance of the environment of the American local political leadership. The character of the municipality, in short, is critical.

The importance of economic level in Yugoslavia can be seen. It alone accounts for 37% of the variance; all of the remaining variables account for less than 22%. Only one other variable increases the amount of variance explained by more than 5%—the degree to which leadership influence is spread among the entire local leadership. Again, this may be a factor in specialization of leadership in the more highly urbanized communes.

Another regression analysis (a free run regression where the sequence of variables is not specified) was run in order to obtain another perspective on the findings. Table 2 presents the three variables in each country that, in the order presented, account for more than half of the variance in activeness in each country. In this analysis, the first two variables entering the regression reinforce what has been said about the relative importance of different categories of variables for explaining activeness in each country.[10]

Table 2—Stepwise Regression on Activeness: Three Steps Accounting for More Than 50 percent of Variance

India		Poland		U.S.		Yugoslavia	
Variable	R^2	Variable	R^2	Variable	R^2	Variable	R^2
1 National commitment (+)	.25	1 Conflicts (−)	.31	1 Economic level (+)	.72	1 Economic level (+)	43
2 Change orientation (+)	.45	2 Division: political views (−)	.46	2 Conflicts (+)	.77	2 Activity: public improvements (−)	.52
3 Conflicts: political groups (+)	.56	3 No obstacles (+)	.56	3 Activity: political organizations (−)	.81	3 Percentage dominant party (+)	.59

In India we find that two values, national commitment and change, together account for 45% of the variance, and, with the addition of conflicts over political views, positively related to activeness, account for over half of the total variance. It has been argued that conflict is the result of leaders' commitment to the nation and change, and, in this case, the conflicts are of a political nature. In Poland, 46% of the variance is contributed by conflicts in general; and divisions over political views; with the addition of the lack of obstacles to the leaders, over half of the total variance is explained. This clearly confirms the critical role of the socio-political factors in Poland. (The next variable of importance in Poland is again socio-political—variance in leadership influence.) In the United States, little needs to be said after the economic level of the city is considered. Again, conflicts accompany a wealthy and active city, as well as the reduced importance of political organizations. In Yugoslavia, wealthy, developed communes have a less active political leadership in public improvements and services; this reinforces the

arguments that where there is more general development, the importance of political leaders is lessened. Further, congruence of party
membership (the League of Communists) among the leaders adds
positively to the explanation of the variance. But this probably reflects
the fact that in urban, more developed communes, the League of
Communists is more important.

This analysis again shows that the values of leaders matter in
India, that socio-political factors (including, of course, an area that was
not treated in this analysis, the national developmental policies)
dominate in Poland, that the economic base and political structure are
decisive in the United States, and that the urban-economic development base, with a leadership that does not need, presumably, to be
active in public improvements and services, is crucial in Yugoslavia.

Conclusion

The most striking finding from these data is the *diversity* of the
explanatory patterns of activeness across the four countries. Although
the general sets of variables examined have cross-national relevance,
the variables that have a role in the explanation of activeness are
specific to each system. Of the general variables, it appears that socio-
political conflict, although operating in quite different ways in each
country, provides one of the more cross-nationally important variables.

Contrasts in relationships at the local level in each country can
only be understood in the broader context of the political system of
which the local political units are a part. The local political system is
not something that has an independent or autonomous role in the
society. The macro-processes in the explanation of activeness should
not be surprising, for it is the patterns of interaction that form the
very basis for defining the political system. It is these processes that
make cross-system analysis essential for testing theories of social
behavior.

What seems to be true in all four countries is that some major
processes in the country provide the critical source for the variation in
activeness. In India, the values of nation-building and change, and
activity in economic development seem to dominate the patterns,
especially as they find their way into the local leadership. These factors,
tied to the local leadership, provide the hard core of the structure of
explanation in India. In Poland there is a national plan for the economic
and social development of the country, which overwhelms the interrelationships between the variables. Besides this, there is a residue of
political problems, especially as they are manifested in conflict and

divisions over political views. But the national plan dominates, although it is interfered with by questions that are manifested in conflicts in the powiats. The United States pattern is permeated by its "urban problem." The question of urban life in America is a national issue, but these patterns suggest that there is no single urban problem. There is a multiplicity of structures, all of which are covered under the label of "city." Although no large urban center or metropolitan center was included in this study, the high degree of functional and structural fragmentation among the middle-sized American cities—working-class cities, declining textile centers, southern cities, suburbs, and the recently arrived city in the far west—seems to be a part of all these relationships. Yugoslavia is undergoing rapid urbanization and economic development. The patterns of activeness can be understood only in terms of this pervasive set of forces in the Yugoslav political system.

This study of the local political system provided a means whereby the forces of the political system could be examined. There were differences within systems, and, more importantly, across the four countries. These differences have not been explained; they have only been interpreted. It is clear that behavior within systems can only be understood in terms of the contexts in which it takes place. Building these contexts into the analysis is the basic tenet of comparative social inquiry.

Notes

1. This was actually done for Yugoslavia, where activeness scores were adjusted to the mean of the three republics. This score was not used in analysis. This approach, however, calls for construction of regionally specific measures, not regionally based scores.

2. See Chapter 7.

3. See Chapter 2.

4. The correlation between participation in voters meeting and membership in the League of Communists is − .09

5. See for example O. P. Williams *et al.*, *Suburban Differences and Metropolitan Policy*, Philadelphia: University of Pennsylvania Press, 1965.

6. This is a discussion of *likely* causal models for the explanation of activeness in each country. Although a causal analysis was not done, the partial order correlations and the interrelationships between variables that are themselves related to activeness suggest the most salient causal paths. See H. Blalock, *Causal Inference in Non-Experimental Research*, Chapel Hill, N.C.: The University of North Carolina Press, 1964.

7. The importance of conflict can also be seen in the detailed breakdown of the conflict categories contained in the open-ended questions.

8. See the section on the general model, Chapter 9, for the explanation of activeness.

9. Of course with this number of variables much of the variance would be explained, even by random numbers. Further, in a forced regression of this kind there are the problems of statistical interaction and multicollinearity. Statistical interaction occurs when the relationship between the independent and the dependent variables are not additive, and tends to reduce the size of the multiple correlations. Multicollinearity, the intercorrelations among the independent variables, is a difficult problem to handle. One approach is to reduce all of the independent variables to uncorrelated dimensions, such as may be achieved through a factor analysis with orthogonal rotation. This leaves the problem of interpreting the factors, especially when the variables are a heterogeneous lot, such as these. The biases resulting from these problems were not adjusted; thus, this regression must be treated with great caution. In the case of free run (not forced) regression, reported below, since the variables are handled independently—as they correlate with the dependent variable—these problems are not present.

10. Seven other variables were added to this analysis in order to give a broader perspective on socio-political variables.

Conclusion

CHAPTER 11

Values, Leadership and Development

This chapter was written by Jacob and Teune in an attempt to sum up the implications of the findings.

An active community, vibrantly responsive to varied pressures for social change, can be the work of human leadership motivated by a particular set of values. This is one strand of a complex web of findings from the International Studies of Values in Politics. But these human factors are conditioned by the political system, economic resources, and to a lesser extent, the range of social conflict in the community.

Whether such situational factors overwhelm the importance of the leader and his values differs among countries. In general, the evidence points to cross-national diversity in the imperatives of developmental change as a fundamental conclusion of this inquiry.

But national differences in the determinants of development do not mean that it is the peculiarities of a national culture or system which have intervened to direct a particular course of social change. Even greater differences were found within countries than among them in some of the major variables of the study. One needs to reach below the peculiarities of nations to explain the patterns of development occurring within them.

Such explanation must be sought close to the lives of the people who are confronted by pressures for change, namely at local levels of government and in the social activities of individuals in communities. This is where the action is, or the inaction, that may make up the development process. This is also the place where the evidence of human diversity is most striking.

The Process of
Activeness

Activeness was found to reflect a general social process in all four countries. The distinctive characteristic which underlies this process is the interrelated capacity of local political units to mobilize their resources for collective purposes and to involve the population in their institutional and organizational structures.

As a phenomenon, activeness in all countries intertwines the social and political, the individual and collective. A local unit, able politically to muster community resources, has a population joined together socially in activities and institutions. Such is the case, despite national and local differences in the economic base—from village agriculture to industrial and service activities; differences in social structure—from caste relationships to enforced egalitarianism; and differences in political system—from highly centralized to highly decentralized. Evidence that resource mobilization and popular involvement are related in each of these diverse countries is the basis for stating that activeness is both a general and a basic social process, characteristic of human activity, perhaps everywhere.

Activeness was conceived as an aspect of the developmental process, a basic aspect, observable and interpretable at the local level of political organization—the first point where human behavior is aggregated for significant collective action. As such, the concept of activeness is a way of getting hold of the primary inputs of general developmental processes normally identified only at more complex levels of human activity—economic regions, nation-states, or international associations. Local political units provide sufficient proximity for individual involvement, and at the same time sufficient complexity for diversified collective action necessary for development. In all four countries there were not only systematic and interpretable differences among the local political units, but also systematic and intelligible explanations of activeness, indicating that activeness is a viable local counterpart to general processes of development.

Although the phenomenon of activeness is a common and basic process in all four countries, the explanation of why some communities are more active and others less, differs across these countries. These national differences in explanatory patterns reflect the fact that activeness is inextricably tied to the distinctive processes of change transforming each of these countries: in centralized Poland, national decisions on development; in rural India, value commitments of the local leadership to innovation and the nation; in urbanized United States, the changing economic base of the city; and in urbanizing Yugoslavia, the process of social differentiation and increasing wealth, accompanying a shift away from a primarily rural society. Activeness is a general process; but the ways in which this process is shaped are defined by configuration of other general social, economic, and political factors which find expression in the nation-state.

The Relevance of Value
Commitments

The role of values influencing social action shows extraordinary cross-national variation. Not only is there great difference among countries in the patterns of commitment of leaders to particular values, but also in whether their values have any independent impact on the activeness and development of their communities.

In India, the degree of leaders' commitment to nation and the extent to which they can tolerate conflict seem crucial in determining whether their communities will be active in an innovative sense. In Poland, they seem to have no influence at all; while in the U.S. and Yugoslavia leaders' values mirror the wealth of the community.

What this clearly means is that the dynamics of developmental change is not universally and systematically predictable from the values espoused by the leadership, thus undermining the principal hypothesis which prompted these studies. One must now be suspicious of broad-scale acceptance of Max Weber's theory of the developmental dynamic of the "protestant ethic", as well as of other theories which link social change to the force of certain patterns of values. In particular, the idea that "traditional values" consistently inhibit social change must be discounted. What is evident are *alternative patterns of developmental change*, in which values may or may not play a vital role. The convergent evidence from the U.S. and Yugoslavia suggests the possibility of a modal pattern in which social values and economic privilege are inter-locked as developmental imperatives—with other patterns emerging as mutations. Thus, a hospitable culture for change would be one where a community enjoyed relative affluence and its leadership (1) valued change, (2) disparaged economic equality, and (3) discounted social harmony and consensus. This combination generates that special kind of change often described as "modernization" which stresses the importance of technological innovation, and material gains.

Then how to explain India, where the wealth of a community seems to have little bearing on development in comparison with the value commitments of leaders to national goals and tolerance of conflict? Perhaps the economic component of change is neutralized by a lingering concern for the maintenance of close communal ties, the longstanding devotion of the nation's most respected leaders to social egalitarian ideals and the dissociation of a commitment to social change from a personal propensity to act.

The Polish "mutation" demonstrates the capacity for strong-willed central determination of social and economic policy to override the processes of change operating at the base of the society. Both local influence and leaders' values cease to function as significant forces for community activeness when confronted with a set plan, executed by a disciplined apparatus and backed by substantial control over vital resources.

The inescapable conclusion is that the role of leaders' values in generating development is conditioned by dominant socio-political attributes of the national environment in which development is being nurtured.

Cadres for Change :
Leaders Who Lead

Social change is the product of human decision, constrained to be sure by the myriad pressures of physical and social environment. But certain types of persons are more "change-oriented" than others; and they differ in their motivation for change. Some put foremost a concern for economic equality, others stress broadened political participation, and a third group sees strengthening the nation as the primary object of change. Some are committed to all three goals. The number of leaders in each of these camps differs greatly among the four countries. Far fewer Americans target their interest in change on economic equality than leaders in the other countries. Indians tend to shun political participation; large numbers of Yugoslav and U.S. leaders espouse it. Poles are the most inclined to link change to the advancement of national goals.

The imprint of national culture on motivation for change is matched, however, by a factor which cuts across all four countries: the amount of formal education a leader has had. This specifically affects his disposition toward economic equality. Surprisingly, the *less* educated leader is the *more* concerned to reduce economic disparities. The educated leader, while espousing change, is committed to *in*equality and differential rewards as an incentive for developmental change. This finding stands out because there are so few other characteristics, personal or environmental, which consistently identify the kind of change to which leaders are disposed, and whether they are change-oriented at all. Most of the demographic and status factors familiarly cited as correlates of progressive or conservative social action have not proved significant in all four countries; few apply in any of the countries. Even age does not consistently separate the conservative from the progressive.

What happens when the change oriented leaders, of one type or another, enter on the stage of their communities' responsibilities, is strongly affected by the social and political context of the country. The portrait of the Indian leader who leads active communities is sharp and clear: educated, young, untied to traditional local influence groups, but politically literate, party-oriented and committed to national goals with an emphasis on industrialization. He is undeterred from change by concern over community conflict. Thus, activeness is directly related to a particular kind of leader with "developmental" characteristics, including commitment to the developmental ideology of the Indian national political system.

In Poland, it is virtually impossible to identify a developmental "cadre" at the local level—except for the fact that he is an import (reflecting the fact that the more active communities are in the newly settled western territories) and that he is a conflict-avoider. But whether a leader welcomes change or not has nothing to do with whether his community develops or not; nor does any other personal trait.

In the U.S. and Yugoslavia, the leaders of active communities are similar in two respects; they are better educated and less inclined to let conflict stand in the way of change. They differ in that the American has a higher regard than his counterparts in less active communities for public participation in developmental decision-making, while the leader of an active Yugoslav community, compared with the others, tends more to doubt the ideal of economic equality. However, the dominant conclusion in both countries is that leaders do not really lead; they preside over urban, wealthy communities in which development flows from other factors.

The Nation: Seedbed of
Social Change?

The question we must finally confront is how far the imperatives of social change, as evidenced in this study, are universal, or on the contrary, rooted in systems of human interaction distinctive of a particular nation, or group of nations. Do essentially the same set of influences induce or inhibit the same kinds of change across countries which differ in other respects?

What has already been said makes it abundantly clear that the principal thrust of the evidence is in the direction of diversity rather than universality. Let us sum up:

(1) The local leadership differs country-to-country in their degree of commitment to certain values; especially those most relevant to change. This results in sharply different proportions of leadership in each country dedicated to different kinds of change, even though most everyone professes a general desire for change.

(2) Influences found to shape leaders' values in one country are often not significant in others.

(3) Of crucial importance is the fact that the role of values in explaining activeness, and indeed the entire pattern of explaining activeness, is not the same in the four countries. Only in Yugoslavia and the United States does a comparable explanation emerge: in these two countries the factor of community affluence overwhelms leaders' values and all other factors in accounting for community activeness.

These conclusions strongly suggest that the nation, as a system of distinctive social processes, specific in time and place, dominates the course of developmental change.

On the other hand, there are at least three aspects of the value-orientations of leaders where similarity among all four countries is so pronounced that a presumption of universal applicability is warranted:

(1) The ways in which values configurate are remarkably similar. Leaders who are committed to one value tend to be committed to certain others, regardless of the country they live in. There are corresponding "syndromes" or interrelated sets of values in the four countries. If a leader is highly concerned about change, he is likely to place high value on economic development, economic equality and self-lessness, whether he be Indian, Pole, American or Yugoslav.

(2) The amount of diversity among leaders on the politically relevant values they espouse is nearly uniform in the four countries, whether they are looked at as a national sample, or as the leadership of particular communities. There is about as much consensus, or dis-sensus, within Indian blocks as within U.S. municipalities, within Polish powiats as within Yugoslav communes.

(3) The impact of formal education on some of the critical values related to change is, we have seen, much the same in all four countries:

and there is some correspondence in the influence of other demographic characteristics on the values of local leaders. Also, the fact that a wide range of other plausible factors have *no* influence on the socialization of leaders' values in any of these countries, should be added to the evidence for cross-national uniformity.

These commonalities suggest that the domain of human values is governed at least in part by forces which transcend the boundaries of particular nations, or operate similarly *within* the confines of many nations; consequently, differences in values espoused by leaders may be the result not so much of differing characteristics of their countries as of their own diverse personal experiences and social attachments. Hence, to the extent that values, or conflicts of values, do enter into the development process, one should expect to find the roots of social change more universal, than national.

A third base of the dynamics of social change is suggested by the finding that a "developmental ordering" affects the commitment of leadership to certain change-oriented values. The concern for economic development, and also for reducing economic disparities, varies *inversely* with the country's level of economic development. The wealthier the country and the more it produces, the less its leaders put a premium on these values as standards of public policy. In a country which has little, like India, local leadership values both national and local development, and is much more concerned with narrowing the gap between poor and rich. Viewed from this perspective, it is not the political system or cultural character of a nation, but its material endowment and momentum—its GNP in short—which dictates how its leaders will regard change.

One must recognize however that overall GNP is *not* the all powerful determinant of whether a country's leadership values will carry over into developmental action at the community level. To be sure, at the low end of the scale—in India—we know that certain values are among the strongest predictors of activeness (though interestingly, not those values which are directly concerned with development). In the world's richest country, values are subservient to local affluence as a development influence; but this is also the case in Yugoslavia which is as yet closer to India than the U.S. in its economic status, although its rate of growth is more dynamic. Poland, on the other hand, demonstrates that community activeness can be made fully subject to *political* direction, setting aside materialistic determinants at both national and local levels. Neither GNP nor the economic condition of the community seems to control the decisions of central political authority on the direction of socioeconomic change within the country.

What emerges from these studies is the cross-national uniformity or equivalence, of major phenomena involved in processes of social change; but diversity in the way these variables are *linked* to change. Community activeness, values and aspirations of leaders, local economic development, the structure of social influence, cleavages and conflicts, governmental competence and autonomy (formal and perceived), sense of political efficacy—these phenomena have all been identified as present in the countries investigated, and demonstrated to be essentially the same "thing" in each country. But what is related to what—and how much influence each exerts in the mobilization of social action—this, with exceptions as noted, varies.

We have found that such variation in the patterns of developmental change may be the outcome of existing differences in the material conditions of life, or of the imposition of a distinctive system of political organization. But such differences are insufficient to explain systematically the full range of the alternative courses of development being pursued. We are pushed toward a fuller exploration of the vast diversity of dispositions discovered among the human beings who compose the political leadership at the base of these societies. Individual and collective behaviors in local communities simply do not conform enough to the economic, political or social orderings of countries to verify a neat deterministic model of social change. The mix of "determinants" must allow for the variety of personal characteristics which evidently influence leaders to radically different conduct within the same country and the same community, under the same institutions of government, social structure and material environment. It is still possible for a human being to put a peculiar stamp on the evolution of his society, despite the magnitude of the constraining and conforming pressures which bear down on him from the society he has had to grow up in. Man is not the total prisoner of his environment.

The Leadership Survey

The introductory material was written by Sheth and Teune.

𝕋he major data-gathering instrument was a questionnaire. The purposes of the questionnaire were to assess the values of local political leaders, the leaders' perceptions of the social and political structure of their local community, their role behavior, and certain background data.

Design

The final questionnaire contains six open-ended questions. Two of these are intended to elicit value responses—qualities of good leaders and hopes for the country; the remaining four asked about the leader's role in a specific recent decision, his perception of his efficacy, and problems and conflicts in the community. Two multiple-response questions asked for a self-appraisal of activities and influence in different functional decision-making areas. The leaders were also requested to identify the support groups to which they turn when making decisions. Perceptions of community cleavages and local autonomy were assessed in two multiple-response questions. There were two final value questions: the first asked the leader which levels of government ought to undertake various functions; the second requested a partial ranking of eight of the nine values assessed by the forced-choice items. Most of the questionnaire items were designed to assess values by forced-choice responses. There were 69 value items used in all countries, plus several nation-specific items. The final tally of forced-choice value items was: India, 114; Poland, 96; the United States, 108; and Yugoslavia, 122.

All the questions, except approximately one-third of the forced-choice value items, and the specification of support groups, were identical in all four countries. The nation-specific and common (international) forced-choice value items were used to construct nine value scales.[1] Each scale was composed of a minimum of four, or a maximum of ten international items. In all countries, except Poland, a set of items on political responsibility was also included.

Pretests

Developing the final version of the questionnaire involved a preliminary pilot study and two major pre-tests. The purpose of the pilot study, conducted during the spring of 1965 in India and the United States, was to define a universe of values relevant to local political leaders. As the purpose was to explore the range of values, 15 open-ended questions were used, all but one designed to elicit values. Four pairs of questions asked the leader to identify what he considered "good or bad" decisions, "admirable or bad leaders," and types of people who would be "desirable or undesirable" local leaders. After the leader stated what he considered desirable or undesirable, he was asked why. Responses to this probe were coded for values. The seven other questions asked for personal, community, and national hopes and fears; a personal statement of principles and ideals; and a description of actions the leader would most like to undertake. In addition, there were 20 forced-choice questions designed to measure the values of "selflessness" and "impartiality" (later "equality"), and a set of single-word items on economic development, national unity, etc. In the United States eight local- vs. national-orientation items were included.

The analysis of 114 respondents in India and 40 in the United States (four states were included in India and two areas were included in the United States[2]) identified frequently mentioned values, scalable value items, and special value clue words on which there was some variance. The coded responses to the open-ended questions, as well as the individual scale items, were intercorrelated. One result of this analysis was the identification of four open-ended questions that elicited consistent (intercorrelated) value responses, and several scale items. The frequency of value responses was used to determine what kinds of values scale items would be appropriate for the first general pre-test.

The first four-nation pre-test was designed in June 1965 and executed that fall. The bulk of this questionnaire was 104 value items intended to measure eight values. These items were cast into five different forced-choice formats. The four open-ended value questions that produced intercorrelated responses in the pilot questionnaire were retained. These questions asked for desirable and undesirable traits of local leaders, and good and bad recent local decisions. A broad range of questions on the leaders' roles and perceptions of his community were also included.

Because of the time required to complete this questionnaire, it was administered to two separate groups of local leaders. The first part was composed of 104 value items plus the four open-ended value questions. This part was administered to the following number of respondents: India, 119; Poland, 60; the United States, 96; and Yugoslavia, 63.

The responses were coded in a common format and analyzed in the United States.[3] An item analysis, based on intercorrelations within scales and a lack of correlations out of scale, was undertaken to select those items to be included in the questionnaire. Respondents from all countries were pooled for analysis, in addition to being analyzed separately. Every item was identical for each country except for the names of the local communities that were used in the open-ended questions. The second part of the questionnaire, on community decisions and the leaders' roles, was administered to a smaller number of respondents. As the purpose was to ascertain which items discriminated between respondents, analysis was confined to frequencies.

The results of this pre-test led to reconceptualizing the value scales, discarding many items as either ambiguous or not scaling with other items (poorly intercorrelated), and restructuring the questions on leaders' roles and decisions. The conclusion of these evaluations was that another pre-test was necessary.

The third international pre-test questionnaire was written in January 1966 and administered in the early spring. The primary goal of this pre-test was to improve the international comparability of the value scale items. To this end, 168 items were administered to at least 60 respondents in each country. At least 40 of these items in each country were nation-specific, or items adapted to particular countries. Again, because of the time required to respond to this number of items, each country was given the option of administering the questionnaire in two parts—the value scale items and the questions on the leaders' role and perceptions. Further, for the value scale items only, local leaders, gathered at schools or institutions for instruction, were tested in some cases. In India and Poland, the entire questionnaire was given to 60 local leaders in the field. In Yugoslavia and the United States, the value items were administered to local officials congregated at institutes and training centers. Fifteen leaders were given the second part in the United States and 20 in Yugoslavia.

A pooled analysis of all respondents was undertaken for the identical or international value items, and an independent analysis, including the nation-specific items, was undertaken for each of the countries.[4] Informal criteria of clarity and formal criteria of variance were applied to the second part of the questionnaire. The value items were intercorrelated in order to purify the value scales and to discard poorly correlated items.

After these operations, the final questionnaire was edited and constructed. The value items were then scrambled for administration.

Translation

The questionnaire required six translations—Gujarati, Hindi, and Marathi in India; Serbo-Croatian and Slovenian in Yugoslavia; and Polish. Most of the items, of course, had already been translated for use in the pre-tests, and "translation" of the final questionnaire was largely a matter of editing questions previously translated. The questionnaire used for translation was a standard English version, which was administered verbatim in the United States.

Each question was interpreted with a set of notes and interviewer instructions. These were to serve as guidelines for the translators. Although the translations were to be "as literal as possible," many of the questions, and particularly certain words, were interpreted according to their intent and meaning. In India and Yugoslavia, where more than one translation was required, the translations were standardized by retranslation into each of the three Indian languages and the two Yugoslav languages. In addition, 20 interviews were conducted in Gujarat in order to check the translation. In all countries the translations were retranslated into English.

In the pre-tests, certain key concepts, such as "cost," "conflict," "influence," "community," and "decision" provided difficult translation problems. Modifications had to be made in the literal translations in order to conform to a common meaning. "Cost" in Poland is not a general name for sacrifice; rather, it is a name for only economic cost. "Influence," literally translated in the Indian languages, implies ability to get things done by personal power and contacts, rather than having an impact on social or political processes. "Community," in India, would often be interpreted as caste, village, or religious group. "Conflict" in most countries is a strong word indicating sharp antagonisms, whereas in the United States conflict can refer to general disagreement.

Administration

A common set of instructions on securing the interviews and limiting interviewer intervention was given to each interviewer. The directions included, for example, "if a respondent asks what is meant by a question, avoid completely rephrasing," "try first repeating the question as worded," and "avoid reacting in any way to responses." In addition, specific instructions were given for each question on the interpretation allowed and emphases desired. Specific formats and instructions were provided for recording responses. Interviewer evaluations of the interview itself were required.

The following chart gives the period of administration and organization of the interviews. In the United States the research was contracted to a professional organization, the National Opinion Research Center. The research staff, however, interviewed in two of the sample

Country	Date of Interview (1966) (Maximum Time)	Type of Interview Organization	Supervision	Number of Interviewers	Type of Interviewers (Majority)
India	Sept. 15– Oct. 31	Staff of centers	Project directors	19	M.A. in scoial science
Poland	Oct. 10–25	Specially recruited	Team heads	37	Students in sociology
U.S.	Sept. 21– Dec. 15	NORC—28 cities (contract) two cities by staff	Central editing of first two interviews	66	Professional staff (super-visors and first assistants in each city)
Yugoslavia	Nov. 11– Dec. 1	Specially recruited by three centers	Team heads and center staff	60	Students in sociology

cities nearest Philadelphia. Seven weeks was the maximum time span in which the interviews were conducted. All interviews were completed within the three-month period of September 15, 1966 through December 15, 1966.

Although several devices were used to maintain similarity in the style of interviewing, such as a common questionnaire format, the organization and training of interviewers, interviewer instructions, and the like, the actual administration of the interview (particularly its organization and supervision) was adapted to the country and capabilities of the research centers. For example, although it is possible to execute a national survey from one center in Poland without incurring extraordinary expenses or lack of control, in the United States and India the cost would obviously be prohibitive.

One problem with this type of research is that the cost of executing a survey within local units limits the procedure of assigning interviewers to the units. Ideally, interviews and interviewers should be randomly assigned, to remove the influence of interviewer bias on community scores. In India, some attempt was made to have interviewers work in all of the blocks in one state. This was accomplished by having the entire research team in each state interview in two blocks at the same time, thereby allowing each interviewer to interview in at least half of the blocks. In Poland, two and three-person teams were assigned to each powiat. In the United States it was not possible to distribute interviewers across the cities. In three cities one interviewer was used, in 24 cities two interviewers, and in 3 cities, three interviewers. In the two cities covered by the staff, six interviewers mixed their assignments in both. In Yugoslavia, as in India, three separate interviewing groups of about 20 each were recruited, each one being under the direct supervision of a member of the research staff. Teams of four persons were assigned to at least two and, in some cases, three communes; through this method each interviewer was "spread" between at least two communes. The fact remains, however, that interviewer bias and community characteristics are to some extent coterminous.

Coding and Processing
the Responses

There was an international code prepared for all of the forced-choice responses prior to the actual administration of the questionnaire. Each center coded the data according to this format. The code for the open-ended questions was constructed after the interviews were completed. After preliminary coding of responses to the open-ended questions, an international code was prepared. Each center then applied this code. Finally, a review of these results led to the construction of the final code.[5]

Because most questions had a closed-ended response format, it was possible to have exactly the same code for each country, and to punch the data for analysis immediately after completing the interviews. The only exception to this was the six open-ended questions.

The experience gained in the first two pre-tests (University of Colorado in 1965 and Polish Academy of Science in 1966) made it possible to begin a common analysis of the data within three weeks of receiving the last questionnaire. The first of these analyses was done in December 1966 and January 1967 at the Indian Institute of Technology, Kanpur. This international analysis, with individuals participating from all countries, produced the following outputs: (1) intercorrelations of all value items, for all countries together on the international items, and for each country separately for all items; (2) a factor analysis of the international value items for all countries, and of all value items for each country; (3) individual scale scores; and (4) community level scores. After this first international analysis, responsibilities for further analysis were centered in Philadelphia and Warsaw.

Notes

1. See Chapter 3 for the scales.

2. The states in India were Gujarat, Maharashtra, Rajastan, and Uttar Pradesh. Denver and Philadelphia were the two areas in the United States.

3. This analysis was conducted at the University of Colorado, under the direction of Professor W. A. Scott.

4. This analysis was done at the Polish Academy of Sciences, Warsaw.

5. A sample of the responses of community leaders to the open-ended questions was coded by coders from at least two different countries. For purposes of the community-level analysis, 26 categories were formed by collapsing certain of the original coding categories. To compute the international inter-coder reliability, the ratio of the total number of coding agreements to the total number of possible choices in classifying responses to a given question was used. For example, in the United States, in coding responses to Part A, Question 1 of the survey (community problems) there were 82 instances in which the coder from another country agreed with the coder from the respondent's country, on whether to put a response in a given set of categories (forming one of the collapsed analytical categories) or not to put it in that set. There were 91 possible choices (including the possibility that none of the collapsed categories was considered appropriate). Hence the inter-coder reliability coefficient was 0.90. The *mean* inter-coder reliability coefficient for all of the test coding was 0.90, with a range from 0.80 to 0.96.

The Questionnaire
(STANDARD ENGLISH VERSION)

Code for abbreviations
Country to which question is
applicable

INTL = International
IND = India
POL = Poland
U.S. = United States
YUG = Yugoslavia

Direction

P = Positive
N = Negative

Value Scale items are starred

Part I Problems and Leadership
Activities

1. What do you think are the most important problems facing this community now?
2. Here is a list of areas of activities of community leaders. Will you check those on which you are particularly active?

_____(1) Industrial and economic development—new plants, electrification, employment, labor supply, etc.

_____(2) Agriculture—mechanization, fertilization, co-operatives, etc.

_____(3) Housing—urban renewal, slum clearance, zoning, etc.

_____(4) Public improvements, services and utilities—transportation, roads, streets, parks, sewage, etc.

_____(5) Health—hospitals, sanitation, dispensaries, epidemics, etc.

_____(6) Culture, recreation, and sports—libraries, clubs, theatres, etc.

_____(7) Education—including social education, school construction, curriculum problems, adult education, etc.

_____(8) Social improvement and welfare—child and women welfare, problems related to racial, ethnic, caste, religious, civil conflicts, crime, delinquency, care for the old, handicapped, poor people, etc.

_____(9) Political organization activity—party, political associations, nominations, recruitment, etc.

_____(10) Collection and distribution of public revenue—tax collection, budget distribution, etc.

3. We would also like to know in which areas you feel you have influence on what is accomplished. Would you examine the same list of activities and indicate those in which you feel you have a great deal of influence, only some, or none at all.

	Great Influence	*Some Influence*	*None*
(1) Industrial and economic development			
(2) Agriculture			
(3) Housing			
(4) Public improvements, services and utilities			
(5) Health			
(6) Culture, recreation and sport			
(7) Education			
(8) Social improvement and welfare			
(9) Political organization activity			
(10) Collection and distribution of public revenue			

4. In the areas where you feel you have a great deal of influence, what was the single most important recent action here in which you participated, and how did you participate?
5. What do you feel are the main obstacles, if any, which limit your effectiveness as a local leader?

Part II Value
Scales

The following 3 formats will be used in administering these questions:

FORMAT A

Below are some questions faced in the daily life of political leaders. Please examine the list closely and check the extent to which you agree or disagree with them.

	Strongly *Agree*	*Agree*	*Disagree*	*Strongly* *Disagree*
(1) _____				
(2) _____				
(3) _____				
(·) _____				
(·)				
(n) _____				

FORMAT B

How important do you think it is to achieve or avoid each of the following when making political decisions?

	Very *important* *to achieve*	*Somewhat* *important* *to achieve*	*Somewhat* *important* *to avoid*	*Very* *important* *to avoid*
(1) _____				
(2) _____				
(3) _____				
(·) _____				
(·)				
(n) _____				

Hypothetical situations presenting choices of action.

— · — · — · — · — · — ·

Unless otherwise noted in the list of questions which follows, Format A will be used.

ECONOMIC DEVELOPMENT

	Country applicable	Direction
1. The economic development of the nation should take precedence over immediate consumer gratification.	*INTL	P
2. A high standard of living should be the most important (ultimate) goal of a society.	*INTL	P
3. The long term economic development of the nation should be considered as its most important goal.	*INTL	P
4. Economic development should not be pursued if it means hardships for the people.	INTL	N
5. After obtaining a certain standard of living further concern with economic growth is not required.	INTL *(scaled YUG only)	N
6. Only economic development will ultimately provide the things required for the welfare and happiness of the people.	*INTL	P
7. It is not necessary for the political leaders to be concerned about the economic development of the community.	IND	N
8. One should encourage private industrial enterprise among small industries.	IND	P
9. Efficiency in economic production. (Format B.)	*IND	P
10. Technological education. (Format B.)	*IND	P
11. Less should be spent on social welfare programs so that more resources are available for economic development.	*POL	P

	Country applicable	Direction
12. A quiet peaceful life should not be exchanged for a few material goods.	POL	N
13. Efficiency in economic production. (Format B.)	POL	P
14. Technical competence. (Format B.)	POL	P
15. It is not necessary for political leaders to be concerned about the economic development of the community.	U.S.	N
16. A rising standard of living is not an important sign of progress.	U.S.	N
17. There is too much emphasis in our country now on obtaining a high economic growth rate.	*U.S.	N
18. Economic progress. (Format B.)	*U.S.	P
19. The government may reduce incomes in order to insure economic prosperity.	YUG	P
20. The present generation should have the right to consume what it produces without regard to the economic well-being of future generations.	*YUG	N
21. People should not in any way be forced to contribute to the long term development programs of the community.	YUG	N
22. The decisions of the local government on material development should be based on the long term interest of the citizens.	*YUG	P

CONFLICT RESOLUTION-AVOIDANCE

23. If there is disagreement about a program, a leader should be willing to give it up.	*INTL	P
24. Public decisions should be made with unanimous consent.	*INTL	P
25. It is desirable in reaching political decisions to reconcile as many conflicting interests as possible.	INTL	P

	Country applicable	Direction
26. Leaders who are over concerned about resolving conflicts can never carry out community programs successfully.	INTL	N
27. Preserving harmony in the community should be considered more important than the achievement of community programs.	*INTL	P
28. A good leader should refrain from making proposals that divide the people even if these are important for the community.	*INTL	P
29. Reduction of community conflicts. (Format B.)	INTL *(scaled IND/U.S. only)	P
30. Maintenance of friendly relations among the people who have to make the decisions. (Format B.)	INTL	P
31. Any decision that threatens to alienate a sector or group in the community should be postponed.	*IND	P
32. A decision should not be taken until all disagreements have been fully resolved.	*IND	P
33. Use of violence. (Format B.)	IND	N
34. A leader should modify his actions to keep consensus.	*POL	P
35. It is not necessary for a leader to try and smooth over conflicts that naturally arise in a community.	POL	N
36. Use of violence. (Format B.)	POL	N
37. A leader should modify his actions to keep consensus.	*U.S.	P
38. Conflict is a sign of a healthy community.	U.S.	N
39. It is important for a leader to get things done even if he must displease people.	*U.S.	N
40. A leader should modify his actions to keep consensus.	*YUG	P

	Country applicable	Direction
41. An effective leader is one who is not overly concerned in obtaining agreement of citizens on all controversial issues.	YUG	N
42. It is important for a leader to do as much as possible even if thereby he displeases people.	YUG	N
43. If we waited for all groups in a community to accept a program, it would not be possible to get anything done.	YUG	N

PARTICIPATION

	Country applicable	Direction
44. The complexity of modern day issues requires that only the more simple questions should be considered publicly.	*INTL	N
45. Widespread participation in decision-making often leads to undesirable conflicts.	*INTL	N
46. Most decisions should be left to the judgment of experts.	*INTL	N
47. Only those who are fully informed on the issues should vote.	*INTL	N
48. Only those who are competent on an issue should speak about it.	*INTL	N
49. Participation of the people is not necessary if decision-making is left in the hands of a few trusted and competent leaders.	*INTL	N
50. To have decisions made by people who are experts on the matter under consideration. (Format B.)	*INTL	N
51. Participation by everyone in decision-making regardless of their knowledge of the issues involved. (Format B.)	*INTL	P
52. Decision-making activity need not be the concern of all the people in a community.	*IND	N

	Country applicable	Direction
53. Allowing too many (all) people to have their say in community matters will only interfere with getting things done.	*IND	N
54. A citizen should always be willing to participate in community affairs even if he feels his opinion does not count.	IND	P
55. Protecting leaders from day-to-day interference by the people. (Format B.)	IND	N
56. Participation of all citizens in decision-making even if it takes a lot of time and expenditure. (Format B.)	IND	P
57. An issue should be presented to the general public only after experts have made a decision on it.	*POL	N
58. Decisions on important matters affecting the entire community should be taken only after broad general community discussion.	POL	P
59. Modern work organization is so complex that widespread participation of citizens in decision-making is impossible.	*POL	N
60. Interest in public affairs occurs where there is no confidence in public authorities.	POL	N
61. Citizen panels should be established to review the day-to-day operations of administrative agencies, such as the fire and police departments.	U.S.	P
62. An issue should be presented to the general public only after experts have made a decision on it.	*U.S.	N
63. Even if it takes twice as long to reach a decision, it is nonetheless important that everyone has his say.	U.S.	P
64. Modern work organization is so complex that widespread participation of citizens in decision-making is impossible.	*YUG	N

	Country applicable	Direction
65. A member of the communal assembly should not be under the obligation to comply with the views expressed by the voters.	YUG	N
66. Even if it takes twice as long to reach a decision, it is nonetheless important that everyone has his say.	*YUG	P

SELFLESSNESS

	Country applicable	Direction
67. Everybody should look after his own interest first.	INTL	N
68. A leader should not be concerned about his own status, only about doing a good job.	*INTL	P
69. Sacrificing oneself for others is the highest value a man can achieve.	*INTL	P
70. One should work to the best of his ability regardless of whether his services are adequately rewarded.	*INTL	P
71. If leaders can get things done, the people need not bother whether or not they are selfish.	INTL *(scaled U.S. only)	N
72. Sacrificing oneself for the benefit of others. (Format B.)	*INTL	P
73. A society where a person can pursue his own interest without being required to sacrifice for others. (Format B.)	INTL	N
74. Subordination of one's own interest in the interest of a higher cause. (Format B.)	*INTL	P
75. No one should expect a political leader to be absolutely selfless in his actions.	*IND	N
76. A community can develop without having selfless leaders.	*IND	N
77. A leader can never hope to serve the people if he does not sacrifice all his personal interests.	*IND	P

	Country applicable	Direction
78. To sacrifice one's own opportunities in life is necessary for the sake of the well-being of one's community. (Format B.)	*IND	P
79. A leader can never hope to serve the people if he does not sacrifice all his personal interests.	*POL	P
80. A community can develop without having selfless leaders.	POL	N
81. To sacrifice one's own opportunities in life is necessary for the sake of the well-being of one's own community. (Format B.)	*POL	P
82. Only impractical idealists will sacrifice themselves for others.	U.S.	N
83. A man should not be expected to provide for others in greater measure than for himself.	U.S.	N
84. A leader should act in accordance with common interests regardless of possible adverse material consequences for his family.	*YUG	P
85. A member of the community should subordinate his own interest to the interests of the community.	*YUG	P
86. A member of a work community is asked to transfer to another workplace where he can be more useful than at his present job, but at the new workplace he would earn a lower income. He refuses to move. Has he acted properly or not? Yes____; No____ . (Format C.)	YUG	

LOCAL-NATIONAL ORIENTATION

	Country applicable	Direction
87. National goals should not be obtained at great costs to local communities.	*INTL	P
88. Although national affairs are important, people here should first worry about their own community problems.	*INTL	P

		Country applicable	Direction
89.	Community progress is not possible if national goals always have priority.	*INTL	P
90.	We should not worry so much about national problems when we have so many in our own community.	*INTL	P
91.	The existence of local governments can be justified only in terms of their contribution to national objectives.	INTL	N
92.	Local leaders should always be prepared to adjust their programs to national goals and policies even if this is disadvantageous for the community.	*INTL	N
93.	It is necessary to forego development of one's own community to help the development of the rest of the country.	*INTL	N
94.	It would be better if the national government would allow the local community to do more things for itself.	IND	P
95.	National goals should always receive priority over the requirements of the local community.	*IND	N
96.	In case of conflict the needs of the local community should receive preference over national objectives.	*IND	P
97.	Local leaders' over concern with achieving national goals is not desirable for the development of their own area.	*IND	P
98.	A man does not have to go outside of his community to find opportunities for a full and happy life.	IND	P
99.	A man owes his primary responsibility to his own local community.	*IND	P
100.	Improving conditions of life in your own community is the best way to serve the nation.	IND	P
101.	Unity of local community. (Format B.)	IND	P

	Country applicable	Direction
102. Looking at politics from a purely local standpoint is harmful to the national interests.	POL	N
103. The development of the whole country should not be accomplished at the cost of submerging local and regional differences.	POL	P
104. A proper political leader puts the interests of his community foremost.	*POL	P
105. It is desirable to forego development of one's own community in order that some less well-developed can be helped.	*POL	N
106. Local leaders must realize their communities will stand or fall on the performance of the national government.	POL	N
107. The development of each community is above all the responsibility of the people within it.	POL	P
108. Making the community self-sufficient so that people don't have to go outside.	POL	P
(Format B.)		
100. Local government officials must realize that they stand or fall on the performance of the national government.	U.S.	N
110. When in doubt, local officials should always resolve a government's conflict in favor of what they feel to be the national objectives.	U.S.	N
111. The interest of particular communities should not be allowed to go so far as to interfere with national goals.	*U.S.	N
112. National laws should take precedence over all other laws and social practices.	*U.S.	N
113. Although we may not understand why national leaders make certain decisions, usually their decisions turn out to have been correct.	*U.S.	N
114. Local government should not attempt to gain a share of central funds for		

	Country applicable	Direction
desirable, but not essential local needs.	U.S.	N
115. On the whole, questions of national importance should come first in the minds of local government officials.	*U.S.	N
116. Local governments, under present conditions, should be allowed to care for their own affairs.	U.S.	P
117. It is important to bear in mind the interests of the whole society when making any decision in the local community.	*YUG	N
118. Local governments should not attempt to gain a share of central funds for desirable but not essential local needs.	YUG	N
119. When in doubt, local leaders should decide in favor of the national government's objectives rather than local.	*YUG	N
120. The interest of particular communities should not be allowed to go so far as to interfere with national goals.	*YUG	N
121. Leaders born and brought up in a community can serve it better than those coming from the outside.	YUG	P
122. A proper political leader puts the interests of his community foremost.	*YUG	P
123. It is important to site a large enterprise in one's own commune, although from the point of view of the national interest to site such an enterprise in another commune would prove more useful.	YUG	N

ACTION PROPENSITY

124. I prefer to stop and think before I act even on trifling matters.	*INTL	N
125. I usually check more than twice to be sure that I am not overstepping my tasks.	*INTL	N

	Country applicable	Direction
126. One should be concerned with what he has rather than with what he could get.	*INTL	N
127. The secret of happiness is not expecting too much out of life and being content with what comes your way.	*INTL	N
128. Only irresponsible leaders would risk community resources for possible but not certain future gain.	*INTL (not IND)	N
129. Quick decisions should be taken on important matters even at the risk of bad results..	INTL	P
130. Action should be delayed until it is certain that it will bring the desired results.	*INTL	N
131. Long deliberation over an issue should be avoided if it causes delay in action.	IND	P
132. Rather than doing things in a hurry, it is better not to do them at all.	*IND	N
133. Delaying action on important matters before complete information is available. (Format B.)	IND	N
134. It is important to make plans for one's life and not to accept just what comes.	POL	P
135. With things as they are today, an intelligent person ought to think only about the present and not worry about what is going to happen tomorrow.	POL	N
136. A leader who wants to accomplish something should not waste time examining all of the alternatives connected with every action.	POL	P
137. It is better to give up an action if it is not carefully prepared.	*POL	N
138. There is no progress without risk.	U.S.	P
139. With things as they are today, an intelligent person ought to think only		

	Country applicable	*Direction*
about the present and not worry about what is going to happen tomorrow.	U.S.	N
140. Untried, but possibly desirable programs.	U.S.	P
(Format B.)		
141. A leader who wants to accomplish something should not waste time examining all of the alternatives connected with every action.	YUG	P
142. It is better not to act at all than to try unproved ways of doing things.	*YUG	N
143. Decisiveness is the most important characteristic of political leaders.	YUG	P

HONESTY (TRUTHFULNESS)

144. Honesty and truthfulness must never be compromised at any cost.	*INTL	P
145. Leaders should present the truth no matter what the consequences are.	*INTL	P
146. If a person is requested by his superiors to present a false impression of certain matters, he should be willing to comply.	*INTL	N
147. If a leader knows that the truth will harm someone, he should conceal certain facts.	*INTL	N
148. Local officials should cover up situations which may embarrass their superiors.	*INTL	N
149. In order to achieve community goals, it is permissible for leaders to present facts in a one-sided way.	*INTL	N
150. It is not necessary for a leader to be strictly honest in public dealings if he knows this will interfere with getting his work done.	*INTL	N
151. If a leader in local government is highly skilled, one should overlook minor instances of dishonesty.	*INTL (not IND)	N

	Country applicable	Direction
152. In order to avoid misunderstanding by the people, a leader should not disclose certain facts.	*POL	N
153. Unblemished honesty is the most important trait of a good political leader.	*POL	P
154. A local political leader has an obligation to speak out publicly against the wrongdoing of all, even of the highest leaders.	*YUG	P
155. Local leaders should always publicly and truthfully speak facts about their failures in performing social affairs.	*YUG	P
	CHANGE ORIENTATION	
156. A community should not accept programs which upset the settled ways of doing things.	INTL	N
157. People who are dissatisfied with the way things have been done forget that doing things in a new way may bring about even worse conditions.	INTL	N
158. One cannot learn how to improve things by continually referring to the way problems were solved in the past.	INTL *(scaled IND/POL)	P
159. If society is to progress, newer solutions to problems are essential.	*INTL	P
160. The most reasonable approach toward social development is to accept changes which do not substantially alter the established order.	INTL	N
161. There is nothing inherently superior in the past.	*INTL (not IND)	P
162. The people in this community must continually look for new solutions to problems rather than be satisfied with things as they are.	*INTL	P

		Country applicable	Direction
163.	Even if the newer ways conflict with the way things were done in the past, they are absolutely necessary and desirable.	*INTL	P
164.	Changes are desirable even if they do not seem to contribute as much as one might expect.	*INTL	P
165.	While changes are desirable, they should never be implemented at the cost of our past values and traditions.	INTL	N

EQUALITY

166.	Rich people should pay more for the support of community projects than poor people.	INTL *(scaled POL/YUG)	P
167.	There should be an upper limit on income so that no one earns very much more than others.	*INTL	P
168.	The government has the responsibility to see that nobody lives well when others are poor.	*INTL	P
169.	Underprivileged people (low income people) should not be given any special consideration.	INTL *(scaled IND only)	N
170.	In every situation poor people should be given more opportunities than rich people.	*INTL	P
171.	Avoiding spending on luxuries is necessary to minimize distance between social groups.	*INTL	P
172.	Discrepancies in salaries should be continually reduced.	*INTL	P
173.	It is their own fault that some sections of the society are backward; therefore, the government should not make special provision for their uplift.	*IND	N
174.	Equal provision of funds for higher education of women as for men. (Format B.)	*IND	P

	Country applicable	Direction
175. No one should be privileged because he happens to be more useful than others.	POL	P
176. Differences in salaries should depend upon the size of the family.	*POL	P
177. Young people with special talents should be favored for exemption from the armed services.	U.S.	N
178. No one should be denied the opportunity for a college education.	U.S.	P
179. A son should not be allowed to use the position achieved by his father.	YUG	P

POLITICAL RESPONSIBILITY

(The use of this scale is optional for each country)

180. It is quite justifiable for a leader to avoid taking clear-cut positions on important issues if it threatens his career.	IND U.S. YUG	
181. Only a highly impractical leader will work for his convictions at a cost of popular support.	IND YUG	
182. It is better for a leader to lose his position than to do things against his better judgment.	IND YUG	
183. Even though the citizens may not appreciate what a leader has tried to do for them, the leader is obligated to work in their interests.	IND YUG	
184. A leader should first consolidate his own political position before expressing his views on sensitive political issues.	IND YUG	
185. A leader is obligated to follow the wishes of the community even if he thinks the citizens are mistaken.	IND U.S. YUG	
186. A local leader should only implement the demands and expectations of the citizens and not act independently.	IND U.S. YUG	

	Country applicable	*Direction*
187. The most important thing for the leader is to follow his convictions even if this is different from what the constituency expects.	IND YUG	
188. If the leader is himself convinced of what is the best action, he must try to implement this even though he has to use some pressure on the citizens.	IND YUG	
189. It is permissible for a leader to act sometimes in an unauthorized manner if he is convinced his action is ultimately for the good of the people.	IND YUG	
190. If a leader can preserve his position he can do more for the people than if he lost it by being frank and outspoken.	IND	
191. Only by learning to compromise one's personal convictions with the demands of reality can one ever hope to become a successful leader.	IND	
192. No purpose is served by leaders making personal sacrifices as long as the people did not appreciate them.	IND	
193. A responsible leader should never forget the interests of his friends and loyal supporters.	IND	
194. A leader should never forget that selfless work alone will not help keep his position.	IND	
195. It is essential that a leader act according to clear principles rather than make decisions based primarily upon the circumstances at hand.	U.S. YUG	
196. Strong opposition to policies should not in the least deter political leaders from acting.	U.S. YUG	
197. A good leader will wait until he has won over most of the opposition before he will act on controversial questions.	U.S. YUG	

		Country applicable	Direction

198. The most important quality of a political leader is deep dedication to his goals. — U.S. YUG

199. If a leader is convinced that a particular program is the right thing to do, he should be willing to force it on the people. — U.S. YUG

200. A leader can decide on whether or not to support a program by asking himself if the program is morally right. — U.S.

201. It is foolish for a leader to fight for his own advancement. — U.S.

202. Pressures of office do not in the least excuse a leader of his personal responsibility for his actions. — U.S.

203. No matter how unpleasant, a leader must adhere to his principles. — U.S.

204. It is the responsibility of a political leader to act according to what he feels is best despite whether or not anyone agrees with him. — U.S. YUG

205. Good programs should be pursued even if the public can be convinced of their merits only after they are in effect. — U.S. YUG

206. Leaders should not permit public opposition to discourage them in attempts to advance their programs. — U.S.

207. The job of a political leader is to do exactly as his constituents want. — U.S. YUG

208. Same as 195.

209. Same as 197.

210. For effective implementation of a program in the commune a support of a simple majority is sufficient. (over 50%) — YUG

211. Same as 196.

212. Same as 199.

213. Same as 204.

214. Same as 205.

215. Same as 207.

	Country applicable	*Direction*
216. Same as 198.		
217. When some important problems are in question a leader should not pay attention to the fact that the majority of the people in the community oppose him.	YUG	
218. In undertaking any action a leader cannot expect to have the support of more than 10% of the citizens.	YUG	

Part III Values, Qualities and Aspirations of Leaders

1. (*a*) Below is a list of values and ideals which some leaders feel are important. Please tell us which three of these are most important for you, if you were to make a choice.

LIST C

Most important

_____ (1) To work for economic development of society. (U.S.: to work for higher standard of living for people.)

_____ (2) To avoid conflict and maintain good relations among people.

_____ (3) To sacrifice your own interests for the interests of others.

_____ (4) To give priority to the national goals over the requirements of the local community.

_____ (5) To keep public leaders honest and truthful about public affairs.

_____ (6) To promote citizen participation in deciding about community affairs.

_____ (7) To equalize differences and distinctions based on economic and social discrimination.

_____ (8) To look for new solutions to problems rather than be satisfied with things the way they are.

1. (*b*) Now, please tell us which one of these you have chosen is most important for you.   (Number___)

2. What are your wishes and hopes for the future of our country? If you picture the future of (name of country) in the best possible light, how would things look, let us say, ten years from now?

OBLIGATORY PROBE: Anything else?

(*Note:* in translation—secure exact wording of this question as used in each country for Hadley Cantril's survey of "Hopes and Fears for Self and Country".)

3. What kinds of people would you like to see as political leaders? That is, what do you think are the most important qualities for a good leader to have?

OBLIGATORY PROBE: Anything else?

Part IV Conflicts and Cleavages: Support and Reference Groups: Government Responsibilities and Autonomy

1. In many communities there are conflicts which interfere with effective action to meet community problems. What are some major conflicts, if any, that interfere with getting things done in your community? (Name one or two.)

2. To what extent do these conflicts come in the way of the development of your community?

_____ very much

_____ some

3. To what extent do differences such as the following tend to divide people in your community?

LIST D CLEAVAGES IN THE COMMUNITY

	Very much	*Some- what*	*Not at all*
(1) Differences in education			
(2) Differences in income			
(3) Differences in religious belief or affiliation			
(4) Differences in political views			

	Very much	*Some-what*	*Not at all*

(5) Differences between city and country (urban-rural)
(6) Differences between managers and employees
(7) Differences in racial and social origins
(8) Differences between those desiring social change and those opposing it.

4. (*a*) Of the following groups, whose interests and welfare do you as a community leader feel the *most* strongly committed to advance? (alternative: "public official" for "community leader")
Please choose one:
_____ (1) Your political party
_____ (2) Your friends and loyal supporters
_____ (3) The people in your community
_____ (4) The nation as a whole
_____ (5) Another group; specify which_____

4. (*b*) What is the next most important group for whose interests and welfare you feel responsible?
_____

5. (*a*) When you as a leader (official) are in a situation in which support from others is necessary, to whom do you usually turn? Please check: (See List E.)

LIST E

	U.S.A.	Poland	India	Yugoslavia
(1)	Local party leaders	Powiat Committee of PZPR or ZSL	Your local party organization	Committee of the League of Communists in the commune
(2)	Local elective officials	Praesidium of Powiat Peoples Council	Elected leaders in the community	Deputy (M.P.) elected in the commune (including president)
(3)	Local newspapers	Leaders of social organizations	Leaders of other organizations (cooperatives, voluntary associations, etc.)	Voluntary associations (social organizations)
(4)	Higher level party leaders	Higher level party leaders	Higher level party leaders (ministers, party bosses, etc.)	Higher level party leaders
(5)	City manager or top administrative officials at local level	Top administrative officials of Powiat	Appointed officials in the community	Administrative officials in the communal assembly
(6)	Local civic, professional or reform groups concerned with local politics	Colleagues from your institution or profession	Respected and influential people	Representatives of different local institutions
(7)	Special groups in local party organization	Local party councilmen	Your own supporters in the party	Communal Committee of Socialist Alliance
(8)	Administrative colleagues at own level	Committees of the Councils	Co-workers	Professional organs of communal assembly

LIST E (*continued*)

	U.S.A.	Poland	India	Yugoslavia
(9)	State, county or higher administrative officials	Higher leaders (wojewodship authorities)	Appointed official at higher levels	Professional and administrative bodies at higher levels
(10)	Local business groups such as Chamber of Commerce	Managers of local enterprises and industrial plants	Factory owners and managers (urban)	Managers of enterprises and cooperatives
(11)	Local trade unions	Trade union activists	Trade union leaders	Different professional groups
(12)	Public or citizens generally	Majority of citizens	Majority of citizens	Population generally
(13)	Local ethnic, religious or racial groups	Agricultural activists	Certain caste or groups in the community	Representatives or individual settlements (local communities)
(14)	Lower income or lower social status people	Workers	Poor people	Workers
(15)	Well-to-do people (wealthy upper class)	Peasants	Rich people	Farmers
(16)	Close friends and supporters	Intelligentsia	Close friends and supporters	Intelligentsia

5. (*b*) Of those you have checked, which three are the most important?

6. Regardless of how things are done now and who now has the resources to do the things on this list, who in your opinion *should* have the *major* or *primary* responsibility to undertake them?

LIST F AREAS OF GOVERNMENT RESPONSIBILITY

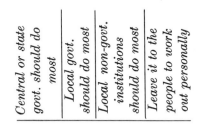

(1) Solve housing problem
(2) See to it that every man who wants a job gets a job
(3) Building schools
(4) Providing clinics, dispensaries, health centers
(5) Supporting art (painting, music) (and culture—Yugo).
(6) Providing electricity services
(7) Solving problems of youth (juvenile delinquency, vocational guidance)

7. In which of these areas does the local government here lack enough power and autonomy to act effectively?

Local government lacks powers and autonomy

Yes   *No*

(1) Solving housing problems
(2) See to it that every man who wants a job gets a job
(3) Building schools
(4) Providing clinics, dispensaries, health centers
(5) Supporting art (painting, music) (and culture—Yugo).

| | *Local government lacks powers and autonomy* | |
	Yes	*No*

(6) Provide electricity services

(7) Solving problems of youth (juvenile delinquency, vocational guidance)

Part V Background Data

1. Present position:

2. How many years (or months) have you held your present position as _____ (name post)?

3. Nation-specific: word to get at political heritage
   (for instance: Did your father also hold governmental or political positions, or perform functions such as yours? If yes, what was this position?_____)
   (or, Was your father active in politics?_____If yes, how?)

4. Nation-specific:
   (India, U.S.)   What political party do you support?
   (Poland)   Which party do you belong to?
   (Yugoslavia)   Are you a member of the party?

5. What has been your principal occupation during your life?

6. What was the principal occupation of your father?

7. How many years have you lived in this place?

8. Were you born in this place?_____Somewhere near?_____
   farther away?_____(Please check appropriate box)

9. How old are you?

10. Nation-specific:
    (U.S.)   What was the highest grade (level or class) of school you completed?
    (India)   What was the highest examination you passed?
    (Poland)   What was your education?
    (Yugoslavia) What was the highest grade (level or class) of school you completed?

11. (Sex)_____ Male_____ Female

Optional with each country

12. (*a*) What was the first public position you held?
Position_____ Year_____

12. (*b*) What other major public positions have you held since?
Position_____ What years held_____

Position_____ What years held_____

13. In your occupation, what position do you hold (or did you hold) before you took your present public office?

14. Nation-specific:
(Questions relating to exposure to mass media, such as:
(*a*) How often do you have a chance to read newspapers? Which?
(*b*) How often do you listen to the radio for news? (rural only)
(*c*) Are there any magazines or journals you read regularly?

15. (Rural respondents only)
Have you lived for some time in a city?_____How long?_____

16. Nation-specific:
(U.S., India) What is your religious preference, if any?

17. Nation-specific:
(Yugoslavia) What is your nationality?
(India) Interviewer record: *caste*
(U.S.) Interviewer record: *race*

International Code

(RESPONSES TO OPEN-ENDED QUESTIONS)

Frequencies reported are the total number of distinguishable references by respondents to the given category. One or more references may have been coded for each respondent. Total number of respondents from: India—954; Poland—888; United States—905; Yugoslavia—1124.

Perception of Community Problems
(question I/1)

What do you think are the most important problems facing this community now?

	India	Poland	U.S.	Yugoslavia
General principles of social and economic organization (code nos. 0100–0190)	19	14	3	57
Concern for general welfare, betterment of life, economic development (code nos. 0200–0300)	33	34	19	41
Basic living standards and productivity; poverty (code no. 0400)	109	5	7	58
Need for economic stability (code no. 0500)	57	6	20	21
Lack of resources; tax problems; inequitable allocation of resources (code nos. 0600–0610)	104	116	345	205
Problems of agricultural development				
In general (code no. 0700)	199	253	0	92
Irrigation (code no. 0710)	462	65	0	14
Food (code no. 0720)	173	21	0	6
Mechanization and other improved agricultural practices (code no. 0730)	97	126	0	78
All other specific problems (agricultural) (code nos. 0790–0791)	80	240	1	145
	1011	705	1	335
Industrialization and related problems				
In general (code no. 0800)	82	167	8	285
Developing industries (large) (code no. 0810)	8	106	16	1
Developing industries (small) (code no. 0820)	75	115	4	33
Attracting industry (excluding tourism), loss of industry (code no. 0830)	0	56	85	155
Business and commerce (code no. 0840)	3	77	16	32
Employment (code no. 0850)	153	315	38	350
Shortage of qualified skills (code no. 0870)	1	59	15	159
All other specific problems related to industrialization (code nos. 0860, 0890–0893)	13	56	15	103
	335	951	197	1118

	India	Poland	U.S.	Yugoslavia
Problems of urbanization				
In general (code no. 0900)	0	21	18	19
Housing (code no. 0910)	43	282	123	203
Urban renewal (code no. 0930)	0	10	195	3
All other specific urban problems (code nos. 0920, 0990)	4	92	150	62
	47	405	486	287
Utilities				
In general (code no. 1000)	2	37	27	89
Water, sewage, sanitation (including air pollution) (code nos. 1010–1011)	139	87	149	194
Electricity (code no. 1020)	111	12	8	73
Transport and communications (code no. 1030)	271	108	175	335
Other (code no. 1090)	6	19	22	10
	529	263	281	701
Social services				
In general (code no. 1100)	1	5	44	0
Health and medical (code no. 1110)	61	101	28	182
Family planning and population problems (code no. 1120)	21	1	45	8
Education (code no. 1130)	283	197	131	539
Cultural and recreation (code nos. 1140, 1191 YU)	0	88	45	167
Social welfare and security (code no. 1150)	7	17	24	116
Other (code nos. 1160, 1190)	1	24	19	15
	374	433	336	1027
Social and cultural problems				
In general; and including problems of backwardness, traditionalism, and social inequality (code nos. 1200, 1210, 1220, 1221. 1230)	73	39	33	26
Inter-group conflicts				
In general; and specific relationships not mentioned below (code nos. 1240, 1242–1244, 1246, 1249, 1250, 1253, 1270, 1291)	31	39	60	46
Conflict between new and old, modern and traditional ideas (code no. 1241)	1	2	6	1
Racial (code no. 1245)	0	0	98	0
Education (code no. 1247)	0	0	79	1
Social origin (including caste) (code no. 1248)	14	0	0	0
Conflicts of personal interest (code no. 1254)	4	0	16	0
Rural-urban (code no. 1260)	12	11	1	70
	135	91	293	144

	India	Poland	U.S.	Yugoslavia
Political problems				
In general; and specific problems not mentioned below (code no. 1300)	3	3	16	7
Problems of government administration (including inefficiency, bureaucracy, lack of coordination, lack of authority, interferences by politicians and others, lack of competent personnel, lack of time) (code nos. 1310–1320)	151	40	179	48
Problems of participation (including people's attitudes towards government, apathy, ignorance) (code nos. 1330–1334)	18	12	59	74
Problems of leaders' conduct (including dishonesty, personal political ambitions, interests (code nos. 1340–1344)	50	1	17	4
Conflicts between political groups and interests (including party, factionalism among different governmental bodies and levels of government) (code nos. 1350–1360)	19	4	90	57
	241	60	361	190
Miscellaneous (including all others not categorized above) (code nos. 1400, 1798 IND, 1410)	67	1	13	7
Total Problems Mentioned	3061	3084	2362	4191

Obstacles to Effective Leadership
(question I/5)

What do you feel are the main obstacles, if any, which limit your
effectiveness as a local leader?

	India	Poland	U.S.	Yugoslavia
Principles of social and economic organization (code nos. 0100–0190)	2	5	15	13
General welfare development (including standard of living) (code nos. 0200, 0410 YU)	0	3	0	2
Need for economic development (code no. 0300)	3	1	0	1
Basic living standards (including low productivity, poverty) (code no. 0400)	68	0	0	1
Need for economic stability (code no. 0500)	8	5	1	2
Lack of material resources (code no. 0600)	215	142	36	328
Problems of agricultural development (code no. 0700)	30	30	1	10
Problems of industrialization				
In general and other categories not specified below (code no. 0800)	3	26	3	49
Developing industry, loss of industry (code no. 0810)	0	12	1	2
Shortage of skills (code no. 0870)	1	32	1	53
Obstacles related to urban conditions (including housing) (code no. 0900)	3	20	19	8
Utilities (code no. 1000)	68[1]	20	19	8
Social Services (code no. 1100)	30	23	4	73
Social and cultural problems				
In general (code no. 1200)	6	5	1	15
Backwardness, traditionalism (code nos. 1220–1230)	157	9	40	27
Inter-group conflicts (code no. 1240)	109[2]	31	49	55
Political				
General and categories not specified below (code no. 1300)	12	30	44	9
Obstacles related to governmental administration and performance (code no. 1310)	344[3]	378	209	141
Lack of competent personnel (code no. 1318)	23	73	51	4
Inadequate time at disposal of leader (code no. 1319)	19	247	171	179
People's attitudes; lack of participation; ignorance (code no. 1330)	145	91	178	182
Leader's conduct (code no. 1340)	73	48	22	22
Conflicts between political groups and interests (code nos. 1350–1360)	209	49	106	122
Miscellaneous (code no. 1400)	66	33	167	39
Obstacles not mentioned, or stated not to interfere with leader's effectiveness (code no. 3100)	99	142	000	202

[1] Includes 56 (code no. 1030).
[2] Includes 30 social origin, caste (code no. 1248).
[3] Includes 140 Inefficient administration (code no. 1311); 95 Bureaucracy (code no. 1313); 52 Interference in government by politicians, etc. (code no. 1317).

Aspirations for Country
(*question III/2*)

What are your wishes and hopes for the future of our country?
If you picture the future of (name of country) in the best possible
light, how would things look, let us say, ten years from now?
    Obligatory Probe (after respondents' initial answer): Anything
else?

	India	Poland	U.S.	Yugoslavia
Principles of social and economic organization				
General; and categories not specified below				
(code nos. 0100–0190, except 0120)	24	76	88	96
Equality—economic and social (code no.				
0120)	101	19	151	188
Concern for improved general welfare, higher				
standard of living, economic development				
(code nos. 0200, 0300, 0401 YU)	276	650	376	765
Attain basic living standards, eliminate poverty				
(code no. 0400)	282	56	91	269
Economic stability (code no. 0500)	12	30	118	177
Provision of resources (including lower				
taxes, more equitable allocation of				
resources) (code nos. 0600, 0610)	11	41	16	32
Agricultural development				
General; and other categories not specified				
below (code nos. 0700, 0710–0792, except				
0730)	438	231	3	22
Mechanization and other improved agricultural				
practices (code no. 0730)	15	125	0	32
Industrialization and related hopes				
In general and other categories not specified				
below (code nos. 0800, 0810–0892, except				
for 0810, 0830, 0850)	261	341	54	113
Developing, or attracting industries				
(code nos. 0810–0830)	33	91	1	25
Employment (code no. 0850)	89	64	80	100
Urban amenities, and related hopes				
In general and other categories not specified				
below (code nos. 0900, 0920, 0930, 0990)	4	49	19	11
Housing (code no. 0910)	39	171	19	34
Utilities				
In general and categories not specified				
below (code nos. 1000, 1010, 1011,				
1020, 1090, 1091)	78	68	50	54
Transport and communication (code nos. 1030,				
1410 US)	99	66	0	20

	India	Poland	U.S.	Yugoslavia
Social services				
In general and categories not specified below (code nos. 1100, 1120, 1150, 1160, 1190, 1191 YU)	30	78	43	23
Health (code no. 1110)	46	41	51	22
Education (code no. 1130)	321	205	184	123
Cultural including recreation (code no. 1140)	1	98	33	19
Social and cultural advancement (code nos. 1210–1231)	46	—	5	130
Elimination of inter-group conflict (code nos. 1240, 1241–1292)	31	86	178[1]	32
Improve the moral character of the people (code no. 1691)	93	145	75	37
Political hopes and wishes—National				
General references; and categories not specified below (code nos. 1500, 1690)	30	24	36	13
Concerning governmental performance (code nos. 1510, 1516, 1520, 1530, 1531, 1532)	40	20	65	5
Concerning form of government; balance government (code no. 1540)	4	0	23	5
Democratic or representative government (code no. 1550)	36	4	33	15
Participation of people in public life (code no. 1551)	10	10	63	131
Decentralization of power (code no. 1552)	3	—	71	5
Non-partisan politics (code no. 1553)	0	—	1	0
Socialistic government (code no. 1560)	41	18	0	63
Freedom (code no. 1570)	11	6	48	15
Law and order, political stability; internal peace (code nos. 1580, 1590)	23	16	71	23
National unity, patriotism (code nos. 1610, 1620)	72	29	73	148
National power, prestige, self-sufficiency, independence (code nos. 1660, 1630, 1640, 1650)	388[2]	125	105	44
Political hopes and wishes—World				
Peace (including references to disarmament) (code nos. 1710, 1720)	12	78	463	152
Friendly relations with all countries; more international cooperation; help other nations (code nos. 1730, 1740, 1760)	7	27	154	41
Non-alignment; neutrality (code no. 1750)	0	1	2	8
Miscellaneous aspirations having to do with international relations (code nos. 1790, 1770)	9	24	30	19

[1] 95 of these references concern racial conflict.
[2] For India: Defence (1620) 117; Self-sufficiency (1640) 209; Prestige (1650) 48.

Qualities of Good Leaders
(question III/3)

What kinds of people would you like to see as political leaders? That is, what do you think are the most important qualities for a good leader to have? Obligatory Probe (after respondent's initial answer): Anything else?

	India	Poland	U.S.	Yugoslavia
Moral				
Humanity (code no. 11)	65	47	40	75
Honesty (code no. 12)	500	461	505	772
Sincerity (code no. 13)	44	59	87	31
Righteousness (dedication to principle) (code no. 14)	39	39	76	89
Selflessness (including putting public responsibilities ahead of personal "careerism") (code no. 15)	496	207	161	228
Morality (code no. 16)	120	97	289	117
Simplicity, humility (code nos. 17, 18)	36	69	20	62
Fearlessness, outspokenness (code no. 19)	68	42	87	171
Religious (code no. 20)	7	0	36	0
Non-violence, peace loving (code no. 22)	33	—	0	11
Other (code no. 21)	13	112	50	19
Working qualities				
Diligence (code no. 30)	52	67	76	145
Self-initiative (code no. 31)	2	38	22	27
Propensity toward the new (code no. 32)	10	7	32	32
Other (code no. 33)	16	65	65	1
Knowledge as a quality				
General intelligence (code no. 61)	38	115	200	79
Education (code no. 62)	115	228	166	202
Professional knowledge (code no. 63)	63	357	260	368
Other (code no. 64)	20	54	94	94
Qualities of leadership				
General leadership abilities (code no. 41)	159	146	266	189
Authoritativeness (code no. 42)	33	167	30	50
Tactfulness (code no. 43)	15	39	16	48
Impartiality (code no. 44)	140	81	114	90
Ability to harmonize interests (code no. 45)	20	18	25	8
Cooperative behavior (code no. 46)	70	28	69	111
Good relationship with people (code no. 47)	348	254	228	400
Dedication (to job, duty; interest in "social work"; voluntary service to public) (code nos. 48, 51)[1]	182	199	200	172
Attachment to national goals (code no. 49)	201	39	39	157
Attachment to local goals (code no. 50)	28	54	57	7
Political activity, ideological education and consciousness (code nos. 52, 53)	5	139	12	168
Respect the laws; not misuse his position; discipline; do what is expected by his superiors (code no. 54)	9	16	6	31
Other (including tolerance) (code no. 57)	50	153	121	17

[1] Of this number 123 (IND) and 109 (YU) expressed interest in social work.

Perception of Community Conflicts
(question IV/1)

In many communities there are conflicts which interfere with effective action to meet community problems. What are some major conflicts, if any, that interfere with getting things done in your community? (Name one or two.)

	India	Poland	U.S.	Yugoslavia
Conflicts over lack or allocation of resources (code nos. 0600, 0610, 1292 (YU))	5	53	120	1
Conflicts among social groups, differing in regard to:				
Attachment to new and old, modern or traditional ideas and practices (including new vs. old residents) (code nos. 1230, 1241, 1243)	22	42	111	39
Race (code no. 1245)	6	0	74	0
Education (code nos. 1130, 1247)	20	28	30	33
Social origin, including caste affiliation (code no. 1248)	177	4	0	0
Income (code no. 1249)	56	48	17	10
Functional activity (code nos. 1250–1253)	29	—	14	8
Personal interests, including property rights (code no. 1254)	85	—	61	36
Conflicts among other groups and generalized references to social conflicts in the community (code nos. 1240, 1242, 1244, 1246, 1260, 1270, 1280, 1291, 1278 (IND), 1290)	82	451	114	50
Political issues				
General and categories not included below (code nos. 1310, 1300, 1314, 1315, 1319, 1320, 1350, 1354, 1360)	85	54	72	17
Issues of governmental administration and performance (code nos. 1311, 1312, 1313)	8	118	45	64
Interferences in government operations by politicians and others (code no. 1317)	1	9	35	2
Competence of personnel (code no. 1318)	0	44	22	28
People's attitudes; issues of participation, apathy, political consciousness (code nos. 1330–1334 (YU))	19	166	197	36
Leaders' conduct (including conflicts over dishonesty, corruption, personal ambitions, misuse of power) (code nos. 1340, 1316, 1341, 1342, 1343, 1344 (YU))	102	126	88	69
Political party rivalries (code no. 1351)	233	9	20	2
Factionalism (code no. 1352)	132	19	67	60
Conflicts between local government (includes party leaders) and the population (code nos. 1353, 1356)	46	64	18	36
Conflicts between levels of government (code no. 1357)	2	28	24	23

	India	*Poland*	*U.S.*	*Yugoslavia*
Conflicts among local political and governmental bodies (including between elected bodies and the bureaucracy) (code nos. 1355, 1358)	21	14	18	182
Special interest groups vs. general community interest (code no. 1359)	22	6	104	7
Miscellaneous (code nos. 0100–0500; 0700–0891; 0900–1090; all 1100 except 1136; 1200–1224; 1396; 1400)	21	10	159[2]	0
No conflicts stated to interfere with community action (code no. 4200)	236[3]	133[3]	81[3]	472[3]

[1] Included in code no. 1358.
[2] Includes 45 references primarily concerned with zoning and other land use conflicts/urban/.
[3] Number of respondents.

Sampling and Selection of Units of Observation

This report was written by Sheth and Teune.

The sampling problem for this research was establishing whether there was a level of local governmental units in the four countries that would constitute a single universe of local governments, that is, whether the units selected could "truly" vary on the defined dimensions of activeness, and whether some of this variance could be accounted for by leader characteristics. Ideally, each unit in the four-country universe should have equal freedom to vary on each of the dimensions in the study. If the units were generally equal in their powers and functions, a basis for treating them, at least conceptually, as a universe, would be established.

Primary Sampling Units:
Local Governments

In order to select local governments that would not only be appropriate for the questions of this research but also would be as similar as possible and would thus constitute a universe of local units, criteria based on the political system were chosen. These were both structural and functional: *structural* in the sense that they would be located in approximately the same place in the political system hierarchy; *functional* in that they had the power to make essentially the same type of decisions in all four countries. This resulted in some probability of a similar pattern in the mobilization of social resources and initiative. The units selected on the basis of these criteria were cities in the United States, powiats in Poland, communes in Yugoslavia and blocks in India.

Whether blocks, powiats, cities and communes in fact form a single universe of local governments depends on whether the units are at the same level in the system of local governments, with similar kinds of relationships to both the central government and the population of citizens. Specifically, the units would be "comparable" if the leadership of the local units had some immediate contact with the local population as well as a major responsibility for similar administrative and decision-making functions.

Although the decision to select the local governmental units was made on criteria derived from the political system, additional criteria of selection could have been incorporated into the definition of units of observation. Some of the more obvious of these are rural-urban population, size and economic level. Since the inclusion of additional criteria would require the expansion of the number of observations, it was necessary to limit the sampling criteria to those most relevant to the dependent variable "activeness." Other characteristics that could have been used as criteria of selection could vary freely in the sample, which made it possible to have findings of a general nature, rather than findings confined to particular types of local governmental units, such as large or small units. As the purpose of this study was to generalize about the relationships between leaders' characteristics and local decision-making processes, the best basis for such a generalization was units that allowed for maximal variation in this relationship.

*Stratification of
the Units*

There were several considerations and constraints, in addition to the problem of obtaining structurally and functionally similar local governmental units in four countries; these included the need for a statistically stable number of community level observations, the high cost of collecting data for each governmental unit, and the question of the representativeness of the units selected. Considerations of cost and statistical stability were resolved by deciding to have 30 units in each country.

In order to get the maximum representation of variation in this limited number of units, it would have been desirable to be able to array all of the governmental units on their "activeness" and to sample on this stratification. This would have allowed for the explanatory variables to be related to the widest possible variation of the activeness of local units in each country. The variation would have been "built into" selection of the units, and would have assured variation in the dependent variable, even with a limited number of cases. However, to stratify the units on the basis of activeness, it would have been necessary to have the measure of activeness developed prior to interviewing. When it became clear that some of the data necessary for the measure of activeness could only be secured in the field, another basis of stratification had to be chosen.

The most obvious alternative criterion for stratification was a variable hypothesized to be of major importance in the explanation of activeness. The variable believed to account for a substantial amount of the variance in activeness was the economic level of the local units. Since economic data are generally available at central sources, it was feasible to stratify the units prior to the selection of the sample.[1]

The goal was to have a purposive sample, rather than a representative one. Although the purpose of the sample was to differentiate communities on the basis of activeness, an alternative basis of sampling had to be chosen. This was the major independent variable of the design—economic level.

Another goal of the sample was to have a number of units adequate for the analysis of differences in activeness in each country. This could be accomplished if the units were drawn from some widely defined base in each country. In Poland and the United States, this base was the national universe of all units of the type selected. In India and Yugoslavia, however, where regional influences are strong, a small nationally based sample (necessitated by limitations on resources, especially in India) would not adequately reflect regional differences. Thus the units sampled were drawn from a limited number of regions—states and republics. The three regions in India were Gujarat, Maharashtra and Uttar Pradesh. In Yugoslavia the Republics were Bosnia, Serbia and Slovenia.

The actual sampling procedures followed in each country depended on the availability of data for stratification, the capabilities of the research organizations in reaching various parts of the country, and limitations on resources. The framework in which these procedures were adopted was designed to have as similar a sample in each country as possible—an adequate number of units for analysis, stratification on economic level, and a representation of some large territorial and population segment of each of the countries.

The unit on which data are most readily available below the state level is the district. Because of the decision to stratify blocks on economic level, and because of the lack of resources to gather data prior to the survey, the first cut of blocks on economic level was done on a district basis. In order to incorporate regional differences into the sample, an equal number of blocks (two) were selected from each of the three states.

In each state all districts were grouped into three categories on the economic development criterion. The grouping into "high," "medium," and "low" was based on a study using 1961 census data by Pal and Subramanian.[2] This study calculated an economic development score for every district in India. The score was based on a factor analysis using the first principal component of 17 indicators. The variables were a mixture of urban, industrial and agricultural measures. Additional scores and ranks were computed for each district in Gujarat and Maharashtra. In Gujarat this score was a combined index based on per capita income, density, and proportion of total income contributed by the secondary and tertiary sectors.

In Maharashtra two other rankings of districts were calculated. The first was a summary rank based on eight indicators, largely agricultural ones. The second was a summary rank of general social development indicators—hospital beds, doctors, females literate, income, establishments with electricity, all per capita. These different approaches to ranking districts more or less ended up with the same overall groupings of high, medium and low.

After the districts were grouped, two districts, one from the high group and one from the low, were selected in each state. This, hopefully, provided a cluster of high and low blocks for each state.

The next step in the sampling procedure was the selection of five blocks from each of the selected districts. The goal was to sample the range of differences in economic level in each of these districts. As data could be gathered at the headquarters of the selected districts in Gujarat and Maharashtra, all of the blocks in each of the districts were ranked on the basis of economic indicators discussed in Chapter 7. Ten blocks were chosen for each state, through the use of a random start with interval sampling, from the continuum of the rankings. However, in Uttar Pradesh the development block is not a revenue unit, that is, a taluk or tehasil, as is the case in Gujarat and Maharashtra, and hence, not an official data aggregation unit. The data necessary for an economic level score had to be gathered at the block headquarters at the time of interviewing. Thus, informants were used to rank the blocks, and a selection was made on the basis of the overall ranking.

The blocks selected are a sample of blocks in six Indian districts, stratified according to economic level. As the districts represent a cluster of high and low economically developed districts, the blocks selected should represent a broad range of variation in economic level. Although technically this is not a sample either of Indian blocks or of blocks in three states, those selected may reflect the full range of variation in the collective characteristics of blocks in three Indian states, especially with regard to economic level. The sample for India is appropriate for inferences about relationships between variables, rather than descriptive for inferences about blocks in India.

Table 1—Sample Design: India

State	Districts	Districts Chosen	Mean Number of Blocks per District	Blocks Chosen
Gujarat	17	one high	(16.4)	5
		one low		5
Maharashtra	25 (Bombay excluded)	one high	(11.7)	4
		one low		6
Uttar Pradesh	54	one high	(16.2)	5
		one low		5

POLAND

The entire population of Polish powiats was sampled. Powiats are of approximately the same size and have identical powers and functions. Data from the Central Statistical Office for 1960 were used for the measure of economic level on which the entire universe of 391 powiats was ranked. In order to maintain a certain degree of homogeneity among the units, the 317 mixed urban and rural powiats were chosen, and exclusively urban powiats were removed from the population of units to be sampled. A table of random numbers was

Table 2—Universe and Sample Characteristics: Poland (1960)

	317 powiats: (mean)	Sample (N = 30): (mean)
1 Area	697.7 km²	879.5 km²
2 Population	68,500	66,800
3 Population density	70.7 per km²	75.9 per km²
4 Urban population	18,400	21,300
5 Nonurban population	50,000	45,500

then used to select a sample of 30 powiats in a way that allows for sampling the full continuum of powiats arrayed according to economic level.

The Polish sample is representative of the full range of differences in economic level for all mixed-urban and rural powiats, and generalization from the sample to the universe is possible.

UNITED STATES

Since the United States is predominantly urban, and since the municipality is the primary contact of the vast majority of the population with the local government, the universe of local units selected was that of municipalities. In drawing a sample of these units, we had to take into account the great variations in their size, ranging from 2,500 to several million. The size factor was important for two reasons. First, in all other countries the population of the units ranged from a few thousand to slightly over 100,000. If a random sample were taken of all municipalities in the United States, the average population would have been approximately 20,000, with a few units over 500,000. Secondly, a variety of studies of the aggregative characteristics of cities have stressed the importance of size as a major factor for predicting other characteristics.[3] For these reasons, the populations of municipalities and cities were stratified to emphasize middle-sized cities for comparability. Both small and large cities were excluded from the universe because of the particular problems they would pose in the analysis, both within the United States and across countries.

The sampling procedures involved several steps. First, on the basis of data provided by the 1962 City and County Data Book, all municipalities and urban places were scored on the 4 indicators of economic level. The 681 cities scored were the universe of all incorporated and unincorporated municipalities and urban places on which the necessary data were available. Although 714 cities are reported for 1960, the data were taken directly from the Census tapes, and certain units were excluded because of missing data or errors on the tape. Second this universe was stratified into three categories of size: (1) 25,000–50,000; (2) 50,000–100,000; and (3) 100,000–250,000. Third, since interviewing was being conducted by the National Opinion Research Center of the University of Chicago, each of the municipalities in the sample of about 200 cities of 25,000–250,000 population was placed into the three categories of size, and arrayed from high to low on the economic level scores. Municipalities were selected by using a random start in each of the three categories; through this method, each city in each of the three size categories was given an equal probability of entering the sample.

Because of this stratification, larger cities are systematically over-represented. The sample, however, can be weighted to represent the universe of cities of 25,000 to 250,000. The weights would be "4.4" for cities of 25,000–50,000, "2" for cities of 50,000–100,000, and "1" for cities of 100,000–250,000.

The two parameters that defined the universe are compared with the sample characteristics below. It can be seen that the mean size of the cities selected is above the mean for all cities within this size range in the United States. Since the economic level score was computed for all cities and the sample was drawn randomly from a major portion of the universe, the mean scores are very similar for the universe and sample.

Table 3—Sample Design: United States (1960)

	Universe	Sample
1 Size	(Mean, all cities)[1] 25,000–250,000	(Mean)
	$N = 714$	$N = 30$
	56,600	86,100
2 Economic level	(Sample of 200 cities 25,000–250,000)	
	$N = 681$	$N = 30$
	50.00	50.71

[1] Out of the 114,727,899 people living in urban areas above 2,500 population in 1960, 40,438,940, or 28%, live in cities between 25,000–250,000.

In the United States, all municipalities in each of the three categories of size had an equal chance of entering the sample. The sample, therefore, is representative of cities of the three size categories and, if weighted, would be representative of all American cities from

25,000–250,000. Further, the full range of differences on economic level are reflected in the sample.

The universe of local units in Yugoslavia is the mixed urban-rural communes in Bosnia, Serbia and Slovenia. As in Poland, exclusively urban communes were excluded. The 339 communes were then scored on two indicators of economic level: per capita income in 1964 and retail trade per capita in 1965. This score was intended to be only an estimate of the economic level score that was developed later and entered into the analysis. Both of these indicators, however, have a dominant role in the overall measure of economic level for Yugoslavia.

The economic stratification score, a mean of the scores on the two indicators, was used to rank all of the 339 communes together, as well as the communes in each of the three Republics separately. A sample of ten communes was drawn from each of the three Republics in such a way as to reflect the range of differences in economic level. This selection procedure resulted in a sample of 30 communes that corresponded closely to the rankings of all communes without regard to Republics. Thus, of the sample of 30 (ten selected from each of the three Republics) 15 of them are above and 15 below the median of the estimated economic level score for all 339 communes.

Table 4—Sample Design: Yugoslavia

Republic	Number of Communes (excluding urban)	Number in Sample	Number above Median	Number below Median
Bosnia	103	10	2	8
Serbia	179	10	4	6
Slovenia	57	10	9	1
Total	339	30	15	15

Selection of Leaders

The design of this research assumes that local leaders can influence community activeness. On the one hand, it is obvious that not all local community leaders defined as "influentials,"—second- and third-level administrators and officers of organizations—will be relevant to what happens in a local governing unit. Even among those leaders who are influential, many will be influential in minor ways, and only infrequently. On the other hand, individual leaders do not necessarily have to have an equal influence on what happens in a community. For the analysis of the behavior of local units, differences in the influence of individual leaders and their characteristics is not as important as differences in the *leadership structure* of the local unit itself. Although it is important that leaders selected have significant leadership roles, it is more important that those roles be a component of the local leadership nexus, in order to justify aggregation of individual leader characteristics into characteristics of the leadership structure.

Ideally, leadership roles could be located in each community in the following ways: first, examination of the formal leadership structure, largely legally defined, which assigns responsibilities and powers for decisions of relevance to activeness; second, identification of local decisions of significance for activeness, and at the same time, identification of the leaders who participate in those decisions; third, an assessment of the relative importance of various leadership roles for these decisions. For the concept of activeness, this would mean a description of the local political decision-making structure in each community, an examination of a sample of local governmental decisions with impact on resource mobilization and popular involvement, and the ranking of leadership roles in terms of their relative importance for these decisions. Preliminary explorations to identify the important and relevant local leadership roles were conducted in each country through case studies of "activeness" decisions. In addition, the formal legal structure was studied in each country.

Research required to identify these leadership roles in local governments in four countries would have been a major research task in itself. To facilitate this task, certain procedures of identification were adopted. These procedures were derived from knowledge that had been accumulated from the exploratory studies and familiarity with the legal decision-making structures.

The first step was to identify the strategic leadership roles in the local decision-making structure. Three major types of decision-making roles were chosen for all countries: elected officials, appointed officials, and organizational leaders, especially those in the local political party organizations. The second step was to differentiate leadership roles in terms of their relative importance in local decision-making generally, and in terms of decisions related to activeness specifically. Those positions with relatively more discretion in policy-making and implementation were of primary importance. Practically, this meant choosing all elective policy-making positions, top administrative positions, and the most salient positions in organizations. For example, all positions on the local decision-making councils or committees of larger elective bodies, heads of local administrative departments and agencies, the presidents of organizations, and in the case of political parties, the secretaries or their equivalents were automatically included for all countries.

Although the same leadership roles were specified for all of the local units in each country, an attempt was made to take local differences in decision-making structures into account. A specified number of leaders were selected on the basis of information gathered in the process of interviewing. Thus, differences in the importance of local organizations and the presence or absence of certain leadership roles and administrative units were incorporated into the selection of leadership roles for a specific community.

Application of these criteria in the selection of leadership positions more or less resulted in the identification of roughly the same kind of roles in each country. Whether these leadership positions are comparable or not will depend on the extent to which the selected leadership roles reflect the general decision-making structure at the local level.

SELECTION PROCEDURES: THE TARGET POPULATION AND
RESPONSE RATE

The general considerations outlined above were translated into operational procedures for each country. The basic strategy in each country was to define a target population for all local units, or, as in the case of the United States where there are substantial differences not only in the role of leaders but also in the names, to define specific target populations for each community. The interviewers were then given instructions explaining how to locate these leaders. Even in the case of positions defined in terms of local conditions, either specific names or instructions for identifying them were given to the interviewers.

Since local leadership positions were carefully defined with no substitutions of positions allowed, and since it was desirable in the community-level analysis to have approximately the same statistical stability in the community scores (the same number of observations), response rate was given special emphasis. Instructions were given to interviewers in each country to make several attempts to locate the targeted leader.

Table 5—The General Categories of Leadership Roles

India	Poland	U.S.	Yugoslavia
1 President and Vice-president of Block Council	1 All members of the Praesidium of Powiat Peoples' Council	1 Administrative heads (mayor and city manager)	1 President of the Communal Assembly
2 Chairman of Block Committees	2 All chairmen of the commisions of the Powiat Peoples' Council	2 City council members	2 Vice-President of the Communal Assembly
3 Block development officer	3 All secretaries of the Powiat Committee of the United Workers' Party (Alternative: all members of the Powiat Committee—about ten)	3 Department heads making significant decisions (commission members where appropriate)	3 Presidents of the councils and commissions of Communal Assembly
4 District development officer		4 Party officials—all parties (co-chairmen city chairmen, and appropriate other positional party leaders)	4 Presidents of the Neighborhood Community
5 Departmental heads at Block or Extension offices (including Agriculture, Cooperatives, Education, etc.)			5 Secretary of the Communal Assembly
6 Member of Legislative Assembly	4 Presidents of United Peasants' Party and Democratic Party	5 Representatives and senators from the city to state legislature where they have significant import on local decisions	6 Secretary and members of the executive committee of the League of Communists in a community
7 Block representative to district panchayat	5 All heads of main departments of Powiat Peoples' Council (Alternative: include only the department head who is chairman of Powiat Planning Committee—one)	6 Members from the city to county commission, board of supervisors or council	7 President and members of executive committee of Socialist Alliance of Working People in a community
8 Presidents of cooperatives in Block Council			
9 Chairman district panchayat			
10 Party executives at Block			8 President(s) and Secretary(ies) of Chamber(s) including president of cooperative
11 District party executives		7 Other strategic formal position holders in city	
12 Opposition leaders in Block Council	6 Other significant strategic position holders in the Powiat		9 Other leaders who have significant formal positions in decision-making processes in community, including president or secretary of Trade Union Council.
13 Coopted leaders in Block Council			
14 Other.			

INDIA

The following table presents the leadership roles targeted for India and the number of respondents interviewed. This is a specific list of the positions interviewed.

Interviewers were given lists of leaders to be interviewed. In some cases names and addresses were secured in advance from the Block Development Officers. Additional leaders were chosen after information was gathered from those initially interviewed.

Table 6—Selection of Leaders in India—Thirty Blocks

Positions	Gujarat	Maharastra	Uttar Pradesh	Total
1 Presidents and Vice-Presidents of Block/Taluka Samiti	20	20	21	61
2 Elected members holding offices in Block/Taluka Samiti[1]	147	91	108	346
3 Coopted members in Block/Taluka Samiti	57	25	27	109
4 Members of legislative assembly from the Block/Taluka constituency	8	6	8	22
5 Presidents, Vice-president and members in the municipality in the Block/Taluka Area	4	17	—	21
6 Taluka/Block Development Officer	10	10	10	30
7 Extension (Departmental) Officers in the Block/Taluka	74	48	68	190
8 Administrative Officers for the Block/Taluka	—	4	2	6
9 Political Party Leaders President, Secretary of Block and District Units	25	64	24	113
10 Other influential organization leaders	—	25	32	57
	345	310	300	955

[1] Gujarat: Elected from cooperatives and members of the executive. Maharastra: Members of the Panchayat Samiti and opposition members, and Sarabanan. U.P.: Members and block representatives of the Zilla Parishad.

POLAND

The uniformity of local leadership structure in Poland made the task of identifying and selecting leaders less complex than this same task in India and the United States. The following table is a summary list of the targeted leadership populations and the number of interviews secured.

Table 7—Selection of Leaders in Poland—Thirty Powiats

Position	Approx. no. holding Position in each Powiat	Total Number targeted	Number Interviewed
1 Members of the Praesidiums of the People's Council	6	180	165
2 Presidents of Committees of the People's Council	8	240	230
3 Secretaries of the Powiat Committees of the Polish United Workers' Party	4	120	117
4 Presidents of the Powiat Committees of the United Peasants' Party and the Democratic Party	2	60	54
5 Heads of the Major Departments of the People's Council	5	150	187
6 Other persons holding key positions	5	150	138
	30	900	891

One of the problems in determining the numbers of Polish leaders to be interviewed in each category was the initial overestimation of the numbers of Praesidium Members and Presidents of the Committees of the People's Council, and the underestimation of the numbers of Major Department Heads of the Powiat Council. Several of the Praesidiums of the People's Councils had more than five Department Heads, and several of the People's Councils had less than six members. In addition, several individuals held more than one office—a practice that is discouraged in the other countries, but permitted in Poland. Thus, the number of "other influentials" initially targeted was increased for all powiats.

A total of nine persons refused to be interviewed. These refusals left 891 leaders out of a total targeted population of 900 who were to be interviewed—an exceptionally high 99 % response rate.

UNITED STATES

The United States, in contrast to Poland, has a heterogeneous pattern of local leadership structures. For example, the number of officials elected as heads of administrative departments varies according to municipal charters. In several respects, the type of government, such as mayor-council or city-manager, will predict the kinds of other local offices present in the municipality. A special sheet of names and addresses and a list of positions for each of the cities in the sample was prepared for the interviewers. This sheet was based on information contained in the *Municipal Yearbook* and other sources. Some discretion was allowed to identify "other key influentials." The following table presents the targeted population of leadership roles and the actual number interviewed.

Table 8—Selection of Leaders in the United States—Thirty Cities

	No. Targeted	No. Interviewed
1 City executives (mayors, vice-mayors, managers)	46	43
2 City Councilmen	225	188
3 Elected administrative officials (treasurer, clerk, etc.)	13	12
4 Appointed administrative officials	281	253
5 State representatives residing in municipality	30	38
6 County officials residing in city	30	23
7 Party officials	190	158
8 School: President and member of school board and superintendent of school	90	89
9 Leaders of major organizations (Chambers of Commerce and Service Club)	60	62
10 Other influentials	30	39
	995	905

The targeted population of leaders in Yugoslavia was more detailed than in any other country. This was possible because the structure of leadership in the commune had recently been redefined. In addition, the presence of certain organizations in every commune enabled the research centers to specify each leadership role. The following table

Table 9—Selection of Leaders in Yugoslavia—Thirty Communes

	No. in each Commune	Targeted Total
1 President and Vice-President of the Communal Assembly	2	60
2 President of Communal Council	1	30
3 President of the Council of Workers' Communities	1	30
4 Chairmen of Councils of the Communal Assembly	4	120
5 Secretary of the Communal Assembly	1	30
6 Heads of the Economic and Education and Culture Divisions of the Commune	2	60
7 Desk Officers: Communal Affairs and Public Health and Social Welfare	2	60
8 Chairman of Commission of Complaints of the Communal Assembly	1	30
9 First and Second Secretaries of the Communal Committee of the League of Communists and Member of the Communal Committee for Ideological Questions	3	90
10 President, Secretary, and a Member of the Communal Committee of the Socialist Alliance	3	90
11 President of the Communal Trade Union Council	1	30
12 Presidents of the Communal Councils for the Social Activity of Women and Youths	2	60
13 A National or Republic Deputy living in the Commune	1	30
14 Director of the People's University (Slovenia and Serbia only)	1	20
15 Managers of Enterprises	2	60
16 Principal of the School in Center of Commune	1	30
17 Head of Public Health Centers	1	30
18 Managers of Agricultural Cooperatives (if none, then Presidents of Workers' Council or Manager of Enterprise)	2	60
19 Presidents of Local Communities within the Commune	9 (est.)	270
		1190
Total number secured		1179

presents the roles and targeted number for every commune. In Yugoslavia, 40 leaders were targeted for each commune, more than in the other countries.

In selecting heads and managers of enterprises, the interviewers were instructed to choose the largest or most important enterprise in the commune. Although almost every commune has some agricultural population, some do not have agricultural co-operatives. In those cases, the interviewers were instructed to select the President of the Worker's Council. This choice reflected the counterpart of the Agricultural Co-operatives.

*The Population of
Local Leaders*

A variety of adjustments had to be made for the political systems. These system differences are sharply evident when dealing with roles and names of roles in the system itself. In making comparisons it is necessary that the phenomenon—the leadership structure at the local level—be at least conceptually equivalent in all systems. The specific components of this leadership structure, of course, had to be defined in a language specific to each of the four countries. The procedures for identifying the components of the leadership structure were similar in all of the countries. The question that remains is whether the procedures followed in applying the criteria have resulted in a comparable base of observation.

The application of the criteria of selection resulted in three generic types of local leaders in each country: official policy-makers, usually elected; heads of the major administrative departments, usually appointed; and party leaders. The similarity of the local leadership structure in the four countries is reflected in the fact that approximately the same proportions of these categories of leaders were chosen. Indeed it was difficult to locate many more leaders with formal positions in the local unit than were selected unless minor leaders of minor organizations were included.

All of the leadership roles selected were formally defined. No attempt was made to locate informal leaders, that is, individuals with influence on policy but no formal position. Decision-makers—individuals who have roles with rights to bind the collectivity—were emphasized in the selection criteria. Although several individuals who held roles with no or little formal powers to bind the collectivity were also included, those who occupied these roles, by virtue of their position, were considered to have a place in the total leadership structure. Party leaders fell into this category of "influentials," since these positions were of some importance in the processes of policy formation.

In one sense, the roles selected are a universe of the local leadership. In another sense, they can be considered a sample of all of the individuals holding leadership roles in the local unit. What constitutes the universe of leadership roles in each community is a question of fact. The assumption made here is that the leaders selected constitute the entire population of the leadership roles in the specified communities in three decision-making sectors of the leadership structure: the decision-makers, the administrative officers, and the political organization of the local government.

In order to execute a community-level analysis, the characteristics of local leaders were aggregated into community scores. The scores are "means," "proportions," or "variances" of the entire leadership group interviewed in a community. In aggregating individuals, two questions arise: can these individual characteristics be legitimately aggregated, and how stable is the community characteristic derived from the aggregation?

The legitimacy of aggregating individual leadership characteristics depends on whether the individuals on which the collective characteristics are based indeed constitute a group. This can only be argued *ex hypothesis*. The assumption underlying aggregation in this study is that the leaders interviewed constitute a group in two senses. The first is that all of the individuals belong to the same community or are members of the same local unit. The second is that each of them occupies a role in some common structure—the local community leadership structure. In contrast, for example, if a random sample of the general population in each community were aggregated into a community characteristic, the only basis for calling this a group characteristic would be that the individuals all came from the same community. However, the leaders selected for this study, at least in principle, are linked together by a set of roles in a common social and political structure.

The second question is a matter of the number of observations in each community. In all countries, about 30 leaders were interviewed in each unit. This number begins to approach the area where the assumptions required for calculating means based on a normal distribution are approximated. In addition to reasons of no response, it was not possible to interview an identical number of leaders in each community because of the absence of certain leadership roles or incumbents. However, in every community in Yugoslavia, over 30 leaders were interviewed. The lowest number of observations for communities in the other countries is 24 in India, 22 in Poland, and

25 in the United States. In over two-thirds of the remaining cases, over 30 interviews were secured.

An Evaluation of the Sample of Local Governments and
Selected Leaders

The primary focus of the sampling procedures was to represent variation in the dependent variable of activeness at the local governmental level. No attempt was made to sample local political leaders in the *country* as a whole; rather, the representation of the full range of characteristics of the position-holding local political leadership within each of the sampled local governmental units was attempted.

The sample of units is drawn from one or more major strata of local governments in each of the countries. In India it is the rural level of local government in three states; the non-urban strata in Poland and Yugoslavia, and the middle-size urban strata in the United States were chosen. In all countries except the United States the lowest level of government—local communities within the local government—were excluded, as well as major regional and intermediate governmental units, such as states and districts. In all countries certain forms of local government are set aside in recognition of the basically different nature of urban and rural governmental problems. The rural stratum is included in India and excluded in the United States to reflect the preponderantly urban or rural nature of the countries. In both Yugoslavia and Poland, where approximately half of the population is urban and half rural, local governmental units with a mixture of urban and rural population were included and urban powiats and communes excluded. Despite these exclusions and inclusions of strata of local governmental units in defining a universe of local governmental units in the four countries, those strata selected manifest, or perhaps even represent, the major decision-making processes at the local level. These are the processes in which local political leaders interact with the population; leadership behavior required for mobilizing individual resources for collective purposes and for involving the population in the community can at least, in principle, take place.

The leaders who were interviewed represent basically 30 strata of local political leaders in each of the four countries—the 30 units selected for study. The definition of the universe of local governmental units prescribes the kinds of local leaders who had some chance of entering the universe of leaders in each country. In India leaders had to be members of three levels of strata in order to have a chance of entering the universe of leaders. They had to reside in one of three, out of a total of 16, Indian states; they had to be located in one of six, out of a total of 96, districts; they had to hold an office at either the village or block level in one of those six districts. In Poland, a wide stratum of local political leadership had some probability of being included into the group of leaders interviewed. Holding any official position in any mixed urban-rural powiat in Poland gave the individual a chance of entering one of the thirty strata defined by the powiats that entered the sample. Of all the local officials in the United States, an individual leader had to hold a position in a city of 25,000–250,000 in order to have any chance of being selected. The probabilities of being selected, as has been discussed, were greater if the leader held a position in one of the larger of these cities. Of all of the individuals in Yugoslavia holding official positions below the federal level, only those holding positions in a mixed urban-rural commune in one of three republics had any chance of being included in the population interviewed. Because of the different number of kinds of communes in the three Republics, the probability that a Slovenian commune leader would be selected was about twice that of Bosnian leaders and three times that of Serbian leaders.

The procedures for selecting leaders allowed a significant segment of local leaders to be chosen in each country, and provided an adequate base for reflecting some variation of the attributes of local leaders in each country. Generalizations about the leaders, however, must recognize the various strata of local leadership from which leaders were selected and within which observations were made.

Notes

1. In the United States the population of cities ranges from a few thousand to several million. This is not the case in the other countries, where the size of the units are circumscribed by statutes and practice. Thus, in the United States size was used both to define a universe of roughly comparable units—municipalities varying between 25,000 to 250,000—and to stratify the units for selection.

2. See, M. N. Pal and C. Subramanian, "Regional Disparities in the Level of Development in India," New Delhi, India Statistical Institute, 1965 and M. N. Pal, "A Method of Regional Analysis of Economic Development with Special Reference to South India," *Journal of Regional Science* Vol. 5 (1963), pp. 41–58. For details of this procedure, see Third Report to A.I.D. Science Director, *A Study of Social Values and Political Responsibility in Developing Countries,* Philadelphia: University of Pennsylvania, 1967.

3. See J. Hadden and E. Borgatta, *American Cities: Their Social Characteristics,* Chicago: Rand McNally & Co., 1965.

APPENDIX Ⓒ

Measuring Values

This report was written by Jacob and Singh.

The strategy adopted by the ISVIP to measure values was designed to meet the following criteria:

1. identification of values relevant to the public decision-making functions of the respondents;

2. discrimination of each value from the others;

3. measurement of the intensity of commitment of respondents;

4. assurance that the values measured were cross-nationally equivalent, in order to permit comparisons of commitment among respondents from different countries.

Four interrelated procedures were used, leading, in the end, to the construction of multi-item scales. The reliability was demonstrated by inter-item correlation, and independently by factor analysis; the validity of these scales was supported by the congruence of the results secured by the different procedures.[1]

1. *Open-ended questions* ascertained which qualities were considered the qualities of "good" leaders and what were considered meritorious public actions; these questions also asked individuals to spell out

their hopes and fears for their country. This provided a pool of un-structured value-laden statements representing a spectrum of political values *as expressed by political leaders themselves.*[2]

2. Concrete, *forced-choice* statements in several formats elicited the respondent's degree of commitment to, or repudiation of, ten values selected as peculiarly relevant to political decisions concerned with local development.[3]

Two sets of such questions were prepared. One set, identically worded for all four countries, provided a core of items that were at least semantically uniform. The other set, adapted to conditions, experiences, and language familiar to the leaders in each country, contributed to validity by seeking cultural relevance. By statistically demonstrating the equivalence of the identical and the nation-specific questions, cross-national *comparability* can be presumed, both in the substance and the measurement of the value.[4]

3. *Factor analysis* of responses to all the forced-choice questions demonstrated the homogeneity and independence of most of the value scales. Responses clustered in a way that paralleled given value scales, much as we had conceived and defined them. In some instances, however, there was no clear counterpart of a value scale; this made it doubtful that these scales represented an independent, unidimensional value. The factor analysis further pointed to the existence of certain important cross-nationally comparable value patterns that had not been foreseen.

4. *Content analysis* of major speeches and other documentary records of political discourse demonstrated standards of evaluation commonly expressed in public life; these findings were independent of any influence attributable to the interview situation. Such a general view of dominant value themes provided a frame of reference within which the significance of the particular values on which this study has concentrated could be fixed.

Scaling
Values

The development of value scales involved an arduous process of interaction between the definition of a value conceptually and the testing of questions designed to draw forth different degrees of com-mitment to the value. Although we are indebted to previous studies for many relevant test items, some of which proved to be good in-dicators of values as defined in this study,[5] no ready made scales were found suitable for the measurement of the values at issue for local political leaders in these different countries. Hence, new scales had to be constructed. The procedure was as follows:

—The collaborating scholars from the four countries decided on a mutually meaningful description of each value to be measured.

—They then attempted to write (or to borrow) questions that would relate to one value and one value only and that would also have the power to discriminate different degrees of commitment within each country. As noted above, two sets were prepared—the international set, which was identical for all countries, and, after the first pre-test, a set specific to each country.

—These items were pre-tested on leaders in each country similar to those to be interviewed in the final survey.

—Pre-test responses were conceptually and statistically analyzed; a complete inter-item correlation of the responses was included. Questions were then discarded on three grounds—if they failed to generate sufficient variation to assure an adequate distribution of respondents; if they had a low homogeneity ratio, that is, they did not correlate sufficiently with the rest of the questions designed to form the scale; and, if they were reported to be confusing to respondents or, on second look by investigators, they appeared ambiguous.

—The value *concepts* were then thoroughly re-examined, and their definitions were refined to make the value concepts correspond more precisely with the items retained.

—Additional questions were written, others revised and the pre-test repeated. Altogether, two pre-tests were conducted in each country and three were conducted in two countries, with a total of 830 respondents in all.

—Upon completion of the final survey, the "purification" process was again repeated. After choosing the best set of internationally identical questions for each value from a pooled analysis of all respondents, those nation-specific items that had the highest correlations with the international set were added to compose nine purified scales.[6]

The homogeneity and reliability of the scales as finally selected is reported in Table 1. Their stability, validity and comparability will be evaluated later after considering the results of the factor analysis and other evidence.

Table 1—Homogeneity and Reliability of the Value Scales[1]

	India n = 952		Poland n = 888		U.S. n = 905		Yugoslavia n = 1179	
	(a)	(b)	(a)	(b)	(a)	(b)	(a)	(b)
1 Innovative Change	.143	.451	.211	.570	.149	.462	.230	.588
2 Action Propensity	.134	.454	.128	.505	.183	.572	.112	.462
3 Economic Development	.129	.424	.181	.518	.206	.601	.224	.665
4 Economic Equality	.134	.540	.221	.662	.300	.680	.271	.685
5 Participation	.155	.709	.145	.599	.192	.651	.203	.712
6 Conflict Avoidance	.167	.556	.197	.549	.160	.567	.096	.345
7 National Commitment	.217	.728	.163	.604	.140	.629	.212	.751
8 Selflessness	.126	.514	.201	.636	.116	.470	.176	.574
9 Honesty (truthfulness)	.131	.473	.160	.655	.251	.726	.216	.729

[1] Column (*a*) notes the mean coefficients of inter-item correlations. Values .088 and above are significant at the 1% level for a sample of 900 or above. Column (*b*) notes the Kuder-Richardson coefficients computed by the formula

$$r_{tt} = \frac{n}{n-1} \times \frac{s_t^2 - \Sigma s_i^2}{s_t^2}$$

where s_i is the standard deviation on a given question in the scale and s_t^2 is the test variance

$$[(\Sigma s_i)^2 \bar{r}_{ii} - \Sigma s_i^2 \bar{r}_{ii} + \Sigma s_i^2]$$

See G. F. Kuder and M. W. Richardson, "The Theory of Estimation of Test Reliability," *Psychometrica*, 2, 1937, 151–166.

Responses to all the forced-choice value questions in the final survey (including those that were dropped from the purified scales) were subjected to three or more forms of factor analysis for each country.[7]

One important result of the factor analyses was the sustenance of the integrity of five of the scales within all four countries. Most of the items selected for the scales of commitment to Participation, Nation, Innovative Change, Honesty and Economic Equality tend to cluster together in single, independent factors, so that one clearly interpretable factor corresponds closely to each of these value scales.[8] The same is true in India for Conflict Avoidance. Although there is a mix of other out-of-scale items in some of the factors, the core of each factor is composed of in-scale items. Also, most items that were omitted from the purified scales turn out to have low loadings in the factor analysis, thus further confirming the criteria of scale purification.

A broader mix of items, going beyond a particular scale, is most noticeable in a general factor involving the issue of integrity in public life as opposed to an inclination to justify opportunism or expediency (see Table 2, Factor A and discussion below). However, the core of the factor in all countries is the Honesty scale, as almost all items in this scale are highly loaded on this particular factor.

Furthermore, there is almost perfect accord between the anticipated direction of the responses to the scale questions and the actual direction of the responses as found in the corresponding factors. If questions called for a positive response to indicate agreement with a value, they are positively loaded on the factor. If a negative response was required to be consistent, the loading is indeed negative. (In only one instance was the loading the reverse of what was expected.)

This analysis strongly supports the conclusion that the scales do in fact measure stable and consistent elements in the leader's value orientations.

The cross-national comparability of these values is a second significant conclusion of the factor analysis. The parallelism of the factor structure among all four countries (each with a common core of internationally identical items), as demonstrated in Table 2, tends to validate the assumption that we are dealing with equivalent value dispositions of local political leaders in these nations.

A third finding is the presence, in all countries, of an important value, more general than those scaled, that is interpreted as a concern for "principled" conduct in public life, as opposed to an opportunistic or

Table 2—Value Factors—International

Questions (with relatively high loadings)	India	Poland	U.S.	Yugoslavia
FACTOR A[1]		*Percentage of Variance*		
Commitment to Principled Conduct	10.40%	14.99%	18.03%	22.25%
in Public Life		*Loadings*		
#71 If leaders can get things done the people need not bother whether or not they are selfish	.372	.449	.494	.134
#146 If a person is requested by his superiors to present a false impression of certain matters he should be willing to comply	.273	.342	.443	.389
#147 If a leader knows that the truth will harm someone he should conceal certain facts	.394	.325	.348	.475
#148 Local officials should cover up situations which may embarrass their superiors	.297	.358	.524	.495
#149 In order to achieve community goals, it is permissible for leaders to present facts in a one-sided way	.358	.505	.482	.333
#150 It is not necessary for a leader to be strictly honest in public dealings if he knows this will interfere with getting his work done	.531	.472	.567	.392
#151 If a leader in local government is highly skilled one should overlook minor instances of dishonesty	.514	.417	.610	.449
FACTOR B[2]		*Percentage of Variance*		
National Commitment	10.12%	13.10%	18.14%	13.22%
		Loadings		
#87 National goals should not be obtained at great costs to local communities	−.348	−.334	−.349	−.251
#88 Although national affairs are important, people here should first worry about their own community problems	−.494	−.405	−.475	−.280
#89 Community progress is not possible if national goals always have priority	−.540	−.451	−.415	−.525
#90 We should not worry so much about national problems when we have so many in our own community	−.552	−.329	−.378	−.271
#92 Local leaders should always be prepared to adjust their programs to national goals and policies even if this is disadvantageous for the community	.376	.247	.117	.600
#93 It is necessary to forego development of one's own community to help the development of the rest of the country	.387	.145	−.161	.443
FACTOR C[3]		*Percentage of Variance*		
Commitment to Change	11.32%	13.26%	6.40%	9.86%
		Loadings		
#159 If society is to progress, newer solutions to problems are essential	−.287	−.498	−.428	−.392
#162 The people in this community must continually look for new solutions to problems rather than be satisfied with things as they are	−.285	−.495	−.433	−.372
#163 Even if the newer ways conflict with the way things were done in the past, they are absolutely necessary and desirable	−.455	−.473	−.362	−.391
#164 Changes are desirable even if they do not seem to contribute as much as one might expect	−.410	−.292	−.248	−.295

FACTOR D[4]	India	Poland	U.S.	Yugoslavia
Commitment to People's Participation in		Percentage of Variance		
Decision-Making	9.56%	8.87%	6.70%	12.10%
			Loadings	
#45 Widespread participation in decision-making often leads to undesirable conflicts	.254	.330	.257	.336
#46 Most decisions should be left to the judgment of experts	.259	.307	.455	.515
#47 Only those who are fully informed on the issues should vote	.358	.332	.448	.473
#48 Only those who are competent on an issue should speak about it	.353	.473	.462	.343
#49 Participation of the people is not necessary if decision-making is left in the hands of a few trusted and competent leaders	.495	.357	.329	.365
#50 To have decisions made by people who are experts on the matter under consideration (is important to achieve when making political decisions)	.245	.330	.377	.491
#51 Participation by everyone in decision-making regardless of their knowledge of the issues involved (is important to achieve when making political decisions)	.396	.441	.480	.393

FACTOR E[5]		Percentage of Variance		
Concern for Economic Equality	11.32%	11.01%	12.36%	15.21%
			Loadings	
#167 There should be an upper limit on income so that no one earns very much more than others	.365	.571	−.213	.522
#168 The government has the responsibility to see that nobody lives well when others are poor	.350	.528	−.280	.390
#170 In every situation poor people should be given more opportunities than rich people	.533	.333	−.307	.479
#171 Avoiding spending on luxuries is necessary to minimize distance between social groups	.239	.472	−.323	.285
#172 Discrepancies in salaries should be continually reduced.	.198	.475	−.370	.461

[1] Several additional questions relating to honesty and selflessness in public conduct loaded above .300 for particular countries, as follows: India 3, Poland 1, U.S. 3, Yugoslavia, 6. Beyond the common core, this factor includes, for some of the countries a set of items that appear to represent a particular ideological commitment, or concept, of general principles held to characterize a "good" leader in that particular country. In Yugoslavia for instance, the factor includes 11 items indicating concern for economic development, acceptibility of social change, and commitment to public participation in decision-making. In the United States, several of these same items load heavily on the factor, indicating commitment to a similar set of principles associated with legitimate public conduct. But in the United States, unlike Yugoslavia, there is also an element of *opposition to economic equality*, making this an integral component of the ideology of political responsibility.

[2] Additional nation-specific items relating to the concern for local, as opposed to national interests load above .300 on this factor as follows: India, 3, Poland, 2, U.S., 1, Yugoslavia, 3.

[3] In most of the countries, this factor also includes selected items referring to concern for economic development and action in decision-making. In India, this factor merges with Factor V (economic equality).

[4] Additional items relating to this theme load .300 or above on this factor as follows: India, 3, Poland, 1, U.S., 1, Yugoslavia, 2.

[5] In India this factor merges with Factor III (Change).

expediential approach that would compromise truthfulness, the public interest or ideological considerations to achieve self interests. This factor, loaded heavily in the direction of Honesty and Selflessness in all countries, also draws in a set of items that varies from country to country, and appears to reflect what is the prevalent or orthodox view of "good" or "proper" ends in that particular society. Accounting for up to 22 % of the variance, the factor cutting across national differences, obviously uncovers a prime dimension of values, as political leaders confront their decisions and make their choices.

Aside from the factors that are similar in all countries, the *analysis has singled out others that are distinctive of particular countries.* In India, there is the concern for community consensus or conflict avoidance already mentioned. In Poland and the United States, the local-national factor splits in two, indicating that leaders make a distinction between the issue of the importance of national over local interests and the importance they attach to the problems and development of the local community *per se.* (In India, by contrast, leaders tend to relate most of the local-national questions to a single dimension). In India, there is a specific factor that can be interpreted as acceptance of the *status quo;* this is a positive commitment to the value of things as they are. The desirability of change is viewed as a separate issue, not necessarily opposed to an appreciation of tradition and stability. In Yugoslavia no such distinction occurs, the concept of change being associated clearly with rejection of the *status quo.* In India and, to some extent, in Poland, factor analysis reveals a distinction between the personal and public spheres of conduct in regard to the values of Honesty, Selflessness, and similar principles. In addition to the general factor of "principled" conduct in public life, there is another factor that pulls together those items that apply more to individual life or interpersonal relations.

The overall result of the factor analyses is the establishment of considerable confidence in the reliability of most of the basic measures of values, while at the same time suggesting refinements of the others.[9]

Value Content
Analysis

The use of thematic content analysis to identify the dominant patterns of values in the political culture and, especially, to secure a basis for comparing the values of local leaders with those espoused by the top national level of leadership was not as extensive as originally intended.

A method was developed and tested to identify, classify, and measure the frequency and intensity of values expressed in any form of verbal political communication. A pilot study succeeded in applying this method to derive a tentative value profile of certain Indian and U.S. national leaders from a limited selection of their major policy statements on development issues.[10]

It was not possible to complete a sufficient amount of analysis, in any of the countries, to document the kind of national profile desired, nor was it possible to secure enough reliable records of statements by local leaders to permit an analysis of the values they expressed in the normal course of their public life. This left us without one of the expected independent means of validating the value responses secured in the survey.

Nevertheless, the preliminary results suggest some of the dominant concerns that the national leadership in two of the countries chose to emphasize in the year prior to the ISVIP survey. A comparison of these concerns with the survey indicates large areas of mutual relevance, and warrants some tentative conclusions for India and the United States concerning the vital question of whether the local leadership accepts the values propounded by the top.[11]

Establishing Priorities
Among Values

The most difficult measuring problem, and the one least adequately solved, was ascertaining which values would prevail when leaders had to choose among conflicting values. What "good" holds priority over other "goods" when you cannot secure them all?

Scale scores, of course, provide a useful overall assessment of the relative strength of commitment to different values, but they do not necessarily indicate which values will prevail in situations in which issues are sharp and clearly pit one value against another.

Many of the questions, as phrased, required respondents to choose between adherence to either one value or another, and turned out to have strong discriminating power. For instance:

Q.4 *Economic development** should not be pursued if it means *hardship for the people.*

Q.28 A good leader should refrain from making *proposals that divide the people* even if these are *important for the community.*

Q.45 *Widespread participation* in decision-making often leads *to undesirable conflicts.*

Q.71   If leaders can *get things done*, the people need not bother whether or not they are *selfish*.

Q.93   It is necessary to forego *development of one's own community* to help the *development of the rest of the country*.

Q.147 If a leader knows that the *truth will harm someone*, he should *conceal certain facts*.

Q.150 It is not necessary for a leader to be strictly *honest* in public dealings if he knows this will interfere with *getting his work done*.

* Italicized statements identify different values that are pitted against each other.

But the alternatives posed did not always relate directly to the specific values being scaled, and there was no systematic pairing of alternatives that would have permitted Thurstone's method of paired comparison or similar ordering.

An attempt was made to devise a battery of situation-specific questions in which the respondent was asked to decide what he would do in concrete political controversies. This proved futile, however, as we got few reliable interitem correlations; this made across country comparisons hazardous, in view of the wide contrasts in the nation-specific situations.

Finally, in pursuit of the respondent's hierarchy of values, one direct question was asked, posing a forced-choice among a set of verbal statements representing eight of the values scaled. While the abstract format of these statements detracts from the reliability of this approach, the results are worth reporting because they do indicate a definite ordering (see Table 3). This ordering does not correlate consistently with the intensity of commitment to particular values as measured by scale scores but nevertheless there is considerable congruence between these two quite independent measures of priority (compare Table 3 with Table 4, Chapter 3). With one exception, the four values ranking highest in importance in each country are ones to which the scale scores indicate strong positive commitment by the leaders; with four exceptions, the four values ranking highest in each country on the priority question are also among the four having the highest scale scores.

On the other hand, as will be seen, the *operational* impact of values on the leaders and their communities does not depend on their abstract priority. For instance, the values of National Commitment and Economic Equality have in some countries a closer association with other leadership characteristics and with community activeness than their place in the priority list would suggest. Commitments to values that may not be considered the most philosophically important can be more significant in the actual making of decisions

Table 3—Value Priorities

Value Ranked	Means* and Rankings for							
"Most Important"	India	R	Poland	R	U.S.	R	Yugoslavia	R
1 Economic Development	.947	1	1.053	1	.737	3	.997	1
2 Conflict Avoidance	.504	3	.477	4	.234	5	.388	5
3 Selflessness	.468	4	.167	8	.153	7	.172	7
4 National Commitment	.435	5	.337	6	.029	8	.088	8
5 Honesty	.795	2	.505	3	.967	1	.807	2
6 Participation	.193	8	.314	7	.735	4	.380	6
7 Equality (Social and Economic)	.398	6	.356	5	.187	6	.611	3
8 Change	.254	7	.834	2	.883	2	.572	4

* This table reports means of the means secured for the leaders in each community (rather than for the leaders pooled nationally). "Action propensity" was not included in this question because it did not lend itself to single statement exposition as clearly as the others.

than the values that people profess to hold in higher esteem when responding to a question of this type (honesty, for instance).

Validification

Before concluding, we must admit that none of the measures we have used can, by themselves, establish that the values identified do actually influence political action, that is, have an *operational* effect. These are measures of *professed* values. Whether leaders act in a way consistent with their professions, and whether, in turn, there is carry-over into community performance must be determined by other means. Indeed, validification in this fundamental sense has been the overall task of the project; we have tried to discover how far one can predict from leader's professions of values to their political behavior and the developmental activity of their communities. Other sections of this study discuss the extent to which linkage was discovered between the values expressed and various types of individual and collective action, that is, how far these values were verified by practice in public life. In general, the evidence lends credibility to the proposition that professed values, as measured here, can have a definite bearing on behavior; scores on at least some values correlate with some kinds of action in some countries. This conclusion is corroborated by related studies of a similar type.[12]

In the limited sense of *concept validity*, the internal consistency of respondents in answering the survey questions in all four countries, indicates that we were measuring something that was commonly perceived and understood, and that meant the same thing to almost everyone. Factor analysis, as we have seen, gave such evidence of concept validity in the conceptually coherent clusters of items that corresponded to many of the scales.

Additional confirmation of the fact that our measures, especially the scales, tapped specific values that were recognized as such by the respondents was secured by testing the "discriminant validity" of the scales. Examining the extent to which the responses to questions correlated more highly outside a scale than within, we found that, in every case, only a few of the items included in a scale (always less than half) correlated more highly with items in any other scale than with the average of correlations within the scale (the homogeneity ratio as reported in Table 1).[13] This means that most respondents clearly linked a particular question to the value we were seeking to identify rather than to another value; thus, it was demonstrated that in their eyes, as well as ours, these values were conceptually distinct, and that their distinctiveness could be effectively expressed through the kinds of questions we had devised.

All this points to the existence of these values as a definable and integral element of the leader's dispositional structure.

A Methodological Critique of Value Scales and Profiles:
by The Yugoslav Group

The Yugoslav participants have two basic criticisms of the value scales as they have been interpreted and used in constructing value profiles. First, the value scales are not unidimensional, especially in Yugoslavia. Second, the use of a single cutoff point in the scales (as defined and measured) for dividing leaders into those committed and those against a particular value is not warranted.

There is evidence, especially in Yugoslavia, that some of the scales cannot be interpreted in a unidimensional manner. First, and most importantly, there is the nature of the items included in the scales—their content. Second, on the basis of a special study done in Yugoslavia, which asked the respondents for their understanding of particular items, it is clear that some of them interpreted items differently from what was intended by the investigators.[14] Third, there is the pattern of inter-item correlation. These points are especially applicable to the value scales of commitment to Nation, Participation, and Economic Equality.

The scale of commitment to Nation contains items asking for endorsement of national programs and goals, espousal of the importance of the local community, and a choice between national and local interests. It is not only possible for an individual to endorse national goals without prejudice to local interests, and vice versa, but, also, the analysis of the respondents' interpretation of these items shows that the promotion of local interests has no necessary implication for national goals and programs. The scale score, in short, is not unidimensional but rather multidimensional.[15]

Participation, in a similar manner, asks for endorsement of popular participation and for the participation of experts. Again, the analysis of the respondent's understanding of these items in Yugoslavia demonstrates that approval of popular participation carries no implications for participation of experts. It is possible to be in favor of participation of both the citizens and experts; that is, expert participation is not in conflict with democratic decision-making.[16]

The problem with the scale of Economic Equality lies in the interpretation of the scale. The items in the scale and the respondent's understanding of items indicate that what is being assessed is the reduction of economic differences in society, and not a commitment to the absence of economic differences. The interpretation of this scale in one part of the text is limited to the reduction of economic disparities. In other parts, the scale is interpreted as economic egalitarianism and is used to infer economic radicalism. We believe that the interpretation of this scale should be confined to the character of the items and the respondent's understanding of them, which, in Yugoslavia at least, is the reduction of economic inequalities.[17]

Also, the basic issue in the construction of value profiles is the use of a single cutoff point and the "black and white" interpretation of those individuals who fall on either side of this cutoff point. This has been previously noted in considering the strategy of explanation for leaders' values (see Chapter 4, p. 105n. 28). There are several problems. First, such cutoff points, if they are to be used, should be adjusted to the nature of particular scales, and not applied to all scales without regard to their content. In particular, use of such cutoff points for the scales of National Commitment and Participation, with their multidimensional properties, is inappropriate. Secondly, the consideration of a respondent with a score of 2.6 as one who has declared himself on one side of a value and a respondent with 2.4 on the other, opposite side, is an arbitrary designation that ignores the scalar properties of the way in which the values were measured—ordering individuals from high to low. Similarly, the decision that respondents scoring 2.5 are neutral, and therefore should be eliminated from the analysis, distorts the patterns of value profiles in countries where leaders expressed themselves in a less categorical manner. Yugoslavia had the largest deletion of cases. Thirdly, due to the way in which the profiles were constructed, it is not at all surprising that they could not be explained by the characteristics of local communities, or demographic characteristics of the respondents or their perceptions.

Notes

1. For an overview of methods previously used in measuring values, see Allen Barton, *Measuring the Values of Individuals*, New York: Columbia University, Bureau of Applied Social Research, Reprint No. 354 and his working paper, "Value Measurement and the Analysis of Behavior," prepared for the First International Roundtable of the ISVIP (ISVIP Doc. US/19).

2. See Chapter 3 for a description of the questions and Appendix A for the international code that was constructed from the responses.

3. See Chapter 3 for a description of these values.

4. This method, which is believed to be an innovation for assessing similar phenomena in culturally heterogeneous populations, was not originally programmed; instead it was devised as the national teams worked together to resolve this most persistent dilemma confronting cross-cultural research. The approach is explained more fully in Chapter 2. The rationale and operational procedures were propounded by A. Przeworski and H. Teune in "Equivalence in Cross-National Research," *The Public Opinion Quarterly*, Vol. 30, Winter, 1966–1967. As it turned out, the approach proved not to be as critical in this survey as expected. Correlations between the two sets of questions, international and nation-specific, were high; only a few of the nation-specific questions survived the process of "purification" whereby items that did not correlate significantly and positively with the other items in a scale were eliminated. However, this strategy makes it possible to have much more confidence in the validity of the final results, than if only common questions had been used.

5. We are specifically indebted to Joseph A. Kahl and Milton Rokeach for permission to use certain questions from their respective scales of "fatalism" and "dogmatism."

6. The approach to scaling values adopted by the ISVIP generally followed that applied by William A. Scott in studying the values of American college students. See his *Values and Organization*, Chicago: Rand McNally, 1965.

International items were selected if (a) they correlated positively with each other in all countries and (b) their average correlation with other items in the scale was above .08 (significant at the .01 level). Nation-specific items were selected if (a) they correlated positively in that particular country with every other scale item, international as well as nation-specific and (b) their average correlation with other items in the scale was above .08. In the following scales, one international item that did not fully meet these criteria in one country was added (as indicated) in order to strengthen the scale in the other three:

Action Propensity	(Yugoslavia, question 124)
Economic Development	(India, question 1)
Conflict Avoidance	(Yugoslavia, question 23)
National Commitment	(U.S., question 90)
Selflessness	(India, question 70)

See Appendix A for full list of questions included in the purified scales (note the starred items on the survey questionnaire).

Scores were originally computed on a 4-point basis: 1 = strongly agree, 2 = agree, 3 = disagree, 4 = strongly disagree. An individual's score on a given value was computed by dividing his total score on the items finally selected for a scale (adjusted for the direction of the question) by the number of items to which he responded.

Midpoint is obviously 2.50, though no option was provided for this position, or for "no opinion." Conceptually, the significance of a 2.50 score is that it is equidistant from the maximum possible agreement with the items in a scale, and maximum possible disagreement with those items. In analysis and interpretation, we have inferred that those scoring below 2.50, as originally computed, tended to accept the value, those scoring above 2.50 tended to reject it.

To clarify reporting in this publication, the original scores have been reversed so that a *high* score denotes a high commitment *to* a value, a *low* score denotes rejection of the value, or at least a relatively low degree of commitment to it. A score of 4.00, therefore, indicates the maximum possible acceptance of a value, a score of 1.00 the maximum possible rejection.

7. In the analysis reported herewith, all items (except those relating to the political responsibility scale) were analyzed separately for each country by a factor iteration program that sequentially rotated all principal components with an eigen-value greater than 1.00. This produced the following number of factors: India (8), Poland (9), U.S. (8), Yugoslavia (6).

8. In the Indian analysis, when only six factors were rotated, items from both the Change and Economic Equality scales tended to merge into the same factor (see Table 2); when the number of rotations was increased, however, these two sets of items separated into distinguishable factors.

9. The presumption of reliability is strengthened by evidence from a subsequent study conducted by Kailash K. Singh in Uttar Pradesh using some scales that were largely composed of questions identical or very similar to those used in ISVIP. Responses from a sample of leaders that overlapped with the sample in the ISVIP were consistent with those obtained earlier, in what amounted to a partial re-test situation. See Kailash K. Singh, *Values, Leadership and Development*, Report to the Research Programmes Committee, Planning Commission, Government of India. Kanpur, India: Indian Institute of Technology, June, 1968.

The factor analysis provided evidence of a flaw in the construction of the survey questionnaire, at least in reference to India. One whole group of items, cast in Format B, that asked respondents to designate whether a given proposition was important to achieve or to avoid was found to load on a single factor in most countries. This is attributable to a response set to which this format appears especially susceptible, at least in India. Fortunately, only a few of these items were used in the purified scales.

10. See K. Krippendorff, "A Preliminary Inquiry Into the Expression of Values in Political Documents," ISVIP Doc. USA/68 for elaboration of the technique. Coding instructions are available in ISVIP Doc. USA/72. See also, P. E. Jacob, "Progress Report on Value Content Analysis of National Leadership: U.S., and India," ISVIP Doc. USA/71. This report is based on analysis of ten major speeches on "Great Society" issues by President Johnson, 1965–1966, and ten speeches on domestic issues by Prime Ministers Shastri and Gandhi during approximately the same period.

11. As would be expected, in view of the completely different methods of inquiry, there is a considerable range of issues on which even rough comparisons are not possible. Values emerged from the content analysis that had no counterpart in the survey. Also, some of the values pointed up in the survey were not echoed in the particular set of national statements that were content analyzed. It is hoped that in further research, value content analysis of local leaders' speeches and other communications corresponding to the kind of material gathered for national leaders may be undertaken.

12. See, for instance, the study undertaken for the Research Programmes Committee of the Planning Commission, Government of India, by Kailash K. Singh of the Indian Institute of Technology, Kanpur: *Values, Leadership and Development, op. cit.*, especially pp. 98f. The results showed evidence of a definite relationship between discrete values expressed by leaders and their personal performance in role responsibility; this is based on an intensive survey of 431 respondents from 60 villages in Uttar Pradesh and covers three levels of government organization—village, block and district.

13. In Yugoslavia, there was evidently considerable conceptual overlap between certain items in the Conflict Avoidance scale and items in the Participation, National Commitment, and Change scales; this is true also between items in the Action Propensity scale, and the Honesty and National Commitment scales. In India, three of the items in the Honesty scale also correlated highly with several items in the Participation scale.

The discriminant validity test was not performed on the Polish scales.

14. Results of this study, including an item-by-item tabulation and analysis of responses, are reported by Z. Puric in ISVIP Doc. YU/76, and summarized in a subsequent memorandum by the Yugoslav group, in Doc. YU/197.

15. This is carefully emphasized for Yugoslavia in the aforementioned item analysis by Z. Puric, who notes that most of the answers to the relevant questions are not categoric (respondents shun the extreme positions of "strongly agree" and "strongly disagree"). She concludes that "the respondents replied to what we had asked them, and we asked them two different things. It seems clear enough that the majority does not oppose these two interests one to the other."

16. The point is made by Puric as follows: "Analyzing these questions logically we have established that no other category of bearers of decision making was explicitly opposed to experts. Accordingly, leaders themselves, rather than citizens, can be understood as confronting experts, especially as the respondents were leaders. A respondent might reason something like this: 'Well, why should I mix in *expert problems*, let experts think of and decide on that. If political problems were involved, then that would be different. There, both myself, as an official, and organs of self-government should take part'." ISVIP Doc. YU/76 *op. cit.*

17. The evidence for this conclusion, and its implications for the interpretation of the results of the ISVIP are elaborated in Z. Puric, "Propensity to Removing Disparities in Wealth Among the People," Belgrade: Institute of Social Sciences, January, 1970. Unpublished manuscript, ISVIP Doc. YU/196.

The Measurement of Activeness

NOTES ON INTERPRETATION OF THE ACTIVENESS FACTORS

The first note was prepared by Teune, on the basis of interpretations commonly agreed upon by the authors of the chapters on Activeness: Bosnic, Mlinar, Ostrowski, Sheth. The second note, "A Dual Pattern of Activeness," was prepared by Jacob.

The table at the end of this Appendix presents the factor loadings that were used to score the local communities. The factor interpreted as activeness, a mixture of popular involvement and resource mobilization indicators, was discussed in Chapter 8, with a summary of the measurement operations followed. The purpose of this appendix is to present some interpretation of the results of the factor analysis.

Both India and Poland have clear factors of popular involvement. The highest loading indicators in India (Factor III) are individual efforts to build facilities in the locality, such as drinking wells, manure pits, and latrines. In Poland all of the indicators that load highly and consistently in this factor (Factor II) refer to organizational affiliation. The high loading items in the United States can be characterized as individual monetary contributions to local organizations, and continued increases in these contributions. If some American indicators are reconceptualized as performance of civic duty, such as libraries and recreational facilities, and the factor is interpreted as "civic-mindedness," at both individual and collective levels, then a clear dimension can be identified in this factor. Such an interpretation, however, would depart from the definition of popular involvement.

The resource mobilization dimension is the most disappointing. A clear factor of resource mobilization can be found only in the United States (Factor I). The factor that resembled resource mobilization in Yugoslavia contains items loading inconsistently with their hypothesized relationships. In India and Poland there was an interpretable factor, but it was composed of only a very limited number of highly loaded indicators. The Indian resource mobilization factor (Factor IV) includes schools and improved seeds. In Poland (Factor IV) two important indicators concern increases in powiat services—education and retail outlets. The third most important indicator, loading just below these presented, is increase in medical services, more physicians. The resource mobilization factor in the United States is almost entirely made up of expenditures, including changes in expenditures and revenues. The dominance of municipal expenditure indicators in this factor, however, perhaps reflects the fact that most of the collective efforts at the local level are reflected in the municipal budget.

In India and Poland, the loadings are above 75% of that predicted for popular involvement indicators. In the United States the consistent loadings on the resource mobilization factor are 75% of that predicted. In Yugoslavia there is a clear activeness factor, but there are no factors that are easily interpreted as ones corresponding to the definitions of popular involvement or resource mobilization.

One consideration in evaluating activeness scores from a particular rotation is to the extent to which they are independent of each other. Excluding Yugoslavia, because of the inconsistently loaded items, activeness correlates .45 with resource mobilization in India and .64 with popular involvement in Poland. The other correlations indicate less than 9% (r^2) of the variance in common.

A second consideration is to the extent to which the activeness scores based on one kind of rotation of the principal components (orthogonal) would have been different if different rotations had been used. In all countries except Poland correlations were run between scores based on oblique, oblimin, and orthogonal rotations, in addition to an orthogonal analysis on random numbers for the same number of variables used in the activeness measure. In the United States, correlations are .99 between the three kinds of rotations and −.32 for the random numbers. In Yugoslavia, correlations were .98 between rotations and −.19 for random numbers. In India, oblimin-orthogonal correlation is .81, the oblique-orthogonal .91, and activeness-random numbers, −.22. Thus it appears that the type of rotation used would not affect the activeness score in the United States or Yugoslavia, but would have some effect in India. Furthermore, the correlation between the random numbers and the data in the United States indicates some error in the activeness score, as does the low percent of variance explained.

In three of the countries there are bipolar factors with indicators loading positively and negatively. There is a difference of judgment as to whether to interpret these factors (Factors II in India, the United States and Yugoslavia) or not. The authors of the Activeness sections, Bosnic, Mlinar, Ostrowski, Sheth, and Teune, believe that it is not prudent to interpret these factors in *the context of factor analysis used to measure activeness as it has been defined*. Jacob argues that these factors show a "dual pattern of activeness," an argument he will elaborate below. The arguments for avoiding interpretation are based on the conceptual nature of the definition of activeness, the interpretation of scores derived from the loadings (the purpose of this factor analysis), and the necessity for examining alternatives to a bipolar interpretation.

Technically, bipolar factors are those that have approximately an equal number of negative and positive loadings of about the same magnitude. Conceptually, a bipolar factor is one in which the positive and negative loadings cannot be interpreted in terms of the hypothesized dimensions. Bipolar factors are to some extent a function of both the positive and negative directions of the correlations and the number of rotations. Every indicator was conceived to belong to a common domain, activeness, which has two dimensions. Thus, any factors in which the indicators are juxtaposed, producing bipolar factors, cannot be interpreted as belonging to a common domain. However, if a typology of activeness were intended, and if the loadings did not reverse the directions of correlations, it would be possible to use these bipolar factors to develop typologies.

It is almost impossible to interpret a score based on a bipolar factor. Scores are usually interpreted in a unidimensional manner: the higher the score the higher the attribute. If bipolar factor loadings are used as coefficients for scores, the scores reflect the position of a particular case on several indicators, some of which are positively and others negatively weighted. Thus high scores would tend to be given to those cases that fall into the upper range on the positively loaded items, but into the middle range on negatively scored items; low scores would tend to be those cases that fall into the upper range on negatively loaded items and into the middle range on those positively loaded. Midrange scores would either be high on both positive and negatively loaded items or in the midrange on both. The scores in effect would reflect a typology, a position on several dimensions, rather than a position on a single dimension. Thus, it would be difficult to characterize a case in terms of these substantive dimensions from the scores.

In terms of alternatives, the activeness indicators and a particular type of factor analysis (indeed, a specific rotation of the components) were chosen to obtain the "best fit" with the definition of activeness and its components. No attempt was made to test whether there was a "dual pattern of activeness;" rather, we only tried to discover whether popular involvement and resource mobilization indicators had some variance in common. This was found in all four countries, and in several of the countries there are identifiable dimensions of the two types of indicators in the factor analysis. To establish more would require use of some alternative indicators, perhaps alternative kinds of factor analysis, and some demonstration that certain extraneous factors did not compound the error, as in the case of urbanism and the activeness measure in Yugoslavia. Exploration of the alternatives would have involved more hypothesis-testing than the one hypothesis required in the definition of activeness— resource mobilization and popular involvement indicators have some variance in common.

A Dual Pattern of
Activeness

Analysis of the data on community activeness, as interpreted by this investigator, indicates that, at least in India and Yugoslavia, there are alternative modes of collective behavior that are radically different from what has been cited in the body of this report as the common, cross-nationally comparable phenomenon of "activeness." At least two general types of activeness can be identified in each of these countries, rather than one; also, the two types tend to be contradictory. That is, communities that demonstrate high activity along one line are likely to score low on the other. This means that we are dealing with two different phenomena rather than one, each reflecting fundamentally different mixes or clusters of indicators. Thus it would be inappropriate to characterize a community as highly active, without specifying the specific form or structure of activeness being measured. A community could be classified in one of three categories: (a) active with respect to Type I (the mixed factor consistently referred to in this book); (b) active with respect to Type II (an alternative mixed factor wherever it emerges); or (c) inactive in both respects. As noted above, the evidence shows that no community is likely to be active on both Types I and II.

The substantive significance of this finding emerges when one examines the sets of activities that cohere to form the respective patterns. In India, Type I, the pattern referred to throughout this volume, is heavily oriented to innovation and the acceptance of practices based on technical knowledge—adoption of scientific methods of agriculture, animal husbandry, population control and public health. It also includes a rise in adult literacy and exposure to public communication (through the presence of radio facilities). Type II includes none of these as significant components, but demonstrates a major commitment of manual effort to the physical cultivation of the land, for instance, in the amount of irrigation and use of improved ploughs. *Rejection* of family planning practices such as insertion of loops, and the lack of motorized equipment such as pumping sets, are strong negative components of this measure.

In Yugoslavia, Type I, as previously expounded is characterized by an orientation toward developmental change (especially as stimulated by public investment at the local level), exposure to public means of communication, and by formal general membership in the main instrument of political influence, the League of Communists. Type II engages more vigorously in local political activities—especially where individuals can participate, as in nominations of candidates and attending voter's meetings. They pay their local taxes but they are not active in a variety of cultural and educational activities, for a reason that becomes quickly apparent when one discovers that these are communities that are *poor* and *rural* as compared with Type I. The fact is that some of the programs used to measure activeness in Yugoslavia were simply nonexistent in the less developed regions and communities. In other words, there was a definite economic bias in the selection of the indicators of activeness. S. Tomic, who conducted the ISVIP project in Bosnia, notes that the indicators were unusually weak on "voluntary participation" activities, which would be the principal channel for poor, rural communes to demonstrate initiative and progress in social and economic development. (The problem in the inclusion of such indicators was the difficulty of securing comparable data for all the communes in the sample.)

I do not concede that the validity of this alternative measure of activeness is necessarily destroyed by an element of bipolarity in the factor on which it is based—as contended in the preceding note. Nonaction can be as significant an indicator of a phenomenon as action. Indeed, bipolarity is a function, in part, of how each indicator was originally conceived to fit the overall pattern, and how the input of data was organized. Suppose, for instance, going to the movies had been considered a frivolous waste of time, rather than a positive demonstration of community activeness in Yugoslavia. Then we would have reversed our input of data on movie attendance (using low attendance as a sign of "high" activity) and this indicator would have emerged as a high loaded item on the second factor, rather than a negatively loaded item, eliminating at least this one aspect of bipolarity. What the evidence of bipolarity does refute, it seems to me, is the original assumption that guided our research on activeness, namely, that there was only one dimension of activeness, and that it would be demonstrated by the consistent interrelationship of the various items that we, in our untested wisdom, thought would be indicators of that dimension. Not only did the facts demonstrate that some of these items failed to correlate with the set that did fit our original conception; they produced an alternative set, with which the *opposite* of some of our intended indicators was highly correlated. The test of validity is the *conceptual coherence* of the indicators actually forming the factor; I would submit that the second factor can be interpreted as a measure of activeness just as coherent as the first—and sharply distinguishable from it. (I would grant the point that an independent test of this *ex post facto* hypothesis has not yet been undertaken, and should be.)

What makes the hypothesis of a dual pattern of activeness seem even more plausible is the extraordinarily large number of significant correlations between the various independent variables and the second activeness factor in both India and Yugoslavia. Indeed, the number considerably exceeds those found for the factor chosen as the standard measure. Furthermore, the correlates have an impressive coherence of their own, as they identify both ecological characteristics and a type of leadership that distinguishes the community ranking high on the second measure, and low on the standard measure.

In India, for instance, the leaders of communities that are active in the conventional ways of a manual agricultural society, are essentially *harmonizers*, in contrast to the *innovators* who lead the other type of active communities:

(1) they are greatly concerned with the avoidance of conflict;

(2) they are unusually conflict-conscious, asserting more than others, that conflicts beset their communities, and interfere with their development;

(3) they are also cleavage-conscious, noting many differences that divide people in their communities;

(4) they are far less convinced of the desirability of changing the established ways of coping with community problems;

(5) they tend to blame and to shun government:
—they see "bureaucracy," maladministration, corruption (outside, or up above) as major obstacles to their leadership,
—they favor leaving problems up to the people to resolve, rather than calling upon any level of government, even local, to take a hand;

(6) they are unusually attached to local bases of support—official and nonofficial (including "poor people" as well as the "respected and influential");

(7) conversely, they are allergic to political party and political life:
—they profess not to seek support from higher party leaders,
—they state minimal concern for advancing party interests,
—far fewer than in other communities claim membership in the Congress Party,
—they don't recognize or admit partisan conflict to be an obstacle to their leadership,
—an unusually small number indicate that they are either active or influential in political organizations;

(8) these people are preeminently agriculturalists; they quite clearly concede that they are neither active nor influential in general economic development. They do take a lively hand in the area of community services.

The leaders of the poor, rural communes in Yugoslavia are as different from those of the wealthier, urbanized communes as is their pattern of activeness. They are more highly committed to the values of Economic Equality, Economic Development, and Political Participation. They are more nationally (centrally) oriented. They identify themselves as active in agriculture and *political organization*. There are other indications of a high degree of political socialization; they are unusually strong in declaring their *support for party* (even though in their communities, membership in the League of Communists is much lower than in the other type of active communities), and they look primarily to the party and related organizations as their base of support, rather than to nonpolitical sources, such as institutional representatives, voluntary associations, or the intelligentsia. The leadership in communes that are active in this second sense see their communes as unusually wellknit, with few divisions and cleavages, few conflicts, especially of a political nature, and few obstacles to their leadership. In other words, these are, in their own eyes, self-confident leaders of purposive, integrated communities, although ones that are having a tough struggle to compete with those that enjoy a better resource base. Consistent with this picture, these leaders put their hopes for their country in generalized welfare, industrialization and national unity and solidarity. They significantly reject or deemphasize economic *stability*, and political or governmental change. They want their communes included in *general* progress in development, not left to sink in the backwash of the progress of the better-off; they see commitment to national (central) initiatives and vigorous party activity as their principal means of leverage in contending with the more privileged. They recognize the need for political influence to secure a lift from the rest of the country, even while their communities try to pull themselves up from their condition of economic backwardness by their own bootstraps. One might add that these leaders tend to have less education than those in other communes, again a reflection of the fact they come from the less developed, rural areas of the country.

What this all suggests is that community activeness is *not* unidimensional. Especially in less developed countries, there may be one pattern that thrives on innovative change, and another that functions within constraints established by lack of resources or settled political traditions. Communities may be no less energetic, but may feel that they must seek different channels of activity than those that readily adopt new ways. Perhaps the anticipated rewards for alternative forms of activeness, as well as the character of the leadership, affects the path that will be chosen.

Table 1—Activeness and its Dimensions

This table reports the rotated factor loadings of a principal component analysis using the varimax criterion.

For India, U.S. and Yugoslavia the loadings reported are for the rotation of four components; for Poland, the first four factors of an eight-component rotation are given.

India

Resource Mobilization		Factors		
	I	*II*	*III*	*IV*
Fertilizers	.940	−.042	−.156	−.025
Radios	.708	−.535	.141	.112
Pumps	.540	−.314	−.099	−.271
Schools	−.077	.214	−.107	.741
Seeds	−.104	.036	.330	.577
Plows	−.150	.877	.082	−.079
Irrigation	−.157	.744	−.027	.083

Popular Involvement	*(I)*	*(II)*	*(III)*	*(IV)*
Literacy	.909	−.119	−.167	−.005
Inoculation of Cattle	.843	.210	−.015	.026
Sterilization	.744	−.145	−.050	−.278
Smallpox Vaccinations	.605	−.337	.167	−.177
Artificial Inseminations	.439	.374	−.027	.031
Latrines	.019	−.143	.760	.046
Manure Pits	.012	.253	.788	.038
Loops	.004	−.605	.272	−.066
Co-ops—Members	−.042	.805	.289	−.006
School Enrollment	−.053	−.252	−.001	.589
Co-ops—Capital	−.120	.568	.639	−.147
Wells	−.178	−.155	.838	.104
Percentage of Total Variance	23.4	19.0	14.2	7.8

Poland

Resource Mobilization	*I*	*II*	*III*	*IV*
Investments/Capita	.891	.079	.062	.168
Investments/Total	.853	.031	.184	.177
Expenditures/Capita	.743	.422	−.253	−.182
Industrial—Agricultural Investments	.692	.121	.361	−.061
Pupil Change	.219	−.030	.218	.781
Investment Change	.147	−.095	.850	.013
Physicians Change	.027	.034	.104	.315
Inhabitants/Shop Change	−.016	.157	−.151	.877

Popular Involvement	*(I)*	*(II)*	*(III)*	*(IV)*
Investment Proposals	.750	.104	.065	−.072
Pathfinders	.727	−.107	−.143	.146
Peasant Party	.521	.570	−.036	.118
Polish United Workers	.487	.360	.037	.168
Union of Rural Youth	.470	.294	−.002	.225
Union for Freedom and Democracy	.346	.671	−.751	.133
Library Cards	.239	−.074	.021	−.051
Typhoid Vaccinations	.235	.001	.071	.124
Volunteer Fire Brigades	.192	.758	.035	.014
Union of Socialist Youth	.122	.523	−.236	.116
Polish United Workers Party—Change	−.033	.116	.774	.037
Organizational Proposals	−.076	.141	−.013	.135
Donations to Schools	−.094	.206	.004	.020
Peasant Party Change	−.123	.862	.162	.013
Agricultural Circles	−.127	.128	.273	.072
Percentage of Total Variance	28.8	14.7	8.9	7.1

United States

Resource Mobilization	III	I	II	IV
		Factors		
Pupil Expenditure	−.918	+.006	−.098	−.085
Parks and Rec. Expenditure	−.709	−.173	+.190	+.163
Library Expenditure/Capita	−.656	+.079	−.063	+.424
Law and Order Expenditure/Capita	−.200	−.480	+.620	+.124
Law and Order Expenditure—Change	−.098	−.189	+.638	+.290
Library Expenditure—Change	−.098	+.105	−.082	+.535
Public Health Expenditure/Capita	−.092	+.096	+.790	−.036
Pupil Expenditure—Change	−.083	+.165	+.181	−.002
Parks and Rec. Expenditure—Change	+.004	+.152	+.446	+.083
Rev. from Property Taxes	+.054	+.640	+.453	.000
Total Expenditure, Government	+.084	−.110	+.855	+.061
Non-public Hospitals Revenue	+.104	−.412	+.090	−.013
Intergov. Revenue—Change	+.124	+.717	+.175	−.157
Value of Poverty Program	+.146	+.393	+.684	−.058
Public Health Expenditure—Change	+.150	+.243	+.509	−.156

Popular Involvement	(III)	(I)	(II)	(IV)
League of Women Voters	−.869	−.065	−.035	−.164
Mean Pres. Vote	−.450	+.423	−.427	−.001
Y.W.C.A. Contribution	−.235	+.007	+.155	+.577
Y.M.C.A. Volunteers—Change	−.177	+.003	+.162	−.217
Mean Referenda Voters	−.154	+.505	−.145	−.007
Boy Scout Volunteers—Change	−.043	−.691	−.058	+.027
United Fund/Capita	−.008	−.265	+.017	+.769
United Fund/Capita—Change	+.021	+.146	+.293	+.770
Change in Boy Scouts Membership	+.093	−.527	−.045	−.201
Mean Total Vote	+.113	+.630	+.017	+.252
Y.M.C.A. Contributions	+.135	+.014	+.041	+.758
Y.M.C.A. Board and Comm. Members	+.317	+.258	−.064	+.391
Percentage of Total Variance	11.6	12.7	13.9	11.4

Yugoslavia

Resource Mobilization	I	II	III	IV
		Factors		
Books	−.683	+.105	+.158	−.083
Local Investments/Capita	−.680	−.096	−.474	−.124
Local Investments/National Income	−.419	−.247	−.586	−.031
School Budget	−.351	−.117	−.599	+.054
Unpaid Taxes	−.160	+.847	+.061	+.143
Classroom Space	−.142	+.074	+.842	+.004
Total Budget	−.056	+.152	+.427	+.353
Physicians	+.082	+.685	+.046	−.237
School Teachers	+.236	−.161	−.663	−.193
Buildings completed	+.294	+.711	+.020	+.185

Popular Involvement	(I)	(II)	(III)	(IV)
League of Communists	−.831	−.140	+.106	+.340
Cinema Attendance	−.827	+.339	+.215	+.110
Voters in Assembly elections	−.377	+.291	+.141	−.713
Socialist Alliance	−.291	+.061	+.113	+.761
Cultural and Educational membership	−.215	+.850	−.001	−.048
Voters' Meetings held	−.153	−.384	+.493	−.013
Voters' Meetings initiated by Assembly	+.216	+.263	−.717	+.138
Candidacy Meetings	+.388	−.565	+.154	+.165
Percentage of Total Variance	18.3	18.5	17.5	8.7

The loadings reported are those that came directly out of the analysis. The definition and the logic of assessment of activeness required that the direction of the loadings (positive and negative signs) be interpreted in terms of the predicted direction of relationships and the scores based on the loadings. In India and Poland the positive loadings made it possible to read a high score as an indication of more activeness; in the United States and Yugoslavia, high *negative* scores on the mixed factor used for comparisons had to be interpreted as an indication of more activeness. These interpretations are incorporated in the tables and discussion in the Activeness chapters (8, 9, 10).

The Analytical Variables: Summary Tabulation of Data[1]

Variables	India		Poland		United States		Yugoslavia	
	x̄	s	x̄	s	x̄	s	x̄	s
A. COMMUNITY CHARACTERISTICS								
Ecological:								
Economic level	see Chapter 7 for measures of level of development							
Size (in 1000)	109.5	39.9	67.7	30.1	86.1	46.5	26.7	21.3
Density (km²)	580.2	≈34.2	86.7	56.2	146.2	11.3	82.9	5.9
Socio-Political Structure I:								
Problems (% of leaders reporting):								
Agricultural	78	9	56	14	0	0	23	13
Industrial	18	12	54	15	18	14	50	21
Employment	15	11	35	19	4	1	29	20
Utilities	46	20	—	—	59	14	60	15
Service	34	11	54	15	38	12	66	13
Conflicts	4	4	17	3	23	17	8	7
Cleavages (max. score = 2.00):								
Education	.78	.23	.99	.17	.90	.23	.85	.21
Income	1.17	.21	1.18	.18	.96	.25	1.16	.16
Religious Beliefs	.76	.21	.92	.16	.48	.19	.51	.26
Political Views	1.22	.22	.83	.14	1.01	.24	.50	.19
Rural-Urban	.77	.24	.71	.13	.36	.30	.64	.23

[1] Reported herewith, except where otherwise indicated, are means of the 30 community means in each country for the principal variables used in the analysis of community activeness; and also the standard deviation of the 30 communities from these intercommunity means.

Where the variable involves an attribute of the leaders who are interviewed, the mean for the total sample of respondents has been found to closely approximate the result obtained in averaging the distributions within communities for each country. Despite this similarity, the execution of analyses at the individual level, as reported in Chapters III and IV, was nationally performed, using individual data, rather than community aggregates.

Variables	India x̄	India s	Poland x̄	Poland s	United States x̄	United States s	Yugoslavia x̄	Yugoslavia s
Manager and Employee	.74	.19	.83	.11	.64	.22	.76	.17
Racial and Social Origins	.99	.17	.33	.15	.82	.44	.32	.12
Those desiring change and those opposing it	.95	.22	.97	.17	.78	.25	.57	.16
Mean Sum of Areas of Division	.92	.16	.84	.09	.74	.17	.67	.19²
Conflicts (% of leaders reporting):								
Social Groups	38	23	37	14	30	14	19	11
Political Groups	48	16	17	7.7	27	15	26	10
No Conflicts	25	22	15	9.6	9	11	40	15
Extent of perceived community conflict (Max. score = 2.00)	1.14	.39	1.02	.16	1.42	.25	.74	.22
Socio-Political Structure II								
Areas of Leaders' Activity (Max. score = 1.00):								
Economic Development	.43	.13	.35	.12	.51	.10	.34	.08
Agriculture	.84	.07	.46	.09	.06	.07	.32	.13
Housing	.42	.15	.33	.09	.56	.14	.24	.07
Public Services	.68	.10	.29	.09	.63	.09	.42	.11
Health	.66	.08	.24	.09	.76	.18	.25	.07
Culture	.50	.15	.40	.10	.59	.12	.37	.08
Education	.78	.07	.40	.08	.51	.12	.46	.08
Welfare	.54	.14	.31	.14	.59	.10	.37	.10
Political Organization	.60	.13	.53	.09	.54	.10	.79	.10
Finances	.55	.11	.23	.07	.44	.10	.28	.10
Mean Sum of Areas of Activity	.60	.06	.35	.09	.49	.06	.30	.09²
Areas of Leaders' Influence (Max. Score = 2.00):								
Economic Development	.61	.20	.77	.16	.83	.17	.63	.08
Agriculture	1.35	.21	.88	.20	.11	.09	.68	.25
Housing	.56	.21	.75	.11	.93	.23	.61	.12
Services	1.10	.22	.82	.10	1.10	.18	.92	.18
Health	.95	.13	.64	.18	.70	.16	.57	.14
Culture	.78	.20	.95	.14	.89	.23	.77	.16
Education	1.26	.15	.97	.12	.83	.19	.91	.14

² Estimated as x̄ of SD.

Variables	India		Poland		United States		Yugoslavia	
	$\bar{x}$	s	$\bar{x}$	s	$\bar{x}$	s	$\bar{x}$	s
Welfare	.84	.21	.89	.11	.97	.19	.75	.11
Political Organization	.95	.21	1.19	.13	.92	.21	1.30	.17
Finance	.78	.16	.76	.11	.82	.19	.72	.15
Mean Sum of Areas of Influence	.92	.10	.85	.09	.81	.13	.79	.98
Reference Groups (from which leaders seek support)								
Total no. of groups (Max. score = 19.00)	9.2?	2.13	6.14	1.01	4.88	.99	4.40	1.06
Specific Groups (Max. score = 2.00)								

India:

	$\bar{x}$	s
Local party organization	1.39	.16
Elected leaders in the community	.98	.18
Leaders of other organizations (cooperatives, voluntary associations, etc.)	.77	.19
Higher level party leaders (ministers, party bosses, etc.)	.66	.28
Appointed officials in the community	.77	.23
Respected and influential people	.86	.18
Your own supporters in the party	.76	.18
Co-workers	1.25	.16
Appointed official at higher level	.64	.13
Factory owners and managers (urban)	.21	.14
Trade union leaders	.28	.13
Majority of citizens	1.15	.18
Certain caste or groups in the community	.33	.13
Poor people	1.10	.20
Rich people	.40	.4
Close friends and supporters	.89	.6

Poland:

	$\bar{x}$	s
Powiat Committee of PZPR or ZSL	1.45	.20
Praesidium of Powiat Peoples Council	1.26	.19
Leaders of social organizations	.47	.13
Higher level party leaders	.33	.13
Top administrative officials of Powiat	.45	.14
Colleagues from your institution or profession	.71	.18
Local party councilmen	.25	.12
Committee of the Councils	.47	.14
Higher leaders (wojewodship authorities)	.61	.15
Managers of local enterprises and industrial plants	.34	.15
Trade union activists	.37	.16
Majority of citizens	.44	.16
Agricultural activists	.21	—
Workers	.14	—
Peasants	.19	—
Intelligentsia	.20	—

United States:	x̄	s
Local party leaders	.35	.17
Local elective officials	.72	.25
Local newspapers	.78	.24
Higher level party leaders	.16	.07
City manager of top administrative officials at local level	.80	.28
Local civic, professional or reform groups concerned with local politics	.65	.18
Special groups in local party organization	.15	.10
Administrative colleagues at own level	.62	.20
State, county or higher administrative officials	.44	.15
Local business groups such as Chamber of Commerce	.70	.21
Local trade unions	.17	.15
Public or citizens generally	.92	.23
Local ethnic religious or racial groups	.17	.15
Lower income or lower social status people	.07	.08
Well-to-do people (wealthy upper-class)	.08	.06
Close friends and supporters	.76	.21

Yugoslavia	x̄	s
Committee of the League of Communists in the commune	.59	.15
Deputy (M.P.) elected in the commune (including presidents)	.58	.09
Voluntary associations (social organizations)	.39	.10
Higher level party leaders	.05	.04
Administrative officials in the communal assembly	.26	.11
Representatives of different local institutions	.15	.06
Communal Committee of Socialist Alliance	.49	.13
Professional organs of communal assembly	.17	.07
Professional and administrative bodies at higher levels	.37	.10
Managers of enterprises and cooperatives	.24	.09
Different professional groups	.07	.04
Population generally	.42	.08
Representatives of individual settlements (local communities)	.23	.11
Workers	.24	.10
Farmers	.17	.10
Intelligentsia	.13	.06

413

Variables	India		Poland		United States		Yugoslavia	
	x̄	s	x̄	s	x̄	s	x̄	s
Socio-Political Structure III								
Autonomy of Local Government as perceived by leaders: (score 0 = sufficient autonomy 1 = lacks autonomy)								
Housing	.72	.19	.59	.15	.39	.16	.16	.10
Employment	.77	.23	.50	.15	.52	.17	.25	.09
Building Schools	.31	.14	.65	.12	.16	.12	.15	.12
Health Services	.46	.13	.45	.15	.23	.10	.24	.13
Culture	.38	.17	.29	.12	.20	.15	.16	.12
Electrification	.76	.22	.55	.15	.26	.19	.15	.14
Youth Problems	.55	.28	.15	.07	.24	.11	.13	.10
Mean Sum of Areas Lacking Autonomy	.55	.15	.54	.07	.29	.09	.18	.07
Obstacles to Effective Leadership (% of leaders reporting):								
Governmental Performance	30	11	32	15	22	8	14	6
Public Participation	15	9	10	8	19	9	15	7
Conflicts—Political	20	15	6	5	11	8	7	7
No Obstacles	10	7	16	10	12	10	17	8
Party Membership (% belonging to dominant party)	61	11	82	6	64	12	84	8
Preferred Organ of Responsibility for action in above areas (Max. score = 7.00):								
Central Government	3.31	.58	1.47	—	1.32	.69	2.29	.76
Local Government	2.44	.45	4.82	—	2.93	.49	3.27	.62
Local Non-governmental Institutions	.57	.16	.50	—	1.83	.55	.88	.26
Leave it to the People	.62	.32	.18	—	.77	.28	.46	.37

B. LEADERS' CHARACTERISTICS

Leaders' Values (scale scores 1.00 to 4.00):

Economic Development	1.29	.08	1.89	.13	2.17	.10	1.54	.16
Conflict Resolution	1.83	.18	2.58	.11	2.87	.09	2.15	.11
Participation	3.17	.22	2.74	.08	2.25	.10	2.26	.19
Selflessness	1.43	.10	1.77	.11	1.85	.07	1.78	.12
National Commitment	2.56	.15	2.70	.07	2.28	.10	2.65	.18
Action Propensity	3.38	.15	2.85	.10	2.51	.11	2.94	.09
Honesty	1.67	.19	1.86	.08	1.72	.08	1.52	.14
Change Orientation	1.53	.12	1.67	.11	2.16	.09	1.72	.17
Economic Equality	1.50	.09	2.26	.13	3.28	.13	1.96	.20

Value Priorities (Max. score = 2.00)

Economic Development	.94	.25	1.05	.14	.74	.18	1.00	.17
Conflict Resolution	.51	.17	.48	.12	.23	.09	.39	.18
Selflessness	.45	.19	.17	.07	.15	.10	.17	.08
National Commitment	.43	.18	.34	.11	.03	.04	.09	.06
Honesty	.81	.22	.51	.11	.97	.17	.81	.17
Participation	.19	.12	.31	.13	.74	.13	.38	.17
Change	.26	.12	.83	.15	.89	.14	.57	.18
	.40	.18	.36	.13	.19	.12	.61	.14

Traits of Admired Leaders (% of leaders reporting):

Honesty	53	13	52	16	58	11	66	11
Selflessness	54	13	40	8	33	9	16	7
Knowledge	22	7	66	12	56	12	50	11
General Leadership Abilities	17	8	16	8	29	6	16	7
Impartiality	14	9	9	5	13	6	8	7
Good Relations with People	36	13	29	11	25	8	34	10

Variables	India		Poland		United States		Yugoslavia	
	$\bar{x}$	s	$\bar{x}$	s	$\bar{x}$	s	$\bar{x}$	s
Aspirations for Country (% of leaders reporting):								
Improved Welfare	51	13	72	15	48	11	53	11
Industrialization	32	11	49	15	11	6	18	8
Social Services	36	14	36	15	28	9	13	11
Improved Governmental Performance	16	8	8	9	33	12	21	8
National Unity	38	14	17	9	20	10	16	8
World Peace	3	—	15	—	60	—	14	—
Congruence of Values I (Average SD on 9 value scales)	.43	.03	.46	.03	.37	.04	.35	.03
Congruence of Values II (Average SD on 3 value scales)	.46	.06	.46	.02	.37	.06	.37	.05
Leaders' Loyalties: (Max. score = 2.00)								
Political Parties	.51	.22	.97	.22	.16	.10	1.00	.25
Friends	.08	.07	.04	.02	.30	.15	.02	.03
People in the Community	.73	.22	.51	.14	1.31	.16	.55	.24
Nation	1.34	.24	1.39	.16	1.04	.17	1.36	.15
Background:								
Age[3]	3.90	.25	4.25	.29	4.42	.31	3.42	.27
Education[4]	2.25	.28	[6]4.69	.30	2.80	.24	2.36	.28
Years in Community[5]	3.82	.27	1.72	.34	3.67	.56	3.35	.40

[3] Coded: 1 = under 20, 2 = 20–29, 3 = 30–39, 4 = 40–49, 5 = 50–59, 6 = over 60.
[4] Coded: 1 = low (primary), 2 = middle, 3 = high, 4 = professional.
[5] Coded: 1 = under 5, 2 = 5–9, 3 = 10–20, 4 = longer than 20, 5 = "all my life".
[6] Measured on a scale from 1 to 6 in Poland.